INNOCENCE
SLAUGHTERED

*Gas and the transformation
of warfare and society*

edited by
Jean Pascal Zanders

UNIFORM
PRESS

Published by Uniform Press
An imprint of Unicorn Publishing Group
101 Wardour Street, London W1F 0UG
www.unicornpress.org

www.uniformpress.co.uk

A catalogue record for this book is available from
the British Library

5 4 3 2 1

ISBN pb 978-1-910500-41-5
ISBN E-Pub 987-1-910500-43-9
ISBN Pdf 978-1-910500-44-6

Cover design Uniform Press
Typeset by Vivian@Bookscribe
Printed and bound in Spain

Maps based on content kindly provided by
In Flanders Fields Museum. Created by Battlefield Design.

The Monument to the first victims of a gas attack at Steenstraete. This telling monument
by sculptor M. Real del Sarte and architect P. Bourin was inaugurated in May 1929 near the
northernmost end of the line of the German gas offensive of 22 April 1915. Only 12 years after its
inauguration, on 8 May 1941, it was dynamited by German occupation forces, only to be replaced
by a high cross many years after the Second World War. (In Flanders Fields Museum, Ypres)

CONTENTS

AUTHOR BIOGRAPHIES

Dr Maartje Abbenhuis is assistant professor in Modern European History at the University of Auckland, New Zealand. She researches the history of neutrality and internationalism, particularly in Europe in the period 1815–1919. Her main publications on this are *An Age of Neutrals. Great Power Politics 1815–1914* (2014) and *The Art of Staying Neutral. The Netherlands in the First World War, 1914–1918* (2006), a book on the maintenance of neutrality by the Netherlands in the First World War.

Dominiek Dendooven (Brugge, 1971) is a researcher at In Flanders Fields Museum, Ypres. Among his publications on the First World War are *Menin Gate & Last Post. Ypres as Holy Ground* (Klaproos, 2001), *World War One. Five Continents in Flanders* (Lannoo, 2008).

Bert Heyvaert studied history and archaeology at universities of Leuven and Sheffield. From 2005 until 2007 he was a staff member at the In Flanders Fields Museum, Ypres and the memorial museum Passchendaele 1917. Since 2008 he has worked as an archaeologist in Flanders, specialising in conflict archaeology. He is a member of the organising committee of the annual 'Conflict in Contact' conference for conflict archaeology in Belgium.

Olivier Lepick holds a PhD degree in International History and International Politics from the Graduate Institute of International Studies of Geneva (Geneva University). His PhD dissertation was dedicated to strategical, tactical, scientific and industrial aspects of chemical warfare during the First World War. He is a Research Associate at the Foundation for Strategic Studies in Paris and his research has centred around chemical and biological weapons. He is the author of numerous articles and books on these issues: *The Great Chemical War 1914–1918* (1998, Presses Universitaires de France), *Chemical Weapons* (1999, PUF), *Biological Weapons* (2001, PUF), *Non-conventional terrorism: chemical, biological and nuclear* (2003, PUF).

Dr David Omissi is Senior Lecturer in Modern History at the University of Hull, where he teaches British imperial, Indian and military history. Before moving to Hull, he was a Prize Research Fellow at Nuffield College, Oxford. He is the author of *The Sepoy and the Raj: The Indian Army, 1860–1940* (1994), and editor of *Indian Voices of the Great War: Soldiers' Letters, 1914–1918* (1999). His article 'Europe Through Indian Eyes: Indian Soldiers Encounter England and France, 1914–1918', *English Historical Review*, 122 (2007) was recently nominated as one of the 35 'most respected' articles published in the EHR since the periodical's foundation in 1886.

Dr Gerard Oram is a tutor in the war and society programme at Swansea University. His research interests include the relationship between conflict and legal structures and his approach often combines historical inquiry with criminology. He has published widely on morale and discipline in both military and civilian contexts. Recently he has been acting as an advisor to the BBC for the World War One at Home project.

Julian Putkowski is a 68-year-old university lecturer and broadcaster with a long-established interest in British military discipline and dissent during the First World War. Since 2009 he has been a member of the Scientific Committee of the In Flanders Fields Museum, Ypres, but lives and works in London. His contributions to the study of mutinies and military 'collective bargaining' is recorded in https://www.marxists.org/history/etol/revhist/backiss/vol8/no2/part4-intro.html. With Julian Sykes, he wrote *Shot at Dawn* (1989) and supported the ensuing campaign that in 2006 secured posthumous conditional pardons for soldiers executed by the British Army during the First World War. His views about the campaign feature in *Murderous Tommies* (2011), co-authored with Mark Dunning, and independently in a commemorative pamphlet, entitled *Three Uneasy Pieces* (2014).

Dr Leo van Bergen (Venlo, the Netherlands, 1959) is a medical historian specialised in tropical medicine and 'war and medicine'. He has written numerous articles on medicine in the First World War in peer-reviewed journals and has written the articles on medical care in the Cambridge History of the First World War and the Online Encyclopaedia of the First World War. His monograph on the subject, *Before my Helpless Sight. Suffering, dying and military medicine on the Western Front* (2009), is generally regarded a must read.

Peter van den Dungen has been at the Department of Peace Studies at the University of Bradford since 1976 and is now an honorary visiting fellow.

A peace historian, he is general coordinator of the International Network of Museums for Peace (INMP). On the occasion of the centenary of the Women's International League for Peace and Freedom (WILPF, founded in The Hague in April 1915), he organised a small exhibition on WILPF's campaign against chemical warfare in the 1920s and 1930s at the Organisation for the Prohibition of Chemical Weapons (OPCW).

Luc Vandeweyer is Doctor in History. He studied at the University of Leuven and has specialised in history of the Flemish movement and peace movement. In recent years he has published a lot of books and articles about the history of Belgium and the Belgian Army during the wars in the first half of the 20th century. He was asked many times by press, radio and television to comment on the commemoration of the First World War.

Dr Wolfgang Wietzker was born in former East Prussia in 1941, from where his family was forced to emigrate in 1944, and grew up in Northern Germany. He spent his professional life as an officer in the German Army. After retirement he studied new history and political sciences at the Heinrich-Heine University in Düsseldorf. He received his PhD degree in 2006. He has published several books on how political circumstances in Germany affected people's personal lives.

Dr Jean Pascal Zanders is an independent researcher/consultant on disarmament and security questions. He heads *The Trench*, a research initiative dedicated to the future of disarmament. He holds Masters degrees in Germanic Philology-Linguistics (1980) and Political Sciences (1992) and a PhD degree in Political Sciences (1996) from the Free University of Brussels. He was Project Leader of the Chemical and Biological Warfare Project at the Stockholm International Peace Research Institute (1996–2003); Director of the Geneva-based BioWeapons Prevention Project (2003–08) and Senior Research Fellow at the European Union Institute for Security Studies (2008–13). He has participated as an expert to the EU Delegations in the BTWC and CWC meetings since 2010.

FOREWORD

The year 1915 saw a turning point in the history of modern warfare. It was then, on 22 April, in the fields near Ypres in Belgium that chlorine gas was first deployed on a large scale as a weapon. Chemical warfare was born that day, and before the First World War drew to a close, it had claimed, by some estimates, more than a million casualties.

Chemical weapons did not have the decisive impact that military planners in the First World War might have hoped for. But the horrific and indiscriminate suffering they caused, transformed how we think war can and should be waged. No-one was left in any doubt about the inhumane nature of chemical warfare in the aftermath of the First World War. Hence, the Geneva Protocol, which prohibits the use of chemical weapons, was concluded in 1925. It took, however, seven more decades to establish a global ban on the production and use of these brutal weapons.

Since the Chemical Weapons Convention entered into force in 1997, significant progress has been achieved in the elimination of existing stockpiles of these weapons. Ninety per cent of them have so far been destroyed under international verification. The verification regime set up by the Organisation for the Prohibition of Chemical Weapons (OPCW) has also played an important role in preventing the re-emergence of chemical weapons. I am confident that the States Parties to the Chemical Weapons Convention will continue to stand against the use of chemical weapons or toxic chemicals as a weapon by anyone under any circumstances. The historic Ieper Declaration, which they issued in April 2015 at a meeting to commemorate this first large-scale chemical attack, firmly expresses their resolve to that effect.

I am grateful to Dr Jean Pascal Zanders for his contributions over many years, as a historian and expert, to our shared goals. This volume offers a remarkable compilation of materials, rich in detail and edited in the finest traditions of highly readable scholarship. Its appearance is a timely reminder – in the centenary year of the Ypres chemical attacks – of the terrible legacy of chemical warfare, and of the extraordinary effort by which we seek to overcome it.

Ahmet Üzümcü
Director-General
Organisation for the Prohibition of Chemical Weapons

Gas Attack - Thursday 22 April 1915

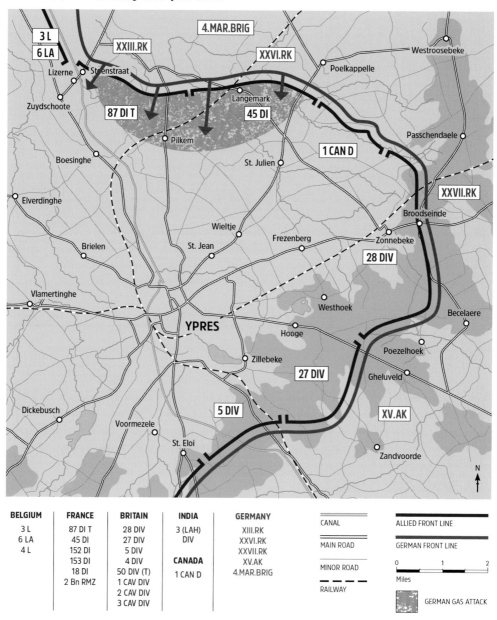

Gas Attack - Saturday 24 April 1915

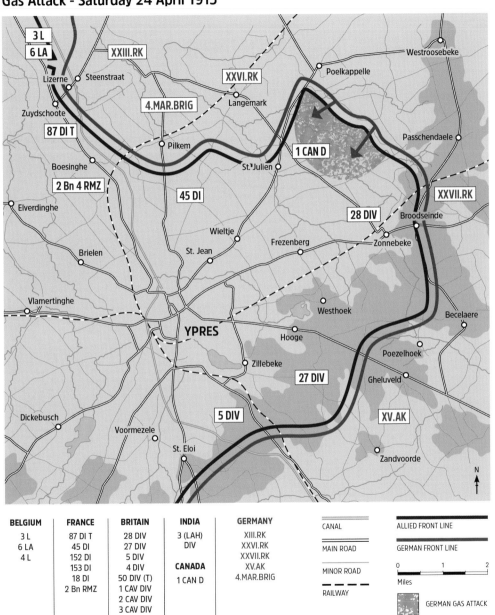

BELGIUM	FRANCE	BRITAIN	INDIA	GERMANY
3 L	87 DI T	28 DIV	3 (LAH)	XIII.RK
6 LA	45 DI	27 DIV	DIV	XXVI.RK
4 L	152 DI	5 DIV		XXVII.RK
	153 DI	4 DIV	CANADA	XV.AK
	18 DI	50 DIV (T)	1 CAN D	4.MAR.BRIG
	2 Bn RMZ	1 CAV DIV		
		2 CAV DIV		
		3 CAV DIV		

CANAL

MAIN ROAD

MINOR ROAD

RAILWAY

ALLIED FRONT LINE

GERMAN FRONT LINE

0   1   2

Miles

GERMAN GAS ATTACK

Gas Attack - Saturday 1 May 1915

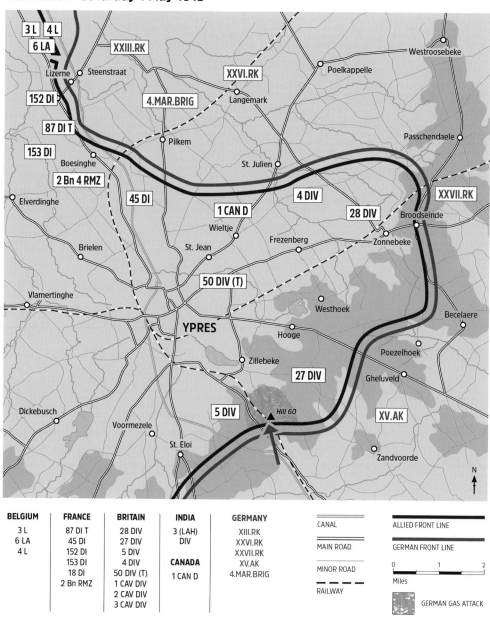

BELGIUM	FRANCE	BRITAIN	INDIA	GERMANY
3 L	87 DI T	28 DIV	3 (LAH)	XIII.RK
6 LA	45 DI	27 DIV	DIV	XXVI.RK
4 L	152 DI	5 DIV		XXVII.RK
	153 DI	4 DIV	**CANADA**	XV.AK
	18 DI	50 DIV (T)	1 CAN D	4.MAR.BRIG
	2 Bn RMZ	1 CAV DIV		
		2 CAV DIV		
		3 CAV DIV		

CANAL

MAIN ROAD

MINOR ROAD

RAILWAY

ALLIED FRONT LINE

GERMAN FRONT LINE

0   1   2

Miles

GERMAN GAS ATTACK

Gas Attack - Sunday 2 May 1915

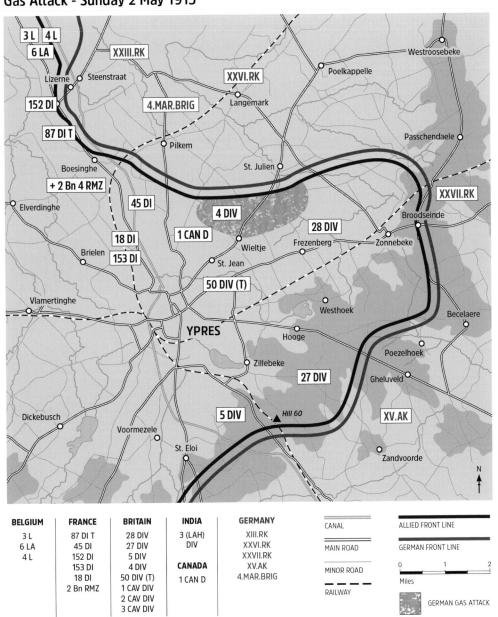

BELGIUM	FRANCE	BRITAIN	INDIA	GERMANY
3 L	87 DI T	28 DIV	3 (LAH)	XIII.RK
6 LA	45 DI	27 DIV	DIV	XXVI.RK
4 L	152 DI	5 DIV		XXVII.RK
	153 DI	4 DIV	**CANADA**	XV.AK
	18 DI	50 DIV (T)	1 CAN D	4.MAR.BRIG
	2 Bn RMZ	1 CAV DIV		
		2 CAV DIV		
		3 CAV DIV		

CANAL

MAIN ROAD

MINOR ROAD

RAILWAY

ALLIED FRONT LINE

GERMAN FRONT LINE

0   1   2
Miles

GERMAN GAS ATTACK

N

Gas Attack - Wednesday 5 May 1915

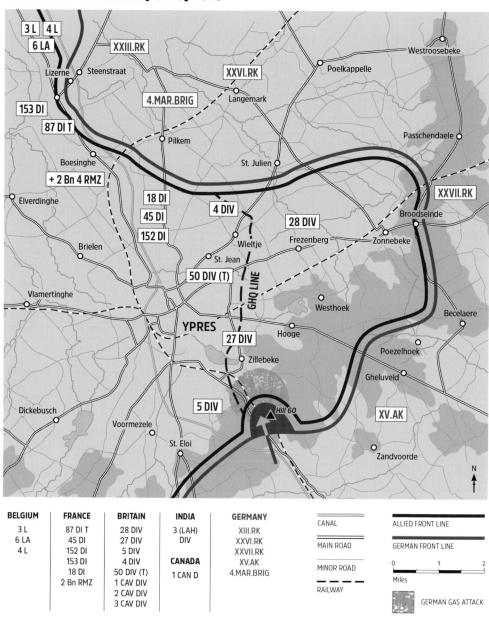

BELGIUM	FRANCE	BRITAIN	INDIA	GERMANY
3 L	87 DI T	28 DIV	3 (LAH)	XIII.RK
6 LA	45 DI	27 DIV	DIV	XXVI.RK
4 L	152 DI	5 DIV		XXVII.RK
	153 DI	4 DIV	**CANADA**	XV.AK
	18 DI	50 DIV (T)	1 CAN D	4.MAR.BRIG
	2 Bn RMZ	1 CAV DIV		
		2 CAV DIV		
		3 CAV DIV		

CANAL

MAIN ROAD

MINOR ROAD

RAILWAY

ALLIED FRONT LINE

GERMAN FRONT LINE

0   1   2
Miles

GERMAN GAS ATTACK

Gas Attack - Monday 10 May 1915

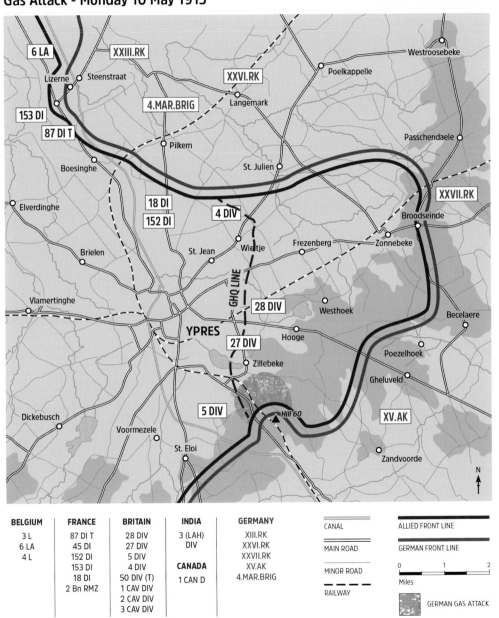

BELGIUM	FRANCE	BRITAIN	INDIA	GERMANY
3 L	87 DI T	28 DIV	3 (LAH)	XIII.RK
6 LA	45 DI	27 DIV	DIV	XXVI.RK
4 L	152 DI	5 DIV		XXVII.RK
	153 DI	4 DIV	**CANADA**	XV.AK
	18 DI	50 DIV (T)	1 CAN D	4.MAR.BRIG
	2 Bn RMZ	1 CAV DIV		
		2 CAV DIV		
		3 CAV DIV		

CANAL

MAIN ROAD

MINOR ROAD

RAILWAY

ALLIED FRONT LINE

GERMAN FRONT LINE

0   1   2
Miles

GERMAN GAS ATTACK

Gas Attack - Monday 24 May 1915

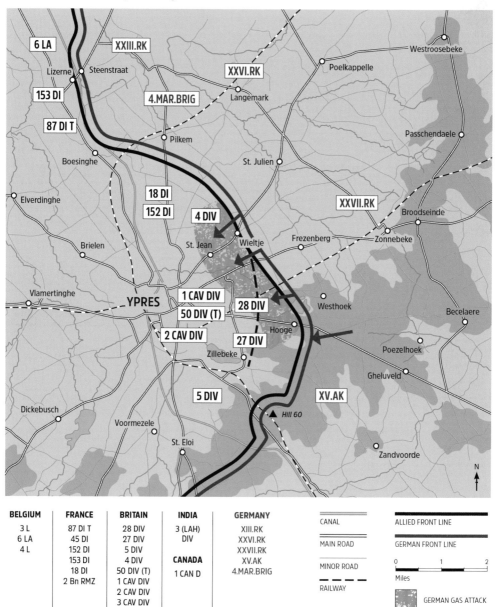

BELGIUM	FRANCE	BRITAIN	INDIA	GERMANY
3 L	87 DI T	28 DIV	3 (LAH)	XIII.RK
6 LA	45 DI	27 DIV	DIV	XXVI.RK
4 L	152 DI	5 DIV		XXVII.RK
	153 DI	4 DIV	**CANADA**	XV.AK
	18 DI	50 DIV (T)	1 CAN D	4.MAR.BRIG
	2 Bn RMZ	1 CAV DIV		
		2 CAV DIV		
		3 CAV DIV		

CANAL

MAIN ROAD

MINOR ROAD

RAILWAY

ALLIED FRONT LINE

GERMAN FRONT LINE

0   1   2
Miles

GERMAN GAS ATTACK

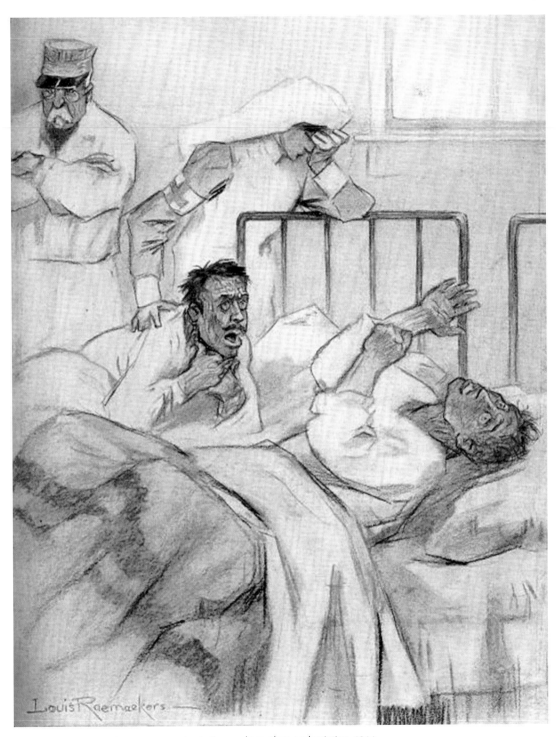

Louis Raemaekers: Slow Asphyxiation, 1916.

INTRODUCTION

In November 2005 In Flanders Fields Museum, Ypres organised and hosted an international conference in Ypres, entitled *1915: Innocence Slaughtered*. The first major attack with chemical weapons, launched by Imperial German forces from their positions near Langemarck on the northern flank of the Ypres Salient on 22 April 1915, featured prominently among the presentations. I was also one of the speakers, but my address focused on how to prevent a similar event with biological weapons. Indeed, it was one of the strengths of the conference not to remain stuck in a past of – at that time – nine decades earlier, but also to invite reflection on future challenges in other areas of disarmament and arms control. Notwithstanding, the academic gathering had a secondary goal from the outset, namely to collect the papers with historical focus for academic publication.

The eminent Dutch professor and historian Koen Koch chaired the conference. He was also to edit the book with the historical analyses. Born just after the end of the Second World War in Europe, he sadly passed away in January 2012. He had earned the greatest respect from his colleagues, so much so that the In Flanders Fields Museum, Ypres, set up the *Koen Koch Foundation* to support students and trainees who wish to investigate the dramatic events in the Ypres Salient during the four years of the First World War. The homage was very apt: Professor Koch had built for himself a considerable reputation as an author of studies on the First World War. Most remarkable: The Netherlands had remained neutral during the conflagration, which adds to the value of his insights.

Death, unfortunately, also ends projects. In the summer of 2014, while doing some preliminary research on the history of chemical warfare, I came across the manuscripts of the chapters that make up the bulk of this book. They were in different editorial stages, the clearest indication of how abruptly the publication project had screeched to an end. Reading them I was struck by the quality of the contents, rough as the texts still were. Together, the contributions also displayed a high degree of coherence.

One group of papers reflected on the minutiae of the unfolding catastrophe that the unleashing of chlorine against the Allied positions meant for individual soldiers and civilians. They also vividly described German doubts about the effectiveness of the new weapon, and hence its potential impact on combat operations. These contributions also reflected on the lack of Allied response to the many intelligence pointers that something significant was afoot. In hindsight, we may ponder how the Allied military leaders could have missed so many indicators. Yet, matter-of-fact assessments of gas use by Allied combatants recur in several chapters, suggesting either widespread anticipation of the introduction of toxic chemicals as a method of warfare or some degree of specific forewarning of the German assault. Gaps in the historical record, however, do not allow a more precise determination of Allied anticipation of chemical warfare. Still, a general foreboding may differ significantly from its concrete manifestation. From the perspective of a contemporary, the question was more likely one of how to imagine the unimaginable. Throughout the Second Battle of Ypres senior Allied commanders proved particularly unimaginative. In the end, the fact that German military leaders had only defined tactical goals for the combat operations following up on the release of chlorine, meant that they had forfeited any strategic ambition – such as restoring movement to a stalemated front, seizing the Channel ports, or capturing the vital communications node that Ypres was – during the Second Battle of Ypres, or ever after. The surprise element was never to be repeated again. Not during the First World War, not in any more recent armed conflict.

The second group of papers captured the massive transformation societies were undergoing as a consequence of industrialisation, science and technology, and the impact these trends were to have on the emergence of what we know today as 'total war'. Chemical warfare pitted the brightest minds from the various belligerents against each other. The competition became possible because the interrelationship between scientists, industry, politicians and the military establishment was already changing fast. But chemical warfare also helped to effectuate and institutionalise those changes. In many respects, it presaged the Manhattan Project in which the various constituencies were brought together with the sole purpose of developing a new type of weapon. In other ways the competition revealed early thinking about racial superiority that was to define the decades after the Armistice. The ability to survive in a chemically contaminated environment was proof of a higher level of achievement. In other words, chemical defence equalled survival of the fittest. Or how Darwin's evolutionary theory was deliberately misused in the efforts to justify violation of then existing norms against the used of poison weapons or asphyxiating gases.

During and in the immediate aftermath of the war, opposition to chemical warfare was slow to emerge. In part, this was the consequence of the appreciation by soldiers in the trenches and non-combatants living and working near the frontlines that gas was one among many nuisances and dangers they daily faced as its use became more regular. Defences, advanced training and strict gas discipline gave soldiers more than a fair chance of surviving a gas attack. The violence of total war swept away the humanitarian sentiments that had given rise to the first international treaties banning the use of poison and asphyxiating gases in the final year of the 19th century. Those documents became obsolete because people viewed modern gas warfare as quite distinct from primitive use of poison and poisoned weapons or the scope of the prohibition had been too narrowly defined. By February 1918 chemical warfare had become so regular that a most unusual public appeal on humanitarian grounds by the International Committee of the Red Cross (ICRC) badly backfired on the organisation. Throughout the 1920s the choice between an outright ban on chemical weapons and preparing populations for the consequences of future chemical warfare would prove divisive for the ICRC. In contrast, peace and anti-war movements in Europe campaigned against war in all its aspects and consequently refused to resist one particular mode of warfare before the Armistice. It is instructive to learn that opposition to chemical warfare specifically first arose far away from the battlefields – northern America and neutral Netherlands – and among a group of citizens not directly involved in combat operations: women. And perhaps more precisely, women of science who protested the misapplication of their research and endeavours to destroy humans. Just like the chlorine cloud of 22 April 1915 foreshadowed the Manhattan project, the Women's International League for Peace and Freedom presaged the Pugwash Conferences on Science and World Affairs, who would bring together scientists, academics and political leaders to counter the growing menace of nuclear war and find solutions to other threats to peace and security.

It was clear to me that I should not remain a privileged reader of the manuscripts. They contained too much material and insights that the broader public should have access to. Piet Chielens, curator of the In Flanders Fields Museum, Ypres, and Dominiek Dendooven, researcher at the Museum, could not agree more, and so a new publication project was born. However, since the centenary of the chlorine attack was only a few months away, reviving the academic product Koen Koch had been working on was initially not an option. So, the decision was to exploit modern communication technologies and produce the volume as a PDF file in the first instance. However, by the time the electronic edition was ready for online publication, In Flanders Fields Museum, Ypres, had found a publisher willing and able to produce a formal edited volume before the end of the centenary year of the first modern gas attack. My gratitude goes to Ryan Gearing of Uniform Press for his guidance and concrete assistance in making this book a reality.

Time for preparing this publication was very short. To my pleasant surprise, every author in this volume responded favourably and collaboration over several intense weeks – both in the preparation of the original PDF version and the subsequent book project – proved remarkably gratifying and productive. Some contributors even took the time to introduce me to certain concepts widely accepted among historians, which I, with my background in linguistics and political science, had interpreted rather differently. For the experience in preparing this volume, I indeed wish to thank every single contributor.

22 April 1915 was not just the day when the chlorine cloud rolled over the battlefield in Flanders. It also symbolises the confluence of often decade-old trends in science, technology, industry, military art and the way of war, and social organisation. That day augured our modern societies with their many social, scientific and technological achievements. However, it was also a starting point for new trends that eventually led nations down the path of the atomic bomb and industrialised genocide in concentration camps. It also highlighted the perennial struggle of international law and institutions to match rapid scientific and technological advances that could lead to new weapons or modes of warfare. This volume captures the tree dimensions: the immediate impact of poison warfare on the battlefield, the ways in which the events in the spring of 1915 and

afterwards shaped social attitudes to the scientification and industrialisation of warfare, and the difficulties of capturing chemical and industrial advances in internationally binding legal instruments. Indeed, there can be no more poignant reminder that our insights into the trends that brought the chlorine release 100 years ago are crucial to our understanding of trends shaping our societies today and tomorrow.

Yes, the world has moved on since the First World War, even if the use of chlorine in the Syrian civil war one century later may seem to challenge the thought. Yet, one institution may unwittingly have come to symbolise the progression. Fritz Haber, the scientific and organisational genius who led Imperial Germany's chemical warfare effort in 1915, was awarded the Nobel Prize for Chemistry in 1918. Typical for the day, the Nobel Committee detached scientific achievement from moral considerations. His contribution to the development of a synthetic fertiliser for agricultural use, for which he got the prize, equally enabled Germany to continue munition production in the face of an Allied blockade denying it access to foreign raw materials. Haber's part in chemical warfare too fell entirely outside the Nobel Committee's considerations. Ninety-five years later, in 2013, the Organisation for the Prohibition of Chemical Weapons received the Nobel Peace Prize for its progress in eliminating the scourge of chemical warfare. The decision represented a strong moral statement, for it reflected the (Norwegian) Nobel Committee's views that today chemistry, and science in general, should serve peaceful purposes. Therefore it is indeed painfully paradoxical that the successful elimination of the most toxic substances developed and produced for warfare has resulted in the return of chlorine, today a common industrial chemical, as a weapon of choice in the Syrian civil war that started in 2011.

We indeed still experience the consequences of 22 April 1915: this dichotomy between the application of science and technology for life and their mobilisation for war continue to characterise our societal development today. This realisation explains why I thought that the papers, initially prepared under the guidance of Professor Koen Koch, should see the light of day. Particularly now.

Jean Pascal Zanders
Ferney-Voltaire,
October 2015

THE ROAD TO THE HAGUE

Jean Pascal Zanders

Before the First World War the prohibition on the use of poison or poisoned weapons was one of the least controversial regulations in the laws of war. Between 18 May and 29 July 1899 the world's foremost powers convened in The Hague for the first Peace Conference. The 26 participating states concluded their deliberations with three conventions and three declarations. Convention (II) with respect to the Laws and Customs of War on Land captured much of the then existing customs and laws of war. Article 23 listed poison and poisoned weapons as the first of seven outlawed modes of combat.[1] This document the participants adopted unanimously. At the second Hague Peace Conference in 1907 the 44 participating powers reaffirmed this ban when adopting the Hague Convention (IV) respecting the Laws and Customs of War on Land.[2]

The First International Peace Conference, The Hague, May–June 1899. (HU67224)

The three declarations of the 1899 meeting touched upon novel weapon developments: discharge of projectiles and explosives from balloons, asphyxiating gases, and expanding (dum dum) bullets. Under Hague Declaration (IV, 2) the Contracting Powers agreed to abstain from the use of projectiles the object of which is the diffusion of asphyxiating or deleterious gases.[3] The United States refused to sign it, and so did the United Kingdom on the principle that the document lacked consensus.

From a toxicological or physiological viewpoint no difference between poisons or asphyxiating gases exists: both harm living organisms through their direct toxic action. The adoption of two documents, one of which proved controversial, by the same group of diplomats points to different conceptions the negotiators had of poisons and asphyxiating gases. The former were naturally occurring substances; the latter the product of scientific and technological advancement. Concern arose towards the end of the 19th century the chemical revolution was not only fundamentally altering the nature of warfare, but also placing more agrarian societies at a distinct disadvantage.

After opening the valves of chlorine-filled cylinders near Ypres on 22 April 1915, questions sprang up as to whether the German Imperial forces had violated international law. Given the rather narrow focus on projectiles in Declaration (IV, 2), many officials and commentators on both sides of the conflict expressed the opinion that at a minimum Germany had not violated the letter of the agreement. More intriguingly, few people viewed the German chemical attack as falling foul of the Hague Conventions, whose ban on the use of poisons and poisoned weapons in combat was wholly uncontroversial. It seems that science, technology and industrialisation not just stimulated codification of the laws of war, but also reframed the ways in which the international community was to interpret the newly codified rules. International law on the eve of the First World War had not yet matured sufficiently to fully capture the impact of new weapon developments on it. Furthermore, it left sufficient ambiguity to effectively constrain the application of novel modes of warfare on the battlefield, particularly in circumstances when military objectives demanded ingenuity to overcome setbacks on the frontline.

Constraining poison warfare

If on the eve of the First World War people generally viewed poison weapons with abhorrence, it was because the constraints on their use as a method of warfare were already multifaceted and long-standing.[4] On the one hand, the physical properties of the warfare agents and their dependence on environmental mediation in order to reach the target have always limited their military utility. For instance, the introduction of firearms, such as muskets and canon, moved enemy formations beyond the reach of the (poisoned) arrow. On the other hand, poisons upset the social order. Any person who had the knowledge and skills to prepare and apply them also had the power to kill even the most trained and best equipped fighter. Particularly in medieval Europe a poisoned arrow or crossbow bolt could kill a knight irrespective of his investment in armour or lifelong training. The victim's death was a virtual certainty. Consequently, psychological and moral objections meant that a user always faced harsh punishments.

The first statements against the use of poisons and poisoned weapons in combat expressed a particular society's moral values. Compiled in the second or first century BCE, the *Manu Smrti* (the Tradition of Manu), which forms one of the foundations of Hindu code, contained the earliest recorded prohibition. It exhorted a king not to use poisoned weapons.[5] Religions have had a restraining influence on the conduct of war and on the use of poisons in particular. Fundamental writings such as the Bible or the Qur'an do not discuss poisoning, and consequently do not contain formal prohibitions, but the Jewish, Christian and Islamic inspired constraints were derived from other sources.[6] The origins of contemporary laws of wars can be traced to the teachings of the Prophet Mohammed in the 7th century and the influence of Christianity and chivalry on the conduct of war in the Middle Ages.[7]

The Renaissance in Europe stimulated the articulation of constraints on warfare, which, in some cases reached back to Roman law. The Spanish theologian Francisco de Vitoria (1480–1546) condemned the barbaric practices, including the mutilation or massacre of prisoners, the total destruction of villages, perfidy, and the poisoning of weapons.[8] Albericus Gentilis (1552–1608), an Italian who fled to England, likewise enumerated the employment of poison, veneniferous substances and magic as acts prohibited in war. 'Magic', a term also used in the *Manu Smrti*, refers in older writings to hallucinating substances. He also condemned the use of serpents.[9] According to the Dutchman Hugo Grotius (1583–1645) a belligerent may kill all enemy subjects, but his means to do so are not unlimited. He deemed the use of poison and poisoned weapons prohibited because it augmented the perils of wars too much.[10] These writers and later authors testified to certain practices in war that either were or ought to be banned.

Certain military formations adopted such prohibitions as part of their code of conduct. A pledge taken by German gunners in the late Middle Ages included an explicit prohibition against the construction or use of poisoned balls, 'because the first inventors of our art thought such actions as unjust among themselves as unworthy of a man at heart and a real soldier'.[11] Article 70 of the first US Army Field Manual (1863), also known as the Lieber code, similarly stated that 'the use of poison in any manner, be it to poison wells, or food, or arms, is wholly excluded from modern warfare. He that uses it puts himself out of the pale of the law and usages of war'.[12]

However, such unilateral expressions of behaviour on the battlefield did not bind other civilisations or political entities. The 1648 Peace of Westphalia gave rise to the sovereign state, and shortly thereafter the first international accord constraining the use of poisoned weapons in war was concluded. According to Article 57 of Strasbourg Agreement of 27 August 1675, the French and German forces, and their respective allies, agreed to prohibit the firing of poisoned bullets and to severely punish any soldier using such munition.[13] The Strasbourg Agreement was valid for the duration of the war, during which Louis XIV tried to establish French control over Lorraine. In general, however, no tacit or expressed comprehensive agreement on the conduct of war existed between states until the 19th century. Each then existing political unit – a feudal lord, a city state or hanseatic city, a religious empire, a nation, etc. – or military formation had the discretion of issuing unilateral rules to govern its conduct or to seek an understanding with an adversary.[14]

Major transformations took place during the second half of the 19th century. The sovereign state established itself as the dominant form of social organisation. As each state became recognised as an equivalent unit in the international system, the opportunities for entering in bi- or multilateral contracts increased. Furthermore, industrialisation and technological innovation rapidly changed the nature of warfare, as a consequence of which the leading powers began codifying the customs of war. They reached a milestone with the St. Petersburg Declaration of 1868 prohibiting the use of explosive, fulminating or incendiary projectiles weighing less than 400 grammes. The agreement soon became obsolete, but it was the first time a multilateral treaty referred to the custom that the 'employment of arms which uselessly aggravate the sufferings of disabled men, or render their death inevitable' is 'contrary to the laws of humanity'.[15] This fundamental principle would be repeated in all future international agreements limiting the use of weapons in armed conflict.

Over the next three decades, the codification process accelerated. The Brussels Declaration of 27 August 1874 stated that belligerents do not have unlimited power in the adoption of means to injure an enemy. Among other instruments of war, poison or poisoned weapons are especially forbidden.[16] However, not all 15 participating European governments were yet prepared to accept it as a binding convention. Lack of ratification meant it never became binding upon them. Nevertheless, together with the Oxford Manual (which proposed to outlaw the use of poison in any form whatever),[17] it laid the foundation for the agreements to be achieved at the Hague Peace Conferences in 1899 and 1907. Furthermore, towards the end of the 19th century the outcomes of the many meetings striving to codify the laws of war (even when they did not produce a treaty) increasingly began to be reflected in national instructions guiding the conduct of armed forces in combat.

Emerging science and technology and their impact on warfare

As already noted, the introduction of firearms reduced the utility of poisoned kinetic weapons. That, however, did not prevent ideas for using of chemicals to force defenders from fortifications from emerging. The same technological developments also reduced the military utility of incendiary weapons: units began engaging each other at distances outside the traditional range of flaming projectiles. The incorporation of more non-combustible materials in armour and defensive constructions, too, decreased their usefulness. Not until the First World War would scientific progress be able to overcome these obstacles.[18]

Before 1914 armies used smoke only sporadically. In one rare instance, King Charles XII of Sweden crossed the Dvina River in the face of Polish-Saxon foes under the protection of a smoke screen generated by burning large quantities of damp straw.[19] However, in the 19th century smoke generated by the increased use of black powder reduced visibility over the battlefield, thus hampering military operations. Although smokeless powder remedied the problem by the time of the American Civil War, the earlier experiences nonetheless retarded development of artificial smoke as a tactical instrument of land warfare. Only in the summer of 1915 did the belligerents commence to utilise smoke on any regular basis. Naval tactics, in contrast, had recognised the importance of concealment before the outbreak of the First World War.[20]

During the 18th and early 19th centuries, the evolution of weapon technology and fortification design rekindled interest in asphyxiating clouds in Europe. The idea of using of toxic chemicals to dislodge defenders from fortified positions was in and of itself not new. Archeological field investigations and contemporary literature have documented several incidents in Antiquity. Around 1600, Italian doctor and physicist Leonardo Fioravanti proposed an oil distilled from turpentine, sulphur, asafetida, human faeces and blood, etc., whose stench would have driven anybody from his position in a fortification so attacked.[21] A Yugoslav writer on chemical warfare claimed that a poisonous cloud saved Belgrade from the Turks in 1456.[22] During the French North African campaign in 1845, Lieutenant-Colonel Aimable Pélissier ordered the burning of green wood to suffocate the tribe of Kabyls, whose members had sought refuge in caves at Ouled Ria (south-east of Algiers).[23] In response to the outrage in Europe, the French Minister of War had to issue a public apology and recalled Pélissier to Paris (which did not prevent him from being appointed Governor-General of Algeria in May 1951 and promoted to Marshal following victory at Sebastopol during the Crimean War in September 1855).

The growing application of the scientific method to chemistry and the nascent

Thomas Cochrane 10th Earl of Dundonald.

industrialisation in the first half of the 19th century called forth more sophisticated proposals. The British naval officer Thomas Cochrane (later Admiral Cochrane, Lord Dundonald) suggested in 1812 to drive the Napoleonic forces from the coastal fortifications at Toulon by burning ships filled with sulphur.[24] The resulting sulphur dioxide had been known since Antiquity to be unbreathable as Egyptians, Greeks, Hebrews and Romans used it for fumigating buildings. Poisonous fumes were also part of tunnelling and counter-tunnelling operations under the walls of besieged cities. Recent archeological investigation, for example, discovered the skeletons of 19 Roman and one Sassanid (pre-Persian) soldiers under the walls of the ancient city of Dura-Europos, whose ruins lie on the banks of the Eufrates on the Syrian–Iraqi border. In the 3rd century, the Sassanids, who were trying to collapse the city walls, ignited sulphur and naphtha to frustrate a Roman counter-mining operation.[25] Yet, armies had apparently never employed the gas in pure form in siege operations or manoeuvres before Cochrane's proposal.[26]

Described as 'a man of wide observation and no mean chemist,' Cochrane observed during a visit to the Sulphur Kilns on Sicily in July 1811 how the fumes produced during the sulphur extraction process destroyed all surrounding vegetation and endangered animal life to a great distance. People were forbidden to sleep within three miles of the kilns during the melting season. He immediately sought to apply the observed phenomenon to military and naval purposes.[27] A committee appointed by the British government to study the proposal expressed doubts about its feasibility because of the variable, uncontrollable factors of wind, weather, currents and tides. In 1846 he resubmitted his plan with the added feature of using a smoke screen to obscure the sulphur ships. A new government-appointed committee again rejected the idea, this time on grounds that the use of sulphur dioxide would be against the rules of warfare and because of the fear that after initial British use other armed forces would swiftly adopt the method against them. The admiral revived his ideas during the Crimean War, but they were refused once more *inter alia* for the added reason advanced by the scientist Michael Faraday that it would not be difficult for the defenders to provide respirators.[28] Another attempt the next year also failed. Early in September 1914, one month into the war, Lt. Gen. Lord Dundonald submitted his grandfather's plans to drive the enemy from his position by noxious fumes to Field Marshal Horatio Herbert Kitchener. After being rebuffed on grounds that the plans were of no use in land warfare since they had been invented by an admiral, he turned to Winston Churchill, then First Lord of the Admiralty. After several months of consideration, consultations, and even experiments, Churchill decided that while a technical committee would further investigate the matter, especially as regards smoke, Britain could not depart from the accepted laws of war.[29] The date was 21 March 1915, almost to the day one month before the Germans launched their first major gas attack.

The Crimean War (1854–56) presaged the impact technology, industrial power and military organisation was to have on the conduct of warfare. In addition, the frustrations of a stalemated battlefield stimulated military inventiveness. A significant aspect of the British chemical warfare ideas throughout the 19th century – few as they still were – was their continuity in development rather than being discrete proposals as had been the case previously. Their submission to scientific or technical committees before the government made its policy decision undoubtedly furthered this progression. When Cochrane initially suggested the sulphur dioxide screens, the British forces had been employing smoke balls, composed of a mixture of saltpetre, coal, pitch, tar, resin, sawdust, crude antimony and sulphur for quite a long time. These weapons were declared obsolete only in August 1883. Their purpose was threefold: concealment, signals, and for suffocating or expelling the enemy from casemates, mines, or between decks of naval vessels. At the time apparently nobody commented on the similarity between the smoke balls and Cochrane's proposals.[30]

However, one committee member to whom Lord Dundonald's proposals had been sent and who had rejected them was the chemist Lyon Playfair. In two respects he played an important role. First, he preserved all of Lord Dundonald's papers and in 1886

Lyon Playfair.

transferred them to the admiral's grandson, who later submitted them to Churchill in the first months of the First World War.[31] Second, he also became interested in the subject of chemistry in war and suggested, in contrast to Lord Dundonald's smoke proposals, two types of chemical shell for application in the Crimean War. The first one was to contain – in a significant move away from the simple burning of sulphur – the highly poisonous organo-arsenic compound cacodyl chloride to make the operation of guns on enemy ships impossible.

The second shell was to be filled with an incendiary agent based on white phosphorous for use against land targets. The War Department rejected the propositions because it equated the mode of warfare to poisoning the enemy's water. His ideas were far ahead of his time and, because the chemical industry had not yet reached the stage of large-scale production of either compound, it is doubtful that the British forces would have been able to utilise the shells widely if the government had responded favourably.[32]

Around the same time Scottish chemist John Stenhouse designed two types of gas mask based on a filter of powdered wood charcoal, which was known to remove unpleasant odours from decaying meat if strewn over it, and furnished with a velvet lining for a tight facial fit. He also devised filters to purify air entering rooms.[33] As with Faraday's comments about protective masks on Dundonald's proposals, the military significance of defence against gas was grasped only decades later. In other countries too, gas mask development, especially for work in mines and the chemical industry, progressed considerably before any large-scale offensive use of the latest industrial toxic substances was contemplated.[34]

In the United States, individuals were also experimenting with noxious chemicals. In 1825, James Cutbush, professor of chemistry and mineralogy at West Point, published a book entitled *System of Pyrotechny, Comprehending the Theory and Practice, with the Application of Chemistry; Designed for Exhibition and War*. He thought of a whole range chemical, incendiary and smoke devices, most notably stink balls for harassing enemy troops. The idea turned up again during the Civil War to drive the enemy from trenches. Although the Confederates were apparently able to produce the devices if ordered to do so, suggesting that it was not a novel contraption, no evidence of actual use is on record.[35] As this war, like the Crimean War, stimulated innovation, many other proposals emerged. Interestingly, all but one of these ideas originated with the Northerners, an indication of the growing disparities regarding the application of science and technology to warfare between industrialised and essentially agrarian societies.[36] In a letter to President Lincoln,

Forrest Sheppard proposed the mixing of acids, the heat of which would produce a mist of hydrochloric acid that then rolled towards the enemy entrenchments. While not possessing the lethality of later warfare agents, it would have nonetheless forced the soldiers to abandon their positions. John Doughty sent in August 1862 sketches and a detailed description for a chlorine shell. The characteristics of the chemical in the field, combined with the slow rate and inaccuracy of artillery fire, would have prevented the achievement of sufficient density over the target to be effective. Chlorine – but then liquefied in cylinders – was the agent the Germans were to release during their initial cloud attacks in April 1915. The sole known Southern idea on chemical warfare was to chloroform the ironclad Monitor. It arose after a naval battle with the Southern Merrimac had ended in a draw. Whether the suggestion was made in seriousness or jest is unknown.[37]

Even though very much on an individual basis, some military thinkers were considering delivery of toxic chemicals as a means of overcoming evolving defensive technologies. Most of the historical research concerns the British Empire and the United States, but evidence of similar interest in other industrialising countries would not surprise. An interesting feature of the trend is that officials, particularly in Great Britain, did not reject the proposals outright on grounds of violation of the laws and customs of war, but started to submit them to committees for consideration. It signified the scientification of policy-making. Moral or legal considerations entered the deliberations when science or technology offered marginal benefits at best or long-term advantages were in doubt. This trend was the clearest in Great Britain because of the continuity of thinking, one of its characteristics being repeated submissions of ideas and their consideration by successive committees. Ultimately the ideas failed to gain any traction, partly because the science or technology was still immature, or because of age-old bureaucratic prejudices. The rejection in 1914 of a proposal for the use of noxious fumes in land warfare because the idea came from a naval officer was a case in point. No other designs are known to have been proposed before the First World War, except for some irritant substances the French filled into bullets for riot control and similar British developments.[38]

A different trend was rising independently from military considerations. Many of the toxicants introduced to the battlefields during the First World War derived from developments in chemistry and chemical industry for more than a century. Chemical warfare as understood today was a distinctive outgrowth of the second industrial revolution, which originated from an increasingly utilitarian application of scientific principles driven by an economic rationale during the second half of the 19th century. This transformation, long in the making, ultimately took place in a relatively short span of time: 'About 1880 physical chemistry was not yet a formally established academic discipline; a generation later it was transforming the industry [...].'[39] The foundations for this revolution were laid more or less simultaneously in several countries, including Great Britain, France, Germany and the United States, all already belonging to the industrial centre.

Greek fire – from the The Madrid Skylitzes, a richly illustrated manuscript.

Some chemicals that were to become notorious during the First World War had been discovered many decades earlier. Chlorine, the agent used near Ypres in April 1915, was first prepared by Swedish chemist Carl Wilhelm Scheele in 1774 (even though only recognised as a distinctive element by the British chemist Humphry Davy in 1810).[40] Davy also first synthesised phosgene in 1811.[41] Another British investigator, Frederick Guthrie first described mustard agent and several of its toxic effects in two contributions published in 1860–61.[42] Later laboratory research in Germany yielded more information on its deleterious actions, as well as alternative production methods. Initially both the Germans and Allies ignored its effects and failed to consider the compound as a potent warfare agent.[43]

The real challenge was their production on an industrial scale once their utility in other processes had been established, a capability only achieved towards the end of the 19th century. Chlorine, for example, found widespread use in the manufacture of bleaching powder for the paper and textile industries, but liquefaction for industrial purposes only became possible in 1888.[44] Only seven decades after the discovery of phosgene did Germany, then the sole country to have realised its importance as an intermediate in the dyestuff manufacture, begin its production on an industrial scale. On the eve of the First World War, France and Britain too possessed the equipment for phosgene production. For diverse reasons, including access to overseas raw materials and the search for alternatives, the chemical industry developed at markedly different rates in those countries.

During the final years of the 19th century the various trends in chemistry, chemical industry and the application of technology in military art were clearly converging. Investment in science by the industry promoted applied research and preferred integrated work by one or more research teams over individuals at academic institutes. Still, remaining largely absent was systematic cross-fertilisation between civilian scientists and the new industries, on the one hand, and the military establishment, on the other hand. With the growing impact of technological innovation on military affairs, the latter group tended to rely more on its own ability to anticipate and solve technical problems. The new explosives appearing towards the end of the 19th century, however, required advanced knowledge of chemistry, which the civilian sector could provide.[45] It would nonetheless take the continuance of the First World War for the military establishment to prioritise scientific innovation. Indeed, that war provided the real stimulus for focused military-oriented research into chemical compounds with the prime purpose of exploiting their poisonous characteristics against humans or their habitat. A British and a German source denied any concerted offensive chemical warfare preparations before 1914.[46]

If military officers steeped in tradition lacked technological imagination, science fiction presaged the future battlefield. The presentation of deadly gases as high-technology weaponry in many military science-fiction novels in different countries around the turn of the century – for instance, H. G. Wells' *The War of the Worlds* (serialised in 1897) – reflected the chemical industry's growing impact on societies. Scientific, technological and industrial developments occurred relatively independently, but at different pace in different countries. The Crimean, American Civil and Franco–Prussian Wars each demonstrated the impact of those trends on the battlefield. Novel weapon designs and the degree to which a state was able to mobilise its technological and industrial base in support of warfare increasingly segregated agrarian societies from the rising industrial powerhouses. The then theoretical possibility of employing novel toxic substances as a potentially decisive weapon of war, as well as recent war experiences, caused sufficient concern for the powers to consider legal constraints on emerging military technologies. The 1899 Hague Peace Conference was to be the first one in a long line of efforts.

Going beyond poison: the prohibition on asphyxiating gases

Vocabulary tends to reflect the rapid changes in a society. Multiple words get coined to delineate specific phenomena. To a large degree they will be synonymous, yet also display semantic differentiation. Certain groups with a political interest in maintaining a sharp characterization of their field of activities will come to challenge some emerging referent meanings. In contrast, some terms, while fully synonymous, will claim an exclusive space, because groups want to isolate their field of activities from broader debates to avoid political interference.

Biotechnology is today in the middle of such a process as, for example, various stakeholders debate the implications of certain types of genetic modification of pathogens for future biological warfare or terrorism with biological weapons. 'Gain-of-function' research investigates how infectivity of a given pathogen may be augmented in order to understand future disease threats. In several respects the work mimics natural genetic evolution in a laboratory. However, in the process it creates artificial disease variants with no natural equivalent. Their escape out of a laboratory could cause an epidemiological disaster. Their potential development for military use or falling in the hands of terrorists rank among some of the worst human-made nightmares. Researchers began objecting to the utilisation of 'gain-of-function' in a security framework because it carried negative connotations for many analogous routine investigations. Government officials and security analysts consequently adopted the term 'dual-use research of concern', which connects easily with the broader threat framework of proliferation of dual-use technologies to unsavoury governments or terrorist entities. Yet they do not wish the term applied to exactly the same type of investigation in genetic modification carried out in government and private contractor laboratories as part of mostly secret biodefence programmes, which has been labelled 'science-based threat analysis'.[47]

Just like biology and biotechnology today, chemistry and chemical industry at the end of the 19th century brought forth a strong sense of scientific and technological achievement and power as well as of existential dread. Captains of industry strongly resisted any governmental regulation of their activities, but at the same time sought governmental contracts and support to maintain their international market share. As noted earlier, a large chemical industrial base contributed to the projection of military might. Concerns about this shifting balance of power led agrarian states, Russia in particular, to call for an international meeting to curb this qualitative armament dynamic, the 1899 Hague Peace Conference. In international forums the type of semantic skirmishing described above plays out on even more levels, as a diplomats interpret a given concept in function of their nation's value system, commercial, geopolitical and security interests, and threat perceptions too. Its impact is visible in the degree of consensus on any issue that delegates can achieve. Uncontroversial proposals will engender little debate; matters whose impact are still little understood or affect a country's primary interests negatively are less likely to be adopted unanimously or at all.

The Hague Peace Conference ended with the world's leading powers concluding the first multilateral agreements on the conduct of war. The core conventions it produced gained absolute unanimity. However, it was not successful on every count. In particular, the conference failed in its primary objective to curb the armaments build-up and the technological competition between nations. It barely managed three Declarations that touched on novel weapon developments. Only a majority of the twenty-six participating powers adopted the Declarations. The count thus reflected the highest possible level of consensus at that specific point in time. As will be discussed below, in the German perception of the role in international law in warfare, absence of unanimity testified to the immaturity of a particular rule. Consequently, it could be discarded if it conflicted with military necessity on the battlefield. The reasons why consensus proved illusive in the deliberations of proposal to ban the use of asphyxiating gases also clarify how delegates came to view this emerging category of weaponry as distinct from poison.

In diplomacy coercing negotiating parties into accepting positions contrary to their perceived national interests is impossible. The US First Delegate, Joseph F. Choate, recalled the absolute importance of consensus during the deliberations in a lecture given in 1912:

It is always necessary, in considering the work of this Conference, to remember the absolute necessity controlling it at every moment, in order to attain the end of absolute unanimity, to weigh every word in every article proposed, in order to meet any objection that might be interposed from any quarter [...][48]

In his instructions to the American delegation to the 1907 Hague Conference Secretary of State Elihu Root wrote:

In the discussions upon every question it is important to remember that the object of the conference is agreement, and not compulsion. If such conferences are to be made occasions for trying to force nations into positions which they consider against their interests, the powers cannot be expected to send representatives to them. It is important also that the agreements reached shall be genuine and not reluctant. Otherwise they will inevitably fail to receive approval when submitted for the ratification of the powers represented. Comparison of views and frank and considerate explanation and discussion may frequently resolve doubts, obviate difficulties, and lead to real agreement upon matters which at the outset have appeared insurmountable. It is not wise, however, to carry this process to the point of irritation. After reasonable discussion, if no agreement is reached, it is better to lay the subject aside, or refer it to some future conference in the hope that intermediate consideration may dispose of the objections. Upon some questions where an agreement by only a part of the powers represented would in itself be useful, such an agreement may be made, but it should always be with the most unreserved recognition that the other powers withhold their concurrence with equal propriety and right.[49]

Reporting on the work of the preparatory committee of the Final Act, French delegate Louis Renault explained that the various documents accomplished at the first International Peace Conference might bear a different number of signatures because of varying national interests.[50] The level of consensus among the participating states may therefore be taken as an indicator of the strength of a particular interdiction in prevailing international law. At the same time, it underscores the degree to which those states share a common understanding of the nature of new types of weaponry or their potential humanitarian impact on the battlefield.

However, in an especially harsh appraisal of procedures at both Hague conferences, a leading French jurist, Antoine Pillet, wrote in 1918 that the authority of the rules adopted unanimously had more appearance than reality. Disillusioned as he was by the negligible impact of international law on the First World War, he attacked the system of commissions, sub-commissions and special commissions of inquiry, in which small groups composed of the same men negotiated, but rarely achieved consensus. As the proposals moved upward through the commission system, fundamental questions and issues were being ignored. By the time they had reached the plenary session, such questions and issues could no longer be raised since they would have threatened the entire enterprise of the Conference. Meanwhile, where divergencies existed, the required unanimity was obtained by changes in the phraseology, which entailed a broadening of the provision's scope or weakening of its content.[51]

This criticism adds even more weight to the semantic shift that was taking place in the 1890s. Whether one describes a toxicant as a poison or an asphyxiant, from a chemical or physiological perspective no distinction exists. Yet, the progressing semantic bifurcation between poison and asphyxiating gases led to two separate documents. Moreover, one agreement failed to reach consensus. The substance of Pillet's criticism does not appear to have affected the conventional ban on the use of poison. Indeed, the delegates adopted the relevant clause from the 1874 Brussels Declaration without any discussion at all.[52] The declaration on poisonous or deleterious gases, by contrast, failed to obtain unanimity at all levels of deliberations as a consequence of US dissent. Yet, in a paradoxical implementation of Secretary of State Root's instructions to the US delegation, sufficient states thought it worthwhile to agree to and sign the Declaration (IV, 2). While the survival of the proposal through the various negotiation stages weakens Pillet's charge, the lack of unanimous consent nonetheless testifies to the degree of controversy the proposal generated and the subsequent relative weakness of the constraint.

While the consensus factor confirms the existence of the semantic shift, procedural and substantive debates both attested to the nature of the bifurcation. In conformity with the agenda in Count Mikhail Muravieff's letter of 11 January 1899,[53] the Second Commission of the International Peace Conference dealing with the laws and customs of war on land set to review the 1874 Brussels Declaration. Art. 12 of the latter document wanted to deny belligerents unlimited power in the adoption of means of injuring an enemy. Art. 13 applied the principle to poison or poisoned weapons as well as some other modes of warfare. Apart from some phraseological modifications, the Commission maintained the prohibitions in respectively articles 22 and 23 of the regulations annexed to the Hague Convention (II). The Second Commission furthermore united the provisions on the means to injure an enemy and on sieges and bombardments in a single chapter to state unequivocally that the articles regarding the means to injure an enemy are also applicable to sieges and to bombardments.[54] It thus expanded the circumstances applicable to the use of poison.

At the 1907 International Peace Conference in The Hague no amendments to these provisions were submitted to the Second Commission.[55] The Fourth Commission dealing with issues relating to naval warfare, on the other hand, investigated to what extent the Regulations Respecting the Laws and Customs of War on Land annexed to the 1899 Hague Convention (II) might apply to maritime war. A committee of inquiry concluded that the adaptation of these regulations to the war at sea would necessitate fundamental modifications. This required critical examination, a task for which the committee was unprepared.[56] It nonetheless carried out a tentative translation, which was annexed to the Fourth Commission's General Report as the Laws and Customs of

Maritime War. Noteworthy is that the committee declared articles 22 and 23 of the 1899 regulations applicable without any comment.[57] The conference, having failed to produce regulations regarding maritime warfare, still expressed the desire that pending such regulations the Powers may apply, as far as possible, to war by sea the principles of the Convention relative to the laws and customs of war on land.[58] In view of the committee's recorded opinion, little doubt exists that the use of poison or poisoned weapons were also considered outlawed in naval engagements.

The ease with which the ban on the use of poison could be extended to other domains of international law testified to the lack of controversy. Far less agreement existed regarding limitations on the use of asphyxiating gases. One aspect was purely procedural. Count Muravieff's letter of 11 January 1899 limited the agenda for the First International Peace Conference to eight topics. In view of geopolitical realities in Europe, he thus accepted, among other things, that items not contained in the programme were to remain entirely excluded from the talks.[59] In the First Subcommission of the First Commission dealing with *inter alia* the implements of war on land, the issue of prohibiting new means of destruction depending on the application of chemistry and electricity surfaced. The absence of any formal reference in the programme led to it not being discussed. As the second point on the proposed agenda mentioned new firearms, new explosives and more powerful powders, it can be surmised that 'the application of chemistry' did not refer to the production of traditional munitions. Moreover, when the subject came up in the First Commission itself, the German representative, Colonel Gross von Schwarzhoff, accepted Russia's point 'that the existing methods of war are sufficient', but countered successfully that 'we should not tie our hands in advance so that we should have to ignore more humane methods which may be invented in future'.[60] Again, the implication was one of some future implement of war. In other words, the direct application of chemistry to war was too new a proposal to be formally included in the negotiations. Remarkably, the idea of applying chemistry to war itself was not dismissed as revulsive. On the contrary, it might produce a implement of war that was more humane and therefore morally preferable. Had the association with poison been close, the objection to its inclusion in the deliberations may not have been raised. The issue itself might even not have been raised at all.

Another facet of the controversy was one of substance. Asphyxiating gases cropped up during the discussions on new explosives in the Second Subcommission of the First Commission on naval war. When a proposal to prohibit qualitative improvements in explosives was defeated because this would have been to the detriment of smaller powers, the Russian representative, Captain Schéine, substituted it for one to ban the use of 'projectiles charged with explosives which diffuse asphyxiating or deleterious gases.' Following a remark by Count Soltyk of Austria-Hungary that all explosives contain gas that may be injurious, Captain Schéine rephrased his proposition to 'include only those projectiles whose object is to diffuse asphyxiating gases, and not to those whose explosion produces incidentally such gases.' Austria-Hungary, Denmark, France, Great Britain, Portugal and Russia endorsed the proposal on the following grounds:

- the task of the conference being to restrict the means of destruction, it is logical to prohibit 'new' means, above all when they have a barbarous character and partake of treachery and cruelty similar to the poisoning of drinking water;
- directed against a besieged city, they would destroy more non-combatants than ordinary projectiles;
- death from asphyxiation is more cruel than death from bullets;
- means should be sought for putting enemies out of battle, but not out of this world.[61]

The approach to chemical substances as new weaponry differed markedly in both subcommissions. The first rejected any discussion on the formal ground that the weaponry had not been included in the programme. The second interpreted the issue in the context of the fundamental principle underlying the entire codification endeavour: humanity in war. Important for the present discussion is the recognition that asphyxiating gases were a *new* means of destruction and that their treachery and cruelty were *similar* to that of the poisoning of drinking water. Asphyxiating gases thus did not equal poison in the delegates' minds. Rather, they believed that in their action both were perfidious, indiscriminate and cruel, qualities reproved by time-honoured customs of war.

Captain Alfred Thayer Mahan, US naval delegate, vehemently opposed the proposal and cast his vote against it. He voiced his support for the use of toxic gases in the First Commission and before the Conference too, in the process underscoring the differences between poison and gas. In a report to the US government justifying his action, he wrote:

> As a certain disposition has been observed to attach odium to the view adopted by this commission [i.e. the United States delegation] in this matter, it seems proper to state, fully and explicitly, for the information of the Government, that on the first occasion of the subject arising in Subcommittee, and subsequently at various times in full Committee, and before the Conference, the United States naval delegate did not cast his vote silently, but gave the reasons, which at his demand were inserted in the reports of the day's proceedings. These reasons were, briefly: 1. That no shell emitting such gases is as yet in practical use, or has undergone adequate experiment; consequently, a vote taken now would be in ignorance of the facts as to whether the results would be of a decisive character, or whether injury in excess of that necessary to attain the end of warfare, the immediate disabling of the enemy, would be inflicted. 2. That the reproach of cruelty and perfidy, addressed against these supposed shells, was equally uttered formally against firearms and torpedoes, both of which are now employed without scruple. Until we know the effects of such asphyxiating shells, there was no saying whether they would be more or less merciful than missiles now permitted. 3. That it was illogical, and not demonstrably humane, to be tender

about asphyxiating men with gas, when all were prepared to admit that it was allowable to blow the bottom out of an iron-clad at midnight, throwing four or five hundred into the sea, to be choked by water, with scarcely the remotest chance of escape. If and when, a shell emitting asphyxiating gases alone has been successfully produced, then, and not before, men will be able to vote intelligently on the subject.[62]

Mahan's opposition was entirely motivated by the weapon's new technological qualities and the possibility that because of them it may prove decisive in a future war while not causing superfluous suffering. Not unlike Gross von Schwarzhoff's contemplation about the potential contribution of chemicals in war to the humanisation of warfare, Mahan essentially viewed technology as value-neutral. Only the mode of application might be immoral. Yet, the technological imperative, gathering strength with the Second Industrial Revolution, prevailed upon American diplomacy. Traditional norms and values ceded to technocratic arguments, as Ambassador Andrew Dickson White, leader of the American delegation, recorded in his diary at the time of the discussion:

To this [Captain Mahan's argument] it was answered – and as it seemed to me, with force – that asphyxiating bombs might be used against towns for the destruction of vast numbers of non-combatants, including women and children, while torpedoes at sea are used only against military and naval forces of the enemy. The original proposal was carried by a unanimous vote, save ours. I am not satisfied with our attitude on this question; but what can a layman do when he has against him the foremost contemporary military and naval experts? My hope is that the United States will yet stand with the majority on the record.[63]

The lack of unanimity provoked the British refusal to sign the declaration. Six other states had signed the document on condition of unanimity but ratified it nonetheless.[64] At the Second International Peace Conference, Great Britain announced its accession to the agreement in order to achieve the highest degree of unanimity. Several South and Central American countries, which had not participated in the 1899 discussions, also acceded, making the United States the only country at the 1907 Hague Conference opposing the prohibition. Moreover, no country requested in 1907 to revise Declaration (IV, 2), following which it was declared to be of indefinite duration.[65] A state could only denounce it by giving one year's notice in advance. In 1908, Hull concluded rather optimistically that 'this action on the part of forty-three out of forty-four of the world's governments is probably the reason why human ingenuity has not been devoted more conspicuously to the invention or improvement of asphyxiating bombs; and it will doubtless prevent this particular means of warfare from being resorted to in the future.'[66]

The delegates at the First Hague Conference in 1899 made no direct association between poison and asphyxiating gases. They considered the former an ancient, barbarous mode of warfare, whose long-standing customary prohibition generated no controversy. Poisonous or deleterious gases, on the other hand, were clearly perceived by all as a novel development spawned by the growing impact of science on society and industry. At best, the negotiators recognised their perfidy comparable to that of poison and thought that the overall customary rules of humanity in war should apply to their use too. Conversely, technological progress held out the promise of shortening wars or even of rendering them virtually impossible because of the potential decisiveness of new weaponry in combat. The optimism in progress supported the view that – at least theoretically – such weapons would actually contribute to humanity in war by reducing the overall number of casualties. Therefore, they should not be included in the list of implements of war specifically banned by the customs and laws of war.

Declaration (IV, 2) expressed the compromise between both positions. On the one hand, the traditional norms were made applicable to poison gas. On the other hand, the mere act of making poisonous and deleterious gases the object of a separate legal document rather than incorporating them into the regulations regarding war on land in itself constituted their recognition as a novel type of weaponry. Moreover, the document only covered one technology known to the negotiators, namely shells whose sole object is the diffusion of toxic or harmful gases, and made no attempt to cover future developments, for instance by including an explicit reference to analogous or similar methods.[67] The vehement opposition by the United States only underscored the lack of time-honoured repugnance of the use of poisonous or deleterious gases. The stance presaged the debates on the humaneness of chemical warfare after the First World War.

German interpretation of the laws of war

The rise of the sovereign state as the central actor in the international system after the 1648 Peace of Westphalia contributed to the emergence of different principles in the conduct of war than those accepted under natural law. The intellectual debate about which legal doctrine takes precedence over the other contributed significantly to the lack of an unconditional and absolute prohibition on the use of toxic weapons on the eve of the First World War. Current literature by and large ignores past existence of rivalling legal doctrines, partly because the international community has greatly tempered the impact of natural law and partly because of the widespread assumption that war regulations have systematically aimed at restricting the application of violence in combat. Imperial Germany, however, made consistent unilateral statements to the contrary and applied them in the Franco-Prussian war of 1870–71. The doctrine also provided Berlin with the legal framework for resorting to gas after the Western front had stalemated in 1914.

In the late 18th and 19th centuries German literature on *Kriegsrecht*, the law of war, distinguished between *Kriegsmanier*, the conduct of war according to the ordinary customs and laws of war, and *Kriegsraison*, the non-observation of these customs and laws dictated by the necessity of war (*ratio belli*).[68] *Kriegsraison* took precedence over *Kriegsrecht*. All proven means that led to the enemy's impossibility to continue the armed struggle were considered licit; all acts of violence that did not contribute to that goal were illegal and barbarous.[69] The principle also found its justification in the military commander's duty to do his utmost best to achieve victory and responsibility for his men.[70] Its normalcy in German legal thought was probably best reflected in the remark that it was self-evident that all violations of the laws of war (*Kriegsmanier*) authorised the enemy to violate these rules in turn to take reprisals.[71] In other words, acts justifiable by *Kriegsraison* offered no legal grounds for reprisals. The legal position reflected military doctrine too: 'Hurting the enemy shall only be a means to achieve the war aims, thus to weaken the enemy state, so that the opposing willpower may be bent and the claims against him enforced; that is to weaken the enemy state in every respect, because no grounds exist to confine the weakening solely to its armed forces.'[72]

Especially after the Franco-Prussian war *Kriegsraison* came up for international criticism. Professor Karl Lueder of the University of Erlangen, ostensibly in an effort to parry foreign condemnation, deviated from the general understanding of the concept at the time. He stressed that it could only be exceptionally invoked and did not violate the law of war (*Kriegsrecht*) precisely because of that exceptionality.[73] He identified two situations in which the recourse to *Kriegsraison* is legitimate, namely retorsion and extreme necessity. Retorsion is a breach of the laws of war committed by one state upon another as an act of retaliation or reprisal justified by the unfair disadvantage the state against which the original violation was committed would otherwise find itself in.[74] This idea of self-help among states, rooted in the fundamental principle of self-preservation, was recognised by prevailing international law and also governed by rules.[75] Extreme necessity, in contrast, occurred when a belligerent was unable to achieve the war aims or escape an extreme danger while observing the limitations imposed by the laws of war. The belligerent should, according to Lueder, choose to violate international rules if this contributed to achieving the war aims or avoiding that danger. He justified the derogation by claiming that war was too serious a business and that defeat or ruin were unacceptable outcomes for a state.

Lueder thus deviated in two important respects from contemporary German jurists. First, he assumed the primacy of the law of the war and considered *Kriegsraison* to be applicable in exceptional circumstances only. Second, he argued that retorsion was precisely such an exceptional circumstance. In doing so, Lueder exposed himself to other criticism.[76] It was indeed not necessary to justify retorsion since the principle was internationally recognised. The gravest misgiving, however, concerned the notion of 'extreme necessity'. It authorised under given circumstances the use of all means except for absolute prohibitions explicitly adopted by convention or means of warfare subject to long-time condemnation by mankind, such as poison or items infected by disease.[77] Yet, according to the logic, so one critic argued, the principle of 'extreme necessity' might apply to these cases too.[78]

After the conclusion of the 1899 Hague Conference the polemic persisted despite the signing of the conventions and declarations by Germany. Article 1 of the Convention (IV) Respecting the Laws and Customs of War on Land required the contracting states to issue instructions in conformity with the regulations annexed to the convention to their armed forces. When in 1902 the German General Staff issued with governmental approval *Kriegsgebrauch im Landkriege*, the instructions met with severe criticism from American, British and French sources because they appeared to legitimise the 'barbaric forms of warfare of earlier ages'.[79] In particular, it emphasised the place of *Kriegsraison* and made scant, derisory reference to the Hague documents. In the introduction, for example, it warned military commanders against the humanitarian tendencies of the time and referred to the humane principles of the Hague Conventions as 'Sentimentalität und weicheliche Gefühlsschwärmerei' ('sentimentalism and flabby emotion').[80] As such, *Kriegsraison* as an overruling part in *Kriegsrecht* remained a long-standing unilateral statement on the conduct of war from Germany that went against the general trend of evolving international law during the last quarter of the 19th and first decade of the 20th century. The international polemic, however, demonstrated the concept's problematic nature and testified to an active conventionalisation process. After the First World War the international community firmly rejected any such interpretation.[81] The United Nations Charter in 1945 repudiated the right of self-help (*Notrecht*) as defined at the time and upheld by several German authors.[82]

Gas warfare and international law on the eve of the First World War

Constraining the use of poisons and poisoned weapons in war during the latter half of the 19th century reflected a steady progression from prohibitions formulated in different locations and at different times to multilateral codification. After the First World War a further evolution took place when the international community began to focus on banning the weapon itself, rather than just its use. This process is still continuing today, not just because of scientific and technological progress, but also because of the changing context in which the treaties must remain valid. An analogous dynamic in the late 1800s created the paradox that confronted the negotiators at the First Hague Peace Conference.

If decision-makers or diplomats formulated a more general principle that because of its generality might be able to retain its relevancy under changing circumstances, then they risked that its application would prove impractical in specific situations. An international prohibition on the use of poison, as contained in the 1899 and 1907 Conventions on land warfare, is essentially useless without national instructions providing for the criminalisation and penalisation of breaches. However, those responsible for overseeing compliance of the prohibition would be the same persons who may decide to employ the proscribed weapon. In those days nobody was considering formal mechanisms, whether national or international, to investigate allegations of poison use or impose international sanctions against the offending state. Any such initiatives would have been *ad hoc* and dependent on the geopolitical coalitions of the moment, as well as the disposition of the offending country to abide by the sanction regime.

If, in contrast, the prohibition is too specific, then it can be easily circumvented or diverse societal and technological processes can render it rapidly obsolete. Gas cylinders avoided the interdiction on asphyxiating gases, because Declaration (IV, 2) limited its application to the dissemination by means of projectiles.

As will be discussed in the final chapter of this book, the legal situation on the eve of the First World War would enable the Germans to deny that they had violated international law when they introduced chemical weapons to the battlefield. The Allies, in contrast, did not accuse the Germans during or after the war of having breached the interdiction against poison and poisoned weapons as formulated in The Hague Conventions of 1899 and 1907. Rather, they charged that the Germans went against the principle of the 1899 Hague Declaration (IV, 2). In 1915, however, the latter rule was too young to belong to the customs of war. Moreover, it had not been unanimously adopted. In other words, according to the German interpretation of international law the document did not represent a well-established and ancient custom.

Notes

1 Convention (II) with Respect to the Laws and Customs of War on Land and its annex: Regulations concerning the Laws and Customs of War on Land, signed at The Hague, 29 July 1899. Available from the International Committee of the Red Cross (ICRC) website at <https://www.icrc.org/ihl/INTRO/150?OpenDocument>.

2 Convention (IV) respecting the Laws and Customs of War on Land and its annex: Regulations concerning the Laws and Customs of War on Land, signed at The Hague, 18 October 1907. Available from the ICRC website at <https://www.icrc.org/ihl/INTRO/195>.

3 Declaration (IV,2) concerning Asphyxiating Gases, signed at The Hague, 29 July 1899. Available from the ICRC website at <https://www.icrc.org/applic/ihl/ihl.nsf/Article.xsp?action=openDocument&documentId=2531E92D282B5436C12563CD00516149>.

4 While today international law distinguishes between chemical and biological weapons, the latter category only received separate recognition with the 1925 Geneva Protocol. The propagation of disease became scientifically understood in the late 19th century. Prior conception of infection did not allow for pathogens as objects to be manipulated, whether for medical treatment or use as a method of warfare. Nevertheless, many acts of war that today would qualify as biological warfare fell under 'poisoning'.

5 G. Bühler (Translator), *The Laws of Manu. Translated with Extracts from Seven Commentaries* (Oxford University Press: Oxford, 1886), reprinted under UNESCO sponsorship in The Sacred Books of the East, vol 25 (Motilal Banarsidass: Delhi, 1975), p. 230. Chapter VII 'The King', verses 87–98 laid down the ruler's conduct in war. The ban on the use of poison, as well as of treacherous and incendiary devices and weapons that cause superfluous injury, is contained in verse 90.

6 As a consequence of the Diaspora, Jewish teachings did not further develop a code against the use of poison in war as the Jews did not have a homogenous territory to defend as a nation. After 1948, Israel has taken up the debate on the legitimacy of chemical and biological weapons as a sovereign state rather than as a religious entity.

7 J. P. Zanders, 'International norms against chemical and biological warfare: An ambiguous legacy', *Journal of Conflict & Security Law*, vol. 8 no. 2 (2003), pp. 392–93.

8 J. Barthélemy, 'François de Vitoria', in A. Pillet (ed.), *Les fondateurs du droit international* (Giard et Brière: Paris, 1904), p. 31.

9 H. Nézard, 'Albericus Gentilis', in Pillet, *ibid.*, p. 59.

10 J. Basdevant, 'Hugo Grotius', in Pillet, *ibid.*, p. 207.

11 C. Siemienowicz, *Grand art d'artillerie* (1650), as quoted in J. Appfel., 'Les projectiles toxiques en 1650', *Revue d'artillerie*, no. 103 (March 1929), p. 234.

12 'Instructions for the Government of Armies of the United States in the Field', prepared by Francis Lieber and promulgated as General Order no. 100 by President Abraham Lincoln, 24 April 1863. Document reproduced in D. Schindler and J. Toman (eds.), *The Laws of Armed Conflicts. A Collection of Conventions, Resolutions and Other Documents* (A. W. Sijthhoff: Leiden, 1973), pp. 3–23.

13 L. Lewin, *Die Gifte in der Weltgeschichte* (Verlag von Julius Springer; Berlin, 1920), p. 563.

14 J. H. Choate, *The Two Hague Conferences. The Stafford Little Lectures for 1912* (Princeton University Press: Princeton, 1913, reprinted by Kraus Reprint Co.: New York, 1969), pp. 20–21.

15 Declaration of St. Petersburg of 1868 to the Effect of Prohibiting the Use of Certain Projectiles in Wartime, signed at St. Petersburg, 29 November–11 December 1868. Document reproduced in Schindler and Toman (eds.), *The Laws of Armed Conflicts*, pp. 95–97.

16 International Declaration Concerning the Laws and Customs of War, signed at Brussels, 27 August 1874. Document reproduced in *ibid.*, pp. 25–34.

17 The Laws of War on Land, Manual adopted by the Institute of International Law at Oxford, 9 September 1880. Document reproduced in *ibid.*, pp. 35–48. Founded in 1873, the Institute of International Law was composed of individual members and associations from different countries.

18 A. M. Prentiss, *Chemicals in War: A Treatise on Chemical Warfare* (McGraw–Hill Book Company, Inc.: New York, 1937), p. 250.

19 *Ibid.*, p. 220.

20 *Ibid.*, p. 221.

21 R. Hanslian, and F. Bergendorff, *Der chemische Krieg: Gasangriff, Gasabwehr und Raucherzeugung* (E. S. Mittler & Sohn: Berlin, 1925), p. 5.

22 V. Vojvodic, *Toxicology of Chemical Warfare Agents*. [Manuscript, intended for the active and reserve forces of the Yugoslav People's Army.] (Belgrade, 1982), p. 7.

23 J. K. Batten, 'Chemical Warfare in History', *Armed Forces Chemical Journal*, vol. 14, no. 2 (1960), p. 17. Vojvodic, *ibid.*, p. 8.

24 C. J. West, 'The history of poison gases', *Science*, vol. 49, no. 1270 (2 May 1919), pp. 412–17. The author reproduced correspondence between Lord Palmerston and Lord Panmure and the enclosed Memoranda by Lord Dundonald, excerpted from *The Panmure Papers* (London, 1908).

25 S. James, 'Stratagems, Combat, and "Chemical Warfare" in the Siege Mines of Dura-Europos', *American Journal of Archaeology*, vol. 115, no. 1 (January 2011), pp. 69–101.

26 W. D. Miles, 'Admiral Cochrane's plans for chemical warfare', *Armed Forces Chemical Journal*, vol. 11, no. 6 (November–December 1957), p. 22.

27 West, 'The history of poison gases', p. 413.

28 Miles, 'Admiral Cochrane's plans for chemical warfare', p. 22; J. B. Poole, 'A sword undrawn: chemical warfare and the Victorian age, Part I', *Army Quarterly* (October 1976), pp. 463–67.

29 W. S. Churchill, *The World Crisis 1915* (Thornton Butterworth Limited: London, 1923, republished by Barnes & Nobles: New York, 1993), pp. 516–20.

30 Poole, 'A sword undrawn, Part I', p. 467.

31 *Ibid.*, p. 467; J. B. Poole, 'A sword undrawn: chemical warfare and the Victorian age, Part II', *Army Quarterly* (January 1977), p. 92.

32 W. D. Miles, 'The chemical shells of Lyon Playfair (1854)', *Armed Forces Chemical Journal*, vol. 11, no. 6 (November–December 1957), pp. 23 and 40.

33 W. D. Miles, 'The velvet-lined gas mask of John Stenhouse', *Armed Forces Chemical Journal*, vol. 12, no. 6 (June 1958), pp. 24–25.

34 L. F. Haber, *The Poisonous Cloud: Chemical Warfare in the First World War* (Clarendon Press: Oxford, 1986), p. 17.

35 W. D. Miles, 'Stink balls, fire rain, and smoke pots – chemical weapons in 1825', *Armed Forces Chemical Journal*, vol. 12, no. 5 (September–October 1958), pp. 34–36. The idea that the stink ball was not an entirely novel development stems from the laconic reply by Lieutenant-Colonel W. Le Roy Broun to a suggestion for trials by Brigadier-General W. N. Pendleton in June 1864: 'Stink balls, none on hand; don't keep them; will make if ordered.'

36 Wyndham Miles of the U.S. Army Chemical Corps Historical Office, who collected much of the historical material about the 19th century, nonetheless sounded a cautionary note: 'This is not to

say that the inventors of the Confederacy lacked ingenuity or interest, but rather that there are fewer Southern records and that they have been subjected to less scrutiny. Our knowledge of Northern ideas is better [...]. Generally speaking we seem to know less about Civil War ideas on chemical warfare than on any other category of munitions.' W. D. Miles, 'Chemical warfare in the Civil War', *Armed Forces Chemical Journal*, vol. 12, no. 2 (March–April 1958), p. 33.

37 *Ibid.*, pp. 26–27 and 33.

38 Regarding fact and fiction, as well as reported research proposals in Great Britain, France, and Germany, see Haber, *The Poisonous Cloud*, pp. 19–21.

39 L. F. Haber, *The Chemical Industry 1900–1930. International Growth and Technological Change* (Clarendon Press: Oxford, 1971), p. 3.

40 *Encyclopaedia Britannica*, Ultimate Reference Suite (Encyclopædia Britannica: Chicago, 2012), 'Chlorine'.

41 *Encyclopaedia Britannica*, 'Phosgene'.

42 F. Guthrie, 'On Some Derivatives from the Olefines', *Quarterly Journal Chemical Society*, vol. 12 (1860), p. 117; F. Guthrie, 'On Some Derivatives from the Olefines,' *Quarterly Journal Chemical Society*, vol. 13 (1860/61), p. 135.

43 Haber, *The Poisonous Cloud*, pp. 117 and 342, note 18.

44 A. S. Travis, *The Synthetic Nitrogen Industry in World War I: Its Emergence and Expansion*, Springer Briefs in History of Chemistry (Springer International Publishing: Cham, 2015), p. 47.

45 M. Pattison, 'Scientists, Inventors and the Military in Britain, 1915–19: The Munitions Inventions Department', *Social Studies of Science,* vol. 13 (1983), p. 524.

46 Foulkes, C. H. (Maj. Gen.), *"Gas!" The Story of the Special Brigade* (William Blackwood & Sons Ltd.: Edinburgh and London, 1936), pp. 22–23; Haber, *The Poisonous Cloud*, p. 20.

47 J. Tucker, 'Biological Threat Assessment: Is the Cure Worse Than the Disease?', *Arms Control Today* (October 2004), available from <http://www.armscontrol.org/act/2004_10/Tucker.asp>.

48 J. H. Choate, *The Two Hague Conferences. The Stafford Little Lectures for 1912* (Princeton University Press, 1913, Reprinted by Kraus Reprint Co.: New York, 1969), p. 37.

49 E. Root, 'Instructions to the American Delegates to The Hague Conference, 1907', 31 May 1907, reproduced in United States Department of State, *Papers Relating to the Foreign Relations of the United States with the Annual Message of the President Transmitted to Congress*, 3 December 1907, Part II, pp. 1129–30.

50 Oral report by Mr Louis Renault on the work of the drafting committee of the Final Act, 25 and 27 July 1899, reproduced in: J. Brown Scott (Under the supervision of), *The Proceedings of The Hague Conferences: The Conference of 1899* (Oxford University Press: New York, 1920), p. 103.

51 A. Pillet, *Les Conventions de La Haye du 29 juillet 1899 et du 18 octobre 1907. Etude juridique et critique.* (Pedone, Editeur: Paris, 1918), pp. 67–68.

52 W. I. Hull, *The Two Hague Conferences and Their Contributions to International Law* (Published for the International School of Peace by Ginn & Company: Boston, 1908, Reprinted by Kraus Reprint Co.: New York, 1970), pp. 232–33.

53 30 December 1898, according to the Julian calendar then still in use in Russia.

54 J. Brown Scott (Under the supervision of), *The Proceedings of The Hague Conferences: The Conference of 1899*, p. 424.

55 Major General Baron Giesl von Gieslingen, Rapporteur, to the Fourth Plenary Meeting of the Second Commission on the amendments proposed to the regulations of 1899 respecting the laws and customs of war on land, in J. Brown Scott (Under the supervision of), *The Proceedings of The Hague Conferences: The Conference of 1907, Volume I* (Oxford University Press: New York, 1920), p. 110.

56 General Report to the Conference Upon the Work of the Fourth Commission, in *ibid.*, p. 259.

57 *Ibid.*, p. 260.

58 Final Act of the Second International Peace Conference, as reproduced in Schindler and Toman (eds.), *The Laws of Armed Conflicts*, p. 55. (Authentic text in French.)

59 Pillet, *Les Conventions de La Haye du 29 juillet 1899 et du 18 octobre 1907*, p. 51.

60 Hull, *The Two Hague Conferences and Their Contributions to International Law*, pp. 180–81.

61 *Ibid.*, pp. 87–90.

62 Captain A. T. Mahan, Report to the United States Commission to the International Conference at the Hague, on Disarmament, etc., with Reference to Navies, in J. Brown Scott, *The Hague Peace Conferences of 1899 and 1907. A Series of Lectures Delivered before the Johns Hopkins University in the Year 1908, Volume II* (The Johns Hopkins Press: Baltimore, MD, 1909), p. 37.

63 A. D. White, *Autobiography, Volume II* (The Century Co.: New York, 1906), p. 89.

64 Brown Scott (Under the supervision of), *The Proceedings of The Hague Conferences: The Conference of 1899*, pp. 366–67; A. Roberts and R. Guelff (eds.), *Documents on the Laws of War* (Clarendon Press: Oxford, 1982), pp. 41–42.

65 Brown Scott (Under the supervision of), *The Proceedings of The Hague Conferences: The Conference of 1907, Volume I*, p. 105. It is interesting to note that the conclusion pertained to both Declaration (IV, 1) on bombardment from balloons, which had a limited duration of five years, and Declaration (IV,2) on asphyxiating gases, while most of the discussion concerned the former document.

66 Hull, *The Two Hague Conferences and Their Contributions to International Law*, p. 466.

67 Such a phrase had been included in a draft convention Russia submitted at the Brussels Conference where fifteen European states met on 27 July 1874 on the initiative of Czar Alexander II: paragraph 12 (A) proposed to prohibit the use of poisoned weapons, or the dissemination by whatever means of poison on enemy territory. The negotiators only retained the interdiction on the use of poison or poisoned weapons, having discarded the second part of the clause for the sake of simplicity. Document as reproduced in A. Mechelynck, *La Convention de la Haye concernant les lois et coutumes de la guerre sur terre* (Ad. Hoste: Ghent, 1915), p. 239.

68 *Kriegsraison* was not a novel concept defined towards the end of the 19th century, but one that became increasingly controversial. It was rooted in natural law, which placed few restrictions on the means to achieve a satisfactory peace. The influential German jurist Georg Friedrich von Martens accepted it in his *Précis du Droit des gens moderne de l'Europe* (Tome II (Guillaumin et Cie, Librairies: Paris, 1864), p. 226; first edition printed in 1788) and quoted a treatise, 'Gründliche Nachricht von Kriegsceremoniel und Kriegsmanier', published in 1745. J. L. Klüber (*Droit des gens moderne de l'Europe*. Revu, annoté et complété par M. A. Ott. Deuxième édition. (Guillaumin et Cie, éditeurs: Paris, 1874), p. 347 – first edition in French, 1819) recognised *Kriegsraison* as part of custom and stressed its exceptionality. He traced the concept to Grotius (*jus s. titulus necessitatis*) and referred to several 17th and 18th century jurists. Grotius's maxim, 'In war things which are necessary to attain the end in view are permissible', exposed the core of the ambiguity: it allowed for both military necessity and a humanitarian interpretation. G. Best, *War & Law Since 1945* (Clarendon Press: Oxford, 1994), p. 30.

69 F. de Holtzendorff, *Eléments de Droit international public*. Traduit de l'Allemand par G. C. Zographos. (Arthur Rousseau, éditeur: Paris, 1891), p. 166.

70 A. Rivier, *Lehrbuch des Völkerrechts* (Verlag von Ferdinand Enke: Stuttgart, 1899), pp. 393–94.

71 Holtzendorff, *Eléments de Droit international public*, p. 167.

72 Rivier, *Lehrbuch des Völkerrechts*, p. 399.

73 The principle was discussed extensively by John Westlake. L. Oppenheim (ed.), *The Collected Papers of John Westlake on Public International Law* (Cambridge at the University Press: Cambridge, 1914), pp. 244–46.

74 This understanding of retorsion appeared several times in the German literature; e.g., von Martens, *Précis du Droit des gens moderne de l'Europe*, pp. 185–86 and the annotation by Charles-Henri Vergé, commenting that retorsion and reprisals must not be confounded, the former being essentially a political measure governed by specific rules of internal public law (*ibid.*, pp. 186–87). John Westlake, a British jurist, noted, however: 'Retorsion in war is the action of a belligerent against whom a law has been broken, and who retorts by breaking the same or some other law, in order to compensate himself for the damage which he has suffered and to deter his enemy from continuing or repeating the offence. Where the same law is broken the proper term is retaliation, but there is no difference of principle between the cases, and the term retorsion covers both.' Oppenheim (ed.), *The Collected Papers of John Westlake on Public International Law,* p. 259.

75 B. Cheng, *General Principles of Law as Applied by International Courts and Tribunals* (Grotius Publication Limited: Cambridge, 1987), pp. 97–99.

76 Lueder's writings were taken as an example because he felt compelled to justify the concept rather than state its existence. It should be noted, however, that no full agreement existed among German jurists on the precise relationship between *Kriegsrecht*, *Kriegsraison* and *Kriegsmanier*, or on their exact definition. These discrepancies may, in fact, reflect the internal ideological debate of a nation adapting to rapid industrialisation and mechanisation of warfare.

77 Holtzendorff, *Eléments de Droit international public*, p. 167. Rivier, *Lehrbuch des Völkerrechts*, p. 400.

78 Oppenheim (ed.), *The Collected Papers of John Westlake on Public International Law*, p. 246.

79 H. Bonfils and P. Fauchille, *Manuel de Droit international public*. Septième édition (Librairie Arthur Rousseau: Paris, 1914), p. 725; J. W. Garner, *International Law and the World War*, vol. 1. (Longmans, Green and Co.: London, 1920), pp. 4–6.

80 J. H. Morgan, *The War Book of the German General Staff* (Translated with a critical introduction) (McBride, Nast & Company: New York, 1915), p. 9.

81 Although Anglo-French sources severely criticised the concept of *Kriegsraison*, after the First World War certain aspects of it gradually gained broader international acceptance as part of total war and the envisaged role for offensive strategic air power therein. Based on the plans for the British air campaigns in 1917 and 1918, Air Marshall Sir Hugh Trenchard developed his theories of an air force capable of hitting the enemy heartland without engaging its military forces. Breaking the enemy's morale, whether military or civilian, became a legitimate military objective:

> [...] the object of all three Services is the same, to defeat the enemy nation, not merely its army, navy or air force.
>
> For any army to do this, it is almost always necessary as a preliminary step to defeat the enemy's army, which imposes itself as a barrier that must first be broken down.
>
> It is not, however, necessary for an air force, in order to defeat the enemy nation, to defeat its armed forces first. Air power can dispense with that intermediate step [...]
>
> What is illegitimate, as being contrary to the dictates of humanity, is the indiscriminate bombing of a city for the sole purpose of terrorising the civilian population.
>
> It is an entirely different matter to terrorise munition workers (men and women) into absenting themselves from work or stevedores into abandoning the loading of a ship with munitions through fear of air attack upon the factory or dock concerned. Moral effect is created by the bombing in such circumstances, but it is the inevitable result of a lawful operation of war – the bombing of a military objective.

C. Webster and N. Frankland, *The Strategic Air Offensive Against Germany* (HMSO: London, 1961) as cited in G. H. Quester, *Deterrence Before Hiroshima: The Airpower Background of Modern Strategy* (Transaction Books: New Brunswick and Oxford, 1986), pp. 52 and 53. It should be noted that during the *Interbellum* air strategists from different countries envisaged an important strategic role for aerial chemical bombardment.

82 Cheng, *General Principles of Law as Applied by International Courts and Tribunals*, p. 101, fn. 11.

TOWARDS TOTAL WAR: LANGEMARCK, 22 APRIL 1915

OLIVIER LEPICK

Late in the afternoon of 22 April 1915 some 150 tonnes of chlorine were released from 5,830 cylinders from the German trenches facing the Ypres Salient. Along a 6km wide front stretching from Steenstraete on the Yser canal to the west of Poelcappelle, the cloud drifted towards the French positions opposite the village of Langemarck. The main target were elements of the French Army detachment in Belgium, commanded by General Henri Gabriel Putz of the 45th Infantry Division (commanded by General Fernand Quiquandon), and the territorial army of the 87th Infantry Division (commanded by General Raymond Roy). The heavy green-yellow cloud rose one metre above the ground and, pushed forward by a slight north-easterly wind, drifted towards the French lines at a speed of 2–3 metres per second. Fifteen minutes later, the German infantry equipped with mouth pads began its advance behind the gas cloud.

German troops preparing a gas attack, 1915. (In Flanders Fields Museum, Ypres)

The effect of the gas was immediate. The front Allied trenches immediately became indefensible; the French troops abandoned them without resistance. Initially, nobody fully realised the situation because the gas clouds, together with the smoke from explosions, almost completely masked the front. Hundreds of terrified and suffocating men were fleeing to the rear in search of breathable air. The asphyxiating gas seemed to set their lungs on fire. They ran towards Poperinghe and Ypres. Nothing or nobody could stop their mad race.

The German troops encountered apocalyptic scenes during their advance. The dead with greenish complexions lay next to the dying, their mouths filling with a yellowish liquid and bodies shaking with violent spasms. The Imperial German Army had just ushered in modern chemical warfare.

The gas cloud shocked the Allies and public opinion. Without any doubt it was one of the most important military acts in the war. For decades the French and German military had prepared for a possible conflict. When it eventually erupted in August 1914, they were convinced that the war would be short. Their opening moves followed previously elaborated plans, but already by October, three months into the war, the Western Front had stalemated. The character of the conflict was changing. Conventional weapons were unable to restore mobility, as a consequence of which minds started searching for alternative means. They looked at science and technology for a breakthrough. In the German mind, gas was one option to restore movement.

Military necessity blotted out political and moral hesitations. Asphyxiating gases – poisons – violated then existing international law, in particular the Hague Conventions of 1899 and 1907.[1] It was a deliberate choice that revolutionised warfare and the ways in which nations organised themselves for war.

Fritz Haber, the father of modern chemical warfare

The German Chief of General Staff Erich von Falkenhayn was very interested in studies on the military use of chemical substances. At that time, a renowned German chemist, Fritz Jacob Haber, director of the *Kaiser Wilhelm Institut of Berlin-Dahlem*, made an astonishing proposal. A vigorous 46-year-old Silesian, Haber was an expert in the handling of compressed gas. It was his invention to synthesise ammonia by way of compressing hydrogen and nitrogen. The so-called Haber process was first applied on an industrial scale in 1913. The invention was to earn him the 1918 Nobel Prize for chemistry. Furthermore, faced with an Allied naval blockade, the process enabled Germany to become partly independent from Chilean nitrates for the manufacture of its explosives. Haber suggested discharging liquefied chlorine from cylinders placed in the trenches. The agent provokes powerful irritation of the respiratory tract and may cause quick death after inhalation. Gaseous above 3°C, the liquid quickly evaporates into a thick light greenish cloud. An additional advantage of Haber's proposal was the element's availability in large quantities because of the German chemical industry's production capacity.

Haber took charge of the German military chemical programme. He was immediately promoted from Corporal to Reserve Captain. He would be decorated with the Iron Cross for his action during the conflict. Notwithstanding, the Nazis later persecuted him because of his Jewish origins. Even though he had converted to Protestantism, he fled into exile after Adolf Hitler came to power in 1933. He first went to Great Britain and then to Switzerland, where he died in Basel in 1934.

Despite some opposition, the General Staff authorised Haber to conduct tests. In early January 1915 some limited trials were held at the artillery test centre in Wahn. The next month more substantial experiments were carried out at the barracks of Beverlo in Belgium, followed by more tests on the military exercise grounds in Hasselt in early April. Haber and many high-ranking officers attended. During the trial, Professor Haber and Major Max Bauer rode without protection on horseback through a small cloud of chlorine to test its effects. This bravado earned them both a two-week hospital stay. Notwithstanding, the tests proved conclusive.

The Germans took the decision to use gas on the battlefield in the middle of January 1915. Many high-ranking officers viewed the idea as a breach of their code of honour. Notwithstanding, von Falkenhayn personally approved the decision in principle. After having obtained assurances from the chemical experts that the Allies would not be able to respond to this type of warfare for many months, von Falkenhayn and his staff started consulting officers in different sectors on the Western Front to determine the most suitable site for the operation. They also considered Galicia (Poland) where a significant offensive was being planned. The staff abandoned the idea, because it did not want to risk an important military operation with an experimental weapon whose impact on the battlefield was unknown. Therefore, after a detailed study of climatic and topographic conditions and in agreement with Major-General Duke Albrecht von Württemberg, commander of the 4th German Army, the *Oberste Heeresleitung* (High Command) decided on the sector occupied by the 4th Army. The initial plan envisaged the release of chlorine in the southern part of the Ypres Salient held by the XV Army Corps commanded by General Berthold von Deimling.

Lethal mist over Langemarck

The German military authorities swiftly requisitioned approximately 6,000 cylinders with chlorine, which then amounted to half of the available stock. They also ordered 24,000 additional units for an overall volume of 700 tonnes of chlorine. To implement the operation, Colonel Otto Peterson, an Engineers officer, was entrusted to form special units. Under his command the 35th and 36th *Pionier Regimente* trained in chemical warfare. The units also included scientists and engineers recruited from other regiments and sometimes from civilian society. Amongst them were the physicians James Franck and Gustav Herz, as well as the chemist Otto Hahn. All three would later become Nobel Prize laureates. Haber retained the technical and scientific supervision of the offensive.

On 25 January 1915, von Deimling was called to the main headquarters in Mézières to confer with von Falkenhayn. The Commander-in-Chief of the Fourth Army was also present. Von Falkenhayn revealed that a new warfare technique was going to be used and that von Deimling's sector had been selected for the first trials. In his memoirs, von Deimling recalled his aversion to poison warfare: 'I have to admit that the mission of poisoning the enemy like rats provoked in me the reaction it should in any honest soldier: it disgusted me.' Those scruples were soon swept aside, however. 'But if those toxic gases were to cause the fall of Ypres, maybe we would obtain a victory that would be decisive for the whole campaign? Before such a great objective, personal objections had to be silenced.'[2]

Peterson's men began installing the heavy pressurised cylinders in von Deimling's sector near the village of Gheluvelt towards the end of February. Located to the east of Ypres, it soon became apparent that as a consequence of the curve in the Salient, the prevailing winds placed the German troops at a high risk of being hit by their own gas. Duke Albrecht of Württemberg of the Fourth Army decided on 25 March to prepare a second release site near the village of Langemarck at the northern end of the Salient. Between 5 and 11 April, Peterson's men completed the installation of 5,830 units holding 150 tonnes of chlorine. Their work was so thorough that replacement

Ypres, April 1915. (In Flanders Fields Museum, Ypres)

units arriving in the trenches did not realise that the cylinders had been buried below their feet.

Haber had initially calculated to produce a cloud density of 30 tonnes of chlorine per kilometre. The volume was reduced to 21 tonnes.

The upcoming German offensive envisaged various tactical objectives. Having been tasked to seize Pilckem Ridge overlooking the City of Ypres, General Otto Freiherr von Hügel, commander of the XXVIth Reserve Army Corps, instructed his troops on 8 April to take the crest along the Boesinghe-Pilckem-Langemarck-Poelcappelle road and then dig in. With no expectation of a strategic breakthrough, the *Oberste Heeresleitung* did not allocate any additional troops or equipment. Major-General Emil Ilse even refused two regiments offered to him by the *Marine-Infanterie-Korps* (naval infantry). The High Command also hesitated about the toxic cloud. While it believed that the gas could eventually break the enemy front, a trial operation was required first to assess its impact. Shortage of confidence in this new weapon was to have severe consequences.

The offensive was initially planned for 15 April, but lack of wind precluded the release of chlorine. The same conditions prevailed on the 19th and 20th. Meanwhile, however, Russian forces were increasing pressure in Galicia. Von Falkenhayn therefore decided to transfer units from the Western Front to the region of Gorlice-Tarnòw from 17 April on. The decision further changed the rationale for opening the Second Battle of Ypres. While allowing offensive action in Galicia, the strength on the Western Front would remain sufficient to defend current positions or to carry out a few limited offensives, so von Falkenhayn thought. He considered it necessary to maintain a certain degree of activity in the West to hide the reduction in German troops for as long as possible. At the same time, straightening the frontline by eliminating the Ypres Salient would decrease the pressure from manpower shortages. A shortened frontline thus acquired strategic importance.

In the afternoon of 21 April weather conditions seemed to improve and orders were issued to commence the offensive the next day at 7am. The attack eventually materialised in the late afternoon. Hügel's 51st Reserve Division took the village of Langemarck in only one hour. The central thrust of the German offensive along the Pilckem Ridge towards the Yser Canal and Boesinghe also achieved considerable success. However, both the northern and southern flanks ran into fierce resistance. The French reserve troops (90th Brigade of Colonel Jean Jules Henri Mordacq and the 174th Brigade of the Territorial Army, commanded by Colonel Couillaud) and the 1st Canadian Contingent had been relatively spared by the gas. Official German records noted that the gas missed its full impact in an area in front of Steenstraete. There, the left wing of the 46th German Reserve-Division encountered strong resistance and only captured the hamlet late in the evening. For this reason, the planned junction with the 52nd and 51st German Reserve-Divisions could only be realised around 10pm, which temporarily stopped the German advance. Shortly before midnight, the German infantrymen received orders to fortify their new positions as strongly as possible. This allowed the Allies to recover and bring up their reserves to re-establish the frontline. The Germans had advanced some 7–

8 kilometres. However, thanks to the 1st Canadian Contingent holding their ground around Saint-Julien and the subsequent involvement of the French 152th and 153th Infantry Divisions, as well as some British units, the Allies succeeded in stabilising the lines and blocking any further German progress.

When the first telephone messages from the frontline units reached Colonel Mordacq in his headquarters in Elverdinghe, he initially thought that his subordinates were suffering from a 'mental disturbance'. However, he quickly saw the horrors of the situation when:

> everywhere distraught fugitives [...], without their greatcoats or widely unbuttoned, ties ripped off, running like madmen, erratically, and screaming for water, coughing up blood, a few even rolling on the ground in their desperate effort to breathe. [...] I had never seen such a spectacle, such a frenzy.[3]

At the beginning of May 1915, Lieutenant Jules-Henri Guntzberger presented the following testimony to the French commission established 'to register the acts committed by the enemy in violation of the rights of the people':

> on 22 April around 5pm [...] at 70 or 80 metres from the advanced German trenches [...] one of my soldiers pointed at steam rising up in front of these trenches. I then saw a green cloud of approximately ten metres high and particularly thick at the base, which touched the ground. This cloud moved towards us, pushed forward by the wind. Almost immediately, we literally suffocated [...]. We then had to withdraw, followed by the cloud. I then saw many men fall, some stumbling up, starting to walk again, falling again, and from fall to fall finally reaching the second line, behind the canal, where we halted. There, the soldiers collapsed and until about three in the morning incessantly coughed and vomited [...]. Today I am still suffering from bronchitis, and many of my men are evacuated every day due to bronchitis and pulmonary congestion.[4]

In his daily report, the British Commander-in-Chief Field Marshal Sir John French wrote:

> after a severe bombardment, the enemy attacked the French division around 5pm, using asphyxiating gases for the first time [...]. What followed cannot be described. The effect of the poisonous gas was so virulent that it completely annihilated the action capacities of the troops who occupied this part of the front. The smoke and the steam covered the theatre of operations and plunged hundreds of men into a comatose state, and subsequently death. In one hour the whole position had to be abandoned leaving behind 50 pieces of artillery. I firmly wish to refute the idea of any responsibility of the French division during these events.

French trench after chlorine attack, 23 April 1915. (In Flanders Fields Museum, Ypres)

Assessing casualty reports

Until today assessing the exact number of gas victims on 22 April remains difficult. Depending on the source, the numbers vary between 200 and 5,000 fatalities and up to 10,000 injured. In 1921, Victor Lefebure advanced the figure of 5,000 fatalities.[5]

Thirteen years later Rudolf Hanslian rightfully accused the Allied forces of having significantly exaggerated their losses.[6] German Army reports prepared on 23 April indicated that German infantrymen found few corpses in the Allied trenches. The Germans obviously tried to minimise the extent of human loss caused by the chlorine. After the conflict, Fritz Haber declared that he saw very few men killed by chlorine on 22 April 1915.

The Official British Medical History of the War, basing itself on reports by the Allied medical services in the region of Ypres, suggested 3,000 fatalities and 7,000 injured as a consequence of the German chemical attacks on 22 and 24 April, and 1 May.[7] These figures too must be treated with caution because no truly accurate evaluation exists. An incomplete French medical report prepared by Dr Célestin Sieur on 25 April only mentions 625 victims. In a letter passed on to Colonel Mordacq, a French doctor taken prisoner-of-war wrote that he was led to a German field hospital where he counted 800 severely poisoned men, several of whom died later.[8] Finally, official French medical statistics listed only 469 gas casualties for the whole French Army during the month of April 1915.[9]

These reports justify suspicions about authors claiming a high gas toll from the first chlorine attack. The figure of 5,000 dead must be drastically reassessed downward. According to my own assessment, the number of victims lies between 800 and 1,400 fatalities with 2–3,000 other casualties suffering from more or less severe poisoning.[10]

A wasted innovation?

The next day, in unusual euphoria after hearing about the success of the offensive, Kaiser Wilhelm II expressed his satisfaction to von Falkenhayn with a warm and uncustomary embrace. The German operation achieved tactical success. Von Falkenhayn obtained a considerable narrowing of the Ypres Salient and enhanced security on his northern flank, but he failed to reach all objectives set the day before the offensive.

The General Staff had considerably underestimated the potential impact of the gas attack on the Allied forces, and von Falkenhayn had to admit this: 'the surprise impact was considerable. Unfortunately, we were not able to exploit it properly. The necessary reserves were not in place.'[11] Numerous high-ranking German officers, including General von Deimling, shared these regrets: 'had we disposed of sufficient reserves, our troops could have pierced the front and reached Ypres.'[12] As noted earlier, the German High Command did not foresee sizeable reserves in support of the offensive and considered the gas attack as a battlefield experiment in a smaller operation with

Allied trench Ypres Salient, April 1915. (In Flanders Fields Museum, Ypres)

purely local objectives. To the German military commanders, gas had to prove its effectiveness in the field before they were willing to consider the weapon in a major offensive. Maybe Wilhelm II's enthusiasm on 23 April 1915 would have been tempered if he had realised these facts.

When recollecting this operation after the war, Fritz Haber declared: 'the military commandment recognised afterwards that if they had followed my advice and prepared a major operation, instead of turning Ypres into a vain experiment, Germany would have won the war.'[13] This outrageous statement is not without interest, because it seems legitimate to ponder whether a major offensive on 22 April might have achieved much more significant results. As Professor Julius Meyer rightfully remarked in 1926, 'the impact on the enemy had been enormous and the actual results considerable, but tactically, the success had not been fully exploited because the military command, partisans of their classic training, could not anticipate the powerful action of the gases and were therefore not properly prepared.'

The lack of protection among Allied troops enhanced the impact of the first chemical attack. This advantage the Germans would have never again. Many authors have speculated on whether Germany might have won the war on 22 April. Of course, had the offensive been better prepared and more troops been available, the outcome might have been quite different. To quote German General Erich von Tschischwitz, commanding the XXIII Army Reserve Corps in April 1915, the offensive had been 'a failed firework and it would have been preferable if it had not happened under the given form.' As he rightly assessed, Germany had wasted a weapon that could have been decisive.

French gas casualty, 23 April 1915. (In Flanders Fields Museum, Ypres)

The daily press release by the German staff of 23 April noted the important progress by their units, but did not mention the use of gas. For their part, the British forces revealed the use of noxious chemical agents by the German troops without mentioning the Allied retreat. The outrage provoked by the gas attack was immense in the Allied countries. These methods undoubtedly breached the Hague Declaration (IV, 2) of 1899, which Germany had signed. A violent anti-German press campaign was launched in France and Great Britain. 'Their faces, arms and hands had become grey; and open-mouthed, glassy-eyed, they rocked back to front gasping for air', reported the *London Times* on 24 April 1915. The same paper wrote five days later that this was 'a dreadful method of warfare, for which Humanity would surely hold Germany responsible.' It also used terminology such as 'a deliberate recourse to this abominable method [...], a diabolical inspiration [...], an enormity.' Politicians and the military emphasised the barbarism and the horror these methods provoked, as they could not be reconciled with a soldier's honour. On 23 April 1915, Raymond Poincaré noted with surprising aptness: 'it is the organisation of crime; and will we not be forced alas (!) to use the same methods tomorrow to defend ourselves?'[14] General John J. Pershing expressed a sentiment shared by many when he wrote he had 'the impression that the Germans had abandoned any principle of humanity in the wind of Langemarck'.[15]

Polemics started between the warring factions to determine whether the use of these 'toxic gas clouds' of chlorine was in conformity with the laws of war. The Germans argued that by letting the gas escape from cylinders without using weapons or projectiles, they had not breached the Hague Declaration (IV, 2). A literal interpretation of this document, which prohibited 'the use of projectiles with the sole objective of diffusing asphyxiating or toxic gases', allowed the German lawyers to state quite cynically that the operation on 22 April did not belong to this category as no projectiles had been used. Reporting on a cabinet meeting in a letter to King George V on 27 April 1915, Earl Herbert Asquith, the British Prime Minister, seemed to validate the German interpretation: 'to the extent that the gases were apparently stocked in cylinders and not in projectiles, their use might perhaps not be a breach of the literal terms of the Convention of The Hague.' Quite provocatively, the German paper *Kölnische Zeitung* even went so far as to ask in an article: 'is there a sweeter procedure of warfare, is there a procedure more conform with the rights of the people than to release a cloud of gas that the wind brings to the enemy?'. The German authorities, exploiting the legal vagueness which surrounded the issue of chemical weapons, added that the Allies had started using gas. They also argued that the gases used were not poison and therefore did not fall under article 23a of the Convention of The Hague of 1907. Fritz Haber repeatedly stated during the conflict and in the subsequent years that gases were no crueller than conventional shells. This position was also shared by a certain number of military personnel and historians who spoke out after the end of the conflict.

Conclusion

In mid-May, when the Second Battle of Ypres was drawing towards its end, the city was still in Allied hands. The Germans had lost 35,000 men and had 'wasted' a weapon which could have allowed them to win a decisive battle. Despite the 350 to 400 tons of chlorine used between 22 April and 6 May 1915, no breakthrough was realised as the advocates of the use of chemical weapons had hoped. In hindsight, one could argue that their expectations had probably been correct. The fundamental mistake by the *Oberste Heeresleitung* was that they had not planned for a major offensive near Ypres. Indeed, as soon as gas was revealed as a new weapon and basic protection adopted, gas lost most of its strategic potential to break through enemy front lines. It became another tool in the war of attrition. The warring parties did not realise it at the moment, but the possibility of a breakthrough with gas arose and dissipated in Langemarck on 22 April 1915.

The chemical weapon was not decisive. Initially introduced with the aim of breaking the enemy front and regaining movement, it became one more aspect of a war of slow destruction and harassment. The belligerents, hypnotised by the myth of a breakthrough tool, did not realise that by adopting chemical weapons in a quasi-mechanical way, they had taken the ultimate step towards the totalisation of war. Ten months before the Battle of Verdun (February – December 1916), the start of the chemical warfare already heralded this. It is a paradox that the failure to achieve a breakthrough in the months following 22 April 1915 made this mode of combat the strongest symbol of

Early French individual gas protection. (In Flanders Fields Museum, Ypres)

the totalisation of war. Failing to answer the initial hopes of some strategists, it was nevertheless a quintessential weapon, characteristic of the conditions of combat in the Great War. Even though the chemical weapon never achieved decisive success, at the end of the Great War it paradoxically still appeared to be a weapon of the future, like the aeroplane, the tank or even the submarine.

Notes

1 The Germans claimed this was technically not the case, see further in this chapter.
2 B. von Deimling, *Souvenirs de ma vie* (Paris, 1931), p. 223.
3 H. Mordacq, *Le Drame de l'Yser* (Bruxelles, 1936), p. 65.
4 O. Lepick, *La Grande Guerre Chimique: 1914–1918* (Paris, 1998), pp. 79–80.
5 *Ibid.*, p. 80.
6 R. Hanslian, *Der deutsche Gasangriff bei Ypern am 22. April 1915* (Berlin, 1934), pp. 64, 70 and 104.
7 W. G. McPherson, W. P. Heeringham, T. R. Elliot and A. Balfour, *Official History of the Great War: Medical Services, Diseases of the War* (London, 1923), vol. 1.
8 Mordacq, *Le Drame de l'Yser,* p. 65.
9 Ministère de la Guerre, Direction du service de santé, *Etude statistique chirurgicale, Guerre 1914–18, Les blessés hospitalisés à l'intérieur du territoire, l'évolution de leurs blessures* (Paris, 1924), vol. 2, p. 364.
10 SHAT, Vincennes, SHAT/16N826, 'Rapport du docteur Sieur daté du 25 avril 1915'.
11 E. von Falkenhayn, *General Headquarters 1914–1916 and its Critical Decisions* (London, 1919), p. 85.
12 von Deimling, *Souvenirs de ma vie,* p. 225.
13 Lepick, *La Grande Guerre Chimique: 1914–1918,* pp. 82–83.
14 R. Poincaré, *Au service de la France: 1915, les tranchées* (Paris, 1930), p. 173.
15 J. Pershing, *My Experiences in the World War* (New York, 1931), p. 165.

THE BELGIAN ARMY AND THE GAS ATTACK ON 22 APRIL 1915

LUC VANDEWEYER

For the gas attack of 22 April 1915, the Germans chose a battlefield in a sector where Belgian, British and French forces were active. We will try to answer two major questions about the Belgian Army. First, what did Belgian intelligence know or what could it have known before the gas attack, and how was this knowledge interpreted at the headquarters and implemented at the front? Second, how did the Belgian Army react during and immediately after the German offensive?

The major sources for this research are from the Belgian military archives. The Second World War badly affected these collections. In 1940 the German Army took many files back home for study purposes. Later the Soviet Army recovered the documents and shipped them to Moscow. Some 15 years ago the Belgian Army was able to get them back. Besides those 'Moscow archives', the Army Museum in Brussels also possesses important files on the two infantry divisions involved in the Second Battle of Ypres. These files were analysed too. The personal archives of Charles de Broqueville, Prime Minister and Minister of Defence were also useful.[1] Additional information was found in testimonies and diaries of soldiers and officers involved in the fierce fighting.

Obviously, the German Headquarters had not specifically chosen a battlefield with troops of all the three armies on the Western front. It was by coincidence that Belgian forces occupied positions where the Germans intended to launch their first gas attack. The Belgian troops were not even a prime target. From the German perspective, they were situated to the right of the planned theatre of operations at the northern edge of the Ypres Salient. The area was not ideal for the use of gas. The first Belgian trenches were behind the Yser Canal, which had rather high banks. The German planners were unsure whether the gas cloud would easily cross the water. Furthermore, to the infantry the canal posed an important obstacle. These geographic features contributed to the selection of the neighbouring sector occupied by the French Army Corps.

From a tactical point of view, the canal offered the Belgians better protection than what was available to the French troops. No man's land in front of the French trenches was as good as featureless. In addition, the Yser canal flowed at the rear of their first lines. To cross the waterway, the French infantry had installed many little wooden bridges. German observers had spotted them. The German planners reasoned that if the gas were to knock out the French soldiers, they would have no time and personnel to destroy all these crossings. So, they were confident that their own attacking infantry could use them.

German preparations for the gas attack

What did the Allied, and more specifically the Belgian intelligence services know about the German preparations? In fact, the German High Command, the *Oberste Heeresleitung* first had to convince Fourth Army chief Albrecht, Duke of Württemberg of the operation. On 25 January, a detailed briefing on the characteristics of the new weapon was organised, to which the Generals Emil Ilse and Berthold von Deimling had also been invited. Field preparations began after this meeting. In February, German *Gaspioniere* already reconnoitred the neighbourhood of Steenstraete and Gheluvelt. In March, they began installing the first gas cylinders, a work that was still ongoing at the beginning of April.[2]

The secrecy of the planned gas attack seemed easy to maintain. Belgian air reconnaissance was still very poor and the observers were not yet experienced enough. The documents of the intelligence service, the so-called *Deuxième Bureau* or second section of the General Headquarters, mentioned nothing in this respect. Perhaps no observer was able to recognise the nature of the ongoing works.

Preparations, however, involved more than installing cylinders in trenches. Fear for enemy intelligence kept he first experiments in January on a small-scale on German soil. Larger-scale tests, however, were unavoidable. Hence, from 2 April 1915 onwards, Belgian intelligence had ample opportunity to learn about the German plans for a gas offensive. On that day, the Germans had a try-out at a major training ground between the barracks of Leopoldsburg and the small town of Hasselt in north-east Belgium. Fritz Haber, who had become the driving force behind the preparations to launch a chlorine attack, still needed

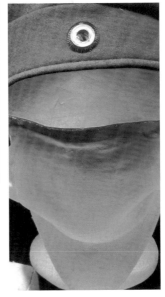

German 'Riechpäckchen', protection against chlorine.
Left: Folded in pouch (Exhibition, In Flanders Fields Museum, Ypres, April 2015)
Right: Display on dummy (OPCW exhibition, Menin Gate, Ypres, April 2015)
(Jean Pascal Zanders)

to convince officers of the *Oberste Heeresleitung* and the staff of the Army Corpses involved in the impending attack. The demonstration was a success. The chemistry professor was so enthusiastic about his cloud that he ran too far and nearly got asphyxiated.[3]

Staff officer Colonel Graf Gottfried von Tattenbach observed the trial and became worried about the prevailing westerly winds, the form of the trench lines and the disruption formed by the canal on his section of the front. He also had questions about protection for his infantry. He had observed how the cloud nearly killed Haber. While other attending officers viewed the incident as proof of the gas' effectiveness, von Tattenbach realised that his soldiers would be as unprotected as Haber.

The next day, 3 April, the immediate preparations on the frontline started under the personal command of Colonel Otto Peterson, chief of the newly created German gas regiment. Research in the archives of Charles de Broqueville and the daily orders of the Belgian Headquarters indicate that the highest decision-making levels remained unaware of these preparations and the demonstration near Leopoldsburg. The imminent gas attack was still a secret. Of course, the expansive training ground and the large number of billeted German troops easily kept prying Belgian eyes at bay. No spy report crossed the Dutch border. Furthermore, I doubt whether any responsible officer would have believed any such messages.

The intelligence picture

However, Belgian intelligence gradually became aware of German large-scale activities in the Salient. Already on 24 February Belgian headquarters received news that the German Fourth Army had ordered some special equipment from a textile factory in Ghent. The news came from the Belgian bureau in Folkestone, the British harbour where the ferry boats from Holland berthed. This bureau was one of the most important recipients and filters of news from the occupied territories of Belgium.

It was the young daughter of the director of the textile factory in Ghent, Louisa D'Havé, who had the courage to pass this information across the Dutch border to Folkestone.[4] Her message read that the German forces had ordered the production of 5,000 'textile pouches'. Within each pouch there had to be rubber to make it waterproof. The pouches were easy to use by troops. Their colour was *feldgrau*, like the German uniforms. Belgian civilian workers were not allowed to fulfil the order, although thousands of experienced textile labourers were available in Ghent. Work had to be undertaken by German military personnel. Hence, she concluded her note with the remark that the pouches had to be very important to the German Headquarters. And how right she was! In her father's factory things did not go as the Germans had wished. Most of the soldier-labourers lacked the right experience for the job. By the deadline, only 2,000 pouches were ready. She noted that the German Headquarters were furious about this delay.

On 5 March she even managed to pass a stolen pouch across the Dutch border. The Belgian bureau sent it to the Belgian Army Headquarters on the continent. On 19 March the next message from Ghent was received: 7,000 additional specimens had been ordered. The priority was so high that the military labourers had to work 24 hours a day, if necessary. Although the daughter tried to gather information about the purpose of this huge production, no German could or would tell her anything.

On 13 April – and this is very important – the next message from Ghent reached Folkestone. A different order had been received. This time the German generals no longer requested pouches, but textile masks for the mouth and nose. They needed 20,000 of them. Once again the young lady was able to steal a specimen and had it sent to Folkestone. The mask had to be carried in the previously produced pouches. These masks had to be kept humid for a rather long time. But why? A German officer had told her that this mask was necessary to protect the troops against the suffocating gas the British were using at the front. She thus accidentally learned that the mouth mask had to be humid to be effective, but had no idea of the composition of the liquid to be used.[5] Notwithstanding, the Belgian officers found it hard to believe that the enemy was preparing for a large-scale gas attack in Flanders.

In the German trenches the soldiers had a hard job. The decision for the attack was taken on 8 April and two days later the infantry began with its preparations. However, wind proved to be a decisive factor in setting the day and hour of the offensive. On the 15th, the weather was bad, so the Germans postponed their attack until the 19th, and then again until the 21st. This meant that the infantry and the *Gaspioniere* had to be on full alert for several days on end, for sure a stressing and fatiguing experience for both officers and men. Apart from this, each delay offered the enemy additional time to uncover the attack plans. Questions also lingered about whether the mouth and nose masks would be ready by mid-April, and whether the field commanders would order the attack before the infantry had received them?

On 14 April, French troops captured a German deserter, August Jäger. He told his interrogators everything he knew and informed them about the gas cylinders and the special unit of engineers. He even provided details about the protective masks. However, the French High Command basically ignored this information.[6]

What about the Belgians? The bureau in Folkestone was convinced of the importance of the messages from Ghent. But was the High Command alarmed? I assume they were at least worried. On 16 April, the Belgian General Headquarters briefed the infantry division headquarters in detail about the 20,000 mouth masks and the pouches to carry them; the fact that the masks had to be humid to protect against suffocating gases; the planned German offensive, which was to involve the use of the new weapon in the sector of the German XVI Army Reserve Corps; the fact that units from this Army Corps had been trained to manipulate cylinders with the deadly gas in the neighbourhood of Roeselare, some 20 kilometres to the rear of the German front; and the fact that the cylinders had been installed in the trenches, 20 units for each 40 metres.[7]

The message's detail was astonishing. Clearly it did not draw solely on the intelligence from Ghent, but probably also used reports from a spy in the neighbourhood of Roeselare. The report also mentioned statements by a German prisoner – possibly Jäger, or a German captured by the Belgians.

Gas attack. (Imperial War Museum, London)

Other rumours came from occupied territory. Hubert Apers, a Belgian civilian, wrote on 12 April that the Germans were producing 'bullets to suffocate' in a factory somewhere near the Belgian town of Boom, halfway between Antwerp and Brussels. He did not operate within intelligence networks, but simply wrote this to his mayor, then an exile in England. There was a serious time lapse, not in the least because the mayor waited too long before passing on the information to the military authorities. Even then, in his letter dated 29 April, he wrote that he did not believe the news, but nevertheless thought it important enough to forward.[8]

In Tielt, a small town not far behind the German lines and headquarters of the Fourth Army, a spy noted on 17 April that the many soldiers there were expecting heavy fighting and consequently were very nervous about being sent to the front. He also mentioned a train arriving from Ghent, consisting of flat wagons holding metal cylinders of about 150 cm high and 35 cm diameter. Was it hydrogen, he asked in his report?[9]

Already before 22 April 1915, the Belgian soldiers realised that daily life in the Ypres Salient was not very attractive. They could hear the thunder of German heavy artillery shelling the historic city. The town had been shelled many times before, but now the firing was really devastating. Most of the remaining civilians, fearing for their lives, fled as soon as they could.[10] In the sector of the 6th Belgian Infantry Division, commanded by General Armand De Ceuninck, 21 April was nevertheless a rather calm day. There were some rifle and artillery exchanges, but nothing more.[11]

In the afternoon of 22 April 1915, the Belgian Headquarters informed the troops that there was no major infantry action and only slight artillery fire in the Belgian sector. However, it reported intense shelling against Allied lines between Steenstraete and Langemarck. This information was followed by the strange remark that the Canadian Contingent of the British Army had reported Germans use of shells filled with suffocating gas against them on 19 April.[12] Whether or not accurate, the Canadian report was another indicator of German intent to use asphyxiating gases as a weapon, which suggests that the Higher Commands of the Belgian, British, Canadian and French forces in the Ypres Salient knew or ought to have known about German intent.

22 April 1915, 5pm

The southernmost Belgian infantry unit was the Grenadier Regiment of the 6th Infantry Division. It occupied the trenches next to the French, some 200 metres north of Steenstraete. The bridge of Steenstraete was in the French sector. The Grenadiers' position was protected by the canal, but the enemy was merely 40 to 50 metres away. The regiment had by then three major lines of defence, spread over several miles and partly protected by water and swampy ground.[13]

On 22 April at 5pm, the Grenadiers saw a strange cloud rolling towards the French trenches. They soon realised it was a deadly and frightening weapon that provoked panic among their neighbours. They smelled chlorine, maybe bromide. Some of them were asphyxiated or became seriously ill, but the Belgian losses remained limited and no panic ensued. They transformed their right flank into a line of battle to prevent the German infantry from entering the Belgian rear. They turned the so-called 'boyau franco-belge', a communication trench between the first and second line some 200 metres north of Steenstraete, into a defensive position. Soon it was even protected by a continuous line of barbed wire. The Grenadiers received support from the other two infantry regiments

Belgian individual gas protection.
(In Flanders Fields Museum, Ypres)

of the 6th Division, the 1st and 2nd Carabineer Regiments. They mostly comprised experienced soldiers, who had occupied these trenches since the middle of March.[14]

The German artillery was unable to knock out the Belgian guns and supply lines. Hence, General De Ceuninck's gunners were able to fire day and night in support of their own trenches, as well as against German infantry advancing in the French sector. The Germans suffered badly on their northern flank. While the support boosted Belgian morale, the constant shelling demoralised the German attackers. It proved to be one of the key factors in the successful defence against the German right flank.[15]

During the first hours of the offensive the German infantry nevertheless advanced extremely fast. Fifteen minutes after the release of the chlorine cloud, the attackers occupied the French trenches with hardly a fight. The gas' efficacy astonished the Germans, who began to hope that it would clear the area of all resistance. That proved an illusion, because chlorine lost its effectiveness after a few kilometres. Weakening artillery support and growing French resistance slowed German progress. Meanwhile, the Belgian artillery continued firing. German infantrymen hoped for a second chlorine cloud on the second day, but unfavourable weather conditions precluded release. The wind was so strong that Belgian air reconnaissance planes were unable to take off.[16]

Gas enveloped the Belgian trenches again in the following night. Some believed the gas had been delivered by artillery shell. Many soldiers became too ill to continue shooting. Officers faced the difficult task of motivating their men to hold their positions.[17]

With mounting losses among Grenadiers and Carabineers, Belgian Chief of Staff, General Maximilien Wielemans ordered the 1st Division under General Louis Bernheim to move up from its reserve position near the coast on 24 April.[18] The reinforcements required some time to reach the combat zone. Surprisingly, Belgian Headquarters did not pass on intelligence reports on the use of gas. Indeed, the *Bulletin d'information* issued in the evening of 23 April already carried the news that the French troops near Steenstraete had been the victim of a deadly gas attack. The report also described the colour and behaviour of the cloud. It hesitated about the means of delivery, listing the options of shells, special projectiles, or cylinders, the so-called '*bonbonnes sous pression*'.[19] Consequently, the reinforcements arrived unprepared for chemical warfare. The higher command echelons apparently still did not believe the reality of the gas cloud.[20]

Adjusting to gas warfare

With improved wind conditions on the 24th, the Germans released a second cloud over the Belgian lines. However, chlorine no longer surprised the Belgian soldiers. They had learned to protect themselves by covering their mouth and nose with wet handkerchiefs. If no water was available, they urinated on the cloth. On that day, General Wielemans suggested for the first time that the troops should carry an improvised wet textile mask. Better protection would arrive soon, he promised.[21]

Later that day he ordered the 1st Division to replace the 6th Division entirely. The replacements were well aware of the ongoing battle. While marching day and night, they clearly heard and saw the artillery to their south. In the morning of 25 April, the 4th and 3rd Infantry Regiments began to take up their frontline positions. A German air observer spotted the 4th Regiment, and it became subject to heavy artillery shelling. Their war diaries still did not mention any use of gas.[22]

Over the next days of fierce fighting, the Germans unsuccessfully tried to force the Belgians from their trenches near the canal. Consequently they were unable to widen the gap in the Allied front.[23] This also meant that the Belgian artillery did not have to retreat and the guns continued to hit the original German jump-off line and the whole field of advance.

The Belgians managed to take prisoners and thus acquire German gas masks and notebooks. Belgian intelligence now quickly learned about the tactical and chemical aspects of the new mode of warfare. The German soldiers told their captors about the cylinders and the suffocated soldiers lying in the trenches. The Belgians also learned a lot from the French and British experiences. Liaison officers worked hard. Most German prisoners carried the pouch with the mouth mask. They told their interrogators that these had been distributed from 20 April onwards. They had trained with the cylinders for the first time on 15 April. At least one German officer told the soldiers about a forthcoming attack with a really poisonous gas instead of the asphyxiating chlorine. They also learned that in the nearby village of Werken, the Germans had tried to throw gas shells with a heavy trench mortar. The shells were 40 cm long and 15 cm thick. After the explosion they could see a yellowish-greenish cloud of the same colour as the chlorine on 22 April. This gas munition was stored near the hamlet of De Kippe.[24]

On 26 April, General Bernheim, commanding the 1st Belgian Infantry Division, ordered the immediate production of mouth masks for his troops. 9,500 masks were distributed, enough for his frontline soldiers He also ordered the installation of permanent water tanks in the trenches. He had a certain salt distributed, to be dissolved in the water in a concentration of 10 per cent. Dipped in the solution, the mouth masks were deemed to offer good protection against the chlorine.[25]

The aftermath

Meanwhile, it became clear that the offensive had not been successful. French and British counterattacks pushed the Germans back. When fighting ceased, the new frontline lay not much in front of the jump-off line of 22 April.

Belgian intelligence could now evaluate the German strategy, its mistakes and its losses. Its sources of information in occupied Belgium were especially interested to learn about the strategic aspects of the German offensive. Near the railroads Belgian civilians saw that the German casualty figures were high. In Ghent, the grand old lady of Belgian literature, Virginie Loveling, wrote in her diary in May that according to circulating news some had seen trains with traces of human blood. Also, many more trains were passing through Ghent than before.[26] And right she was. Belgian

Captured Allied trenches – aftermath of the chlorine attack. (In Flanders Fields Museum, Ypres)

intelligence received several reports of heavy German losses. Some mentioned that on both 22 and 23 April up to 5–6,000 wounded soldiers passed through Roeselare, an important town in the German rear because of the many hospitals and railroad. French, British and Belgian prisoners had also been spotted in the town streets. The wounded soldiers were evacuated by train in the direction of Ghent. On 25 April, fifteen such trains travelled through Ghent in the direction of Germany.[27]

Belgian intelligence quickly determined that more trains with German troops were leaving Flanders for Germany than ones arriving with fresh troops. Already a few days into the Second Battle of Ypres, the Allies concluded that the German Commander-in-Chief Erich von Falkenhayn had never intended to push further. The first gas attack had been nothing more than a large scale test under battle conditions. Absent sufficient reserves, the Fourth Army of Duke Albrecht von Württemberg was never able to push on to the Channel Coast or even to conquer Ypres. The offensive was doomed to bleed to death. The *Oberste Heeresleitung* never sought a strategic breakthrough.[28]

On 4 May 1915, French General Ferdinand Foch visited King Albert I, Commander-in-Chief of the Belgian Armed Forces. He informed him of the French and British preparations for large-scale offensives near Aubers Ridge and Arras. He would appreciate Belgian pressure against the Germans in their sector. Foch told the King that he personally opposed chemical warfare and promised that his troops would not use such weapons.[29]

When the Second Battle of Ypres was over at the end of May, Belgian losses amounted to 30 officers and 1,500 soldiers killed, wounded or missing. Some of the missing had been captured. These were the heaviest casualties since the Battle of the Yser in October 1914 that had halted the German advance in the coastal region.[30]

Gas mask evolution. (In Flanders Fields Museum, Ypres)

Conclusion

The Belgian Headquarters could have been aware of the gas danger before 22 April. Several brave, patriotic civilians in the occupied country and occasional spies informed them of German preparations for chemical warfare in Flanders.

While it would have been difficult to take countermeasures in time, more could have been done. At least, Armand de Callataÿ, a Major in the Grenadiers Regiment who later would become Lieutenant-General, wrote in his memoirs that he was convinced Headquarters knew of this particular threat, but were still unprepared on 22 April 1915.[31]

Notes

1 The so-called 'Russian' archives are mentioned in the footnotes with the number of the box and the dossier. The files of Division Headquarters are indicated by 6 or 1 Inf Div and the number of the dossier and the document. The archives of de Broqueville are kept in the State Archives in Brussels.

2 About this preparation: L. F. Haber, *The poisonous Cloud. Chemical Warfare in the First World War* (Oxford, 1986), pp. 27–28.

3 About this trial on 2 April: R. Hanslian, *Der deutsche Gasangriff bei Ypern am 22. April 1915. Eine kriegsgeschichtliche Studie* (Berlin, 1934), pp. 99–109.

4 After-war testimonies about her are in the archives of the 'Services Patriotiques' I 581, n° 2559 and 2560, State Archives Brussels.

5 Royal Army Museum – Brussels, 'Moscow' Archives: box 249 dossier 185 – 14 – 410, daily reports of the intelligence service during the month of April 1915; especially the dossier of 28 April with a review of the messages that came in from Ghent. This detailed report was written by the chief of the bureau in Folkestone.

6 Gen. Mordacq, *Le drame de l'Yser. La surprise des gaz: avril 1915* (Brussels, 1936). The German deserter's testimony at pp. 25–26 and 219–23.

7 Royal Army Museum – Brussels, 1 Inf Div, 110/8: message of General Bernheim to his commanding officers, 16 April. See also the 'Ordre pour la journée du 17 avril 1915', based on the *Bulletin d'Information* of the General Headquarters that day.

8 Royal Army Museum – Brussels, Moscow' Archives: box 1592 dossier 185 – 14 – 3909, dossier of Intelligence Service, 7 May 1915.

9 Royal Army Museum – Brussels, 'Moscow' Archives: box 249, dossier 185 – 14 – 410, dossier of Intelligence Service, 23 April 1915.

10 State Archives: Reports of the Belgian liaison officer, Major Hougardy, 28 April and 10 May 1915. Files of C. de Broqueville, nr. 520.

11 Royal Army Museum – Brussels, 6 Inf Div, several reports in dossier of 21 April 1915.

12 Royal Army Museum – Brussels, 'Moscow' Archives: box 249, dossier 185 – 14 – 410, reports of Intelligence Service, 22 April 1915.

13 Royal Army Museum – Brussels, 6 Inf Div, several documents in dossier of 21 April 1915.

14 Some officers of the Grenadier Regiment left interesting accounts: A. De Callataÿ, *1871–1955 Souvenirs*, z. p. 2000, p. 68.; Lt. de Mahieu, *Notes et souvenirs de guerre* (Brussels 1923), pp. 76–85.

15 Royal Army Museum – Brussels, 'Moscow' archives, box 4448, nr. 185 – 14a – 3601: extended study, dated 29 November 1915, by General De Ceuninck on defensive tactics, with some lessons and experiences learnt from these operations at the end of April and the beginning of May 1915.

16 Royal Army Museum – Brussels, 1 Inf Div, document 117/30: report by General Maglinse on air reconnaissance on 23 April 1915.

17 Royal Army Museum – Brussels, 6 Inf Div, dossier of 23 April 1915, with reports of eye witness Grenadier Danhieux.

18 Royal Army Museum – Brussels, 1 Inf Div, document 118/18.

19 Royal Army Museum – Brussels, 1 Inf Div, document 117/29.

20 Royal Army Museum – Brussels, 1 Inf Div, document 117/26.

21 Royal Army Museum – Brussels, 1 Inf Div, document 118/15.

22 Royal Army Museum – Brussels, 1 Inf Div, document nr. 1. Field Diary of the III Battalion of the 4 Infantry Regiment, 3 August 1914– 31 August 1915.

23 Royal Army Museum – Brussels, 1 Inf Div, document 116/7: report by Captain Rousseau for General Headquarters, 26 April 1915. document 120/58: report about the fights of Lt. Col. Mahieu of 3 Infantry Regiment. Testimonies by soldiers of these regiments: Georges Hebbinckuys 'Vrijwilliger 1914–1918', Gemeentemuseum van Temse, *Jaarboek 2004*, pp. 72–93.

24 Royal Army Museum – Brussels, 1 Inf Div, document 118/20: *Bulletin d'information*, 24 April 1915, finished at 18.30.

25 Royal Army Museum – Brussels, 1 Inf Div, document 119/35: confidential note of Bernheim for his units, 26 April; document 120/23: about the use of mouth masks by the General Headquarters, 26 April; document 156/25: about the number of masks.

26 *In Oorlogsnood. Virginie Lovelings dagboek 1914–1918* (Ghent, 1999), p. 45.

27 Royal Army Museum – Brussels, 'Moscow' Archives, box 1592 dossier 185–14–3909, files of Intelligence Service 2 and 7 May 1915.

28 Royal Army Museum – Brussels, 'Moscow' Archives: box 1592 dossier 185–14–3909, reports of Intelligence Service of 2 May and report about all the relevant data from agents made by the Bureau of Folkestone, 10 May.

29 Albert Ier., *Carnets et correspondance de guerre 1914–1918*, edited by Marie-Rose Thielemans (Paris et Louvain-la-Neuve, 1991), Carnet: 4 May 1915.

30 Tasnier and Van Overstraeten, *La Belgique et la guerrre. III. Les opérations militaires* (Brussels, 1922), pp. 241–45.

31 A. De Callataÿ, *1871–1955 Souvenirs*, z. p. 2000, p. 68.

22 APRIL 1915 – EYEWITNESS ACCOUNTS OF THE FIRST GAS ATTACK

DOMINIEK DENDOOVEN

This chapter reviews the events of 22 April 1915 by means of eyewitness accounts.[1] Such an overview, however, can never be homogeneous or complete. First, the volume of first-hand stories is far more extensive than what can be presented in a book chapter. Second, the selection presented here has different origins: a German gas pioneer, Allied officers and men, or Belgian civilians. Their respective experiences of the first gas attack vary considerably. Third, some witnesses wrote down their accounts immediately after the events; some did so only years or even decades later. Finally, every narrative bears an imprint of the writer's personality. Every testimony must therefore be necessarily subjective and individual accounts may even contradict each other.

Recreating an as objective as possible picture of the first gas attack is further complicated by the fact that among the many testimonials only few were written by direct victims, namely frontline soldiers who had to confront the chlorine cloud.

Belgian woman with child wearing the British Ph-helmet, 1915–16.
(Imperial War Musuem, London)

French school children posing with their gas masks, 1915–16.
(Imperial War Museum, London)

Particularly on the Allied side few with direct experience survived the attack. Gas masks were not yet available. In fact, the new mode of warfare came as a total surprise to the soldiers occupying the trenches.

It is therefore impossible to reconstruct a full, in-depth overview of the events on 22 April 1915 through the eyes of those who experienced the gas cloud. Notwithstanding, eyewitness accounts are indispensable to understanding the enormity of the event and the ways in which it impacted on the participants in the drama. Eyewitness accounts may offer impressions of what would otherwise remain unexplainable.

For this overview, I have selected unknown or less familiar material. Either these accounts were discovered recently, or they were written down in a language not accessible to most readers, such as Dutch – or more precisely the local West Flemish dialect. Other important witness accounts were previously published in well-known, popular oral histories.[2] With one exception, I will not quote from them. Nor will I quote from Colonel (later General) Jean Jules Henri Mordacq's *Le Drame de l'Yser* (The drama on the Yser),[3] published in 1933, or Dr Rudolf Hanslian's *Der deutsche Gasangriff bei Ypern am 22 April 1915* (The German gas attack near Ypres on 22 April 1915),[4] published in 1934. The debate that originated from both books is worth an entire study in itself. Mordacq, who commanded a brigade in the 45th (Algerian) Division near Ypres in April 1915, published his account of the first gas attack to demonstrate amongst other things '*l'éternelle mauvaise foi germanique*' (the endless Germanic dishonesty).[5] His book was fiercely challenged in Nazi-Germany. Hanslian thus responded by describing the German version of events. He did not deny the gas attack; quite on the contrary, he described it as being justified and reasonable. He only deplored the first gas attack's negative image for Germany in the world.[6]

German eyewitness accounts

Some aspects of the immediate preparations for the gas attack are described in a typescript war diary by Oberjäger Hermann Westermann of the Reserve-Jäger Battalion Nr. 24. I have little information about the author, except for his young age of 17–18 years when he volunteered for the army in 1914 and his pursuit of a military career, ultimately achieving the rank of Colonel in the Bundeswehr after the Second World War. He presumably edited his diary during or immediately after the First World War. At the beginning of April 1915 his battalion was resting in the village of Staden:

> Suddenly during the work service at night we had to bring to the frontline large quantities of large steel bottles, just like carbon dioxide bottles for a beer tap. There, they were put side by side, and pioneers linked them to one another into batteries of 10–12 pieces. They contained a gas, which was to be blown off shortly thereafter in an offensive, and which made the opponent unconscious, and eventually also suffocated him, so that he was overpowered thereby. On one particular night, rumour went that the inventor and technical leader of this gas weapon, a certain professor Haber, wearing an unknown fantasy uniform as major, was in the frontline, to satisfy himself personally of the correct installation and preparations. Lt. Engelbertz, 1st Company, in civilian life a doctor in chemistry, was to become the technical leader for our section of the front – he had already received the commission – however he refused for ethical reasons. He then had to be replaced by lieutenant Paulman, who was also a doctor in chemistry in civilian life. We ourselves received a 'stink pad' (*Riechpäckchen*). This was some kind of bandage, drenched in a chemical substance that was carried in waterproof bags of oilcloth and worn on the left side of the breast between the epaulet and the second button of the uniform jacket. If we were to find ourselves in gas danger, we had to put it over mouth and nose like a moustache strap.[7]

An important witness was Willi Siebert (1893–1972). He is also an interesting figure. When the war broke out he was studying to become a chemist/pharmacist and working as a representative in paints and varnishes. He first served in an infantry regiment but at the beginning of 1915 he became a 'gas pioneer'. Hence, he helped prepare and carry out the gas attack. Later, on the Eastern front, he too fell victim to the gas. He spent the rest of the war behind a desk. In 1921 Willi Siebert moved to California. He wrote down his account in English, even though he was a former German gas pioneer:

Finally, we decided to release the gas. The weatherman was right. It was a beautiful day, the sun was shining. Where there was grass, it was blazing green. We should have been going on a picnic, not doing what we were going to do. The artillery put up a really heavy attack, starting in the afternoon. The French had to be kept in their trenches. After the artillery was finished, we sent the infantry back and opened the valves with the strings. About supper time, the gas started toward the French, everything was stone quiet. We all wondered what was going to happen. […]

As this great cloud of green grey gas was forming in front of us, we suddenly heard the French yelling. In less than a minute they started with the most rifle and machine gun fire that I had ever heard. Every field artillery gun, every machine gun, every rifle that the French had, must have been firing. I had never heard such a noise. The hail of bullets going over our heads was unbelievable, but it was not stopping the gas. The wind kept moving the gas towards the French lines. We heard the cows bawling, and the horses screaming. The French kept on shooting. They couldn't possibly see what they were shooting at. In about 15 minutes the gun fire started to quit. After a half hour, only occasional shots. Then everything was quiet again. […] In a while it had cleared and we walked past the empty gas bottles. What we saw was total death. Nothing was alive. All of the animals had come out of their holes to die. Dead rabbits, moles, and rats and mice were everywhere. The smell of the gas was still in the air. It hung on the few bushes which were left. When we got to the French lines the trenches were empty but in a half mile the bodies of French soldiers were everywhere. It was unbelievable. Then we saw there were some English. You could see where men had clawed at their faces, and throats, trying to get breath. Some had shot themselves. The horses, still in the stables, cows, chickens, everything, all were dead. Everything, even the insects were dead.

We started counting the casualties. This operation was so much bigger than we had ever imagined. That night we guessed over 20,000 French soldiers, and even more town people, had died. The infantry followed us but when they couldn't find any French to fight, they stopped. All of us went back to our camps and quarters, wondering about what we had done, what was next. We knew what happened that day had to change things.[8]

Siebert's poignant account is somewhat reflective and not entirely factually correct. For instance, he overestimated the number of casualties by a large margin. However, it is part of a broader narrative about his war experiences to his son Bill in the early 1930's. Willi Siebert wanted him to know what war really was about after his teacher had recounted some heroes' tales from the American War of Independence. When Bill Siebert visited the First World War battlefields in late 1998 he handed a copy of his father's account to the In Flanders Fields Museum in Ypres. It has largely remained unpublished so far.

French eyewitness accounts

Several French witnesses of the events on 22 April 1915 also wrote down their experiences.

In 1915 Jean-Marie Le Bonhomme, born in 1867 in Trébivan in Brittany, was a Lieutenant with the 73e Régiment d'Infanterie Territoriale, one of the French regiments worst affected by the gas cloud. On 31 July 1915 he described the dramatic events endured by his unit during the first war year in an unpublished speech 'Aux jeunes de la Classe 16' to a new batch of soldiers:

> Finally the 73th after having been brought to the rear area for a few days, abruptly had to board the buses again. It returned to its old positions of Langemarck – Steenstraete – Het Sas (Boesinghe – on the canal) which, by the way, had not changed at all since the hard days of October–November. For some time the situation was quiet on the front it occupied, which paradoxically surprised us more the longer it lasted, and life continued normally, actively, intensely in quasi safety within a few kilometres and even within a few hundred metres from the trenches. Despite the almost daily bombardments, the population was busy at work and trade prospered in Boesinghe, Elverdinghe, Woesten, in sum along the whole line. The awakening was as tragic as it was abrupt. In the afternoon of 22 April, undoubtedly benefiting from the withdrawal of troops partly relieved by the English and sent to the front of Arras for the offensive in May, the Germans in Belgium conceived the system of asphyxiation – you know what occurred. A few hours before the moment of the relief, the 73th and the 74th saw, rising from the German lines, a greenish yellow cloud that fell onto their trenches at the same time as a flood of shells charged with devilish gases. Many of ours had fallen exhausted after having become unwell so that they were unable to hold out under the poisoned cloud. The Germans crossed our first lines with unseen speed, attacked our advanced batteries and subsequently took our second lines, whose defenders were almost all captured [...] But the stupor produced by the incapacitating effect of the asphyxiating gases passed soon. From all sides reinforcements arrived with a remarkable celerity. And then began a second battle of Flanders, even bigger than the first, but within a more restricted area. [...] You can't imagine the noise of the artillery and musketry, which for days on end rang with the echoes over the battlefield of Ypres, the Yperlee and the Yser, the fiery sky at night, the carnage that drenched this region literally paved with dead soldiers in blood. And as the surprise of asphyxiation, this new infernal invention, had missed its effect, the road to Dunkirk remained barred to the soldiers of the Kaiser.[9]

Le Bonhomme's account was clearly part of a speech to remind the fresh recruits of the terrible yet heroic acts in which the 73th had been involved so far. He urged them to continue, just like John McCrae did in his famous poem, written at the Canal Bank near Boesinghe on 2/3 May 1915: 'to you from failing hands we throw the torch – be yours to hold it high!'. The manuscript of Le Bonhomme's speech is still with his family. In Flanders Fields Museum received a copy in the summer of 2004 when his granddaughter handed the city authorities a small bronze bell. Her grandfather had removed it from a local chapel soon after the gas attack. He always intended to return the bell to Ypres, but he unfortunately died in 1919. Only 85 years later his family was able to fulfill his pledge.

Right behind the line at Boesinghe was the 79th Régiment d'Infanterie Territoriale. One of the captains was Joseph Clément, assistant to Colonel Bartéhelemy, the regiment's commander. In the afternoon of 22 April, the regiment's staff arrived from Woesten, where the unit had been resting. Clément reported as follows:

I arrive at Boesinghe around 4pm and install the cooking material in the house of the notary. The colonel takes a room, the captain another one and I the third looking out towards the enemy. All the glass of the widows had been replaced by cardboard, but the bed is good. I even invite my friend Polâtre to come and see it, telling him: 'For once, I will be well'. I have my canteen put up and my orderly prepares the bed. I inspect the kitchen where the dinner simmers all gently. It is perfect! I leave with the second lieutenants when suddenly, a bombardment bursts out. These gentlemen pricked up their ears. I reassure them by telling them that the occurrence is rather frequent. Suddenly, our guns start to roar too; then I conclude that the enemy is attacking. It is currently 4.50pm on my watch. I am in the garden of the notary listening to the infernal din of the shooting and the bombardment.

At this point that a smell comes upon us, which affects the throat and eyes and makes us cry. What is happening? Everyone is surprised. One looks up and we notice, approaching over the canal, a greenish yellow cloud. No doubt: these are the asphyxiating gases. The bullets start to whistle. Everyone gets into the street, with the back towards the houses.

I have the flag taken and keep to the side. The bombardment on Boesinghe starts in a methodical way. The shells fall on the junction of the road to Elverdinghe and Bridge Street. Then the shooting is re-concentrated on the centre. Next to us the roofs are shot to fragments. Debris of all kinds falls around us while the population is fleeing. The first wounded pass, confused; panicking horses gallop randomly.

The situation becomes critical. Then the colonel receives the order to return to Woesten with the regiment. Which way to leave this hell? He decides to cross the park of the chateau. We take the small back door at Julia's and enter the park. The colonel moves towards the chateau. I shout: 'More to the left!' The heavy shells fall like hailstones around the chateau. We leave the park and through the fields we go in the direction of Elverdinghe. We are at least about fifteen in single line. The bullets whistle and follow us for a long time. Everyone is exhausted. We arrive in Elverdinghe where the effect of the gas is still felt and we move on to Woesten. The colonel goes to the division, and we have some cakes at La Casque d'Or, after which we head for Zuidschote.[10]

Captain Clément wrote his account very shortly after the events and it is interesting for its details regarding place and time. The confusion of the regimental staff is clear, though here it seems that the use of gas did not entirely surprise him. He wrote: 'Ce sont les gaz asphixiants!' 'These are the asphyxiating gases!' His preoccupation with food is remarkable: the first thing the French officers do upon arrival in Woesten, after a most dreadful retreat, is to eat some 'gateaux' in 'La Casque d'Or', presumably a pub.

A few kilometres to the south a special witness sat in a captive balloon somewhere between Brielen and Vlamertinghe, just north of Ypres. Edmond Cousin was observing the battlefield when the chlorine cloud attack began. His diary entry for that day reads:

> Calm morning. At 4pm heavy bombardment north east of Ypres. At 5pm the troops are called back from the rear. At 6pm the trenches are pierced at Langemarck,the Germans released an asphyxiating gas in the French trenches. The men had to save themselves, except for the 'joyeux' in the first line who are caught, the alarm is raised, an acrid odour spreads and the debacle starts. The English Army (supply) retreats, the few civilians left in Ypres, Elverdinghe, Boesinghe, Brielen, St Jean are fleeing. We start seeing wounded and fleers. The artillery abandons 46 pieces, the bombardment and firing are intense, around 8pm the Germans reach the canal opposite Boesinghe and Saint-Jean, within 2 kilometres of Ypres. The gendarmes stop the fleers, the regiments are reformed and about 10pm there is a counter-attack against the Germans at Saint-Jean. The struggle is short, they are driven out of Saint-Jean, but they remain in front of Boesinghe and keep Langemarck, one even sees that some have passed the canal, though the larger part of the German Army stays behind. Again heavy shells are falling on Ypres and Elverdinghe, fires ignite and the bombardment continues all the night.[11]

Unlike many other personal accounts, this author offered a broader perspective on the whole event. Again, from Cousin's diary it is clear that chaos was complete among the French troops – he clearly mentions the large number of soldiers running away ('fuyards'), as well as the escaping civilian population. The 'joyeux' he wrote about were soldiers of the 45th Division (mainly North-Africans). Cousin witnessed entire batteries being abandoned. He even saw the first counter-attack after the gas attack, although he confused Saint-Jean with Saint-Julien. Cousin's original diary is in the possession of a family member in the South of France.

INNOCENCE SLAUGHTERED

A captured French trench near Langemarck, as photographed by the Germans. Empty bullet cases bear witness of the fighting that has been going on. (In Flanders Fields Museum, Ypres)

French, Belgian and British prisoners-of-war captured during the Second Battle of Ypres waiting to be sent off, April–May 1915. (In Flanders Fields Museum, Ypres)

A Belgian eyewitness account

North of the Ypres Salient lay the Belgian troops. Especially the Grenadiers Regiment would distinguish itself during those days in April. It defended the northern flank after the German gas attack. A direct witness was Michel Toudy, *Sous-lieutenant auxiliaire* ('auxiliary 2nd lieutenant', the lowest officer grade that existed only in the Belgian Army). He faithfully kept a detailed diary, which included accounts of the first gas attack and all subsequent counterattacks. From his diary Toudy emerges as very dutiful, even severe officer. Michel Toudy died on 8 July 1917 when a grenade depot in his trench exploded.

Some excerpts from his war diary entry for 22 April 1915:

> We are still on picket. Around 4pm a heavy bombardment is heard and we see a large cloud in the direction of Steenstraete. Immediately Van Cauwenberghe receives order to move up front with the company, but I assume command, although I am still ill and declared free from duty by the doctor, but I can't leave the command up to Van Cauwenberghe. The company assembles very quickly, I encourage the men by telling them that this time we will march on to Ghent and that these are our men who are attacking. [...] An aeroplane flies over us, our movements are passed on to the German artillerists. [...] The bullets of machine-guns and rifles fly over the top of our heads by the thousands and the din of the shells is terrible. [...] Finally we arrive at a site between the mill of Lizerne and the bridge of Steenstraete. There, we are subjected to an intense artillery fire – machine gunners, etc. The bombardment which is directed to my trenches is of an extreme violence, it is maddening. [...] Around 8pm we are informed that the Germans have crossed the bridge and the canal and that the French have retreated to Lizerne. The whole night I urge the men to fire without interruption in the direction of Steenstraete in order to prevent the Germans from advancing along this road. The whole night French territorials arrive in our trenches coughing and saying that it is not allowed to attack aged family fathers with asphyxiating gas. What a hell all night and I suffer from fever. Several of my NCOs and my men are killed or wounded and I remain without orders.[12]

From these few extracts it might be clear that this was written pretty soon after the events and that this diary was for private use only. Though not directly affected by the chlorine cloud, Toudy belonged to those Belgian troops who immediately after the gas attack had to make a stand against the German advance. His description of the struggle that night and the following days is extremely detailed. As it would take us too far within the framework of this article, I selected only some excerpts.

A Canadian first-hand account

The above mentioned quotations were German, French and Belgian. However, in the multinational Ypres Salient, the Canadian Army had recently arrived. The Canadians got more or less their baptism of fire during the attack of 22 April.[13] Near Saint-Julien, they were on the north-eastern edge of the attack, and hence did not suffer the full impact of the gas attack. Nevertheless, they also had their experiences. Lyn Macdonald quoted Lance Corporal Keddie from the 15th Battalion Canadian Expeditionary Force (CEF) (48th Highlanders of Canada):

> My company was in the reserve trenches and it was on the afternoon of my birthday that we noticed volumes of dense yellow smoke rising up and coming towards the British trenches. We did not get the full effect of it, but what we did was enough for me. It makes the eyes smart and run. I became violently sick, but this passed off fairly soon. By this time the din was something awful – we were under a crossfire of rifles and shells, and had to lie flat in the trenches. The next thing I noticed was a horde of Turcos making for our trenches behind the firing line; some were armed, some unarmed. The poor devils were absolutely paralysed with fear. They were holding a trench next to a section of the 48th, so the 48th had to move in to hold it also until some of their officers came and made the Turcos go back.[14]

The Turcos mentioned by Keddie were French colonial soldiers, tirailleurs hailing from North-Africa. These troops were also mentioned under even more tragic circumstances in a document from the sound archive of the Imperial War Museum. I quote from an interview with W. Underwood, in 1915 a private serving with the 1st Canadian Division:

> Then we saw coming towards us the French Zouaves. They were in blue coats and red pants and caps and it was a revelation to us, we hadn't seen anything but khaki and drab uniforms. They were rushing toward us, half staggering, and we wondered what was the matter. We were a little perturbed at first, then when they got to us we tried to rally them but they wouldn't stay. They were running away from the Germans. Then we got orders to shoot them down, which we did. We just turned around and shot them as they were running away.
>
> Then, as we looked further away we saw this green cloud come slowly across the terrain, It was the first gas that anybody had seen or heard of, and one of our boys, evidently a chemist, passed the word along that this was chlorine. And he said, 'If you urinate on your handkerchiefs it will save your lungs, anyway.' So most of us did that, and we tied these handkerchiefs, plus pieces of putty or anything else we could find around our faces, and it did save us from being gassed. There were masses of Germans behind this gas cloud, we could see their

grey uniforms as plain as anything, and there we were, helpless, with these Ross rifles that we couldn't fire because they were always jamming.[15]

Accounts by Belgian civilians

Too often in military history, the voice of the civilian remains silent. Yet, the diaries and memoirs by Flemish people and interviews with locals offer a wealth of information hardly ever tapped. For them 22 April 1915 was a traumatic experience too. As indicated by Lieutenant Le Bonhomme's speech, locals continued to live normally, even at only a few hundred metres from the frontline. The gas attack abruptly changed everything. For example, all remaining inhabitants had to leave Ypres soon after 22 April. When the last ones were evacuated on 9 May, the historic place became a ghost town.

Maurice Quaghebeur (born in Boesinghe in 1897, died in Ypres in 1979) experienced the events of 22 April as a 17-year-old. Shortly after the war he wrote his war memoirs:

> On 22 April, around 5pm, we notice in the distance, in the direction of the enemy, a strange yellow-greenish cloud, moving gradually in our direction. Everyone looks at it as if dumb, non-comprehending. A French colonel, billeted with us, joined us and I asked him for the origin of this strange phenomenon. And he reassuringly explained to me that the smoke was caused by the violent activity of the guns.
>
> But at the same time the village was bombarded at ten, twenty places simultaneously, and everything just looked like a sea of fire. All billeted troops were immediately called into battle order. The inhabitants fled in all directions, and a strong odour suffocated everyone in the throat. Soldiers shouted to one another that it was an attack with toxic gases. Many fell stunned to the ground, some never to stand up again. I ran home, where my mother, sister and little brother were ready to leave. My father was absent. I advised them to hide somewhere outside the village till after the bombardment. In the meantime I locked doors and windows, after which I also left the village to protect myself. Everywhere the gun fire was tremendous and it rained shells. There was no question anymore of running away, as we got from one danger into another. And moreover, we were choking – those toxic gases were suffocating us.
>
> In that hail of gunfire I was looking for my family, but I couldn't find them at the meeting place. What now? I could not remain here; that would expose me to too much danger. I decided to go in the direction of Elverdinghe. But held up by violent fire, I didn't make it any further than the pub of René Grimmonprez, where I was advised to spend the night there.
>
> Impossible to describe the fear I felt that night, always thinking of what had become of my family. Were they still in the village, which was now ablaze? If so, what destiny would be theirs? Or had they been able to escape to safety? But where and when would I find them? Questions that could not be answered.

With some neighbours we spent the whole night talking over that dreadful situation, all the time in danger of being killed by gunfire. That night there were terrible fights. If we dared to go outside, we had a spectacle horrifying to see: flashes of the operating guns or explosions of shells, bullets which rustled past our ears, and our village only a blaze. The enemy was apparently very close, as we could clearly hear the cries of savagely fighting soldiers. Horses and guns rushed in gallop towards the enemy, together with whole swarms of fresh attack troops. It was too terrible and even impossible to write it down. Thus passed the most dreadful night I have ever experienced.[16]

The next day Maurice returned to Boesinghe, now in flames. He found his other family members near a small farm on the edge of the village. Despite the danger he went back home briefly to grab some clothes and a few other family belongings. His family was not to return for another 4 years. Boesinghe had been obliterated.

Marie Desaegher was born in Boesinghe in 1888, the eldest of 8 children. She was a young woman working as a servant in Ypres. At the age of 21 she became entirely deaf. Despite her limited education, she recorded her silent war on 13 July 1915. The crucial moment in her memoirs – and most probably in her life – was the evening and night of 22–23 April 1915. The Desaegher family lived at Het Verzet, a crossroads east of Boesinghe. Today it is the site of a small, but moving Breton memorial park dedicated to the victims of the first gas attack. On the morning of the 22nd, Marie and her sister Emma left home for Ypres, where they received their inoculation against typhus:

When I was ten minutes from home – it must have been at around six in the evening – a whole bunch of soldiers and parishioners were in the street. They spoke to us, but we continued. What they said, I did not know.

Suddenly Emma started to give signs of fear and she refused to move on. I asked what was going on and she started a whole story of which I did not understand a single word and I said: 'Come on, you cry-baby, let's move on, as I wanted to be home'.

She was still giving signs, and then I asked: 'Did some shells fall near home?' She said yes, but again a complete story followed. She began to tremble. Then she looked me straight in the face, said some words, which I couldn't understand and then ran off like a hare. I let her go as I was a mere five minutes from home. I saw her fleeing towards the farm of Cyrille Vandenbulcke.

After a few more steps, all of a sudden, the shrapnel was falling only a few metres away from my feet. In a second I became as cold as a dead body. Then I no longer felt my tiredness, but ran as fast as possible straight to the same farm where just two minutes earlier my sister had fled to. During that run, shrapnel flew past me. I jumped across ditches and dikes, over dirt and thorns, in short, across everything in my way. When I arrived at the farm, my first question was for my sister. They said that they had not seen anybody. How was this possible?!

In the courtyard the Zouaves were very nervous. They stood there agitated and were never a second at the same place. [...]

Then I was taken to the kitchen, but I left. Then a soldier took me and led me into the house. There I found a man in his shirt, and another one with his whole head bandaged, people from Pilckem. As soon as they saw me they started talking to me like crazy. As they had such strange manners, I thought that they were drunk.

In the meantime, all the soldiers had fled in the direction of Ypres. I saw that. However, two Zouaves remained. Through the windows I saw a ration wagon fleeing with two black horses and in the wagon there were two Zouaves. All of a sudden the horses were hit by shrapnel and they were killed on the spot. The two Zouaves immediately jumped out of the wagon and fled.

Everything I have described here on that farm, from my arrival up to now, had only lasted five minutes. I must confess that I did not yet know what was imminent. That's how things go when you are deaf... I had already seen so many shells explode and I was not afraid. I could be startled by it, but it was easily forgotten.

Now, as the Pilckem people saw the two horses drop dead, they fled. And there I was, all alone with Julien. While fleeing they made signs to follow them. Why didn't I do it? Even now I don't know why. Julien ran towards me, and with words and signs he told me: 'I will stay with you, Marie'.

I went outside and he followed me. The two Zouaves were there. They ran to the corridor that separated the stables from the farmhouse. I and Julien followed. Hardly arrived in the corridor, I stretched my head slightly forward and saw a group of Germans entering the courtyard. Deadly frightened I looked at the Zouaves saying: 'The Germans are there!' And they started walking towards the Germans without their weapons and with the hands up, whereas I and Julien left the corridor and went to the pig stable, where we hid.[17]

This was only the beginning of Marie's agony. After a dreadful night, Julien Matten, who was her 10-year-old neighbour, and Marie found out that the farm was immediately behind the newly dug German frontline trench. When they were evacuated, Marie got heavily wounded. She did not see Emma or the rest of her family back until the war was over. And little Julien died in 1917 without having seen his parents again. Marie Desaegher died on 6 June 1939, 51 years old, presumably a consequence of her traumatic experiences during the war. Her moving memoirs were posthumously published locally 55 years after her death.

Further afield, in Poperinghe, lived Jeanne Battheu. A young child then, she witnessed the effect the gas attacks had on the soldiers. Decades later, she vividly remembered the dreadful experiences as a child:

Nobody dared to go outside when we saw these clouds. And in the afternoon we went to the town. Yes, we could go to where we lived in the Krombekestraat, everything on foot of course, then we had no bicycles. And there, suddenly two large lorries arrived – it's as true as I say it here – two lorries and there we were watching, about ten children, all going home until the evening. These lorries stood still and some officers and soldiers got off. It was immediately next to the little farm of Vansteene where we had to wait. And out of the lorries they carried those soldiers and we watched and they placed them all in the ditch there. And that I shall never forget, I shall never forget it for the rest of my life. They were all 'gazés', 'gassed ones', people they brought from Ypres and surroundings and who had been struck there by the gas. I cannot imitate it, it is no circus here, they stripped off their clothes and their eyes bulged and their tongue hung down and they were pulling at their clothes and they yelled and they shouted, and we watched. And they laid them all there in a row. 'Come on, children, come on, children' – have I ever been a child – 'come, come, children', and we had to go to these officers. 'With cups of milk you go from one to the other' and we had to go from the one soldier who was there – I will not say just dying, but dying miserably, and we had to go from one to another constantly giving them milk. And there were some who died in front of us, little children, and whole rows of soldiers died there, at Vansteene's. And their eldest, Albert, ran away for three days, they did not know where their boy was, he had run off terrified. And we spent the whole afternoon there going around with buckets of milk and constantly give them a sip. And these soldiers who died there with their tongue hanging down and cried: 'mother, mummy, ma tante, maman', and we: 'here, du lait, du lait, a cup of milk.' I was never a child. If you witnessed that, you could not have been a child. I have already said that a 100 times.[18]

Jeanne Battheu died in 2001. Until her last days she was a very regular visitor of Talbot House in her hometown Poperinghe. In the permanent display at Talbot House's shop, you can hear her voice, telling this poignant witness account. It is also featured on a cd, which Talbot House and In Flanders Fields Museum jointly released.

Finally, as a counterpoint, I will conclude this contribution with the ordinary story of an ordinary man born in the wrong place at the wrong time. When the 90th anniversary of the first gas attack was commemorated in April 2005, the In Flanders Fields Museum received a short e-mail from a local lady. She stated that 22 April 1915 was not only the day of the first gas attack, but also the day her late and beloved grandfather was born.

And indeed, at the very moment of the first gas attack – 22 April 1915 at 5pm – Jacques Lauwers was born in the cellar of a house at Zonnebeekseweg 33, east of Ypres, a mere 5 kilometres from the scene of the chemical attack. His father Marcel was a soldier then and his mother Rachel had no idea of where her husband was. She probably gave birth to her child in solitude at that dramatic moment. On 23 April Rachel left the cellar and fled with her day-old baby. The family was later reunited in

German photograph of a French gas casualty near Langemarck, 23 April 1915.
(In Flanders Fields Museum, Ypres)

Hatfield (England), and returned to Ypres in 1920. Jacques Lauwers would later run a flower shop in Ypres. He died in 1988.

Postscript

It is a policy of the In Flanders Fields Museum to approach the history of the First World War not only by means of facts and figures, but also through the voices of those who lived through the events. Facts and figures, history with a capital 'H', are indeed indispensable to get an overview of a certain event or evolution. However I, and of many of my colleagues, believe that one also needs to hear the subjective voice of the individual to be able to grasp such an enormous event. Hence, I sincerely hope that this presentation of '*documents humains*' will contribute to a better understanding of the impact of the first gas attack.

Notes

1 I use the most common old spellings for the names of town and villages.

2 L. Macdonald, *1915. The Death of Innocence* (London, 1993); M. Arthur, *Forgotten voices of the Great War* (London, 2003).

3 H. Mordacq, *Le Drame de l'Yser. Surprise des Gaz (Avril 1915)* (Bruxelles, 1933).

4 R. Hanslian, *Der deutsche Gasangriff bei Ypern am 22. April 1915* (Berlin, 1934). Earlier that year the book had been published in '*Gasschutz und Luftschutz*', a monthly scientific magazine on the protection of the civil population against gas and air attacks.

5 Mordacq, *Le Drame de l'Yser*, p. 13.

6 Hanslian, *Der deutsche Gasangriff bei Ypern am 22. April 1915*, pp. 80–82.

7 In Flanders Fields Museum, Documentation Centre, 'German Box 5–14', with correspondence by the author.

8 Willi Siebert papers, Typescript, In Flanders Fields Museum, Documentation Centre.

9 Le Bonhomme papers, Manuscript copy, In Flanders Fields Museum, Documentation Centre.

10 Clement diary, transcription, In Flanders Fields Museum, Documentation Centre.

11 Copy of the 22 April 1915 entry in Cousin's diary, General gas file, In Flanders Fields Museum, Documentation Centre.

12 Toudy papers, Manuscript, In Flanders Fields Museum, Documentation Centre.

13 N. Greenfield, *Baptism of Fire. The Second Battle of Ypres and the Forging of Canada* (Toronto, 2007).

14 Macdonald, *1915. The Death of Innocence*, p. 194.

15 Quoted in Max Arthur, *Forgotten Voices of the Great War*, pp. 79–80.

16 Quoted in Aurel Sercu, *Van de oorlog hoor ik niets. Hoe een dove vrouw de oorlog beleefde: Ieper onder vuur, de gasaanval, in Duitse loopgraven..* (Veurne: 1993), pp. 141–43. Maurice Quaghebeur's original memoirs are kept by his son Roger in Ypres.

17 Sercu, *Van de oorlog hoor ik niets*, pp. 122–24.

18 In Flanders Fields Museum and Talbot House, *Will 'ye go to Flanders? Music and soundscapes*, Ieper, 2005, CD reference In Flanders Fields Museum MCD002, track 13.

TOXIC SHOCK: THE BRITISH ARMY'S REACTION TO GERMAN POISON GAS DURING THE SECOND BATTLE OF YPRES

Julian Putkowski

Historians generally recognise the defining characteristic of the Second Battle of Ypres was the German Army's successful employment of chlorine gas as an offensive weapon. In addition to condemning the Germans for breaching the International Hague Treaties many also acknowledge mistakes were made by British generals but are disposed to overlook the extent to which the toxic shock was also used by Field Marshal Sir John French, the Commander-in-Chief of the BEF and some of his senior subordinates to displace and diffuse contemporary criticism of their military ineptitude.[1]

Prelude

Exactly why the British Army came to occupy and stubbornly defend the Ypres Salient tends to be rather a vexed and vexing issue. The arc of trenches was a sacrificial anode, vulnerable to simultaneous bombardment on three sides. Oft-repeated claims about General Erich Von Falkenhayn, Chief of the German General Staff, directing a major offensive to capture the Channel ports lack substance and owed a good deal to wartime propaganda; the gas attack was part of a diversionary exercise to capture Ypres.[2]

The original move was in response to Marshal Joseph Joffre, the French Commander-in-Chief's need to shift French troops from the Salient to take part in the Anglo–French offensive at Aubers Ridge in Artois, scheduled for early May. Field Marshal Sir John French agreed to his forces taking over the trenches vacated by the departing *poilus*.[3] Under the command of General Henri Gabriel Putz, two French divisions remained *in situ*: the 87th Territorial Division, commanded by General Eugene-Jules-Victor Roy and the Groupement d'Elverdinghe, comprising General Fernand Quiquandon's 45th (Algerian) Infantry Division and an assortment of lesser formations, including six companies of Belgian labourers.[4] The abbreviated French front line extended across the northern flank of the Ypres Salient, from the southernmost point of Belgian Army's Yser front at Steenstraete to the Ypres–Poelcappelle road in front of Zonnebeke; the British occupied the remainder of the perimeter.

Operation Order No.7, issued by General Horace Smith-Dorrien's Second Army Headquarters on 1 April 1915, put into effect the extension northwards of the British-held front.[5] Responsibility for carrying it out rested with General Herbert Plumer, the officer commanding V Corps, which had initially consisted of two recently created divisions. The first military 'mint imperial' was 27th Division, which had been pieced together at the end of 1914 by amalgamating thirteen regular army infantry battalions composed of white troops from various overseas garrisons. It also included the Canadian Princess Patricia's Light Infantry. The second was 28th Division, a similar amalgamation of regular army battalions from overseas garrisons and cantonments.[6] Also attached to V Corps was Lieutenant General Edwin Alderson's 1st Canadian Division, composed of war service volunteers and militiamen, many of whom had seen action at Neuve Chapelle. However, they lacked experience at trench warfare and were furthermore handicapped by the Ross rifle, whose loading mechanism was prone to jam during rapid firing.[7]

The British V Corps was poorly provided with trench mortars and had few artillery pieces that could match the German Army's 42-cm siege guns. The British gunners' ammunition supplies were also severely rationed due to poor planning by the War Office and the pressing need to retain a stockpile for the forthcoming Artois offensive.[8]

By 12 April the British had taken over the perimeter on schedule, but senior commanders fretted about the Salient's interior arrangement.[9] The supply network for all three divisions occupying the V Corps perimeter relied on routes fanning out from Ypres, which was already being battered by German artillery. The incoming British infantry also discovered that French trenches and strongpoints were generally inadequate.[10]

Early hints of poison warfare

Much has been made of Field Marshal French and staff failing to heed warnings about German artillery discharging 'high explosive shells which emitted heavy fumes of an asphyxiating nature.'[11] However, the allegations were not particularly novel. In March, troops troops had already been instructed:

> In order to prevent any ill effects from the use of noxious gases, all troops in proximity of the enemy should tie a wet handkerchief over eyes and mouth.[12]

Then, on 4 April, a further warning received from the French Tenth Army, featured in V Corps General Intelligence:

> According to prisoners of the XV German Army Corps the ZILLEBEKE front is provided with iron bottles 5 feet high placed slightly behind the trenches. They have not yet been used but pioneers have been instructed in their use… A favourable wind is necessary. (This is on the authority of III Corps).[13]

In early April a report about the enemy's use of poison gas was even published in the British press, part of what post war critics later insisted were 'a mass' of warnings that were ignored by British military commanders.[14] The British Official History, published in 1927, acknowledged Smith-Dorrien had made tactical preparations, but maintained that 'As the area threatened was clear of the British front, and as the particular gas that might be employed could not be guessed at, no gas precautions were suggested or ordered.'[15]

British officers' disinclination to pay greater attention to the threat of a gas attack may partly be explained by V Corps' poor battlefield intelligence. British intelligence officers remained heavily reliant on information provided by their Belgian and French counterparts.[16] Nor may the latter have always been forthcoming. General Edmond Ferry, commanding the French 11th Division, subsequently maintained he had been censured for sharing intelligence reports with the British, and General Putz had denounced the gas threat as a German deception.[17]

Nevertheless, the French 11th Division did relay a warning to the British.[18] The original draft forwarded to Smith-Dorrien consisted of an ill-composed, unsigned note, scrawled in pencil on a scrap of paper.[19] From the contrasting styles of handwriting, it also appears that two authors may have been involved in its composition. The first wrote:

> Reliable agent of the Detachment of the French Army of Belgium reports that an attack around YPRES has been arranged for night 15/16 April. A prisoner of 234th Regt. XXVI Corps taken on 14 April near Langemarck reports that an attack has been prepared since noon 13th. Reserves have been brought up and passages have been prepared across old trenches existing in the rear of present German trenches to facilitate bringing forward artillery. Germans intend making use of tubes with asphyxiating gas placed in batteries of 20 tubes for every 40 metres on front of XXVI Corps. This prisoner had in his possession a small sack filled with a kind of gauze or cotton waste which would be dipped in some solution to [prevent – deleted in original] counteract the effects of the gas.[20]

The second added:

> The German moral is said to be much improved recently owing to having been told that there is not much in front of them. It is possible that if the wind is not favourable to blow the gases over our lines that the attack may be postponed.[21]

Smith-Dorrien notified the BEF General Headquarters, adding 'All necessary precautions are being taken.'[22] To senior subordinates he said, 'The Army Commander is unable to say to what extent the attached report is trustworthy or not' and directed the Royal Flying Corps to conduct reconnaissance flights over the German lines. He also ordered V Corps and divisional headquarters to be ready to repulse an enemy attack.[23] General Sir Herbert Plumer, commanding V Corps, immediately organised a reserve force ready to move at two hours' notice, and Assistant Directors of Medical Services were also warned to anticipate a heavy influx of casualties.[24] Major General Edward Bulfin, commanding 28th Division, told his brigadiers to anticipate an enemy assault during the evening of 15 April but made no specific arrangements to cope with a gas attack.[25] British senior commanders did not wilfully ignore warnings; Plumer continued to warn V Corps to remain alert for a sudden attack by the enemy but the British seizure of Hill 60 on 17 April and the enemy's efforts to regain control that remained the principal locus of military attention.

The first chlorine attack

At 5.00pm on 22 April the German *Stinkpioniere* opened the valves on their cylinders, generating in less than ten minutes a thick fog of chlorine gas that a light, steady wind ushered into the French lines. Major General Thomas Snow, commanding 27th Division, observed the cloud's progress at a distance:

> At about 5pm… I noticed a whitish blue mist to the northeast of us and behind the French lines. It was the sort of mist one expects to see over water meadows on a frosty night… but it was some time before we realised this was the much talked of gas.[26]

Snow also recorded the appearance and behaviour of the French soldiers escaping asphyxiation:

> Black colonial troops began to filter through Potijze and, although we could not understand what they said, we gathered from the way they coughed and pointed to their throats that they were suffering from the effects of gas and were thoroughly scared…[27]

Twenty minutes after the gas discharge, three German infantry divisions began their advance across the abandoned French trenches. Belgian Army troops at Steenstraete, and the French *poilus* of Colonel Jean Jules Henri Mordacq's 90th Brigade at Boesinghe halted the 46th Division, but German assault troops captured Het Sas and were poised to seize control of Steenstraete.[28]

The first gas cloud did not directly affect the British and comparatively few Canadians. The combined efforts of French *tirailleurs*; Canadian Infantry battalions at Saint-Julien and 10th Battery, Canadian Field Artillery temporarily curbed the German 51st Division's progress before the Canadian gunners had to retire, leaving an undefended 2,300 metre-wide gap to the east of Saint-Julien. The 2nd London

Heavy Battery of 4.7-inch guns at Kitchener's Wood were abandoned. For a while no other artillery formations could directly challenge the German 52nd Division's advance towards the Canadian 3rd Brigade HQ at Shell Trap Farm.[29]

The speed and nature of the German attack delayed and dislocated communications and generated panic. Messages sent by Canadian 3rd Brigade HQ to Lieutenant General Edwin Alderson, commanding the Canadian Division reflected the disarray:

> 6.25pm Left of subsection is 'retiring'.
> 6.30pm Your wire to us is down. Our left driven back, and apparently whole line forced back to Saint-Julien.
> 7.10pm We are forced back to G.H.Q. line; attack coming from the West. No troops left.[30]

It took until 8.25pm, however, before he found out that 3rd Brigade HQ had not been attacked.[31] While British reserve battalions were rapidly mobilised, Canadian staff officers tried vainly to establish exactly when and where the enemy were located. Chaos reigned.

At 9.02pm Smith-Dorrien rather laconically informed General Headquarters: 'Position appears somewhat grave. No reliable information as to position of French'. An hour later he telephoned Field Marshal French and requested him to press General Ferdinand Foch, Commander-in-Chief of the French Northern Army to provide enough reinforcements to enable the Groupement d'Elverdinghe to close the breach.[32] However, rapidly organised counter attacks by infantry taking advantage of the bright moonlit night would have been suicidal. The Germans had furthermore seized 50 *75mm* field guns so any French assault would have lacked covering fire.

The Canadian 3rd Infantry Brigade demonstrated the hazards of a night assault without any clear idea about the enemy's dispositions when they launched an ill-planned and poorly supported counter-attack on Kitchener's Wood at 11.30pm. Shellfire from a solitary field gun failed to prevent German riflemen and heavy machine-gunners aided by illuminating flares and rockets from simply butchering Canadian infantrymen who managed to press their way through the wood.[33] The Canadians tried and failed to recover the four abandoned 4.7inch guns. Survivors eventually had to withdraw from Kitchener's Wood. No amount of consoling rhetoric about their military élan and 'blood sacrifice' could conceal the fact that the overnight counter-attack was an unmitigated bloody fiasco.[34]

Further counter attacks by the Canadians were no less costly. On 23 April two Canadian battalions advanced across 1,500 metres of flat terrain to attack Mauser Ridge. German machine gunners situated on the crest of the ridge could clearly view the extended lines of infantrymen. A thousand Canadians were killed and wounded before orders were issued for the survivors to halt, dig in and consolidate their positions.[35]

Even so, a thinly held perimeter was eventually established and Smith-Dorrien continued to press Field Marshal French for further reinforcements. The latter

Wounded and dead North-African gas casualties waiting te be evacuated by the Germans, 23 April 1915. (In Flanders Fields Museum, Ypres)

responded but stipulated 'Orders for Cav. Corps will be sent through 5th Corps after Cav. Corps has left LA MOTTE,' thereby marginalising Smith-Dorrien. [36] The Second Army commander was furious, and snapped, 'If orders for cavalry are to come through GHQ, would like to be kept informed of same.'[37] French responded by assuring Smith-Dorrien that 'All orders given to them will be repeated to you.'[38]

As well as bickering about command and control with Smith-Dorrien, French vacillated about whether to simply withdraw British forces. However, during a visit to the French Headquarters at Cassel he was persuaded by Foch to hold fast and undertake a combined Anglo-French counter-attack on Pilckem. Unfortunately, neither party planned the attack in any detail. Thus, when the ill-coordinated Anglo-French operation matured on 23 April, it involved troops advancing in extended lines across open fields, yet again with minimal artillery support. The French *Zouaves* were driven back. Lieutenant Colonel Richard Cavendish summarised the British troops' experience:

We were given the very vaguest outlines as to the objective and direction, but the message was so late we had to hurry off […] we had apparently a mile to go in full view of the Germans. It was brilliantly clear, so they had their artillery on us and we began to lose men from the very outset. No details were given us, and of course we had not the slightest knowledge of the ground or the position of the German trenches… Our artillery was conspicuous by its absence and we had unmerciful shelling, it was a wonder anybody got through at all. There was one field with heaps of manure in rows. A lot of fellows thought they could take cover behind them. They are of course not bullet proof, and there was hardly a heap without a dead or wounded man beside it…

At last we got to a ditch which had been improved by the Canadians […] We were just a jumble of about 15 regiments with hardly any officers.[39]

Finally, at 8.52pm Smith-Dorrien called a halt to the day's operations, but Cavendish's experience was to be replicated in virtually every subsequent British counter-attack.

Persistently reacting to gas attacks with hurriedly organised, ill-directed infantry assaults across open ground against well-emplaced enemy machine guns backed by superior artillery was a recipe for military disaster. Other rewards were decidedly meagre. Whatever personal satisfaction Field Marshal French may have derived from his commitment to Anglo-French military solidarity soon evaporated.[40] He shrugged off his own share of responsibility for the debacle by complaining bitterly about having been cajoled and bamboozled by both Foch and Joffre, even though circumstantial evidence suggests French may already have made up his own mind either before or at an early stage of the fateful meeting at Cassel.[41]

British formations' war diaries and reports record relatively little about French operations. As events unfolded, it became clear that the French 87th Division and adjacent Belgian formations had managed to prevent the Germans breaking out of their enclave on the west bank of the Yser. However, the German bridgehead at Lizerne continued to threaten the British lines of communication between Poperinghe and Ypres.[42]

The last week of April

At 4.00am on 24 April the Germans discharged their second toxic cloud against the junction of the Canadian 2nd and 3rd Brigades at Gravenstafel Ridge.[43] The much smaller cloud took about three or four minutes to drift across no-man's land and engulf the Canadian 8th Battalion (Winnipeg Rifles) and 15th Battalion (Canadian Highlanders) with devastating effect.[44] Those Canadians lucky enough to be endowed with quick wits and full bladders quickly urinated or found some water to wet handkerchiefs or cotton bandoliers, and thrust the improvised respirators over or into their mouths. The fumes blinded some; others died immediately or were asphyxiated in the trenches by the heavier than air gas.[45]

The Canadian 15th Battalion was almost completely overcome by the poisonous fog or retreated to reserve trenches. Positions held by 13th Battalion were threatened from the rear by small arms fire from German assault troops advancing behind the gas cloud. A complete collapse of the Canadian-held sector was only averted because the badly gassed 8th Battalion managed to muster enough personnel to inflict a hail of small arms and machine gun fire on the advancing German infantry. Aside from reeling and retching from the effects of the gas, it proved impossible for the Canadian

A captured French trench near Langemarck, 23 April 1915. (Militärhistorisches Museum der Bundeswehr, Dresden)

Captured French defensive positions, probably along the Boesinghe-Langemarck railway, 23 April 1915. (In Flanders Fields Museum, Ypres)

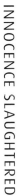

infantrymen to sustain rapid fire with their jam-prone Ross rifles. Heavy shellfire forced what remained of 13th and 14th Battalions out of their trenches, and 7th Battalion was being hard pressed. Chaotic communications between the Canadian brigades and divisional headquarters delayed their relief for three hours.[46]

In the meantime, little could be done to relieve the Canadians, whose already desperate plight worsened.[47] In spite of the best efforts of 2nd Canadian Field Artillery Brigade blasting away over open sights, there were no heavier calibre guns on hand to silence the German howitzers and neutralise well-sited enemy machine guns. The German artillery butchered the Canadians and paralysed communications, isolating battalions and brigade headquarters, and creating delays when not actually severing links between front line formations and senior commanders. Messengers and motorcycle despatch riders had to negotiate congested roads, which enemy artillery also strafed regularly.[48] Even when lines remained intact, coping with the sheer volume of enciphered messages taxed signallers to the limit of their endurance. Communication of information and orders considerably interfered with resistance to the German advance in the vicinity of Saint-Julien, where German shelling prefaced a sustained assault on the Canadian 3rd Brigade.

Stemming, let alone repelling the German advance proved to be a confused and confusing experience, principally for the Canadians. Some soldiers held their ground and engaged in merciless hand-to-hand combat, exacting a heavy toll before being killed. After running out of ammunition and energy others surrendered to the enemy, and an unquantifiable, but substantial number simply fled from the trenches. Poor communications were not a panacea for the behaviour of senior officers during the fighting. General Thomas Snow, 27th Division's irascible commander, complained insensitively about having to 'wet nurse' Brigadier General Currie's Canadians. Brigadier Richard Turner, commanding the Canadian 3rd Brigade, summarily ordered a general disengagement and withdrawal back to the GHQ line. What had been a desperate struggle culminated in a dispiriting Canadian retirement. [49]

By midnight on 24 April over 3,000 Canadians had been killed, wounded or captured, and there remained two or three substantial, undefended gaps along the British front.[50] Field Marshal French's response was robust; he wired Smith-Dorrien, urging 'Every effort must be made at once to restore the situation about Saint-Julien or situation of 28th Division will be jeopardised [...]'[51] Supported by fire from V Corps gun batteries, Smith-Dorrien was ordered to re-take Saint-Julien and drive the enemy back to secure the left flank of 28th Division.[52] The exhortation was also relayed to Plumer, who ordered Lieutenant General Edwin Alderson to assemble an assortment of battalions. Brigadier Charles Hull, commanding 10th Infantry Brigade, 4th Division was delegated to organise and lead the counterattack. Given the time constraints, inadequate communications, overnight rain and nature of military resources with which he was expected to plan and execute the operation, Hull may be excused in some measure for the ensuing disaster.[53] Unlike the gallant deeds of the gassed Canadians that thrilled and were much celebrated by war propagandists, Hull's initiative began ingloriously with a postponement and a premature bombardment of Saint-Julien that alerted the Germans about the forthcoming assault.[54] On 25 April at 5.30am, Hull's force advanced in extended order across the open fields in the light of the rising dawn. Within the hour the infantrymen were shot, shredded by shrapnel, buried or vaporised by exploding shells. It was a bloody catastrophe.[55]

Thereafter, German artillery batteries proceeded to destroy front line trenches and command posts. Exploding shells wreaked havoc with communications and exacerbated the confusion generated by contradictory orders emanating from a dislocated chain of command.[56] Anecdotes testifying to the carnage and courage of ordinary soldiers tend to attract greater attention than equally significant, but more mundane experiences. Thus the 11th Infantry Brigade, despatched to relieve 2nd Canadian Infantry Brigade, ingloriously meandered throught the night without any clear notion of their position. The bulk of the unit established itself shortly before dawn on 26 April on Zonnebeke Ridge, well behind the front line.[57]

Given these disappointing developments, it may have been appropriate for Plumer to have ordered a measure of consolidation on 26 April, including the establishment of a continuous perimeter along the northern flank of the Ypres Salient with the aid of the recently arrived Indian troops of the Lahore Division. Instead, a combined Anglo-French operation was mounted during the afternoon, involving General Putz's forces and the Indian Lahore Division. Putz intended the French attack to commence at 5.00pm. He then cut back the number of originally proposed troops and advanced the time of the attack to 2.00pm.[58] Smith-Dorrien elicited a dusty response from Field Marshal French when he personally complained about inadequate French participation. Yet again, there was insufficient time in which to mount the counter-attack, but he was required to comply with Putz's revised plan of attack.[59] By way of encouragement, Field Marshal French shared his breezily optimistic understanding of the preceding four days' developments:

> Enemy doubtless trying to exploit unexpected success met with on Thursday night, but we know he cannot be very strong in numbers and his troops are very exhausted, and he must have suffered heavily. Tide should turn in our favour this afternoon.[60]

After a forty-minute British artillery bombardment, the Jullundur and Ferozepore Brigades of the Lahore Division went into action at 1.20pm, advancing in two extended lines across a 455-metre front. The first line consisted of white, Irish soldiers, Connaught Rangers, who had been ordered to keep their left flank in contact with French Moroccan troops simultaneously advancing along the opposite side of the Langemarck road. Indian *sipahis* were arrayed in the centre and on the right.[61] Around 360 metres to their rear advanced the abbreviated second line, composed of white, English troops, the 4th Battalion Londons.[62]

The advance went awry from the start, the alignment of the attack was distorted, then at 2.20pm, a two metre high pall of 'gas fumes' halted everything and as the cloud billowed over the brigades, French and Indian, and those who were not felled, ran away as fast as they could manage.[63]

Most published British accounts of the attack make much of Indian troops' general reaction, 'Streaming back [...] shouting, 'Kharbadar, Jehannam pahunche' (Look out, we've arrived in Hell!).'[64] It was hardly surprising, given the *sipahis* had neither been trained nor equipped to cope with enemy gas discharges. Only half of the Lahore Division remained physically unscathed; however, most casualties were sustained before the gas discharge.[65] Using a toxic cloud to repulse an assault was probably entirely fortuitous; it was otherwise employed in an offensive role during the remainder of the Second Battle of Ypres.

The 149th Northumbrian Brigade was also mobilised at 1.30pm to attack German positions at Saint-Julien. With barely an hour to prepare, the territorials advanced over unfamiliar terrain, wholly exposed to enemy guns, and three of the four battalions went into action with insufficient supplies of rifle ammunition. Almost half the brigade was killed or wounded within an hour, and dug in only slightly in front of their starting point.[66]

A preliminary tally of Indian casualties incurred by the Lahore Division and 149th Brigade on 26 April amounted to circa 3,889, roughly the equivalent of an entire brigade.[67] Military historians generally apportion responsibility for these losses more or less equally between French commanders, for having tinkered with the time at which the attack should commence, and Field Marshal French, for having allowed himself to be cajoled by Foch into squandering British soldiers' lives. Smith-Dorrien has also been criticised, albeit for failing to impress Field Marshal French with the folly of going ahead with an ill-prepared plan of attack.[68]

Given the nature and scale of British losses and almost medieval corporate ethos of the British officer corps, it was inevitable that an individual would be identified and saddled with responsibility for the distressing outcome of these initiatives. The pretext took the form of a letter penned by Smith-Dorrien after he had learned about a projected French attack to be launched along the eastern bank of the Yser Canal by an inadequate, ill-supported force.[69] To Lieutenant General Sir William Robertson, the BEF Chief of Staff, he expressed reservations about the French and specifically General Putz:

> I need hardly say that I at once represented the matter pretty strongly to General Putz, but I want the Chief to know this as I do not think that he must expect that the French are going to do anything very great [...] and I am doubtful if it is worth losing any more men to regain this French ground unless the French do something really big.

He advocated a general British withdrawal to the G.H.Q. line, excusing his 'pessimistic' outlook by declaring, 'I think it right to let the Chief know what is running in my mind' and acknowledged the need to avoid jeopardising 'a big offensive elsewhere.'[70] Field

Marshal French dismissed all the concerns expressed in his letter and ordered Smith-Dorrien 'to hand over forthwith to General Plumer the command of all troops engaged in the present operation about Ypres.'[71] The mutual antipathy that had long characterised their personal and professional relationship is well acknowledged by biographers as the principal reason why French relieved Smith-Dorrien of his command.[72]

Smith-Dorrien was a handy scapegoat, diverting attention away from the Commander-in-Chief's own complicity in the developing military fiasco.[73] In his personal diary French confided that 'Smith-Dorrien has, since the commencement of these operations, failed to get a real grip of the situation. He has been very unwise and tactless in his dealings with General Putz.'[74] On both counts the Field Marshal was quite correct; Smith-Dorrien had openly expressed disenchantment with Gallic military 'vigour' and been tetchy in his exchanges with French generals. By sacking the Second Army commander, the Field Marshal got rid of a subordinate he personally disliked; distanced himself from the consequences of his own failures; placated the French, and also demonstrated his authority as Commander-in-Chief. By way of further promulgating the change of command, Field Marshal French sanctioned the creation of 'Plumer's Force', composed of V Corps, the Cavalry Corps, Lahore Division, 50th Division, and three attached brigades, and secretly directed Plumer to plan a staged withdrawal. [75]

Putz was told the British would actively continue to support French infantry attacks, but the assurance was actually an ultimatum. If French attacks failed, then Plumer was mandated to contract the British front line.[76] The contribution of 'Plumer's Force' was mostly confined to artillery bombardment, but the Sirhind Brigade suffered 250 casualties after engaging in a combined operation at the end of the month.[77] The Lahore Division lost 2,689 men in five day's fighting and between 22 April and 1 May; 18,115 casualties in all were suffered by British formations fighting along the north-eastern flank of the Salient.[78]

More ill-conceived actions

Though he had undertaken to review developments with Foch at 5.00pm on 1 May, at 3.45pm Field Marshal French ordered Plumer to begin the planned withdrawal.[79] French responded sympathetically to Foch's angry response to the proposed contraction of the British line and advocated further counter attacks. He then told the Foch the retirement had already started and sought the latter's assurance that the French would maintain a strong enough presence to cover the British left flank. Foch replied he would employ for the purpose 'really good' troops and that only one French division would be withdrawn from the Boesinghe sector. [80]

But what were 'really good' troops? Plumer stipulated 'Not less than three regular French divisions should be kept between the British left and the Belgian right, and that French troops (not coloured) be placed on the immediate left of my troops. The Indian troops which were on my left have now been relieved by white troops.' Foch agreed:

'The part of the front in the immediate vicinity of the English troops is to be occupied only by French troops, to the exclusion of Algerians, Colonial and Native troops.'[81]

Aside from establishing common understanding, their views of non-European troops had a palliative aspect. Military failure could be attributed to the martial inadequacies of French African and British Indian troops. As for white troops, 'The carrying of the position by the French and British was only prevented by the use of asphyxiating gases.'[82] However, there was little evidence that white, British regular army troops, reacted any more robustly than *Zouaves, tirailleurs* or *sipahis*.

Confidence in the martial superiority of white troops was summarily tested at 7.00am on 1 May. A German assault on British-held Hill 60 was prefaced by a heavy artillery barrage for about an hour and a half, which included gas shells. A chlorine gas cloud next enveloped and overcame 1st Battalion Dorsets.[83] An eyewitness vividly recalled: 'The gas attack [...] was so sudden, that the men in the centre of the affected area could not get away at the sides in time, and so ran back into the wood.'[84]

Contemporary reports maintain that the line held because of prompt retaliatory action by two adjacent battalions (1st Battalion Devons and 1st Battalion Bedfordshires) and the gallantry of Private Edward Warner who single-handedly prevented enemy infantry capturing a trench that had earlier been vacated by his comrades from 1st Battalion Bedfordshires.[85] However, a shift in the direction of the wind, accelerating dispersal of the toxic fumes, probably did as much as individual acts of valour to minimise casualties and prevent the enemy seizing Hill 60. Nor may be maintained that the 292 casualties suffered by the Dorsets arose from grappling with German infantrymen because as the unit's war diary acknowledged, 'The enemy apparently made no attempt to cross [no-man's land] [...]'.[86]

Unqualified confidence in British martial superiority was also tested on 2 May. At midday an intense enemy barrage lashed the front held by 10th and 12th Brigades, 4th Division. After discharging some lachrymatory shells, the Germans released a further toxic cloud at 4.30pm. The gas drifted across the lines held by 10th Brigade, which escaped relatively lightly, but to the north of Shell Trap Farm the 'absolutely overpowering gases' devastated the 2nd Battalion Essex and 2nd Battalion Lancashire Fusiliers. 'Officers and men seemed to lose their senses, most of them getting out of the trenches and reeling to the rear.'[87] Only prompt action by 10th Brigade prevented the Germans seizing the unmanned front line trenches.[88]

While some officers and men of the Lancashire Fusiliers remained at their posts, including Private John Lynn, who was posthumously awarded the Victoria Cross for single-handedly holding the line by firing a machine gun blindly into the toxic fog, many of his comrades ran away in much the same fashion as the notionally inferior *Zouaves*.[89] Aside from respirator-less Lynn, those who remained in place were alleged to have survived due to urine-soaked cloth face masks but it was enfilading fire from reinforcements and French artillery shells, rather than Lynn's suicidal gallantry that checked the enemy infantry's subsequent attack.[90] For a couple of hours it had looked as though 4th Division might be compelled to give way but it held on until nightfall.

Casualties of the German gas attack of 22 April 1915.
(Militärhistorisches Museum der Bundeswehr, Dresden)

As for the Lancashires, a handful enjoyed a measure of success with a counter-attack, seizing Listening Patrol Farm but British artillery shells raking the re-captured position nullified their achievement.[91] Although German artillery bombardment continued to plague the British, fortunately for V Corps, major infantry attacks did not materialise and by 3 May, Plumer's formations were ensconced along the GHQ line.

Whether surrendering territory to the enemy is termed a withdrawal, a retirement or a retreat is a matter of military semantics, but it was officially dignified as the end of the Battle of Saint-Julien. For Fritz Haber, if not the German High Command, the withdrawal vindicated the deployment of chlorine gas. Even if bullets and high explosive killed and maimed more soldiers, gas invariably terrified unprotected soldiers. During April and May German artillery also fired many non-lethal, lachrymatory gas shells that did not generate fear and loathing to the same extent as the huge wind-propelled gas clouds.

The three battered divisions crammed into GHQ line trenches that bellied out around Ypres enjoyed a meagre measure of respite until 4 May when repositioned German artillery resumed smashing the trenches; the positions held by the 5th Battalion South Lancashires at Shell Trap Farm disintegrated and 2nd Battalion Monmouths were subsequently assailed by a volley of gas shells.[92] On 5 May, 83rd Brigade reported gas shells had also strafed the East Yorkshires.[93] It was impossible to spot the German guns. Neither forward artillery observers nor the Royal Flying Corps could see or locate the well-camouflaged gun emplacements that scourged 28th Division.[94]

However, Germans broke through the southern flank of British perimeter at Hill 60, during the early morning on 5 May, destroying trenches held by 15th Brigade before discharging a gas cloud, killing many of the 2nd Battalion West Ridings and forcing the remainder to flee.[95] Germans infantry then took over the vacated trenches and repelled all British counter attacks. Brigadier General John Geddes, the 27th Division artillery commander, concluded: 'The Gas at present is defeating us badly, and it is difficult to think of a remedy', but he also qualified his explanation by candidly conceding: 'All day long the [1st Bn.] Bedfords in one of our left trenches were being shelled from the rear [...] the Infantry begged that the 4.7 guns should not fire any more so they were stopped taking any part in the Hill 60 fight.'[96] The majority of the division's heavy artillery guns were worn out and the shell fuzes were unreliable.[97] There was however no ambiguity about the aftermath. For the following two days enemy artillery continued with impunity to pummel the British lines and all efforts to retake Hill 60 were proved unsuccessful.

The German offensive that was directed at the 27th and 28th divisions' positions distributed along the Frezenberg Ridge, the eastern flank of the Salient, did not involve any gas clouds though. However, gas shells certainly figured in the pulverising bombardments discharged by German heavy guns and field artillery. The British formations and the Canadian Princess Patricia's Light Infantry held the line, albeit sometimes more by luck than calculation. Their counter-attacks continued to fail for pretty well the same reasons that have already been identified.

The ordinary soldiers' suffering and narrative accounts about what happened to all the formations on the forward slopes of Frezenberg are well covered in work by Dixon and Cassar. After suffering 9,000 casualties, V Corps was forced out of the shell shattered trenches on the forward slopes of Frezenberg. On 13 May the German onslaught halted.

The tempo and scale of German attacks slackened for the following ten days and the British worked hard to consolidate their defences. In addition to reinforcing depleted battalions and strongpoints, and generally reorganising and improving the defences of the Salient, V Corps acted quickly to develop the strategies to prevent soldiers panicking whenever they were exposed to a gas attack. In addition to muslin and cotton anti-gas masks, Vermoral sprayers and large hand-held fans were distributed with which to neutralise and disperse any accumulation of chlorine gas in trenches. The wind direction was carefully monitored and sentries were detailed to sound the gas alert the first hint, let alone a whiff of chlorine gas.[98]

Final combat operations

At 2.45am on Pentecost Monday, 24 May, the Germans discharged vast cloud of chlorine gas that dispersed along the seven kilometre eastern flank of the Salient instead of meditating on the Holy Spirit. The twelve-metre high fog was produced from banks of cylinders located opposite the British trenches at Hooge and billowed across no-man's

German soldier overviewing a captured French position near Langemarck, 23 April 1915.
(Militärhistorisches Museum der Bundeswehr, Dresden)

land, initially enshrouding the British front lines as far as Turco Farm and Shell Trap Farm.[99] It was bigger than any other gas discharge, a dense, choking fog that diffused into a vast slow-moving plume, extending two kilometres into the Salient.[100] The entire V Corps front was enveloped but during the two hours that it took for the gas to disperse, some formations were more heavily affected than others by the toxic fumes.

The northernmost sector, occupied by 10th and 12th Brigades, 4th Division, was a wedge shaped perimeter of trenches extending from the east of Turco Farm to the Zonnebeke Road. Situated mid-way between these two points, at the apex of the wedge, was the much fought over Shell Trap Farm, defended by 10th and 12th brigades. Though their infantrymen more or less coped with the effects of the gas, they were unable to repulse an incursion by German infantry. The 4th Division War Diary reported soldiers, many unarmed, running away. The Lancashire Fusiliers HQ staff gunned down a few of the fleeing men but failed to stem the panic-stricken exodus.[101]

The 10th Brigade did not give way, possibly because the sentries were alert and thirty minutes elapsed before the gas reached their trenches near Wieltje but the Germans still managed to capture Shell Trap Farm shortly after 6.00am. Brigadier Frederick Anley, commanding 12th Brigade, was assigned to organise a British counter-attack with assistance from the French during the afternoon but the move was postponed due to heavy German shelling and reports that 10th Brigade troops were abandoning the trenches to the south of Shell Trap Farm.[102] These developments and German gas shells prompted Headquarters, V Corps to decree: 'It must be impressed on all ranks that they must not move when gassed.'[103]

Anley's initiative came to naught because General Maurice Joppe, commanding 152nd Division refused to permit French infantry to be used as assault troops and British brigadiers felt pessimistic about the prospects of retaking Shell Trap Farm. Thus the Germans maintained their hold over Shell Trap Farm and took over a substantial wedge of the Salient, including Turco Farm and Wieltje.[104]

General Bulfin's 28th Division, occupied a sector extending from the Zonnebeke Road to Bellewaarde. It was bisected by the Ypres–Roulers railway, to the north of which was 85th Brigade with 84th Brigade on the south side. The massive cloud of chlorine gas cloaked the entire brigade; trenches and the brigade headquarters were simultaneously strafed with lachrymatory gas shells, and then the Germans attacked, 'In no apparent formation after very heavy gun, machine gun and rifle fire.'[105]

The shelling severed telephone lines and the gas cloud disrupted other means of communication. At 85th Brigade HQ the commander recorded: 'We were all coughing and eyes nostrils and throats were painful and smarting […] orderlies who came from the front were all prostrate for a bit […] we suffered principally from the [tear] gas shells the effects of which wear off.'[106] However, the concentration of gas was worse in the trenches, causing two companies of soldiers to flee. Unfortunately, 'The effects of running down wind with the fumes working [sic] them into their lungs was disastrous and all the worst cases of gassing occurred among these men.[107]

Other 85th Brigade troops also 'Retired in disorder thereby losing a great opportunity of inflicting heavy losses on the enemy who had been advancing in masses from the BELLEWAARDE lake.'[108] Chlorine gas corrupted lungs and also corroded soldiers' morale, 'Its strong effects appeared to make the men subjected to it, singularly inert […] It was with considerable difficulty that one could retain the men in the line of dugouts and road, as they were subjected to shellfire in addition to enfilade and frontal rifle fire.'[109]

The 2nd Battalion Buffs was ordered to aid the hard-pressed Royal Fusiliers, including 'certain stragglers', who in their turn tried and failed to re-occupy the trenches north of the railway line that had earlier been vacated by the 2nd Battalion East Surreys. Luckily, by 8.30am the 8th Battalion Durham Light Infantry managed to recover the trenches and seal the gap in the British front line. Thereafter, the Buffs and the Royal Fusiliers managed to establish a line of defences, albeit at Railway Wood, over 350 metres behind the original first line trenches. [110]

The flight of the Fusiliers left exposed the neighbouring southerly sector, held by 2nd Cavalry Brigade, whose headquarters staff was compelled to evacuate because of the gas fumes. Masses of soldiers ran away from their positions, shouting that the gas had driven them out but attempts to round up stragglers were useless because of enemy shellfire.[111] After replacing the 2nd Cavalry Brigade commander, who had been knocked out by gas, Brigadier General William Greenly ordered the 4th Dragoons to reinforce the trenches immediately north of the Menin Road. On arriving the latter found the trenches were already crammed full of British troops and were 'Withdrawn to a position where it was subjected to heavy fire and gas fumes for the remainder of the day.'[112]

The troops who were already occupying the trenches straddling the Menin Road included 'A' Company, the Buffs, who 'Found physical energy difficult and all developed ceaseless coughing'; many dropped out with fatigue *en route* to trenches congested with an assortment of stragglers from nearby positions.[113] The mud-filled trench was uncomfortable and unsafe; the sodden parapets were poor protection from enemy snipers.[114] Many officers had been killed but the line held; surrender was not an option.[115] After dusk, troops slaved away with shovels to improve the trenches while behind the front lines the ground was littered with corpses of terrified soldiers who had run away from the gas cloud, only to perish before they reached Ypres.[116]

During the rest of the day, whenever 28th Division troops gathered launch counter-attacks they were immediately strafed by enemy artillery and machine guns. Even when such initiatives materialised there was little co-ordination between the seriously under-strength battalions. Indecisive skirmishing was still in progress shortly after midday when 80th Infantry Brigade supported a major attack by 28th Division on German lines at Bellewaarde Farm.

General Edward Bulfin, the 28th Division Commander, ordered 80th and 84th brigades to attack across a front that extended from the centre of Bellewaarde Lake to the Menin road. The assault, spearheaded by 80th Brigade, commenced at 12.30am on 25 May. A near-full moon lit the battlefield. They were aided by a bombardment from 1st Artillery Brigade, but lacked essential telephone communications. What followed, however, was by any standards a disorganised shambles. The gunners did their job well, but infantrymen were repeatedly driven back by heavy rifle and machine gun fire.[117] This costly, but otherwise unremarkable rebuff turned out to be the final skirmish before the Germans ceased their offensive. Just as it had determined the date and time when the brawl began, the German Army also decided the time and date on which the Second Battle of Ypres ended.

Responsibility for the debacle

The abrupt and wholly unanticipated German disengagement came as a blessed relief to the British rank and file, but Field Marshal French, his protégés Plumer, Allenby, and their divisional commanders were left with a thorny problem. How were they, collectively and personally to account for ceding ground to the enemy and the massive casualty list sustained under their command? They had repeatedly failed to anticipate the release of any of the gas clouds, and had been responsible for ordering a succession of ill-planned, ill-coordinated and ineffective counter-attacks.

As Commander-in-Chief, Field Marshal French was disinclined to shoulder responsibility for the failure of forces under his command at Ypres and during the Artois offensive at Aubers Ridge, Festubert and Bellewaarde. He colluded with his crony George Moore; Allenby; Colonel Charles a Court Repington and the Northcliffe press to discredit Lord Kitchener, the War Minister, blaming him for the 'Shell Crisis', the shortage of high explosive shells and rendering it politically difficult for the Government to sack French for military ineptitude.[118]

Nor did he admit that the BEF had ever experienced any setbacks. By 21 May and subsequently in his Official Despatch of 15 June 1915, French maintained that the Aubers Ridge and Festubert offensives resulted in 'The capture of a large area of entrenched and fortified ground' as well as providing valuable support for the French Army's 'marked success' at Arras and Lens.[119] As for Ypres, he declared the 'Town and district […] have […] been successfully defended against vigorous and sustained attacks by large forces of the enemy,' supported by a mass of heavy and field artillery, 'Superior to any concentration of guns which has previously assailed that part of the line' and 'A gas so virulent and poisonous a nature that any human being brought into contact with it is first paralysed and then meets with a lingering and agonizing death.' He was no less forthright in condemning Germany's 'Cynical and barbarous disregard of the well-known usages of civilized war and flagrant defiance of the Hague Convention.' He added, 'Poisonous gas fumes materially influenced operations […] until experience suggested counter-measures, which have since been so perfected as to render them innocuous.'[120] The 'counter-measures' to which French referred included the Cabinet's prompt, positive response to French's written demand on 23 April for British-made toxic gas with which to retaliate in kind.[121]

Omitting any reference to his own summary termination of Smith-Dorrien's role as commander, French proceeded to explain that V Corps' troops had experienced, 'Confusion and demoralisation caused by the first great gas surprise and subsequent almost daily gas attacks.'[122] He maintained that it was only after 8 May that 'Effective preventatives had been devised and provided' and explained that the high number of casualties because of the gas attack on 24 May was due to sleeping soldiers failing or being too slow in donning their respirators.[123] Given the proliferation of personal official communiques, censored reports and editorial condemnation of the 'Huns' in the British press between April and June, aside from his exaggeration about the incidence of gas attacks, there was little new in what the Field Marshal had to relate about the strength and ferocity of either the enemy's artillery or sufferings of the gassed soldiers.

However, the succession of fruitless attacks during late April occasioned heavy losses because of other factors, not the least of which was the flat, open terrain and enemy occupation of surrounding high ground that disadvantaged British assault troops, even when the latter did not advance in extended lines. As the perimeter of the Salient contracted, supply, transport and arguably communications may have improved, but trenches and forward positions became congested with troops, providing an abundance of tempting targets for enemy artillery.

Publicly, French and Joffre maintained that they could not relinquish the Ypres Salient because of 'The special political and sentimental value attaching to every acre of the small portion of Belgium remaining unconquered, and the moral effect created amongst neutrals […] by the German paeans of victory on the gain of the smallest parcel of ground.'[124] To the soldiers under his command, Field Marshal French proclaimed with breath-taking insouciance:

> You have fought the 2nd great battle of Ypres, the most desperate and hardest fight of the whole war [...]. I will tell you the reason for that. The Germans have tried all they possibly could to get possession of Ypres – although it was of no use to anybody except from a sentimental point of view.[125]

Few would deny his contemporary assessment of the fighting, but the tactical disadvantages associated with defending the arc of trenches to the east of Ypres were finessed by the Field Marshal and senior commanders' ill-planned and unsuccessful attacks. How many men perished or were maimed defending a town dismissed by French as 'of no use to anybody except from a sentimental point of view' remains a contentious issue.

Calculating the blood price of any battle is a controversial and perplexing process. In the case of the Second Battle of Ypres, it is generally conceded that bullets and explosive shells killed more men than the toxic clouds. It is impossible to estimate the number of casualties generated by artillery shells. Officially, British casualties (all ranks) arising from the fighting at Hill 60 and the struggles around Ypres between 22 April and 31 May were: killed 10,519; wounded 33,234; missing 16,422.[126] However, recent research suggests that the official statistics significantly underestimated the total number of fatalities. Dixon, using 'Soldiers Died in the Great War', calculates that 14,950 (all ranks) died between 17 April and 31 May. Chielens, drawing on the burial registers of the Commonwealth War Graves Commission, concludes that the total is 15,446 (all ranks) died between 22 April and 24 May.[127] The process of estimating British casualties is also bedevilled by the difficulty of reconciling contradictory casualty returns. For example, the heavy casualties recorded by the Lahore Division between 16 April and 7 May, totalling 2,689 (all ranks: killed, wounded and missing) was reduced in the Indian Expeditionary Force (Printed) War Diaries to 463 (all ranks: killed, wounded and missing).[128] There were also an unknown number of men who were picked off by the enemy snipers after adopting the prescribed response when threatened with a chlorine cloud, viz.:

> The important thing is to keep the head as high as possible; the most fatal thing to do is to crouch down. If the enemy attack a trench by gas fumes, the parapet should therefore be manned, and rapid fire opened. This will keep the enemy's fire down and enable men to [adopt?] an upright position. The fact that it distracts the men's attention from the effects of the gas, no doubt assists them to resist the effects.[129]

It also remains impossible to accurately establish the causes of death of soldiers that fell in no-man's land or in bitterly contested fire trenches, or the number of fatalities that were reported to have been exclusively due to gas inhalation. In many cases gas may have been a contributory factor rather than a primary cause of death because semi-asphyxiated soldiers would have been more than usually vulnerable to enemy bullets or bayonets. Nor is it possible to derive from medical returns more than a general impression about the impact of toxic gas inhalation, exemplified by the gas attacks on Hill 60 by Major General Porter, Director of Medical Services, 2nd Army:

> 2nd May [...] About 5 officers and 300 men of the Dorset Regiment affected, most of these cases were only slight. Up to 3 o'clock 2 officers and 25 men had been transferred to Casualty Clearing Stations at Bailleul, 7 of these died soon after admission and the remainder are not expected to recover. 2 died on the journey in from Boeschepe [...] 3rd May Germans again used poisonous gases from their trenches and shells last evening opposite the trenches of the 27th Division and then attacked. A considerable number of men affected also number of men wounded [...] 90 men said to have been killed in the trenches from gas poisoning.[130]

In compiling his own estimates, Foulkes maintained that few of the gassed men admitted to hospital subsequently died:[131]

	Gas casualties hospital admissions	Dead
24 April (Langemarck)	122	11
1 May (Hill 60)	2,413	227
6 May (Hill 60)	557	22
10 May (Hill 60)	79	2
24 May (Menin Road etc.)	3,284	53
Totals	6,455	315

The vast majority of survivors only slightly affected by gas went unrecorded because they remained with their units and returned to duty after some rest. The more acutely gassed cases were taken to casualty clearing stations before being sent for treatment at base hospitals or shipment back to the United Kingdom. The Director of Medical Services, Second Army, also recorded 5,766 Wounded (Gas) cases were evacuated by Second Army between 22 April and 26 May but it is impossible to draw firm conclusions from incomplete data.[132]

'Missing in Action' was a catch-all category, including men who were vaporised, blown to shreds or buried by shell explosions and others, sometimes wounded, who were captured by the enemy. Again, there is insufficient evidence to determine how gas may have influenced the figures of men that were subsequently reported missing. Some of those reported missing would have been summarily killed by their captors, a practice condemned in contemporary British press reports and communiques circulating in the UK and abroad.

The soldiers who surrendered or were captured by the enemy attracted comparatively little publicity yet their numbers may also have been quite substantial. For example, of the 6,036 casualties sustained by the Canadian Division during April, 1,410 men surrendered or were captured. The figure included 627 wounded of whom 87 died from their injuries.[133] However, official enquiries concluded that the captives included only 55 who had been gassed; the majority of gas-affected men, numbering 3 dead and 248 non-fatally affected, escaped being captured. It is difficult to know what to make of such data, other than to conclude that it tends to contradict contemporary anecdotal accounts about the summary killing of wounded men by the enemy, including the alleged gratuitous 'crucifixion' of a captured Canadian NCO.[134]

Rather more specifically, the incidence of casualties after 3 May calls into question the effectiveness of the anti-gas mouth pads, thousands of which had been produced in the UK in response to public appeals by the 'Daily Mail' and 'Times'. They were ineffective when dry and impossible to breathe through when wet. However, against the advice of Professor John Haldane, the British scientist whose gas expertise had been called upon by the Army, many of these useless items were distributed anyway.[135] The provision of 40,000 'naval pattern respirators' that were issued to Plumer's Force; anti-gas mouth pads produced locally at divisional rest stations by RAMC staff and patients, and those manufactured by Second Army were also ineffective, unless dampened and kept moist with repeated application of sodium thiosulphite ('hypo') solution.[136]

Major-General Porter reported that, 'All troops in fighting line have been supplied with some protection against the gases, that is flannel bandages, gauze etc.,' concluding, 'None of which have so far have proved effective'.[137] He reasoned that ready-dampened mouth pads, packaged in waterproof 'Jaconet' bags would be more immediately effective than soldiers relying on a urine-distended bladder or a possibly inaccessible container of hypo solution. He therefore immediately initiated mass production locally, supplementing the daily supply of 10,000 anti-gas mouth pads from the UK.[138]

These developments and the production of the Cluny MacPherson 'Smoke Helmet', a hypo-impregnated flannelette hood equipped with a transparent mica window for vision, prompted Field Marshal French to assert that after 8 May 'Effective preventatives had been devised and provided.'[139] What French omitted to acknowledge was that the mica panel proved too fragile. Until it was replaced with a more durable cellulose window, most troops were therefore still compelled to rely on the minimal protection of anti-gas mouth pads. To be fair, the Field Marshal may have been misled by the relatively low incidence of acute gas cases between 8 May and 23 May. However,

General Porter continued to entertain reservations about the effectiveness of anti-gas mouth pads, including the latest version, the 'War Office Black Veiling respirator'; he attributed low incidence of acutely gassed casualties were due to the wind being 'not very favourable to the enemy.'[140]

The spectacular impact of the 24 May gas cloud provided graphic confirmation of the inadequacy of the issued respirators. However, official embarrassment was avoided because medical officers essentially exonerated both the military hierarchy and manufacturers that supplied the respirators, but not the soldiers who were gassed. Porter reported:

> Men in the firing line not so much affected [...] Men in reserve trenches were asleep when gas came along and had not time to put on their respirators, (3) men were wearing unauthorized pattern respirators, (4) officers took off respirators to give orders, (5) men retired in same direction as gas, (6) respirators had been carried in inside pockets of men's greatcoats, also in front of men's capes and had become dry.'[141]

By the end of May, when Prime Minister Herbert Asquith visited Bailleul, improvised anti-gas mouth pads and equally ineffective Gas Veiling Respirators were being replaced by smoke helmets fitted with acetoid cellulose instead of the original fragile mica viewing panel.[142] However, it was not until 9 June that the Director of Medical Services admitted mouth pads, 'Did not give sufficient protection and recommended that all troops should be provided with a properly prepared smoke helmet.'[143]

Senior British Army commanders aired other explanations to account for casualties incurred during the month's fighting. Of the divisional commanders, General Snow attributed the heavy losses to tactical failure:

> Had we contented ourselves, when we were shelled out of our trenches with digging new trenches and making no attempt at countering, it might have been bad for morale but it would have saved up the enormous casualty roll which resulted from our counter-attack. We had practically no artillery support and we ought to have modified our tactics accordingly instead of which we stuck religiously to the book which never had calculated on such disparity of artillery between the two opposing forces.[144]

For military failures of attacks carried out during May, Field Marshal French blamed reinforcements' combat inexperience; 'slackness' by NCOs and subalterns and 'Neglect by responsible officers, of precautions for the safety of their men and the Army.'[145] Plumer, dubbed the 'Soldier's General', blamed the soldiers, '[...] In some units, or rather in some portions of units, a certain amount of demoralization followed the 'gas' attack.' Echoing French, Plumer warned, 'Failure to meet this new form of attack owing to neglect or carelessness is as culpable for a soldier as misbehaviour before the enemy.'[146]

The Provost Marshal, 2nd Army inaugurated a system of 'Police stops' to round up stragglers. Those classified as 'obviously' gassed were sent for medical treatment. In all other cases stragglers were issued with guns and gas masks and marched back to the firing line. No diagnostic training was provided to assist 'Police stop' personnel to distinguish between a malingerer and a straggler 'obviously' suffering from gas.[147]

For Major-General Henry Wilson, commanding 4th Division the distinction was a straightforward matter. He wrote:

> A very large number of men came into our Dressing Stations without arms or equipment and reported themselves as gassed. Some of these men were suffering appreciably from the gas, [...] in my opinion largely due to their being seized with panic and running away <u>with</u> the gas cloud [...] I think that men who are carried in should be shown as wounded.[148]

Wilson's impatience with ambiguity was also exercised and endorsed via the identification and execution of a scapegoat. By mid-May 1915, approximately 300 soldiers serving with the BEF had been sentenced to death for military offences and Field Marshal French never expressed any reservations about approving the execution of one in ten of the condemned men.[149] The policy of shooting soldiers, summarily or after trial by court martial was already well established, and it was easy to pluck a sacrificial lamb from the flocks of stragglers that had been driven back by the gas cloud released on 24 May.

The soldier who was selected, Private Herbert Chase, was one of a draft of reinforcements sent to reconstitute the gas-decimated 2nd Battalion Lancashire Fusiliers. Chase had only been with the battalion for a few days prior to 24 May, when it was engulfed by gas and shelled out of Shell Trap Farm. Chase maintained he had been feeling ill for some while before 3.00am, when the toxic plume was billowing across the support trenches. He later admitted the gas caused him to flee but could not remember how he came to be spotted at 4.30am, lying by the side of a road near Vlamertinghe in a 'dazed condition and exhausted.'[150] He had been escorted to the Dressing Station, No.12 Field Ambulance, where a mass of soldiers who claimed to have been gassed were examined by a doctor who recalled, 'A proportion were found either by myself or another medical officer to be free from any signs of gas poisoning [...] I considered them fit for duty.'[151] Chase was divested of his rifle and equipment, hospitalized and then accused 'Misbehaviour before the enemy in such a manner as to show cowardice'.

At his trial by Field General Court Martial, Chase spoke briefly in his own defence and was then sentenced to death by the two captains and a subaltern who sat in judgment.[152] Although the written proceedings disclosed little about Chase's behaviour on 24 May, the written addenda by confirming officers expressed their desire to have Chase executed for the sake of example, albeit with some reservations about the paucity of evidence advanced by prosecution witnesses.[153] However, Brigadier Anley was unequivocal in asserting the importance of executing Chase 'The sentence should be carried out without delay.[…] if immediate examples are not made of men who quit their trenches the fighting qualities of the brigade will deteriorate.'[154]

Major General Wilson agreed but was uneasy about the prosecution witnesses' flimsy evidence, so he tucked into Chase's dossier additional depositions by two medical personnel who had not testified at Chase's trial. They claimed to have recognised Chase on 24 May and were of the opinion that he had 'Very little wrong with him' and 'Did not appear to be bad from the gas'.[155] Plumer considered 'Others were equally guilty who have not been arrested […] In this case I recommend the sentence be commuted' but soon reversed his opinion after being told Chase had previously been jailed for desertion.[156] Field Marshal French added his confirmation on 7 June and Chase was duly executed by a firing squad at 4.30am on 12 June in a wood near the Trappist Abbey of Saint-Sixtus in West Vleteren and buried in an adjacent cemetery.[157]

The collective reaction by French and his senior officers to the threat of poison gas was prompted by their own sense of insecurity and perceptions of weak behaviour by the rank and file. Faced with the unfamiliar threat of chlorine gas, they ordered men under their command to carry out poorly supported and ill-planned counter-attacks. They also knew that the anti-gas respirators afforded minimal protection to wearers but continued to punish soldiers who struggled to avoid being gassed. May they have been included in the ghostly company to whom Field Marshal French alluded when he confessed to his mistress that he was haunted by the spirits of his 'glorious' dead friends?[158] Since he took care to destroy his personal papers, we shall probably never know.

* * * * * *

For advice and assistance with references and sources, I thank: Hans Andriessen, Nicky Campbell, Piet Chielens, Simon Jones, David List, Allan Lougheed, and Phil Tomaselli.

Notes

1 See, J. Dixon, *Magnificent but not War* (Leo Cooper: Barnsley, 2003); G. H. Cassar, *The Tragedy of Sir John French* (Associated Universities Press: London, 1985); G. W. L. Nicholson, *Official History of the Canadian Army in the First World War: Canadian Expeditionary Force, 1914–1919* (Queen's Printer and Controller of Stationary, Ottawa, 1962); J. L. McWilliams and R. J. Steel, *Gas! The Battle for Ypres, 1915* (Vanwell: Ontario, 1985); D. G. Dancocks, *Welcome to Flanders Fields* (McClelland & Stewart: Toronto, 1988); E. N. Christie (ed.), *Letters of Agar Adamson 1914 to 1919* (CEF Books: Nepean, 1997); N. M. Greenfield, *Baptism of Fire, The Second Battle of Ypres and the Forging of Canada, April 1915* (Harper Collins: Toronto, 2007); T. H. E. Travers, 'Allies in Conflict: The British and Canadian Official Historians and the Real Story of Second Ypres', *Journal of Contemporary History*, vol. 24, no. 2 (April 1989), pp. 301–325.

2 E. von Falkenhayn; *General Headquarters 1914–1916 and its critical decisions* (Battery Press: Nashville, 1919, repr. 2000), pp. 84–87; U. Trumpener, The Road to Ypres: Beginnings of Gas Warfare, *Journal of Modern History*, vol. 47, no. 3 (September 1975), pp 470–3; 'Eye Witness' Despatch (11 May 1915) in 'How Calais was saved', *Weekly News* (Hull), 15 May 1915, p. 6.

3 R. Holmes, *The Little Field Marshal: The life of Sir John French* (Cassell: London, 1981), pp. 269–71; National Archives, Kew (TNA), War Office, WO158/13, War Office, Military Headquarters: Correspondence and Papers, General Joffre, Correspondence: Report of the meeting at Chantilly, 21 January 1915; Nicholson, *Official History of the Canadian Army in the First World War*, pp. 50–51; Cassar, *The Tragedy of Sir John French*, pp. 202–09.

4 W. Philpott, 'Britain, France and the Belgian Army', in B.J. Bond et al, *Look to Your Front* (Spellmount: Staplehurst, 1999), pp. 128–29; A. D. Lougheed, *Too many Heroes, vol. 1: The translated War Diaries of 1er and 3e battalions de marche d'Infanterie légère d'Afrique, from mobilisation to 2nd Ypres* (Lougheed: Canada, 2012), pp.196–98.

5 TNA, War Office, WO95/270 War Diary, 2nd Army HQ, 1 April–30 April 1915, Appendix 1, p.1.

6 A. F. Becke, *Order of Battle of Divisions*, Pt.1 (HMSO: London, HMSO, 1934), pp. 102, 110.

7 Dancocks, *Welcome to Flanders Fields*, pp. 1–15; 137; B. Rawling, *Surviving Trench Warfare: Technology and the Canadian Corps* (University of Toronto Press: Toronto, 2014 edn.), pp. 28–29; 37–39.

8 D. French, 'The military background to the shell crisis of May 1915', *Journal of Strategic Studies*, 2 (1979), pp. 192–205; P. Fraser, 'The British 'Shells Scandal' of 1915', *Canadian Journal of History*, vol.18, No.3 (1983), pp. 69–86; Cassar, *The Tragedy of Sir John French*, pp. 230–32; I. M. Brown, *British Logistics on the Western Front* (New York, Praeger: New York, 1998), pp. 90–91; A. J. A. Morris (ed.), *The letters of Lieutenant-Colonel Charles a Court Remington, military correspondent of the 'Times', 1903–1918* (London, Army Records Society: London, 1999), pp. 32–34; 229–33.

9 TNA War Office, WO95/270, vol. 4, 2nd Army HQ, 1st to 30th April, 1915, Appendix 2, Details of Moves to be carried out by Corps of the 2nd Army, 2 April 1915.

10 TNA War Office, WO95/270, Summary of Events in the 2nd Army from 7th to 13th April 1915, pp.1–2; Lougheed, *Too many Heroes*, p. 37.

11 TNA War Office, WO95/270, Appendix 9, Summary of Operations of the Second Army,14th to 20th April 1915, p. 3.

12 Christie (ed.), *Letters of Agar Adamson 1914 to 1919*, p. 34.

13 TNA War Office, WO95/270, [J. R.?] Stanhope, Captain for B.G.G.S., 5th Corps. 4 April 1915, p. 53; J. E. Edmonds, G. C. Wynne, A. F. Becke, *Official History of the Great War based on Official Documents, France & Belgium, 1915, Winter 1914–15* (HMSO: London, 1927), p.164.

14 e.g., 'A New German Weapon – Poisonous Gas for our troops', *Times*, 9 April 1915, p. 7; E. Ferry, 'Ce qui s'est passé sur l'Yser', *La Revue Des Vivants* (Paris, 1930); C. H. Foulkes, *'Gas!' The Story of the Special Brigade* (Blackwood: Edinburgh, 1934), pp. 29–35; A. Fortescue-Duguid, *Official History of the Canadian Forces in the Great War 1914–1919* (King's Printer: Ottawa, 1938), vol. 1, Appendices: 180, 321, 323, 327; McWilliams and Steel, *Gas!*, pp. 13–20.

15 Edmonds, Wynne, and Becke, *Official History of the Great War*, p.165.

16 TNA, War Office, WO 95/2267 War Diary: HQ 28th Division, March 1915, Appendices: Memo: Milne, 2 Army to V Corps, 20 March 1915; Edmonds, Wynne, and Becke, *Official History of the Great War*, p.188; L. F. Haber, *The Poisonous Cloud: Chemical Warfare in the First World War* (Clarendon Press; Oxford, 1986), pp. 32–34.

17 Ferry, cited in Foulkes, *Gas!*, p. 33; Edmonds, Wynne, and Becke, *Official History of the Great War*, p. 164.

18 TNA, War Office: WO 95/270 War Diary, vol. 4, General Staff, 2 Army, 1–30 April 1915, 15 April 1915; WO 95/2268 War Diary, HQ, 28th Division, 1–15 April 1915, App. I: Report on Interrogation of German Prisoner Aug. Jaeger (sent with 599 of 14 April 1915); App. II, G 611, 28 Div. to V Corps, 15 April 1915; App. V(a), Translation precis of interrogation of German prisoner taken 25 April 1915, Julius Rapsahl, *4th Landwehr Regiment*.

19 *Ibid.*, WO95/2268, War Diary, Appendix I, p. 3.

20 TNA, War Office, WO 95/270, War Diary, G. S. 2nd Army, April 1915, Precautions against attack on Ypres Salient: GHQ, 2nd Army HQ to GHQ, 15 April 1915 [signed Smith-Dorrien], Enclosure, App. 8: 'Inform. Rec'd. thro L. O.'; Nicholson, *Official History of the Canadian Army in the First World War*, pp. 60–61.

21 TNA, War Office, WO 95/270, War Diary, vol. 4, 2nd Army, Appendix 8: Information received through Liaison Officer.

22 *Ibid.*

23 *Ibid.*, G. S. 2nd Army, April 1915, G 20: Milne to II Corps and V Corps, 15 April 1915; War Diary, 2nd Army, vol. 4, 15 April 1915.

24 *Ibid.*, Precautions against attack on Ypres Salient; Signal: V Corps to 2nd Army, (3.45pm), 15 April 1915; G27 Dobbie for MGGS 2nd Army to V Corps, 15 April 1915; WO 95/743 War Diary, HQ, V Corps, 15 April 1915.

25 TNA, War Office, WO 95/2267, War Diary, HQ, 28th Division, 15 April 1915; 28th Division Order No.30 (3.30pm), 15 April 1915.

26 TNA, War Office, WO 95/2254, Major General T. D. O. Snow, A Narrative of the doings of the 27th Division from the date of its formation to the end of its tour on the Western Front, p. 29.

27 *Ibid.*; Lougheed, *Too many Heroes*, pp. 38; 120–24.

28 Nicholson, *Official History of the Canadian Army in the First World War*, pp. 62–64; Lougheed, *Too many Heroes*, pp. 23–31.

29 TNA, War Office, WO 95/270, War Diary, General Staff Apr–May 1915: Situations, p. 2: Telephone message from Plumer, V Corps & record of conversation; p. 3: G 811 V Corps (2.45am) to 2nd Army (3.10am) intercepted message from Adjt. 13th Bde. RFA reports capture of 2nd London Battery; Nicholson, *Official History of the Canadian Army in the First World War*, *op. cit.*, pp. 62–63.

30 Edmonds, Wynne, and Becke, *Official History of the Great War*, p. 179; A. Fortescue-Duguid, *Official History of the Canadian Forces in the Great War 1914–1919*, Appendices: 347, 351, 357, 370. The GHQ Line 'Ran from Zillebeke Lake, where it was 1½ miles behind the front, northwards to a point half-a-mile east of Wieltje [...] to join a line covering Boesinghe village and railway bridge', Edmonds, Wynne, and Becke, *Official History of the Great Wars*, p. 161.

31 Dancocks, *Welcome to Flanders Fields*, pp. 165–6; Fortescue-Duguid, *Ibid.*; TNA, War Office, WO 95/270, Situations, p. 1: G 797 V Corps (9.00pm) to 2 Army HQ (9.18pm), 22 April 1915; G 799 V Corps (9.45pm) to 2 Army (9.58pm), 22 April 1915.

32 TNA, War Office, WO 95/270, Situations, pp. 1, 2: G231 2 Army HQ 9.02pm) to GHQ; G232 2 Army HQ to GHQ (10.15 p.m); Lougheed, *Too many Heroes*, pp. 113–15.

33 'The Battlefields of Ypres', *Malvern News*, 15 May 1915, p. 5.

34 TNA, War Office: WO 95/270, Situations, p. 6: GA 406 V Corps (12.10pm) to 2nd Army HQ (12.30pm), 23 April 1915 ; WO 95/3772, War Diary, 3rd Canadian Infantry Brigade HQ, 22–23 April 1915; WO 95/3743 War Diary, Divisional Troops, 3rd Canadian Field Artillery Brigade, 22–23 April 1915; Dancocks, *Welcome to Flanders Fields*, pp.172–189; I. Iarocci, *The Shoestring Soldiers: The 1st Canadian Division at war 1914–1915* (University of Toronto Press: Toronto, 2008), pp. 116–19; W. F. Stewart, *'Every inch a fighting man': a new perspective on the military career of a controversial Canadian, Sir Richard Turner* (PhD Thesis, University of Birmingham, March 2012), pp. 63–79.

35 TNA, War Office: WO 95/270, p. 4: G 815, V Corps HQ (7.00am) to 2nd Army HQ (7.25am), 23 April 1915; J 141 Maj. K. S. (8.10am) to 2nd Army HQ (8.31am), 23 April 1915; p. 5: G 261, 2nd Army HQ (10.20am) to GHQ, 23 April 1915; T. Cook, *At the Sharp End, Canadians Fighting the Great War 1914–1916, vol. 1* (Penguin: Toronto, 2007), pp. 129–31.

36 TNA, War Office: WO 95/270, GHQ (8.15am) to Cav. Corps HQ; 1 & 2 Armies (8.55am); OA 938, GHQ (9.30am) to 2nd Army HQ (9.50am), 23 April 1915.

37 *Ibid.*, p. 5: G 258, 2nd Army HQ (10am) to GHQ, 23 April 1915.

38 *Ibid.*, p. 6: OA 943, GHQ (11.15am) to 2nd Army HQ (11.40am); OA 944, GHQ (11.45am) to 2nd Army HQ (12.13pm), 23 April 1915.

39 A. Hodgkinson, *The King's Own T. F., being a record of the 1/5th Battalion, the King's Own (Royal Lancaster Regiment) in the European War* (Lewes Press: Lewes, 1921), pp 23–24; see also McWilliams and Steel, *Gas!*, pp. 91–92.

40 *Situations*, p. 8: G 312 2nd Army HQ (8.52pm) to HQs Northn. Divn. & V Corps; G 833, V The Groupement d'Elverdinghe (7.40pm) to 2nd Army (8.03pm); G 312, 2nd Army to Northumbrian Division & V Corps (8.52pm), 23 April 1915.

41 McWilliams and Steel, *Gas!*, p. 89 Edmonds, Wynne, and Becke, *Official History of the Great War*, p. 201; Holmes, *The Little Field Marshal*, p. 283; A. Fortescue-Duguid, *Official History of the Canadian Forces in the Great War 1914–1919*, Appendix 705.

42 TNA, War Office, WO 95/270, War Diary, vol. 4, 2nd Army, April 1915: Appendix 10, 24 April 1915, p.9.

43 Nicholson, *Official History of the Canadian Army in the First World War*, p. 57.

44 Haber, *The Poisonous Cloud*, p. 35; Edmonds, Wynne, and Becke, *Official History of the Great War*, p. 217.

45 Haber, *The Poisonous Cloud*, p. 70; Cook, *At the Sharp End*, pp. 25–29; Dancocks, *Welcome to Flanders Fields*, p. 4; McWilliams and Steel, *Gas!* pp.104–06.

46 Cook, *At the Sharp End*, pp. 150–54, 156–59; Dancocks, *Welcome to Flanders Fields*, pp. 238–39, 248; Travers, 'Allies in Conflict', (April 1989), pp. 301–25.

47 Cook, *At the Sharp End*, pp. 24–31.

48 TNA, War Office, WO 95/270, Work of Signal Companies 22nd April to 4th May 1915, Appendix 1, pp. 1–2; 'When the wires break', *The Examiner* (Warrington), 27 May 1915, p. 2.

49 *Ibid.*, *Situations*, p. 10: G 365 2nd Army HQ (3.01pm) to V Corps HQ; G 367 2nd Army HQ to GHQ (3.20pm), 24 April 1915; Dancocks, *Welcome to Flanders Fields*, pp. 267–278.

50 TNA, War Diary, WO 95/743, V Corps HQ, 25 April 1915.

51. TNA, War Office: WO 95/270, p.10: OA 959 GHQ (4.15pm) to 2nd Army HQ (4.30pm); p. 11: G 374 2nd Army HQ to V Corps HQ (4.40pm), 24 April 1915.

52 GA 416, V Corps (6.30pm) to Canadian Division, cited in WO 95/743, War Diary, General Staff, V Corps, January–April 1915, 24 April 1915; WO 95/270, War Diary, Copies of miscellaneous letters, messages &c on operations, Telephone message from Major Kincaid-Smith, 24 April 1915.

53 *Ibid.*, WO 95/743, War Diary, HQ, V Corps, 24 April 1915; *Ibid.*, War Diary, vol. 4, 2nd Army HQ, 1–30 April 1915, Appendix 10, April 1915, p. 13.

54 TNA, War Office, WO 95/2, GHQ, BEF, April 1915, Appendix IV: Ypres Battle Reports, 25 April 1915, referring to 10.00am, 24 April 1915.

55 TNA, War Office, WO 95/743, War Diary, V Corps HQ, 25 April 1915.

56 *Ibid.*, WO 95/743, War Diary, V Corps HQ, 25 April 1915.

57 Fortescue-Duguid and Edmonds produced sharply contrasting interpretations of developments about 24–25 April 1915. See Travers, 'Allies in Conflict', pp. 303–17.

58 Travers, 'Allies in Conflict'.

59 TNA, War Office, WO 95/270, War Diary, 2nd Army HQ, Ypres 1915, French Army: Record of Conversation – Captain R. J. Collins with General Putz's Chief of Staff, 9.15pm, 27 April 1915. See also, A.J. Smithers, *The Man Who Disobeyed* (Leo Cooper: London, 1970), pp. 288–89.

60 *Ibid.*, Copies of Miscellaneous letters (&) messages &c on operations, Commander-in-Chief to Smith-Dorrien, Telephone message, am, 26 April 1915.

61 The Lahore Division included white, British battalions and Indian troops See: J. Greenhut, 'The Imperial Reserve: The Indian Corps on the Western Front, 1914–15', *Journal of Imperial and Commonwealth History*, vol. 12, no. 1 (October 1983), pp. 54–73.

62 TNA, War Office, WO 95/3913, War Diary, HQ, Lahore Division, Report No. B-363, Br. Genl. R.G. Egerton, O.C., Ferozepore Brigade to HQ, Lahore Division, 1 May 1915, p.1.

63 *Ibid.*

64 T. Johnstone, *Orange, Green and Khaki* (London, Gill & MacMillan: London, 1992), p. 78.

65 TNA, War Office, WO 95/3913: War Diary: Report, B-366 Egerton to HQ. Lahore Division, 4 May 1915, p. 2; Narrative of operations (round Ypres), p.18; War Diary, May 1915, Appendix 12; Casualty Report: Ferozepore Brigade, in action N. of Ypres, 26 April 1915; E. P. Strickland, OC, Jullundur Brigade: Report on Action taken by Jullundur Brigade in the Operation N.E. of Ypres, April 26th–May 1st, 2 May 1915, pp. 3–5.

66 *Ibid.*

67 M. S. Leigh, *Punjab and the War* (Lahore, Government Printing: Punjab, 1922), p. 206; TNA, War Office, WO 95/2 War Diary, GHQ, BEF, April 1915, Summary of Operations of the 2nd Army, 21st to 30th April (p. 3), records for the period, Officers: Killed 21; Wounded 74; Missing 1. Other Ranks: Killed 340; Wounded 1,720; Missing 168.

68 L. Macdonald, *1915 – Death of Innocence* (Headline: London, 1993), pp. 246–248; Dixon, *Magnificent but not War*, p.136.

69 TNA, War Office, WO 95/270, War Diary, Smith-Dorrien to Putz (Taken personally by Capt. Fitzgerald at 9.10 a.m.), 8.30am, 27 April 1915; WO 95/270, War Diary, 2nd Army HQ, Appendix 10, p. 20.

70 *Ibid.*, Ypres 1915, April, French Army, Putz to Smith-Dorrien, 27 April 1915.

71 *Ibid.*, Priority Telegraph DHX 82 comms, OA976: GHQ, 4.35pm (4.44pm) to 2nd Army, 5.00 p.m, 27 April 1915; Smithers, *The Man who disobeyed*, p. 292.

72 Holmes, pp. 5; 131–33; 272–74; 28–284; G. D. Sheffield and J. Bourne, *Douglas Haig – War Diaries and Letters 1914–1918* (Weidenfeld & Nicolson: London, 2005), pp. 119–20; J. Gooch, 'The Maurice Debate 1918', *Journal of Contemporary History* (1968), pp. 211–28; J. Spencer, *Sir William Robertson and his influence in the BEF in 1915* (MA thesis, University of Birmingham, November 2011), pp. 15–17 and 19–22.

73 Smithers, *The Man who disobeyed*, pp. 209–11; 248–50; 255–57; Cassar, *The Tragedy of Sir John French*, p. 224.

74 Imperial War Museum, Department of Documents: F-M French, Personal Diary, 27 April 1915, cited in Smithers, *The Man who disobeyed*, p. 255.

75 TNA, War Office: WO 95/270, War Diary, PX File, PX7, Notes given by Brig.-General Maurice to General Plumer, afternoon 27 April 1915; *Ibid.*, GX897, Plumer to GHQ, 28 April 1915; PX14, Plumer to Putz, 29 April 1915; WO 158/201, Plumer's Force, 14: Operations of 30th, Genl. Plumer reviews, 30 April 1915.

76 TNA, War Office, WO 95/2, GHQ, BEF, War Diary, Draft Memorandum: OAM987, 28 April 1915 W.R.R. Lt. Gen. CGS (10.00am) to Plumer's Force, 28 April 1915.

77 TNA, War Office, WO 158/201, P193, Knox, Major, GS to Plumer's Force, 9.55am, 1 May 1915; WO 95/3928, War Diary, HQ, 9 Sirhind Brigade, HQ, Sirhind Brigade to HQ, Lahore Division, Report No. 500/5/B. M., 3 May 1915, pp. 5–6.

78 TNA, War Office, WO 95/3913, War Diary, General Staff, Lahore Division, Casualties, Lahore Division, 29 April 1915–3 May 1915.

79 TNA, War Office, WO 158/201: War Diary, Messages: OAM 24, French to Foch, 30 April 1915, pp. 2–3; Plumer's Force, OAM 34, GHQ (W. R. Robertson) to Plumer, 1 May 1915; OAM 34, GHQ (W. R. Robertson) to Plumer, 1 May 1915.

80 *Ibid.*, Note: Foch to Plumer, 1 May 1915; Plumer to Foch, 1 May 1915; OAM 37, Robertson to 2nd Army, 7.00pm, 1 May 1915; Plumer's Force, OAM 58, Robertson to Plumer, 3 May 1915. Cassar, *The Tragedy of Sir John French*, p. 226.

81 *Ibid.*, OAM 62, Memo: Plumer to Foch, 3 May 1915; *Ibid.*, 4388/8, Foch to Field Marshal, C-in-C, British Forces in the Field, 4 May 1915.

82 TNA, War Office,WO 95/3913, War Diary, General Staff, Lahore Division, May 1915, Operations of the Lahore Division near Ypres April 26th – May 1st 1915, p.15. Indian troops were not issued with respirators until early May. See: WO95/3939, Lahore Division, War Diary, 8 May 1915.

83 TNA, War Office, WO95/1572, War Diary, 1st Bn. Dorsetshire Regiment, 1 May 1915.

84 TNA, War Office: WO95/744, War Diary, HQ V Corps, Misc. Gas Reports, Memo: OC, 5th Division to V Corps, 11 May 1915, enclosure [undated, unsigned]; WO95/1572 War Diary, 1st Bn. Dorsetshire Regiment, 1 May 1915 The battalion suffered 187 casualties, of which 35per cent were gassed.

85 *London Gazette*, 29210, 29 June 1915.

86 TNA, War Office, WO 95/1572, 1 May 1915. Sgt. Ernest Shephard maintained the surviving Dorsets were so incensed that had to restrained from launching an attack in the enemy B. Rosser (ed.), *A Sergeant Major's War: from Hill 60 to the Somme* (Ramsbury: Crowood Press, 1987), pp. 40–41.

87 TNA, War Office, WO 95/1501, War Diary HQ, 4th Division, Appendix XIII, Operations: 12th Infantry Brigade, May 1st to 10th, 1915, p.1.

88 *Ibid.*, War Diary, HQ, 12th Brigade, May 1915, Appendix 2, p.1; WO 95/1442, War Diary, HQ, 4th Div, May 1915, Appendix B, Report: 10th Infantry Brigade 4 April 1915–4 May 1915, p.10.

89   *Ibid.*, WO 95/1501.
90   *Ibid.*, Appendix XIII, Operations 12th Infantry Brigade May 1st to 10th, 1915, p. 2. Tyrrell was awarded a Military Cross; Lynn was awarded a posthumous Victoria Cross. *London Gazette*, 29210, 29 June 1915; *Daily Mail*, 28.4.15, p.1.
91   TNA, War Office,WO95/4915, War Diary, 1st Bn. King's Own Lancaster Regiment, 2–3 May 1915.
92   TNA, War Office, WO158/201, Plumer's Force: Summary of Operations, Plumer's Force, May 4–7, 1915.
93   TNA, War Office, WO95/2268, War Diary, 28th Division HQ, Operations Report, 83rd BHQ 4th to 13th May 1915, p.1.
94   TNA, War Office, WO95/2269, Diary of the 28th Divisional Artillery during the Second Battle of Ypres from 22nd April to 14th May 1915, p. 20.
95   TNA, War Office, WO95/1548 War Diary, HQ 13th Infantry Brigade, Report on Operations, 5 May 1915.
96   TNA, War Office, WO95/1521 War Diary, Commander, Royal Artillery (CRA), 5th Division, 5 May 1915.
97   *Ibid.*
98   TNA, War Office, WO 95/1442, War Diary, HQ, 4th Division HQ: HQ, V Corps HQ to HQ, 4th Division: 15 May 1915; 18 May 1915.
99   TNA, War Office, WO 95/2268, War Diary, May 1915 Appendices: Adjutant, 2 Buffs, Report on Operations 'A' Coy. 24/27.
100 TNA, War Office, WO 95/1442, War Diary, HQ, 4th Division, May 1915, Appendix, Gas: Report in reply to GHQ No. OA2/180A/42, Brigadier General Anley, 12th Brigade to HQ, 4th Division, 31 May 1915. See also, Haber, *The Poisonous Cloud*, pp.35–36; 49–50. Letter: Jones to Author, 7 November 2007.
101 TNA, War Office, WO 95/1442, War Diary, HQ, 4th Division, 24 May 1915.
102 TNA, War Office, WO 95/2268, Report on Operations undertaken by the 28th Division on the 24th May, p. 1.
103 *Ibid.*
104 TNA, War Office, WO 95/1442, G 479, Col. A. A. Montgomery, Fourth Division G. S. to V Corps, 11.55pm, 24.5.15.
105 TNA, War Office, WO 95/2278, War Diary, HQ, 85th Brigade, 24 May 1915.
106 *Ibid.*, Private Diary of Gen. Pereira.
107 TNA, War Office: WO 95/2278, War Diary, 85th Brigade HQ, 24 May 1915; WO95/2279, War Diary, 2nd Bn East Surreys, 24 May 1915.
108 TNA, War Office, WO 95/2278, War Diary, HQ, 85th Brigade, 24 May 1915.
109 *Ibid.*
110 TNA, War Office, WO 95/2279, War Diary, 2nd Bn. East Surreys, 24 May 1915: Casualties – Killed 5, Wounded 19, Missing 157; Suffering from Gas Poisoning 24.
111 TNA, War Office, WO95/1112, War Diary, HQ, 2nd Cavalry Brigade (4th Dragoon Guards, 9th Lancers and 18th Hussars), 24 May 1915.
112 *Ibid.*
113 TNA, War Office,WO95/4920, Captain W. G. Barnard, Adjutant, 2nd Bn. The Buffs: Report on Operations, 'A' Coy. 24/7 May [1915], p.1.
114 *Ibid.*, Captain W. G. Barnard, p. 2.
115 *Ibid.*, F. Coleman, *With the Cavalry in 1915* (Samson, Low, Marston: London, 1916), p. 286.
116 *Ibid.*
117 TNA, War Office, WO 95/2254, Report on Operations undertaken by 80th Brigade on the 24th, 25th and 26th May in accordance with 27th Div. No. G. S. 834 by Brigadier General W. E. B. Smith, 29 May 1915, pp. 1–2.
118 Cassar, *The Tragedy of Sir John French*, pp. 240–48.
119 TNA, War Office, WO 95/2277, War Diary, HQ, 84th Infantry Brigade, 21 May 1915. British casualties: Aubers Ridge, circa 11,500 (all ranks); Festubert: circa 16,600.
120 J. D. P. French, *The Despatches of Lord French* (London, Chapman & Hall, 1917), p. 359; Despatch: Supplement to the London Gazette, No.29225, 10 July 1915.

121 TNA, Cabinet Office: CAB 37/127/40, Prime Minister to H. M. King, 27 April 1915; CAB 37/127/43, Prime Minister to H. M. King 29 April 1915; CAB 37/128/1, Prime Minister to H. M. King, 5 May 1915. See also D. Welch & J. Fox (2012), pp. 132–34.

122 In his Despatch, French referred to six gas attacks: 26 April; 1, 2, 5, 10, 24 May 1915, French, *The Despatches of Lord French*, pp. 361–76.

123 *Ibid.,* pp. 369 and 376.

124 Edmonds, Wynne, and Becke, *Official History of the Great War*, p. 271.

125 TNA, War Office, WO 95/270, War Diary, GHQ Second Army, GS Second Army May 1915: General Papers, C-in-C's address to the 83 Infantry Brigade, 21 May 1915, p. 1.

126 French, *The Despatches of Lord French*, p. 355–56.

127 Dixon, *Magnificent but not War*, pp. 299–319, 351–57; Letter: Piet Chielens to Author, 1 May 2005.

128 TNA, War Office, WO 95/391, War Diary, HQ, Lahore Division, 21 April 1915–3 May 1915; India Office Records, British Library, L/MIL/17/5/3119, Casualty Appendices to War Diary, Army Headquarters, India, I. E. F. 'A', vols. 9 & 10, weeks ending: 23 April 1915; 30 April 1915; 7 May 1915.

129 TNA, War Office: WO 95/1548 War Diary, HQ, 13th Brigade, May 1915, Appendices: BA(15) A, Memorandum (sd. A. Hunter, Captain, 13th Infantry Brigade), 5 May 1915; WO 95/744, War Diary, HQ, V Corps, *Ibid.*, Memorandum GX931: From Experiences in the 2nd Army of the recent use by the enemy of Asphyxiating Gases in the fighting around YPRES […]', 5 May 1915, p. 2.

130 TNA, War Office, WO 95/285, War Diary, Director of Medical Services, 2nd Army, 3–4 May 1915.

131 C. H. Foulkes, *Gas!*, pp. 306–07.

132 *Ibid.*, 1–26 May 1915.

133 The captured Canadians included 627 wounded, of which 87 died of their injuries. D. Morton, *When your number's up – The Canadian Soldier in the First World War* (Random House: Toronto, 1993), pp. 207–08.

134 Canadian Army Historical Section survey, cited in Cook, *At the Sharp End*, p. 32; 'With Canadians at Ypres', *North Mail*, 6 May 1915, p. 5; 'Letters from the Front', *Newcastle Daily Chronicle*, 20 May 1915, p. 2; 'Dearly-Bought Success', *Liverpool Weekly Courier*, 12 June 1915, p. 8; 'The Spirit of the Sixth Gloucesters', *Western Daily Press*, 26 May 1915, p. 5; 'The Crucified Soldier' (BBC Channel 4, TV, 4 July 2002).

135 'Rush Job for Women – Respirators for our troops', *Daily Mail* , 28 April 1915, p. 2; 'Respirators Wanted', *Times*, 28 April 1915, p. 10; TNA, War Office, WO 142/91, DGS 23, Haldane to AG, GHQ, 24 May 1915.

136 *Ibid.*, WO142/91, 30 April 1915; WO 95/2256 War Diary, HQ, ADMS, 27th Division, 3–4 May 1915.

137 WO 95/285, War Diary, Director of Medical Services, 2 Army, 3 May 1915.

138 R. S. Jones and R. Hook, *World War 1 Gas Warfare Tactics and Equipment* (London, Osprey Publishing: London, 2007), p. 9

139 *Ibid.*, Despatches, p. 369.

140 TNA, War Office, WO 95/285, War Diary, Director of Medical Services, 2 Army, 3–11 May 1915. Ordnance took over production from the RAMC on 10 May 1915 and all local production of anti-gas mouth pads ceased on 14 May 1915. Jones and Hook, *World War 1 Gas Warfare Tactics and Equipment*, pp. 8–9.

141 *Ibid.*, WO95/285, 24 May 1915; WO 95/744 War Diary, HQ, V Corps, Memorandum: Effects of the gas on our men [sd. W. Tyrrell, Major, RAMC].

142 *Ibid.,* WO 95/285: 26–31 May 1915, 9–10 June 1915; Haber, *The Poisonous Cloud*, pp. 46–47.

143 *Ibid.*, WO 95/285, 8–9 May 1915.

144 Haber, *The Poisonous Cloud*, pp. 53–54.

145 French's Diary, 25 May 1915, cited in G. G. Powell, *Plumer* (Leo Cooper: Barnsley, 1990), p. 126; WO 95/270, Plumer's Force April & May 1915, V Corps Memo (G. X. 113): Imputed carelessness in regard to precautions against gas. For a critique of these early gas masks, see: T. Cook, 'Through Clouded Eyes: Gas masks and the Canadian Corps in the First World War', *Material Culture Review*, vol 47 (Spring 1998), available from URL <http://journals.hil.unb.ca/index.php/MCR/article/view/17732>.

146 *Ibid.*, WO 95/ WO95/270.

147 TNA, War Office, WO 95/1442, War Diary, HQ, 4th Division, Captain A. H. James for Provost Marshal, 2nd Army, Memorandum: Police 'Stops' during an action, 26 May 1915, pp. 1–2. On stragglers' posts and battle stops in and around Ypres during 1914 and 1915, see G. D. Sheffield, *The Redcaps* (London, 1994), pp. 52–55; 58–59.

148 *Ibid.*, WO95/1442, Memorandum A/945: H[enry]. F[uller]. M[aitland]. Wilson to V Corps, 30 May 1915.

149 B. E. W. Childs, *Episodes and Reflections* (Cassell: London, 1930), p.135.

150 TNA, War Office, WO 71/420, Judge Advocate General's Office: Field General Court Martial: Chase, H. [FGCM], Written Proceedings: Testimony of 4315 Private H[arold]. Daws; 317 Lance Corporal A[rthur]. Burton; 2779 Private H[erbert]. Chase, 2nd Bn. Lancashire Fusiliers, 29 May 1915.

151 *Ibid.*, Written Statement 'C', signed by Captain [?] Stewart, RAMC, OC Dressing Station, 12th Field Ambulance, 30 May 1915. On 24 May 1915, Stewart and two lieutenants examined 1200 men, 800 of whom were seriously gassed or wounded, and 200 were classed as: 'Not bad at all and sent back to regiment for duty.' Circa 200, possibly including Chase, were briefly detained at Oosthoek for medical treatment. WO 95/1474, War Diary, Divisional Troops: 12th Field Ambulance, 25 May 1915.

152 TNA, War Office, WO 71/420, *Ibid.*, Brigadier Anley, who convened the Field General Court Martial, explained that no field officer was available to act as president.

153 *Ibid.*, FGCM Schedule and Written Proceedings.

154 *Ibid.*, Memorandum: F. G. Anley to HQ, 4th Division, 29 May 1915.

155 *Ibid.*, Wilson to V Corps, HQ, 31 May 1915, encl.: Written Statement 'A', signed by 12440 Sergeant R[ichard]. Smith, RAMC, 30 May 1915; Written Statement 'B', signed by 6895 Private A[lfred].J[ames]. White, RAMC, 30 May 1915; Written Statement 'C'.

156 *Ibid.*, Plumer to D[eputy].J[udge].A[dvocate].G[eneral], 2 June 1915.

157 *Ibid.*, Plumer to Deputy Judge Advocate General, 3 June 1915; Signal CM2532, 2nd Army A to 4th Division HQ, 2 June 1915; Signal A1108, 4th Division HQ to 2nd Army A, 2 June 1915; Signal A1134, 4th Division HQ to 2nd Army A, 3 June 1915; FGCM Schedule: Written Proceedings.

158 Holmes, *The Little Field Marshals*, pp. 276–7; J. Walker, *'The Blue Beast' – Power & Passion in the Great War* (History Press: 2012), 32–52.

THE INDIAN ARMY AT THE SECOND BATTLE OF YPRES

DAVID OMISSI

Before 22 April 1915

In the summer of 1914, the German advance through Belgium and France seemed unstoppable.[1] The divisions of the British Expeditionary Force (BEF), committed to support the French, had been driven back. The promised contingents from the white Dominions were not yet ready, so the Army in India was the only source of regular reinforcements immediately available within the British Empire. In late August, the Lahore and Meerut Indian infantry divisions were re-directed from Egypt to France.[2] After disembarking at Marseilles, they arrived at the front in October in time for the First Battle of Ypres.[3]

By early 1915, the Indian Corps had its own sector around Festubert and Givenchy. Two Indian cavalry divisions were also serving elsewhere on the Western Front. At the Battle of Neuve Chapelle on 10–12 March, the Indian Corps suffered heavy losses.[4]

The first German gas attack on 22 April opened a gap in the Allied line, creating the danger that Ypres might fall to a determined German assault. On 23 April, the Lahore Division's commander, General Henry Keary (1857–1937), was warned that his troops might have to move north at short notice.[5]

Lahore was a fairly typical Indian division. As well as artillery, cavalry and pioneers, it comprised three infantry brigades, each consisting of one British and three Indian regular battalions. Each brigade had gained a further British Territorial battalion in January 1915 (See Appendix 1).

The Indian Army of this period was recruited according to the 'martial races' theory, which treated only certain Indian communities as 'warlike' and worth recruiting from. Punjabi Muslims were the most numerous 'martial race'; others included Pathans from the North-West Frontier and warrior-caste Hindus.[6] The Commander-in-Chief in India, Sir Beauchamp Duff (1855–1918), had selected what he considered his best divisions for France,[7] so Sikhs from the Punjab, Garhwalis from the Himalayan foothills, and Gurkhas from Nepal – all widely seen as the Indian Army's 'crack troops' – were over-represented among the battalions sent to Europe.

24–25 April 1915

At 1.30pm on 24 April, the Lahore Division started to move from positions in reserve towards Ypres. The troops marched along rutted and cracked roads, arriving after dark in the Boeschepe–Berthen area. They set off again at 7.15 the following morning, over cobbles made slippery by a night's rain. Each man was carrying 60–100 pounds of kit, there had been little food, and there was some straggling. The tired and footsore troops began to arrive at Ouderdom (eight kilometres west-south-west of Ypres) at 10am.[8]

26 April 1915

Once in the Ypres sector, the Lahore Division was placed under the command of General Sir Horace Smith-Dorrien (1858–1930) of Second Army. In the early hours of 26 April, Lahore was ordered to counterattack, its left resting on the Ypres–Langemarck road, which was the dividing line between the French and the British-Indian forces, at 2.00pm that day.[9] The aim of the attack was to recapture the ground recently lost, and to force the Germans back towards Langemarck.[10]

In the morning, the three Indian brigades moved off – closely watched by observers in the German aircraft active over the Salient – reaching their assembly positions between 9.45 and 11am, then deploying for the attack between 12 and 12.30pm.[11] The Jullundur Brigade was on the right.[12] Ferozepur continued the line with its left resting on Ypres–Langemarck road, beyond which was 4th Moroccan Brigade, attached to the French 152nd Division. The Sirhind Brigade was in reserve, to the right rear of Jullundur, south-east of Saint-Jean.[13]

Leichen in einem verlassenen englischen Schützengraben.

A German soldier contemplates British casualties in their captured trench, April 1915.
(In Flanders Fields Museum, Ypres)

The attack was to take place across 1,500 yards of open, shell-swept fields.[14] For the first 500 yards the ground sloped gently up to a crest; it then declined for a further 500 yards, before turning into a natural glacis before the German front line on a ridge.

The initial Allied artillery bombardment opened at 1.20pm and continued steadily until 2.00pm, when all guns directed five minutes of rapid fire onto the German front line, before switching to areas 200 yards behind. The Moroccans and Lahore then started to advance.[15]

The result was a massacre. The Allied gunners had not had enough time to register their guns properly, or to find good observation posts, so their fire had been too inaccurate to subdue the German rifles.[16] Many Allied guns were in the open and clearly visible (particularly to the German airmen), and were subjected to counter-battery fire.[17]

As they approached the unshaken German lines, the Allied troops suffered heavy losses from German shells. On passing the first crest, they came under intense rifle and machine-gun fire.[18] The advancing units tended to bunch for protection behind farm buildings or other cover.[19] Most of Lahore's unwounded survivors were eventually able to creep or rush to within 40–60 yards of the German front line, but could get no further.

The Jullundur Brigade's front line consisted of (from right to left) the 1st Manchesters, the 40th Pathans, and the 47th Sikhs, with the 59th Rifles and the 4th Suffolks in a second line, about 400 yards behind.[20] The original direction of the attack was due north, but the brigade veered slightly left as it advanced, becoming mixed up with the right of Ferozepur.[21]

In the centre, the 40th Pathans moved rapidly, but they soon ran into intense German fire, which one eyewitness compared to:

> a scythe being drawn across the legs of the troops as they advanced. At one moment they were moving forward as if nothing could stop them; the next second they had simply collapsed.[22]

The Pathans' CO, Lt-Colonel Rennick, fell mortally wounded. The battalion suffered about 320 casualties of all ranks; by the evening, its effectives consisted of four British officers and around 120 men.[23]

As soon as the 47th Sikhs began to advance, most of their officers and many of the men were hit. Command of the remnants of the regiment fell to Lieutenant A. E. Drysdale, a subaltern of only five years' service, who led his surviving men forward close to the German front line. He won the Military Cross.[24] The 47th had sent into action 11 British and 10 Indian officers, and 423 other ranks. The next morning, only four officers and 92 men answered a roll call. The losses – nearly 80 per cent – were proportionally the highest of any battalion that day.[25] A wounded survivor lamented: 'The result of the fighting is that corpses grow as thick as straw in watered wheat. If I wrote all day I could not tell you what I have seen'.[26]

As the Manchesters advanced, Corporal Issy Smith (b. Ishroulch Shmeilowitz, 1890–1940) left his company and went forward to assist a severely wounded man, whom he carried for 250 yards, despite being under heavy rifle and machine gun fire. He then brought in several other wounded men. He earned the Victoria Cross for his bravery. The Manchesters pushed on until they reached a road about 60 yards from the German trenches.[27]

The Ferozepur Brigade attacked on a 500-yard front, with the Connaughts on the left, the 57th Rifles in the centre, and the 129th Baluchis on the right.[28] The 4th Londons were in support and the 9th Bhopals in reserve.[29] A Pathan eyewitness recalled:

> The attack began at an hour not suitable for attack. It was two o'clock in the afternoon. The attack started a mile distant from the enemy over an open plain. My regiment [...] was in the front line. There were heavy losses. The enemy's trenches were far away. It was [...] a clear day with the sun shining brightly.[30]

Ferozepur's survivors neared the German front line around 2.17pm.[31]

All the front-line units had by now suffered severely, but worse was to come. At about 2.20pm, devices that looked like fire hoses appeared over the German parapet. These discharged large jets of white smoke which soon turned into the yellowish vapour of chlorine gas. The wind favoured the Germans, and the gas cloud drifted across the Allied front line from right to left, towards the men of the Moroccan and Ferozepur Brigades.[32] Part of Jullundur was also affected.

The troops had no gas masks; but they had been warned what to expect, and they improvised by tying the wetted ends of their *pagris* [turbans] over their noses and mouths. This was of little help, and soon 'the ground was strewn with the bodies of men writhing in unspeakable torture'.[33] The Moroccans and most of the left of Ferozepur gave way. The men fell back down the slope in some confusion – with Moroccans, British and Indians all mixed together. Some found shelter, others continued to La Brique, just north of Ypres.[34]

Just over 100 men – mainly of the Manchesters and Connaughts, with small parties from most of the Indian regiments – clung tenaciously to their positions close to the German lines, although their slightest movement attracted murderous fire. At 2.25pm the Germans followed up the discharge of gas with an infantry counter-attack.[35] Lahore's advanced detachments were forced back about 80 yards, but then held their ground and dug in.[36]

One of the front-line survivors was Mir Dast (1874–1945), a jemadar with the 57th Rifles.[37] As he began to recover from

Subedar Mir Dast VC. Mir Dast won his Victoria Cross on 26 April 1915 north of Ypres and was presented the medal by King George V in person at the Royal Pavillion in Brighton, then in use as an Indian hospital, in August 1915.

Allies casualties, slaughtered in their trenches.
(In Flanders Fields Museum, Ypres)

the effects of gas, he rallied a small group of men, several of them wounded and gassed, and held his position until nightfall, when he was ordered to retire. As he fell back, he found other men sheltering in old trenches; these he helped lead to safety. After dark, he went into the open again, and helped bring in eight wounded officers, British and Indian. While doing so, he was himself wounded. For his actions that day he was awarded the Victoria Cross.[38]

Mir Dast was born in Tirah, in what is now Pakistan. He enlisted in Coke's Rifles, aged 20. Before being decorated in Europe, he had already won the Indian Order of Merit (the highest Indian award for courage before Indians became eligible for the VC in 1911) for his bravery during the 1908 Mohmand expedition.[39] Promoted to Subedar, he was honourably discharged from the Indian Army in September 1917, his health not having fully recovered.[40]

His brother Mir Mast had also been serving in France as a jemadar, with Vaughan's Rifles in the Meerut Division. The war with Ottoman Turkey – the world's leading independent Muslim power – had strained the loyalties of some Muslim soldiers of the Indian Army, and on the night of 3–4 March, Mir Mast had deserted to the Germans, with about two dozen men. The British authorities immediately disarmed Vaughan's remaining 120 Pathans, although they were later returned to duty.[41]

The French and Indian line was stabilised between about 3.30 and 4.15pm; but the ground was still swept by heavy German shell and rifle fire, making it difficult to reinforce the forward units in daylight. Three of Sirhind's battalions accordingly prepared to attack after dark. It was a fine, clear night, and the troops moved forward around 7.45pm. They advanced some 300 yards beyond the British trenches, making contact with the French on the left, and with the surviving parties of the Manchesters and Connaughts.[42] The exact German positions remained uncertain, however, and no other troops were advancing, so the attack was called off.

27 April 1915

The Sirhind Brigade relieved Jullundur in the early hours of 27 April.[43] Ferozepur and Jullundur then withdrew to La Brique, while Sirhind spent most of the night digging in and consolidating the line, helped by a company of 34th Sikh Pioneers.[44] Jullundur had gone into action roughly 2,520 strong; in the 24 hours to 8am on 27 April the brigade had lost around 1,385 men.[45]

On the morning of 27 April it became apparent that another French attack was planned, and arrangements were again made for Sirhind to co-operate. An Allied bombardment was timed to begin at 12.30, with an assault at 1.15.[46] The Moroccans would be to the left of the Ypres-Langemarck road, and Sirhind to the right, with Ferozepur prolonging the Indian line, and Jullundur in reserve around La Brique.[47] The plan was effectively a repetition of the previous day's attack, and, it has been suggested, was no more likely to succeed.[48]

Sirhind advanced over ground strewn with Jullundur's dead from the previous day's fighting. In front were the 1/1st and 1/4th Gurkhas, with the remainder of the brigade in support.[49] The Gurkhas crossed the first crest and immediately ran into heavy German fire. They were soon pinned down about 400 yards from the German trenches in a fierce fire-fight, which lasted until 4pm.[50] The commander of the 4th King's, seeing that the Gurkhas were making no progress, moved his men forward to reinforce them, also at heavy cost.

The Ferozepur Brigade, now down to about 1,800 rifles, started at 12.30pm, from a position further back. On the right were the 9th Bhopals, and on the left the 4th Londons, with the Connaughts in support. Wilde's and the Baluchis – both now very weak from the previous day's losses – formed the reserve.[51] The advance was 'a great calamity', according to an eyewitness, as the leading battalions, particularly the Bhopals, lost heavily.[52] The attack was broken up and checked.

Because the Indians were still some distance from the German trenches, a second bombardment was ordered around 5.30pm. While the guns fired, the Highland Light Infantry and 15th Sikhs advanced. The Moroccan Brigade's commander then planned to deliver a further assault at 7pm, under the cover of heavy artillery fire. The attack began promptly enough, but, ten minutes later, the Indian troops noticed the Moroccans streaming to the rear, half-visible amid clouds of smoke and gas. Some of the Highlanders to their right also fell back. The attack was stopped and Sirhind consolidated its position. The Sikhs and Highlanders took over the line, and the Gurkhas and 4th King's were withdrawn to reorganise.[53]

28 April 1915 and after

From the morning of 28 April the Lahore Division came under the orders of General Plumer (1857–1932), who had been given command of most of the Commonwealth forces actively defending the Ypres Salient.[54]

Over next three days (28–30 April) a series of French attacks were successively planned then postponed. Sirhind several times prepared to act in support, but the German line was very strong, with continuous trenches plus strong-points in farms and other houses, and the brigade was under orders to advance only if the French had

A gassed French Zouave after the gas attack, April 1915. (In Flanders Fields Museum, Ypres)

already been successful. During the night of 29–30 April, the Jullundur and Ferozepur Brigades were withdrawn to Ouderdom, while Sirhind remained in the trenches north-east of Ypres.[55]

Another French assault was planned for the afternoon of 1 May. From 2.15pm, Sirhind advanced in support into the leading Allied trenches. The two Gurkha battalions were in front, the two British units in support, and the Indians in reserve. This time, the artillery preparation was better, but it became clear by 5pm that the German wire entanglement, four yards deep, had still not been cut, so the French wisely decided not to press the attack any further.[56]

After this brief action, the men of Sirhind collected their wounded and withdrew, joining the other two Indian brigades at Ouderdom in the night of 1–2 May. On 3 May the Lahore Division began the march south to rejoin the Indian Corps line in the Neuve Chapelle sector.[57]

Lahore's losses were about a quarter of the division's original strength. (See Appendices 2 and 3.) The counter-attacks had gained little ground; but at least the gap in the line had been closed, and the German advance stopped. Ypres was secure for the time being; and the successful defence of the Belgian city must have influenced wavering neutral powers, which were significant to both the Allied and the German war efforts.

As Indian casualties had mounted in the winter of 1914–15, hospitals for the Indian troops had been set up in various towns on the south coast of England, mainly in Brighton, where several buildings, including the Royal Pavilion, had been converted.[58] In the weeks following the battle, the casualties streamed in.

'Feelings of sacrifice and despondency'

According to the British military censor of Indian mail, soldiers' letters written after the battle expressed 'feelings of sacrifice and despondency'.[59] 'The [Lahore] Division is finished', was one wounded survivor's succinct verdict.[60] Another wrote:

> I cannot give you an account of this hurricane [...] Ask protection from God; there is nothing else to be done. I will tell you the whole tale if I live to meet you.[61]

The censor also noted an increasing 'tendency to indulge in veiled metaphors, or secret writing'.[62] Men compared themselves to 'parched grain' or 'falling leaves', and tried to dissuade others from coming to the front.[63] Indian soldiers' letters also revealed:

> a feeling that the native sepoys are being sacrificed to spare the British troops [...] a sentiment intensified by the severe losses recently experienced by certain native regiments [...] near Ypres.[64]

For example, one man wrote, using a simple code:

> Please do me the favour of letting me know what is the condition of the market for black pepper. That which I brought has all been finished and some more has been sent [...] You probably know that there is lots of red pepper, but they want black.[65]

His letter, and others like it, implied that the Indian troops ('black pepper') were being used in preference to British soldiers ('red pepper').

In general, Indian troops reacted to gas in similar ways to soldiers of other nations: with a mixture of panic and hasty improvisation. There was, however, some grudging admiration for the cleverness of the Germans in inventing the most 'perfect contrivances'.[66] According to one wounded Sikh:

> The German King is very powerful. When there is a new invention it is he who first puts it into practice. The English copy it when they see it. The German King is very clever. He is the master; the English are his disciples.[67]

By the summer, Mir Dast, VC, now in hospital, had been promoted to subedar. Something of his reactions to the battle, and to gas, emerges from a letter he wrote at this time:

> I have been twice wounded, once in the left hand, of which two fingers are powerless. The other injury is from gas – that is dhua [smoke] [...] It gives me great pain and will go on doing so [...] I want your congratulations. I have got

the Victoria Cross. The Victoria Cross is a very fine thing, but this gas gives me no rest. It has done for me.[68]

In August, the King visited the hospitals to comfort the wounded and to present medals. Indian troops seem to have welcomed the King's visit, although we must remember that the men were aware of the censorship. One man wrote:

Yesterday the Emperor inspected this place [...] There was great excitement. He stayed nearly an hour in the hospital and spoke very kindly to the patients, asking about their condition. The sight of the Emperor delighted the hearts of all.[69]

Subedar Mir Dast reacted warmly to the presentation of his VC:

By the great, great, great kindness of God, the King with his royal hand has given me the decoration of the Victoria Cross. God has been very gracious, very gracious, very gracious, very, very, very, very, very [gracious] to me. Now I do not care [...] The desire of my heart is accomplished.[70]

He did, however, ask the King to end the policy of returning wounded men to the trenches once they had recovered.

Men from the Indian Army Corps wearing hypo helmets or British smoke hoods in Fauquissart (France), summer 1915. Some are wearing their turban on top of the hood, some others don't. This Photo was published in the French press with the caption: 'English Infantry ready to repulse a gas attack.' (In Flanders Fields Museum, Ypres)

The Indian Army Corps after the Second Battle of Ypres

The Indian Corps was soon in action again. On 9 May, the Meerut Division attacked German positions on Aubers Ridge, at the beginning of the two-week Battle of Festubert. Meerut suffered heavy casualties, mainly from German machine guns. A night attack by the same division on the evening of 15 May was no more successful.[71]

From June to August the Indian Corps remained in the same sector, enduring a steady trickle of casualties from shell fire and snipers, but seeing no major action.

As the British Army prepared to use gas themselves, several Indian soldiers observed that such retaliation would now be legitimate. One man wrote:

> Look at this German show [tamasha]. They are now using poisonous shells and asphyxiating gas. What is to be done? When things are done with such malevolence, our British Government must follow their example. The proverb 'against blackguards one must be a blackguard' is quite apt here.[72]

The British first used gas, not very successfully, at the Battle of Loos in September, during which the Meerut Division made a diversionary attack. The Indian Corps suffered 3,973 casualties in the battle.[73]

In late October 1915, the two Indian infantry divisions were directed to the Middle East.[74] There were concerns that their morale might not survive another winter in the rain, mud and slaughter of Flanders, particularly after the losses at Loos. However, it also made strategic sense to concentrate India's war effort in the Middle East. The troops would be closer to the Indian ports from which they were supplied and reinforced, and they would be in a theatre of war controlled by the Government of India.[75] Once the Indian infantry had left France, the Indian hospitals in England were closed down.

The two Indian cavalry divisions remained in France, seeing action on the Somme in July 1916, and during the German retreat to the Hindenburg Line and at Cambrai the following year. In the spring of 1918 they were transferred to Palestine to support General Allenby's forthcoming offensive against the Turks.

The Indian Corps on the Western Front (including its British units) suffered a total of 34,252 casualties, or slightly more than the entire strength of the Corps on its arrival. By October 1915, every officer and all but 28 men of the 47th Sikhs' original contingent had been killed, wounded or hospitalised for over ten days.[76]

After the war, Indian soldiers were commemorated according to similar principles as other Commonwealth soldiers – they were remembered where they fell, and in their home country. The main Indian war memorial is the massive arch of India Gate, which anchors one of the central avenues of New Delhi. In Europe, although many Indian names are carved on the Menin Gate at Ypres, the principal monument is at Neuve Chapelle – the site of the Indian Army's most famous (and costliest) action on the Western Front.

APPENDIX 1:
Order of Battle of the Lahore Division, April 1915

3rd (Lahore) Division: Major-General H. D'U. Keary[77]

7th (Ferozepur) Brigade: Brigadier-General R. G. Egerton
    Connaught Rangers (1st and 2nd battalions combined)
    9th Bhopal Infantry
    57th Wilde's Rifles (Frontier Force)
    129th Duke of Connaught's Own Baluchis
    4th London Regiment (Territorials)

8th (Jullundur) Brigade: Brigadier-General E. P. Strickland
    1st Manchesters
    40th Pathans
    47th Sikhs
    59th Scinde Rifles (Frontier Force)
    4th Suffolks (Territorials)

9th (Sirhind) Brigade: Brigadier-General W. G. Walker, VC
    1st Highland Light Infantry
    1/1st King George's Own Gurkha Rifles
    1/4th Gurkha Rifles
    15th Ludhiana Sikhs
    4th King's (Liverpool) Regiment (Special Reserve)

Divisional Troops
    Artillery: 5th, 11th, 18th and 43rd (Howitzer) Brigades, RFA
    Engineers: 20th and 21st Coys, 3rd Sappers and Miners
    Pioneers: 34th Sikh Pioneers
    Cavalry: 15th Lancers (Cureton's Multanis)

APPENDIX 2:
Approximate Strength of the Lahore Division, 23 April 1915

| | Officers | | Rifles | | Sabres | Artillery | | Total | |
	British	Indian	British	Indian	Indian	British	Indian	British	Indian
	421	166	5,439	6,808	475	2,390	281	8,250	7,730
Total	587		12,247		475	2,671		15,980	

Source: Merewether and Smith, *The Indian Corps in France*, p. 340.

The headstone of naik Devi Singh of the 40th Pathans at Railway Dugouts Burial Ground. He was most probably one of the soldiers killed on 26 April 1915 along the Ypres Ramparts when the Indian troops were on their way to the battlefield. (In Flanders Fields Museum, Ypres – Photograph by Rudy Wille)

APPENDIX 3:
Approximate Casualties to the Lahore Division, 26 April–3 May 1915

A: Casualties by Rank and Nationality

		Killed	Wounded	Missing	Per cent
Officers	British	28	105	0	31.6
	Indian	6	57	1	38.6
Other Ranks	British	180	1,096	345	20.7
	Indian	177	1,684	209	24.4
Totals	British	208	1,201	345	21.3
	Indian	183	1,741	210	27.6
Grand totals		391	2,942	555	24.3

B: Casualties by Formation

	Killed	Wounded	Missing	Total
Ferozepur Brigade	138	965	198	1,301
Jullundur Brigade	80	853	159	1,092
Sirhind Brigade	149	929	178	1,256
Divisional Troops	24	195	20	239
Totals	391	2,942	555	3,888
Per cent	2.4	18.4	3.5	24.3

Source: National Archives, War Office, WO 95/3913, Appendix Y. The '29 April' in the original is presumably a typing error.

Notes

1 All documentary references are to the records of the Military Department (L/MIL) of the India Office in the British Library, London, and to the records of the War Office (WO) in the National Archives, London. Tony Henderson, Clare Omissi, Douglas Reid and Simon C. Smith made many helpful comments on earlier drafts.

2 D. E. Omissi, 'Europe Through Indian Eyes: Indian Soldiers Encounter England and France, 1914–1918', *English Historical Review* (2007), p. 122.

3 I. F. W. Beckett, *Ypres: The First Battle* (Harlow, 2004), pp. 103, 106–10, 119, 124–25.

4 J. Willcocks, *With the Indians in France* (London, 1920), Chapters XV–XVI.

5 National Archives, War Office, WO 95/3913, Appendix Y. Two brigades of the British 4th Division were also moved northwards: G. Keech, *Ypres: St Julien* (Barnsley, 2001), p. 51.

6 For the 'martial races' see D. E. Omissi, *The Sepoy and the Raj: The Indian Army, 1860–1940* (Basingstoke, 1994), Chapter 1; L. Caplan, *Warrior Gentlemen: 'Gurkhas' in the Western Imagination* (Providence, RI and Oxford, 1995); and H. Streets, *Martial Races: The Military, Masculinity and Race in British Imperial Culture, 1857–1914* (Manchester, 2004).

7 J. Greenhut, 'The Imperial Reserve: The Indian Corps on the Western Front, 1914–15', *Journal of Imperial and Commonwealth History*, vol. 12 (1983), p. 54.

8 National Archives, War Office, WO 95/3913, Appendix Y; J. W. B. Merewether and F. E. Smith, *The Indian Corps in France* (London, 1919), p. 287.

9 National Archives, War Office, WO 95/3926, Operational Order No. 77, Appendix 91.

10 J. Dixon, *Magnificent but not War: The Second Battle of Ypres, 1915* (Barnsley, 2003), pp. 122, 127.

11 National Archives, War Office, WO 95/3913, Appendix Y.

12 National Archives, War Office, WO 95/3926, Appendix 92.

13 National Archives, War Office, WO 95/3928, OC Sirhind Brigade to HQ Lahore Division [henceforth Sirhind to Lahore], 3 May 1915, Appendix 8; Merewether and Smith, *The Indian Corps in France*, pp. 292–93.

14 Willcocks, *With the Indians in France*, p. 248

15 National Archives, War Office, WO 95/3913, Appendix Y.

16 National Archives, War Office, WO 95/3913, Appendix Y; Willcocks, *With the Indians in France*, p. 255.

17 Dixon, *Magnificent but not War: The Second Battle of Ypres, 1915*, p. 130.

18 Merewether and Smith, *The Indian Corps in France*, pp. 295–98.

19 National Archives, War Office, WO 95/3913, Appendix Y.

20 Report on Action by Jullundur Brigade, 26 April 1915, WO 95/3926, Appendix 90A.

21 National Archives, War Office, WO 95/3913, Appendix Y.

22 Merewether and Smith, *The Indian Corps in France*, p. 302.

23 National Archives, War Office, WO 95/3926, Appendix 90A; Willcocks, *With the Indians in France*, pp. 249–50.

24 Willcocks, *With the Indians in France*, p. 250.

25 Merewether and Smith, *The Indian Corps in France*, pp. 304–05.

26 British Library, India Office Records, L/MIL/5/825/3/376, Jagat Singh (Sikh), 47th Sikhs, Brighton [Hospital], to a friend in India (Gurmukhi), 16 May 1915.

27 Willcocks, *With the Indians in France*, p. 249; Merewether and Smith, *The Indian Corps in France*, p. 299; Keech, *Ypres: St Julien*, pp. 94, 100–01.

28 National Archives, War Office, WO 95/3922, OC Ferozepur Brigade to HQ Lahore Division, 1 May 1915, Appendix 12.

29 Willcocks, *With the Indians in France*, p. 248.

30 British Library, India Office Records, L/MIL/5/825/3/442, Havildar Ghufaron, 129th Baluchis, Pavilion Hospital, Brighton, to Subedar Zeman Khan, Depot 129th Baluchis, Karachi, 4 June 1915.

31 National Archives, War Office, WO 95/3913, Appendix Y.

32 National Archives, War Office, WO 95/3913, Appendix Y; G. Corrigan, *Sepoys in the Trenches: The Indian Corps on the Western Front, 1914–1915* (Staplehurst, 1999), p. 191.

33 Merewether and Smith, *The Indian Corps in France*, p. 312.

34 National Archives, War Office, WO 95/3913, Appendix Y.

35 Willcocks, *With the Indians in France*, p. 253; Corrigan, *Sepoys in the Trenches: The Indian Corps on the Western Front, 1914–1915*, p. 192.

36 National Archives, War Office, WO 95/3913, Appendix Y.

37 A jemadar was the most junior rank of Indian Officer, the next highest being subedar. Mir Dast was seconded to the 57th: his 'home' regiment was 55th Coke's Rifles.

38 Merewether and Smith, *The Indian Corps in France*, pp. 313–14; P. Mason, *A Matter of Honour: An Account of the Indian Army, its Officers and Men* (London, 1974), pp. 416–17; Corrigan, *Sepoys in the Trenches: The Indian Corps on the Western Front, 1914–1915*, p. 193. Mir Dast was the fourth Indian to win the VC.

39 Willcocks, *With the Indians in France*, pp. 251–52.

40 Keech, *Ypres: St Julien*, p. 102.

41 Greenhut, 'The Imperial Reserve: The Indian Corps on the Western Front, 1914–15', p. 62; Corrigan, *Sepoys in the Trenches: The Indian Corps on the Western Front, 1914–1915*, p. 196.

42 National Archives, War Office, WO 95/3922, OC Ferozepur Brigade to HQ Lahore Division, 1 May 1915, Appendix 12; Willcocks, *With the Indians in France*, p. 254.

43 National Archives, War Office, WO 95/3913, Appendix Y; National Archives, War Office, WO 95/9328, Sirhind to Lahore, 3 May 1915, Appendix 8; Merewether and Smith, *The Indian Corps in France*, p. 319.

44 J. L. McWilliams and R. J. Steel, *Gas! The Battle for Ypres, 1915* (Ontario, 1985), p. 196.

45 National Archives, War Office, WO 95/3926, Appendix 90A. This figure includes 314 missing, many of whom presumably later rejoined; see the figures in Appendix 3B.

46 National Archives, War Office, WO 95/3913, Appendix Y; Willcocks, *With the Indians in France*, p. 257.

47 National Archives, War Office, WO 95/3926, Appendix 90A; National Archives, War Office, WO 95/3928, Sirhind to Lahore, 3 May 1915, Appendix 8; Merewether and Smith, *The Indian Corps in France*, p. 322.

48 Dixon, *Magnificent but not War: The Second Battle of Ypres, 1915*, p. 147.

49 1/1st and 1/4th Gurkhas indicates the first battalion of each regiment. Gurkha regiments normally had two battalions, unlike Indian infantry regiments, which were normally of only one battalion.

50 National Archives, War Office, WO 95/3928, Sirhind to Lahore, 3 May 1915, Appendix 8; Corrigan, *Sepoys in the Trenches: The Indian Corps on the Western Front, 1914–1915*, p. 194.

51 National Archives, War Offic, WO 95/3922, OC Ferozepur Brigade to HQ Lahore Division, 4 May 1915, Appendix 13; Merewether and Smith, *The Indian Corps in France*, p. 323.

52 Lance Naik Ram Carup Singh (Rajput), 9th Bhopals, Indian Military Depot, Milford-on-Sea, to Lance Naik Dobi Singh, 16th Rajputs, Calcutta, May 1915 (Hindi), quoted in D. E. Omissi (ed.), *Indian Voices of the Great War: Soldiers' Letters, 1914–1918* (Basingstoke, 1999), Doc. 73.

53 National Archives, War Office, WO 95/3913, Appendix Y; National Archives, War Office, WO 95/3928, OC Sirhind Brigade to HQ Lahore Division, 3 May 1915, Appendix 8; Willcocks, *With the Indians in France*, pp. 260–62.

54 Dixon, *Magnificent but not War: The Second Battle of Ypres, 1915*, p. 159.

55 National Archives, War Office, WO 95/3913, Appendix Y; National Archives, War Office, WO 95/3928, Sirhind to Lahore, 3 May 1915, Appendix 8.

56 *Ibid.*

57 Merewether and Smith, *The Indian Corps in France*, p. 340; Corrigan, *Sepoys in the Trenches: The Indian Corps on the Western Front, 1914–1915*, p. 196; Keech, *Ypres: St Julien*, p. 89.

58 R. Visram, *Asians in Britain: 400 Years of History* (Sterling, VA and London, 2002), Chapter 6; J. Collins, *Dr Brighton's Indian Patients* (Brighton, 1997); Omissi, 'Europe Through Indian Eyes'.

59 British Library, India Office Records, L/MIL/5/825/2/359, Note by Censor [henceforth, NBC], 22 May 1915.

60 Isar Singh (Sikh), 59th Rifles, Indian General Hospital, to a friend, 50th Punjabis, India (Gurmukhi), 1 May 1915, quoted in Omissi (ed.), *Indian Voices of the Great War: Soldiers' Letters, 1914–1918*, Doc. 63.

61 British Library, India Office Records, L/MIL/5/825/3/391, Sepoy Khan Muhammad (Pathan), 40th Pathans, Brighton Hospital, to his uncle, Sepoy Shahwali Khan, Hong Kong Police (Urdu), 19 May 1915. The 'hurricane' appears to refer to the fighting of 9–13 May as well as to Second Ypres.

62 British Library, India Office Records, L/MIL/5/825, NBC, 5 June 1915.

63 Lance Naik Ram Carup Singh (Rajput), 9th Bhopal Infantry, Indian Military Depot, Milford-on-Sea, to Lance Naik Dobi Singh, 16th Rajputs, Calcutta (Hindi), May 1915, quoted in Omissi (ed.), *Indian Voices of the Great War: Soldiers' Letters, 1914–1918*, Doc. 73.

64 British Library, India Office Records, L/MIL/5/825/2/339, NBC, 15 May 1915. See also British Library, India Office Records, L/MIL/5/825/3/385, NBC, 29 May 1915.

65 Lance Naik Ram Carup Singh (Rajput), 9th Bhopal Infantry, Indian Military Depot, Milford-on-Sea, to Lance Naik Dobi Singh, 16th Rajputs, Calcutta (Hindi), May 1915, quoted in Omissi (ed.), *Indian Voices of the Great War: Soldiers' Letters, 1914–1918*, Doc. 73.

66 Havildar Abdul Rahman (Punjabi Muslim) to Raja Sajawal Khan Lumberdar, Jhelum District, Punjab (Urdu), May 1915, quoted in Omissi (ed.), *Indian Voices of the Great War: Soldiers' Letters, 1914–1918*, Doc. 71.

67 British Library, India Office Records, L/MIL/5/825/3/377, Bishen Singh (Sikh), in hospital, England, to a friend in India (Gurmukhi), 14 May 1915.

68 Subedar Mir Dast, The Pavilion Hospital, Brighton, to Subedar [?] Khan, 57th Rifles, NWFP (Urdu), 12 July 1915, quoted in Omissi (ed.), *Indian Voices of the Great War: Soldiers' Letters, 1914–1918*, Doc. 95. The award had been announced in the *London Gazette* on 29 June 1915.

69 Sub-Assistant Surgeon Abdulla (Punjabi Muslim) to a friend in India (Urdu), 23 August 1915, quoted in Omissi (ed.), *Indian Voices of the Great War: Soldiers' Letters, 1914–1918*, Doc. 126.

70 Subedar Mir Dast, VC, to Naik Nur Zada, 55th Rifles, Kohat, NWFP (Urdu), 27 August 1915, quoted in Omissi (ed.), *Indian Voices of the Great War: Soldiers' Letters, 1914–1918*, Doc. 130.

71 Corrigan, *Sepoys in the Trenches: The Indian Corps on the Western Front, 1914–1915*, pp. 205–15.

72 Jaginal Singh (Rajput, 4th Rajputs) to Pensioned Risaldar-Major Jaswant Singh, Hissar, Punjab (Hindi), 7 June 1915, quoted in Omissi (ed.), *Indian Voices of the Great War: Soldiers' Letters, 1914–1918*, Doc. 76.

73 Corrigan, *Sepoys in the Trenches: The Indian Corps on the Western Front, 1914–1915*, p. 235.

74 British Library, India Office Records, L/MIL/17/5/3100, CGS to GOC Force 'D', 29 Oct. 1915, Appendix 70.

75 Greenhut, 'The Imperial Reserve: The Indian Corps on the Western Front, 1914–15', p. 67.

76 Merewether and Smith, *The Indian Corps in France*, pp. 468–69; Corrigan, *Sepoys in the Trenches: The Indian Corps on the Western Front, 1914–1915*, p. 248. These casualty figures do not appear to include those of the two Indian cavalry divisions.

77 Sources: National Archives, War Office, WO 95/3913; Omissi (ed.), *Indian Voices of the Great War: Soldiers' Letters, 1914–1918*, Appendices I and II; Dixon, *Magnificent but not War: The Second Battle of Ypres, 1915*, Appendix III.

PHOSGENE IN THE YPRES SALIENT: 19 DECEMBER 1915

BERT HEYVAERT

The first chlorine use will forever link the year 1915 with the Ypres Salient. The attack on 22 April signalled the start of the Second Battle of Ypres, a period of almost continuous fighting that lasted until the end of May. When operations ceased, for the Allies the frontline had moved uncomfortably close to the historic centre of Ypres.

Quietness, however, did not return fully to the Salient. The new frontline between Saint-Eloi to the south and the Yser Canal in the north experienced bursts of heavy fighting throughout the year. From June till September, fighting raged around the hamlet of Hooge, the most eastern point of the Salient on the strategic Menin Road. On 30 July, special German *Gaspioniere* introduced another horrific weapon: liquid fire. A few weeks earlier, British engineers had exploded an underground mine of unmatched power at the same spot. The onset of the autumn and heavy rainfall brought from October onwards relative calm to the Salient.

However, for 1915 the fighting in the Salient was not completely over yet. On 19 December, the Germans introduced a new chemical warfare agent to the battlefield: phosgene.

Lethal developments

The German scientists working under the direction of Fritz Haber almost immediately considered the lethal potential of phosgene. Especially Carl Duisberg, a leading chemist at chemical industry giant Bayer, was responsible for the research into the use of compound as a weapon of war. While present at a field test with chlorine at Wahn in January 1915, he already recommended the use of phosgene in 20/80 mixture with chlorine. Subsequent experiments demonstrated an excellent build-up of the gas cloud.[1] Being a core industrial compound, the German chemical industry had the capacity to produce sufficient phosgene in time for the first chemical attack on 22 April. As phosgene is about 18 times more lethal than chlorine, such use would have inflicted far more casualties on the Allied side.[2] However, the German scientists had not yet developed an adequate protective device against it with the exception of closed oxygen masks. These were only issued to special troops and they only offered protection for as long as the oxygen supply lasted. A shift in wind direction might thus have proven disastrous for the attackers advancing behind the cloud.

Large-scale production of phosgene began nevertheless. Phosgene was mainly used

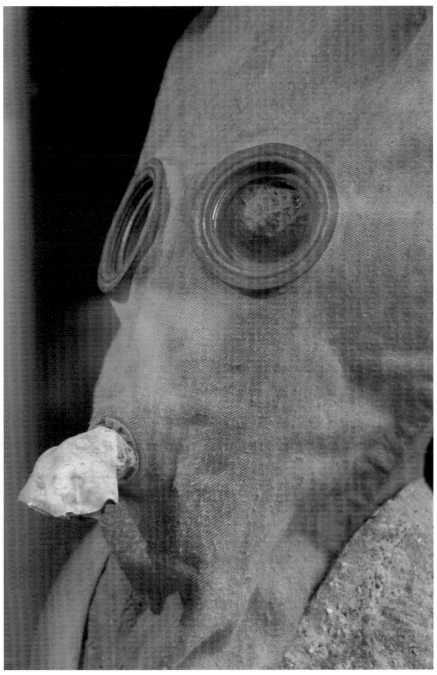

The British PH-type Helmet was the common gas mask in the second half of 1915 and first part of 1916 until it was replaced by the small box respirator. (Jean Pascal Zanders)

in the paint industry, where it was produced by heating carbon tetrachloride. The war economy meant that companies such as Bayer in Leverkusen now produced phosgene for the *Kriegsministerium*.[3] Haber took personal charge of the project to develop a protective mask against phosgene.

Not long after the second battle of Ypres, the German (Gas) *Pionier Regiment nr. 35* was sent to the eastern front in Poland with a first load of the lethal mixture. According to the German author Dieter Martinetz, they introduced phosgene to the battlefield on 31 May. They released almost 240 tonnes of deadly chemicals from 12,000 cylinders against Russian troops at Bolimów, near Warsaw. Although the mixture contained only 5 per cent of phosgene, the effects were devastating. Losses on the Russian side exceeded 3,100, including 1,200 fatalities. A second and a third attack in the east was launched on 12 June and 6 July.[4] Lutz Haber, son of Fritz Haber, is less certain that the first release of phosgene took place on 31 May. If the cloud was indeed released on that day uncertainty exists about whether the phosgene/chlorine mixture was 5/95 or 20/80 per cent. Relevant documents were destroyed. He also suggested that shortage of phosgene might have contributed to the preparation of the mixture.[5] As the autumn set in, the 'Gaspioniere' moved their cylinders back west to the Champagne area and Verdun, where they faced the French Army. Three cloud attacks on 19, 20 and 27 October, inflicted considerable losses on the French: almost 5,700 soldiers fell victim to the gas of whom 500 died.[6] Notwithstanding, the French were able the withstand the infantry attack. On the 19th, they recaptured their lost positions during the night. They lost no ground during the subsequent attacks.[7]

These attacks confirmed what scientists like Duisberg had already claimed: even in small volumes, phosgene was a most lethal weapon. On the whole the effects of the poison initially went unnoticed. Victims developed severe lung oedema only after a few hours. Survivors were at great risk of lasting asthma or other lung damage.[8]

Especially after the Germans turned their new weapon against the French, it became clear to the Allies that phosgene posed a serious threat. The British had no illusions that they would be spared this new weapon. An attack with phosgene on their front was only a matter of time. The almost flat land to the northeast of Ypres was not only strategically one of the most vulnerable areas in the British line, but it also offered one of the most suitable places for a gas attack. The Hypo helmets did not protect against phosgene, and in September the British introduced the improved Phenate Helmet or P Helmet. This was basically a multi-layered and better impregnated Hypo helmet with an exhalation tube and two separate eye-pieces. However, it still did not offer full protection against phosgene and was most uncomfortable to wear, producing a sense of suffocation during the first minutes after adjustment. It tended to leak around the mouthpiece and the eye pieces cracked quite easily. Besides that, distribution was slow, and it was only at the beginning of December that all troops were equipped with the new helmet.[9] In these circumstances, it was feared that a gas attack with a high concentration of phosgene would produce the disaster that had been avoided in April. From January 1916 onwards British soldiers were issued PH helmets that were treated with a phenate-hexamine solution. They gave much improved protection against high concentrations of phosgene.

The Germans, in contrast, were much better protected. In the beginning of September the frontline troops received the *Gummimaske*, the typical rubber face mask with external charcoal filter. The *Gaspioniere*, who needed most protection, received it even earlier. However, the first model did not give sufficient protection against phosgene either. It was only at the beginning of 1916 that the filter was upgraded to offer complete protection.[10]

The preparations and the terrain

At the end of October 1915, *Pionier Regiment nr. 36* started its move from the Champagne region to the Ypres Salient. Its orders were to install gas cylinders around the hamlet of Hooge, the easternmost point of the Ypres Salient. However, due to the unfavourable wind it moved the cylinders a few kilometres north. In late November and early December, it dug them in between the Verlorenhoek road and the Yser Canal.[11]

According to the German *Reichsarchiv*'s official history of the war, General

Richard von Schubert, commander of the XXVIIth Reserve corps, originally proposed an attack against Wieltje and the British lines to the northeast of Ypres. The infantry was to advance behind the cloud. The capture of Ypres was to be the ultimate goal. However, troops and guns for such an undertaking were unavailable. Therefore, von Schubert's superior, Duke Albrecht von Württemberg decided in November to install gas cylinders along entire front of the XXVIth and on the right wing of the XXVIIth *Reserve-Korps*. He intended to launch a cloud attack with strong artillery fire against the British reserve lines, but without an infantry attack.[12] Besides the

A German soldier in a finely reinforced trench, probably a support line, posing with a hand grenade and his gas mask, 1916–17. (In Flanders Fields Museum, Ypres)

lack of sufficient reserves, the inadequate protection against phosgene offered by the German gasmasks may also explain the attack plan. A change of wind direction could have proved disastrous for the attackers.

During the previous six months the theatre of the forthcoming attack had been relatively calm. The landscape still featured trees and hedges, despite the many blackened walls of abandoned, roofless farmsteads. Groundwater levels were much higher here than anywhere else in the Salient. December 1915 was generally warm, but rain made life in the trenches extremely uncomfortable.[13] Having been dug under much dryer conditions in early summer, the excavations lacked a decent drainage system, as a consequence of which soldiers stood knee-deep in water and mud. Especially on the British side, the line represented little more than swamps held by scarce strong points and regular patrols. A soldier of the 1st/6th battalion of the West Yorkshire Regiment described the trenches his battalion was holding between the Pilkemseweg and Morteldje in early December as follows:

> You may think we are in trenches. Disabuse yourself of that idea at once. We are inhabiting canals which are of four varieties: 1. Full of water, 2. full of mud, 3. full of earth 4. drains [...] to keep warm is only possible occasionally – to keep dry a farce.[14]

Illness caused more casualties than enemy action on both sides. For example, during the first two weeks of December 1915, the 1/16 Battalion of the London Regiment, which occupied trenches near Potyze, lost 30 men to disease. This was almost double the number of casualties from German fire.[15] Replacements being unavailable, the frontline battalions became critically undermanned.[16]

Rumours of an upcoming attack

The possibility of a gas attack caused British commanders greater concern than the lamentable state of the trenches and the men occupying them. They increased the number of reconnaissance patrols and small trench raids during the autumn of 1915 to detect any change in German behaviour or activities. Captured soldiers were potentially important sources of information. Thus on 13 November, British raiders brought in prisoners wearing a new type of gasmask. This was taken as a sign of an imminent gas attack. However, it was only when the Germans began installing the gas cylinders at the end of November that German frontline troops received information about the attack planned in their sector.

The Allies also began receiving intelligence from agents behind the enemy lines. Rumours of an imminent German offensive with the aim of taking the channel ports were circulating. Other collected information referred to a potent colourless gas. The strength of the rumours was such that the Dutch – and hence, neutral – newspaper *De Telegraaf* devoted an entire article to them.[17]

It is unclear when the British obtained their first concrete intelligence confirming the many rumours. Given the bad weather and poor state of terrain, raids to take prisoners were difficult undertakings.[18] Brigadier General James E. Edmonds' official British history of the First World War refers to the capture of a German NCO of the XXVIth *Reserve-Korps* in the night of 4–5 December. The unit occupied positions between the Roulers and Staden railways. He reportedly gave the British a first indication of the upcoming attack.[19] However, neither the war diaries of British units, nor the reports from Belgian intelligence officers with the British and French Headquarters in Flanders confirmed this event. In contrast, reported intensification of British artillery fire to the northeast of Ypres around the same time might support Edmonds' claim.

The capture of a German prisoner on 16 December is better documented. One of several raiding parties out in the early hours of that day brought back a soldier of *Reserve-Infantry-Regiment* nr. 240.[20] Two British intelligence officers questioned him at the town hall of Bailleul. One of them, Captain Barley, recalled the event in an interview more than 60 years later:

> Eventually we got an officer who obviously knew something but he wouldn't speak [...] We tried kindness, we tried threats and then we tied him up and put him in the roof of the mayor house which was very cold and finding him Bell and I strapped on our swords and revolvers and spurs and went in. Got him down and said, come and tell us when it is and he answered on the 19th. So, we showed him a map and said, where is that and he said on here, it is here. Now that was what we wanted.[21]

German marines on the Belgian coast posing with several types of gas masks, 1916.
(In Flanders Fields Museum, Ypres)

Another prisoner of *Infanterie-Regiment nr. 143* confirmed the story. Around the same time, the Belgian embassy in The Netherlands reported that according to a traveller who had had a conversation with a director of a dismantled factory, a gas 'without colour or smell, but extremely lethal' was to be used at the first possible opportunity.[22]

These warnings were taken very seriously. When after 15 December the wind turned in favour of the Germans, all troops were placed on the highest alert. Edmonds described the actions taken:

> Standing measures against cloud gas were in force: the directions of the wind were very closely observed by an officer detailed in each corps in the Salient, and whenever conditions were favourable to the enemy, the order 'Gas Alert' was issued. This meant that a sentry was posted near each alarm horn or gong, at every dug-out holding ten men or more, on every group of small dug-outs, and at each signal office; that gas helmets and gas alarms were inspected once every 12 hours; that all ranks wore the helmet outside the great coat, or rolled up on the head, and had the top button of the great coat left undone, so that the helmet might be tucked in; and that special precautions were taken to lubricate the working parts of all rifles, machine guns and guns in forward positions.[23]

In addition, the British held extensive drills, so that every soldier would be able to don the gas helmet and mount the parapet in less than one minute, and know exactly what to do in the event of an attack.[24] An officer in every battalion was tasked to constantly verify the soldiers' gas masks and replace them whenever necessary. The soldiers undertook the drills punctiliously, even to the point that the exercises began to annoy them.[25] The 16th Brigade, resting in Poperinge and Houtkerke in the first half of December, received precise orders in case of an attack on the 6th Division's front during their recuperation. They also received special inspections and training in rapid adjustment of gas helmets 'due to the possibility of gas attack in the near future'.[26]

In a final effort to neutralise the gas threat, on 18 November 4.5 inch howitzers were scheduled to bombard the frontline where German prisoners had told the British the cylinders were deployed. Especially in front of the 49th (West Riding) Division, No-Man's Land was very narrow. At 'International Trench' and 'Morteldje Salient', it was no more than 20–30 metres wide. Where necessary the garrisons evacuated the frontline trenches for safety reasons. Thick fog blocking all observation delayed the planned bombardment until the next day. It allowed the Germans to take the initiative first.

The attack

After the cylinders had been installed, a period of waiting for the right conditions started for the German troops occupying the area. It meant a nerve-racking sequel of standing to and standing down again. Both on 19 and 22 November the attack was postponed, followed by two weeks of unfavourable wind conditions.[27]

On 17 December a heavy German bombardment shattered shelters and trenches across the British front northeast of Ypres. On Sunday, 19 December, the wind finally favouring the Germans, the *Gaspioniere* were ready by 4.30am. At 6.15am, bright red flares spread their ghostly light along the battlefield. With a loud hissing sound, the 20/80 mixture of phosgene and chlorine was forced out of the cylinders.[28] British sentries reported German soldiers coming out of their trenches, bending down apparently to open the taps of the tubes in No Man's Land. Before the sentries could open fire, the gas was upon them.[29]

Over a front almost three miles wide, from Verlorenhoek to the Staden railway, a thick white cloud of over 15 metres high drifted towards the British trenches. Sentries immediately sounded the alarm with claxons and gongs. All ranks responded promptly by putting on their gas helmets. In several places, however, the gas travelled fast at a speed of several metres per second and was upon them in a matter of seconds. Between International Trench and Morteldje, the 2.5-kilometre long front of the 49th Division was so close to the German lines that many men were unable to don their masks properly in time. The 1st/4th West Ridings in and near International Trench suffered worst during the early stages of the attack.[30]

On the front of the 6th Division, stretching from Morteldje to Verlorenhoek, No Man's Land was mostly over 250 metres wide, allowing the garrisons more time to adjust their helmets. Even here, however, many soldiers were overcome by the phosgene. The 1st Leicesters, who were in front of Wieltje, reported that the gas had reached their headquarters at Sint-Jean even before the news of the gas attack had been telephoned through from the front line. The 1st/5th West Yorkshires, who were east of the Pilckem Road and had their headquarters at La Belle Alliance, also reported not having been informed in time.[31]

In general, the British battalions did not react uniformly to the attack. Some immediately opened fast rifle and machine gun fire, while others waited for the German advance, wanting to catch the enemy in the open.[32]

Although the British soldiers obviously feared a massive infantry attack, the Germans did not intend such action. However, all along the front German patrols went forward to investigate the effects of the newly-introduced gas. *Reserve Infantry Regiment nr. 235*, for instance, sent out three patrols led by officers towards Morteldje. They met with fierce fire from the 1st King's Shropshire light infantry facing them. Two patrols were immediately pulled back. One party got through, but the British killed the Lieutenant in charge and three men, while wounding another three of their comrades.[33]

Expecting the German infantry to attack behind the cloud, most British infantry battalions in the front trenches brought their support companies forward. Battalions making up the brigade reserve were also alarmed and moved forward. About 45 minutes after the first release of gas, the Germans began shelling the British trenches and hinterland. Many reserve units had just begun arriving in their frontline positions. Communication lines were cut. Shells particularly hit important points in the British

A first model British hypo helmet (British smoke hood), recovered during an archaeological excavation north of Ypres.
(In Flanders Fields Museum, Ypres)

defence, which German observers had carefully mapped.[34] The British artillery responded, and soon all hell broke loose.

All frontline battalions reported heavy German shelling, but with limited impact. Their reports were misleading, because in fact the German objectives lay in the rear or were approach routes. The German gunners fired vast quantities of T-shell containing tear gas. Their orders were to support the gas attack by saturating a 1000-metre long by 400-metre wide box. At that moment the British support trenches were overflowing with gassed and wounded soldiers. Roads behind the front line too were turning into death traps.

Heavy German howitzer fire continued until 10.30am, but the British reported heavy artillery fire throughout the day. At 2.15pm the Germans re-intensified their bombardment, which they repeated intermittently until the evening of the 21st. In all, the VIth Corps suffered shelling for almost 58 hours.[35]

In the night of 19–20 December, a shift in wind direction blew lingering gas back to the German lines, making casualties there. It briefly created the impression of a British gas counterattack.[36] Reserve battalions relieved the battered British troops.

Gas victims

All official sources tend to comment more on the effects of the gas than on tactical achievements. British troops appear to have stood their ground well and the general conclusion was that the German phosgene release had failed. The intense gas drill of the preceding days seemed to have paid off. Most soldiers were able to overcome the oppressive feeling from the smell of phenol. Those who were unable to resist the sense of suffocation tore off their helmets and died instantaneously. Most officers ascertained that their men were masked before donning their own helmet. This helps to explain the rather large number of officers killed during the early stages of the attack. The need to lift their mask to shout orders may also explain the large number of casualties among officers and NCOs.[37]

Captain A. F. L. Shields, a Royal Army Medical Corps (RAMC) officer attached to the 1st Battalion King's own Shropshire Light Infantry between Morteldje and Hill Top

Farm, described the plight of the British soldier:

> The first feeling on putting on the helmet was one of suffocation and for the
> first 5 minutes it was distinctly uncomfortable, giving one the impression that
> one was being gassed [...] It is important that men should be assured that the
> unpleasant effects at first experienced on putting on the helmet is due to the
> chemical in the helmet and not to gas poisoning, as one man thought he was
> being gassed although his helmet was perfect and well adjusted, but on my
> reassuring him he carried on all right and suffered no ill effects. Other men lost
> confidence in their helmets, removed them, and were gassed during the process
> of putting on their second helmet.[38]

Malfunctioning mouth and eye pieces added to the casualties in the early stages of the
phosgene attack.

Notwithstanding, immediate casualties remained low. Phosgene, however, had
insidious effects that only became apparent many hours after exposure, even in low
quantities. The delayed effects set in during the afternoon of the 19th, when it was
deemed safe for the men to go back about their normal business or for the slightly
gassed to report to the aid posts. Exercise hastened the effects of phosgene. Soldiers who
trudged through the thick mud on their way to the dressing stations felt exhausted,
and many collapsed in communication trenches or by the side of the road. Those in
the front lines repairing damage and filling new sandbags similarly felt exhausted and
collapsed or died on the spot depending on the severity of their exposure. Roads and
trenches thus became strewn with exhausted men and stretcher bearers had to work
until 7am the next morning to bring them all in. Doctors found that they were dealing
with two different kinds of gas victims. The first group reminded them of the chlorine
victims in April and May 1915. The second group displayed completely different
symptoms more associated with cardiac problems rather than pulmonary oedema
typical of chlorine poisoning.[39] Lieutenant Aubrey O'Connor, medical officer to the
8th Bedfords, described his first encounter with a phosgene gas victim as follows:

> The first case I had was that of an officer who came to the dressing station
> in the evening of the 19th about 8.30pm. He said he didn't feel very well,
> but he did not look very bad. I gave him a cup of tea which he drank and we
> talked for a little while. Suddenly he collapsed in the chair he was sitting on,
> and I gave him some oxygen but he died an hour afterwards. His collapse was
> extraordinarily sudden.[40]

Medically, there was not much doctors could do for these victims. The phosgene
replaced the oxygen in the cells and quickly caused an oxygen deficiency within the
body, unconsciousness and death. Treatment ranged from the general 'army tonic nr. 6'
to an atropine injection. Overall, however, rest was the only remedy that really seemed

to help. If not, death was all but certain.

These typical 'secondary effects' of the gas attack lasted for several days. Sudden physical efforts exhausted men abnormally. The 9th Suffolks, who had endured the attack just north of Wieltje, were relieved in the evening of the 22nd. Their medical officer, Captain K. K. Drury, wrote a worrying report to the Assistant Director Medical Services (ADMS) of the 6th Division:

> On the night of the 22nd, when the regiment was relieved, great numbers of men while on the march to the train – about 2 miles – had to sit down for short rests. [...] At this time the strength of the regiment as a fighting force was greatly diminished and if an attack had been made, I have grave doubts that the men would not have been physically able to repel it.[41]

Aftermath and conclusions

Although the British defences did not collapse under the phosgene attack, casualties were not slight. The 6th and 49th Division had 12 battalions in the front lines or support trenches a few hundred metres to the rear. Given that most battalions seemed undermanned, probably 8–9,000 troops directly faced the gas cloud. At least 4 battalions, another 2,750 to 3,000 men, were rushed in as soon as the attack started, making for a total of around 12,000 British soldiers in the forward lines. Official statistics attribute 1,069 casualties to the gas attack. The mortality rate was 24 per cent, which amounts to 265 gas fatalities.[42]

The source for those figures, however, is unclear. A calculation based on casualty figures by the Commonwealth War Graves Commission suggests 183 British dead on 19 December, and another 103 who died from their injuries over the next three days. In all, 296 soldiers were killed in action or died in the aftermath of the 19th. These figures do not discriminate between the number of fatalities from phosgene and those who perished in the 48-hour German artillery bombardment. The official figure appears slightly on the high side, but not that far from the actual number. The highest ranking victim on that day was Colonel E. O. Wright, ADMS of the 49th division, who was killed by a shell while evacuating gassed men.[43]

Edmonds' assessment that about three quarters of the victims belonged to the 49th Division is incorrect.[44] It is true that the 49th Division lost slightly more men in action on the 19th. However, taking into account the men killed during the bombardment of the next day and fatalities in hospitals and aid posts, then the 6th Division seems to have lost more soldiers (156) than the 49th (140).[45] Overall, of 12,000 troops that went into action that day, 296 or around 3 per cent were killed.

Edmonds explains the low fatality rate by pointing to the short period of one hour at the most during which the Germans released the phosgene and the strong winds that drove the gas rather quickly across the British trenches. This may have been fortunate as the gas helmets would not have withstood high concentrations of the agent. The

A church bell used as a well elaborated gas alarm in a German position. The statue of an angel attached to it is a poignant detail. (Militärhistorisches Museum der Bundeswehr, Dresden)

official history of the *Reichsarchiv* also mentions that there was no continuous line of cylinders, meaning that the gas cloud would not have had the same concentration everywhere.[46] The gas cloud reached positions as far as Bailleul, some 19 kilometres behind the front. Canadians on parade there smelled it clearly.[47] The distance has been advanced as evidence of the severity of the phosgene attack, although it appears more likely that the strong winds were responsible for the distribution of the warfare agent over such a great distance.

Had the Germans managed to release a larger volume of gas, or released it for a longer time, or even if they had had a stronger concentration of phosgene in their mixture, British casualties might have been three or four times higher. The gas helmets were far from phosgene proof, and especially the tally of delayed fatalities could have risen sharply under such conditions. A sudden collapse of three or four times as many soldiers, combined with a heavy bombardment of the bridges over the canal, might well have given the German infantry the opportunity to push forward as far as the canal, making the situation in the northeast of the Salient untenable .

The *Reichsarchiv* claims relative success on the German side, as an infantry attack was never intended. However, the phosgene cloud did not boost German morale. Weeks of tension had culminated in what seemed a rather useless attack. However, the British 'jumpiness' in the days preceding the attack, and their artillery response caused quite a few victims among German ranks as well. As the author of the regimental history of *Reserve-Infanterie-Regiment* (RIR) 239 puts it: 'we rather had one big attack than ten of these small ones'. The only thing the German soldiers welcomed was that the gas was now out of their trenches.[48]

The title of Edmonds' chapter on 19 December, 'The first phosgene attack', has misled many to think that this was the first occasion on which the gas was used. By far, this was not the first time phosgene was used on the Western front, although most British regimental histories seem to have interpreted it in this way. The cloud attack of 19 December was not a trial of the phosgene-chlorine mixture. It had already been used in combat and the Germans knew its lethality and effects. If they were testing anything, it would have been the British defences and response.

As for gas drill and lessons learned from this attack, the British proved themselves quick learners. It would be interesting to learn how the French had reacted to their encounters with phosgene just a few months earlier, which lessons they drew from them, and to what extent they were communicated to the British. It would appear that not much had come through about this towards the British, as many doctors operating on the 19th seemed hesitant to attribute the complaints of the gassed patients to phosgene, although the symptoms were obvious.

19 December 1915 was also the day on which Sir John French handed over command of the British forces in France and Flanders to Sir Douglas Haig. The phosgene attack near Ypres has stood in the shadow of this event. In 1916, artillery shell became the main delivery system for phosgene, which meant that units father away from the front could also be targeted. Cylinders with phosgene were used against the British on five more occasions, including three times in Ypres Salient: twice near the village of Wulverghem (30 April 1916 and 17 June 1916) to the south and once near Wieltje (8 August 1916) to the northeast.[49] Even with the improved PH helmet, casualties still rose to 804 during the August attack.

Just six days after the gas attack, German and Allied soldiers lived through another Christmas in the trenches near Ypres. Contrary to the previous year, the British soldiers showed little enthusiasm for the German calls to fraternise. The memories of the gas attack were all too fresh. Artillery and snipers did their work as on any other day.

Acknowledgements

I would like to thank the staff of the In Flanders Fields documentation centre in Ypres, Dr. Luc Vandeweyer (Royal Archives of Belgium), Simon Jones (Liverpool), Jan Vancoillie and Kristof Blieck (Memorial Museum Passchendaele 1917) for their help in supplying information for this article.

Notes

1 D. Martinetz, *Der Gaskrieg 1914/18* (Bonn, 1996), p. 20.
2 R. Harris and J. Paxman, *A Higher Form of Killing, the Secret Story of Chemical and Biological Warfare* (New York, 1982), p. 18
3 Martinetz, *Der Gaskrieg 1914/18*, p. 12.
4 Martinetz, *Der Gaskrieg 1914/18*, pp. 26–27.
5 L. F. Haber, *The Poisonous Cloud* (Clarendon Press: Oxford, 1986), p. 37.
6 Martinetz, *Der Gaskrieg 1914/18*, p. 60.
7 L. F. Haber, *The Poisonous Cloud*, p. 60; O. Lepick, *La Grande Guerre chmique 1914–1918* (Presses universitaires de France: Paris, 1998), p. 139
8 Martinetz, *Der Gaskrieg 1914/18*, pp. 27 and 70.
9 Harris and Paxman, *A Higher Form of Killing*, p. 17.
10 G. Lachaux and P. Delhomme, *La guerre des gaz 1915–1918* (Paris, 1985), p. 115
11 L. F. Haber, *The Poisonous Cloud,* p. 60.
12 *Der Weltkrieg 1914 bis 1918. Die Operationen des Jahres 1915, die Ereignisse im Westen und auf dem Balkan vom Sommer bis zum Jahresschluß*, eds Reichsarchiv (14 vols, Berlin), vol. 9, p. 113.

13 National Archives, WO 95/1605, War Diary 16th Infantry brigade.

14 Captain E. V. Tempest, *History of the Sixth Battalion West Yorkshire Regiment*, vol. 1, p. 60.

15 National Archives, WO 95/1616, War Diary 1st 16th Battalion the London Regiment.

16 National Archives, WO 95/1605.

17 Royal Army Museum – Brussels, 'Moscow' archives:Box 2801, dossier 185–14–6377, *Armée Belge, commandement de l'armée IIe bureau G.Q.G. le 16/12/1915, sommaire des renseignements*; Box 3071, *Renseignements sur l'ennemi, armée Belge commandement de l'armée IIe bureau*, Pièce 656E.

18 Otto Hennig, *Das Reserve-Infanterie-Regiment Nr. 235 im Weltkriege* (Oldenburg, 1931), p. 65.

19 J. E. Edmonds, *Military Operations France and Belgium, 1916* (2 vols, London, 1932), vol. 1, p. 158.

20 A. Mayer and J. Görtz, *Das Reserve-Infanterie-Regiment Nr. 236 im Weltkrige* (Thüringen), p. 197; Royal Army Museum Brussels, 'Moscow' archives, Box 3071, *Renseignements sur l'ennemi, armee Belge commandement de l'armée IIe bureau*, Piece 619E 17/12.

21 Liddle Collection Leeds, Interview Captain Barley; Royal Army Museum Brussels, 'Moscow' archives, Box 3071, *Renseignements sur l'ennemi, armée Belge commandement de l'armée IIe bureau*, Piece 619E 17/12.

22 Royal Army Museum – Brussels, 'Moscow' archives: *Groupe d'Armées du Nord, Etat-Major, II bureau, bulletin de renseignements du 19 décembre 1915*.

23 Edmonds, *Military Operations France and Belgium, 1916*, pp.158–159.

24 P. G. Bales, *The History of the 1/4th Battalion Duke of Wellington's (West Riding) Regiment, 1914–1919* (London, 1920), p. 52.

25 Tempest, *History of the Sixth Battalion West Yorkshire Regiment*, p. 63.

26 National Archives, WO 95/1605.

27 J. Schatz, *Geschichte des badischen (rheinischen) Reserve-Infanterie-Regiments 239* (Stuttgart), p. 74; *Das Res.-Feldart.-Regt. Nr. 51 im Weltkriege* (Kassel, 1932), p. 199.

28 A. A. Fries, and C. J. West, *Chemical Warfare* (McGraw-Hill: New York, 1921), p. 162.

29 H. C. Wylly, *History of the 1st & 2nd Battalions The Leicestershire Regiment In the Great War* (Aldershot), p. 55.

30 Edmonds, *Military Operations France and Belgium, 1916*, p. 159; National Archives, *War Diary 1st 4th Battalion Duke of Wellington's (West Riding) Regiment*, WO 95/2799.

31 National Archives, WO 95/1621, *War Diary 1st Battalion the Leicestershire Regiment*,; and WO 95/2794, *War Diary 1st 5th Battalion The West Yorkshire Regiment*,.

32 Edmonds, *Military Operations France and Belgium, 1916*, p. 160.

33 National Archives, WO 95/1609, *War Diary 1st Battalion the King's Shropshire Light Infantry*.

34 National Archives, , WO 95/2795, *War Diary 1st 7th Battalion The West Yorkshire regiment*.

35 Edmonds, *Military Operations France and Belgium, 1916*, pp. 161–62; Das Res.-Feldart.-Regt. Nr. 51 im Weltkriege, pp. 199.

36 Mayer and Görtz, *Das Reserve-Infanterie-Regiment Nr. 236 im Weltkrige* , p. 197.

37 National Archives, WO 142/99 file 55843, *Report on the attack of 19th December 1915, Capt. Evans RAMC 1/West Yorks*.

38 National Archives, WO 142/99, file 55843, *Report of gas attack, Sunday, 19th December 1915*.

39 National Archives, WO 95/1621, *Report on the gas attack on December 19th 1915*.

40 National Archives, WO 142/99, 55843, *Remarks regarding the gas attack of the 19th December by Aubrey A. O'Connor RAMC*.

41 National Archives, WO 142/99, 55843, *Report on the attack of 19th December 1915 by Captain Drury RAMC*.

42 WO 142/109/DGS/M/64 33715.

43 Edmonds, *Military Operations France and Belgium, 1916*, p. 161.

44 Edmonds, *Military Operations France and Belgium, 1916*, p. 162.

45 Commonwealth War Graves Commission data.

46 Edmonds, *Military Operations France and Belgium, 1916*, p. 161; *Der Weltkrieg 1914 bis 1918*, p. 114.

47 E. Wyrall, *The West Yorkshire Regiment in the war 1914–1918* (2 vols, London), vol. 1, p. 143.

48 Schatz, *Geschichte des badischen (rheinischen) Reserve-Infanterie-Regiments 239*, p. 75; D. F. Lennartz and D. Nagel, *Geschichte des badischen (Später rheinischen) Reserve-Infanterie-Regiments 240* (Thüringen), p. 100.

49 National Archives, WO 142/109/DGS/M/ 54, 33715.

A WAR ON TERROR: GAS, BRITISH MORALE, AND REPORTING THE WAR IN WALES

GERARD ORAM

> To sustain the moral of his own men; to break down the moral of his enemy –
> these are the great objects [of leadership in war].
>
> *Colonel G. F. R. Henderson*[1]

These remarks by one of the most respected British military theorists were written at the end of the 19th century – a time before what we now term *Total War*. Arguably, the American Civil War, with which Henderson was certainly familiar, was the world's first total war, but the First World War was certainly the first total war to be fought in Europe. Even in 1915 Henderson's remarks still encapsulated much of the military strategy of the belligerents on the Western Front where morale remained a major concern. New and terrible weapons were developed to break down the morale of the enemy which, it was thought, would unlock the way to victory. But what Henderson had not anticipated was the extent of total war. Total war meant the dismantling of boundaries and limits. One of the first to be dismantled was the boundary between the war front and the home front as each state mobilised its entire resources – military, political, economic, industrial, technological, scientific and human – for the war effort. The impact of this new kind of warfare, so far as Henderson's teachings are concerned, was that civilian morale took on a greater importance and must, therefore, be viewed on equal terms with that of troop morale.

But what is morale? I have explored the complex concept of morale elsewhere and it would not be appropriate to repeat the process here.[2] However, a concise definition would be salutary. Morale, I have argued, is basically the resolve, determination and willingness to fight or to continue the war effort under the circumstances prevailing at any given time. Therefore, to destroy the enemy's morale would be to bring about an end to that willingness to fight. The result would be capitulation. Notions such as 'the will to fight' or 'the ability to stick it out' were actually commonplace amongst military theorists and commentators during the First World War,[3] but these do appear to imply that morale is a given, something that it fixed. Instead, I have preferred to imply a more negotiated willingness that is fluid, something that can waver, something that can be lost, something that once lost can also be re-found. This model is especially useful in any analysis of civilian morale, but it is also supported by a lot of the scholarly work on troop morale.[4]

In a total war context, the destruction of the enemy's civilian morale could be even more decisive than the destruction of troop morale. The latter might yield position by winning the battle, but the former would yield the war itself. This was not lost on politicians or generals. Once appropriately updated to the exigencies of total war, Henderson's evaluation remained the lynchpin of wartime strategy, not only military and political, but social and economic also. In fact, the gas attack of 22 April epitomised this paradox, because it did destroy troop morale when many of the defenders gave up their willingness to fight and fled. This resulted in some territorial gain, but the loss of morale was limited to a relatively small part of the battle zone and the units that resisted, such as the Canadians, became the focus of an improved morale – especially on the home-front. But we need to examine the impact of the attack in a broader context.

Military reactions

The military reaction to the gas attack was mixed. On the one hand, the telegram sent on 23 April 1915 (the day after the first gas attack) by Field Marshal Sir John French is remarkable for its lack of indignation:

> Germans used powerful asphyxiating gases very extensively in attack on French yesterday with serious effect. Apparently these gases are either chlorine or bromine. Will send further details later but meanwhile strongly urge that immediate steps be taken to supply similar means of most effective kind for use by our troops. Also essential that our troops should be immediately provided

A British machine gun crew wearing the PH helmet, 1915–16. (Imperial War Museum, London)

with means of counteracting effects of enemy gases which should be suitable for use when on the move. As a temporary measure am arranging for troops in trenches to be supplied with solution of bicarbonate of soda in which to soak handkerchiefs.[5]

Commander of the British First Army, General Sir Douglas Haig, was equally restrained in his observation that the French generals only had themselves to blame for being caught out by the German initiative. General Ferdinand Foch – commander of the French Army Group North – and others, he claimed, displayed an 'ignorance of the practical side of war', and that 'they never seem to think of what the enemy will do'.[6]

On the other hand, the Secretary of State for War, Lord Herbert Kitchener, likened the actions of the Germans to the barbarity he associated with the Dervishes, before proceeding immediately to obtain permission from the war cabinet to retaliate in kind.[7] A similar swing from initial indignation to a position of pragmatism was reflected in the reaction of some troops who had witnessed the attack or who had been otherwise directly involved. One account written by a stretcher-bearer who had helped to bring in wounded Canadians recalled:

> They [the Germans] are well supplied with everything, men, money, brains and what is sometimes thought not to be the case, ammunition, and this gas is beyond speaking about. It is deadlier in effect than millions of shells. How we curse that gas. One never knows the minute that the breeze blowing on our faces is going to be turned into one of the deadliest poisons. Britain is too honourable to fight such scum as the Germans but she will have to drop that honourableness if she means to win. We must play them at their own game, and that very soon. If we don't, God knows what will happen.[8]

Even here, though, the dichotomy was evident: to remain 'honourable' or to fight a total war where the boundaries and limits are blurred. The dichotomy, in this case, was resolved in favour of the latter.

In terms of casualties, of course, gas was not a particularly effective weapon – at least not in its original, chlorine, version (later, phosgene and mustard gases were to prove more deadly).[9] However it is clear from the accounts of those directly affected that this weapon certainly had the potential to destroy troop morale. Gas provided the sternest of tests to Britain's morale. Indeed, as Ben Shephard posited: 'Accounts of the effects of these gas attacks are so horrifying that one might wonder why they did not bring the war to and end there and then'.[10]

1915, a year of crises

Moreover, 1915 was a key year for Britain – perhaps even the key year – in its collective willingness to fight. Morale was probably at its lowest and the use in 1915 of a morale-

Ernest Brooks: A gas sentry ringing an alarm at Fleurbaix, 15 miles south of Ypres, June 1916. He is wearing a PH helmet while his tin helmet is hanging from his bayonet. The gas alarm is a larger house or chapel bell. Note the unused duckboards waiting in the background.
(Imperial War Museum, London)

destroying terror weapon such as gas could conceivably have brought about a collapse in Britain's resolve to continue. There was little to cheer politicians, generals, civilians or troops as the enthusiasm and expectations of 1914 were swept aside by a succession of crises. Firstly, there was a military crisis. The initial breakthrough at Neuve Chapelle in March had been squandered. The Second Battle of Ypres in April (where the Germans first released chlorine gas) had resulted in a loss of territory. The gas attack by British forces at Loos in September had failed and the offensive resulted in large casualties especially amongst Territorial Force divisions, widening the casualty list from the regular army to something akin to a citizen army. Away from the Western Front things were hardly any more encouraging. The naval attack on the Dardanelles during March had been ineffective and necessitated the Gallipoli troop landings in April. This too became bogged down and then required evacuation in December. The only good news in the military sphere was the capture of Kut-al-Amara in September but even this had turned sour by the end of the year when the town was placed under siege by the Turks (and of course ended in catastrophe in May 1916 when the garrison surrendered). Then there was a crisis in leadership (both political and military) and by the end of the year there were numerous high profile casualties. In the military, General Sir Horace Smith-Dorrien – II Corps commander – was the first to go, but he was later followed by the man who had pushed him, Field-Marshal Sir John French.

On the political front, in November Winston Churchill was forced to resign as First Lord of the Admiralty after the Dardanelles fiasco, but worse was to come when the Prime Minister himself, Herbert Asquith, was forced into a coalition with political opponents following a split in his Liberal administration in May 1915. There was a crisis of ideology with old liberalism giving way to new as conscription (both military and industrial) became increasingly unavoidable. Asquith was eventually pushed out by Lloyd George in December 1916. But the death of old liberalism was not brought about by Lloyd George's new ministry: it was moribund long before Asquith's resignation and was epitomised by the introduction of the National Registration Act in July 1915. There was an industrial crisis whereupon Britain, the birthplace of the industrial revolution and supplier to the world market, was unable to satisfy the voracious appetite of total war – in this case the shortage of shells.

For the first time, also, Britain's civilian population was deliberately targeted: the naval bombardment of coastal towns in the North-East of England in December 1914 had not only exposed the Royal Navy's inability to defend the realm, but it had brought home to British civilians the reality of total war. Of course, the targeting of civilians was not new and it had been ruthlessly carried out by the invading German armies in Belgium and France in 1914,[11] but for British civilians this kind of war was beyond their experience. The targeting of civilians was escalated in 1915 with Zeppelin raids on King's Lynn, Great Yarmouth and London that left more than 80 civilians dead. But this was dwarfed by the death toll of the sinking of the Lusitania in May (1,192 dead, although reports at the time suggested figures of more than 1,500).

It was not only the extent of total war that precipitated crisis; it was also the nature of that war. In 1915, Britain found itself fighting a new kind of war, a war without limits and, after the chlorine gas attack of 22 April (and use of phosgene gas on 19 December), a war with new and terrible weapons deployed against its troops. It was a war against terror.

From a war against terror into a war on terror

There was every reason to suppose that British morale might have collapsed in 1915. But it did not. To understand why this did not happen we need to consider, once again, contemporary military theory and apply it to a total war context. It was no coincidence that maintaining morale was one of the main themes of a training course for army officers in France towards the end of 1915. In his address, Brigadier-General R. J. Kentish, a former commandant at the Senior Officers' School at Aldershot, acknowledged the continuing relevance of earlier theorists such as Henderson when he stated:

> Moral force in modern [total?] warfare preponderates as greatly as formerly.

He then continued:

> Of the many factors which may create moral force, some of the most powerful [...] [are] success in battle, a great leader, a popular cause.[12]

Britain could hardly lay claim in 1915 to either of the first two of Kentish's 'three moral factors' – as we might term them – but it did have the third and, thanks in part to the actions of the enemy, the popular cause had been transformed into a moral one. Our understanding of the term 'morale' is clearer when channelled through the contemporary practice whereby the word 'moral' was preferred. The two words were interchangeable – synonymous even – and by 1915 British morale became a matter of morality as the war against terror was transformed into a war *on* terror.

To achieve this transformation was hardly difficult given the demonisation of Germany from the earliest days of the war. Atrocity stories were widespread and sat comfortably with the concept of aggressive Prussian militarism, which, juxtaposed with the idea of liberal Britain, had offered justification for entering the war in the first place. Perhaps the best known expression of this was H. G. Wells' essay 'Why Britain Went to War' published on 22 August 1914 in the widely circulated *The War Illustrated*:

> Physical and moral brutality has indeed become a cant in the German mind, and spread from Germany throughout the world. I could wish it were possible to say that English and American thought had altogether escaped its corruption. But now at last we shake ourselves free and turn upon this boasting wickedness ['blood and iron'] to rid the world of it.[13]

Did the British government capitalise on the 'moral war' that confronted it? A concept as abstract as 'morale' is difficult to measure and few have even attempted it. Clearly, any interpretation will be largely subjective. Yet there are some markers or indicators that can be useful to the historian. One of the more reliable markers in the British context is that of recruitment to the army. Britain, of course, was the only one of the major European military powers that did not conscript. Although this was to change during the First World War, the period that we are interested in here (mid 1915) remained one where the British Army relied on the voluntary principle for recruits. Even allowing for the notorious seasonal change in recruiting patterns there does appear to be statistical evidence that the war on terror had bolstered rather than diminished the willingness of the British people to continue the fight: recruitment figures for the month following the gas attack show a significant rise from 119,087 in April to 135,263 in May.[14] With the exception of the total recruited in January 1915, which can be accounted for by the relatively poor return for December 1914 that had caused the processing of applications to be carried over into the new year, May was by far the best month for enlistments in a year when the monthly average was fewer than 107,000.

22 April 1915 was a watershed in British morale because the process of demonising the enemy was complete. Thereafter, even a military reverse would bring about a greater determination to defeat a supposedly immoral Germany. It is therefore significant that

A British and Belgian sentry wearing their gas masks, 1916–17. The British soldier is posing with
the small box respirator, the Belgian with the French masque M2 respirator.
(In Flanders Fields Museum, Ypres)

the only other notable rise in recruitment during 1915 was in October (113,285) and
November (121,793), which can be attributed to this new 'moral effect' (this time arising
from the Battle of Loos). It was also no coincidence that after the first gas attack, there
followed intensification in the telling of atrocity stories both by the press and in personal
communication. The Canadians, who had withstood the attack, were the focus of the
latest round. On 15 May *The Times* reported that during the battle in April a Canadian
soldier had been found skewered to a barn door by German bayonets that pierced his
hands and throat. From this point the story escalated. Within days rumours in private
correspondence had it that it was not one, but six Canadians who had been 'crucified'.
The same correspondent reported that the men in his unit had now been ordered not to
take prisoners, but to shoot or bayonet surrendering Germans.[15] The putative immoral
enemy action provided the preconditions for a highly energised form of morale.

After that first gas attack, the boundary between the actual and the psychological
battlefield had been dismantled and the new struggle for hearts and minds would
probably determine who would win the war. Central to this, in Britain at least, was the

control of information. Early in the war the Asquith government established the War Propaganda Bureau situated at Wellington House, operating under the Foreign Office. Later, Lloyd George would reorganise it into the Department of Information with wider responsibilities for cinema, news and political intelligence.

By 1915 the national press was effectively the official voice of the British government. This had been achieved in typically British fashion, not so much by prescription – though that would follow – but by bringing the press either into government or so close to it that the difference was indiscernible. Local newspapers, though, largely escaped this governmental association and many (especially in remote parts) were even able to continue as if The Defence of the Realm Act 1914 (DORA) did not apply. Consequently, if we want to gauge government concerns we need look no further than the national daily papers, but for the reactions in the country, local newspapers provide an invaluable source. Local newspapers were sometimes in conflict with the official line on the war. Even more striking were the differing reactions to the same events in different parts of Britain. Local newspapers were – and indeed still are – concerned primarily with local news, so, surprising as it might seem, war events were often secondary to apparently mundane local stories. But this could alter if the war news was also local news: if, for example, local units had been involved.

The gas attack of 22 April 1915 provoked widespread condemnation and outrage in much of the British press. In fact, the atrocity stories had started even before the attack with *The Times* reporting rumours of the use of gas almost two weeks prior to its first deployment.[16] After the attack, the sense of outrage was reflected up and down Britain in the various local newspapers. Predictably, the extent of the outrage depended on whether local units had been on the receiving end. But even in areas not directly involved with the events at Langemarck, there existed indignation at this escalation of the war. This continued in the months afterwards with letters and editorials continuing to express outrage at the barbarity of the new weapon. There were, however, some exceptions to this. One such exception appears to have been in south and west Wales. Here, I will argue, social and industrial conditions were such that the gas attacks were not regarded as an escalation of warfare in quite the same way that appears to have been the case in the rest of Britain.

The exceptional case of Wales

In some respects this should not be unexpected. As early as September 1914, David Lloyd George, then Chancellor of the Exchequer, had made what amounted to a direct personal appeal to his fellow Welshmen to support the war effort. In a speech that included references to alleged German atrocities (though, he did acknowledge that not all these stories were true), Lloyd George drew on Welsh military icons such as Glendwr and the martial hymn *Men of Harlech*. 'But Wales must continue to do her duty', he declared, adding: 'I should like to see a Welsh Army in the field'. Most tellingly, though, was his remark that:

We [the Welsh] have been living in a sheltered valley for generations. We have been too comfortable, too indulgent, many, perhaps, too selfish.[17]

The southern half of Wales had undergone a transformation during the second part of the nineteenth century with the industrial revolution and much of the area was given over to the coal industry. There had also been a population explosion as workers were brought in to work the mines or labour in industrial plants and ports on the south and west coasts. All of this would prove to be essential for the nation's war effort from 1914 onwards. Work and life in the area was hard with industrial accidents common place. In 1913 a mining accident at the Universal Colliery near Caerphilly resulted in the death of 439 miners (out of 900 underground at the time) in a single explosion. Remarkably, this came only 12 years after another accident at the same colliery when 81 out of a total of 82 miners had been killed. Not only was this sort of tragedy devastating to the small local community, but it represented a greater loss of life than any British battalion would suffer in the dreadful first day of the Somme offensive in July 1916. The comparison is a most useful one given that the strength of a British infantry battalion was roughly the same as the number of men working underground on that day in 1913. Indeed, the Accrington Pals (11 East Lancashire Regiment) are often cited as an example of the huge losses of the British Army on 1 July 1916 with the associated devastation to the community of Accrington. But total casualties amongst the 'pals' that day was 585, which can be further broken down as 351 wounded, 141 missing, and 95 killed.[18] According to Robin Prior and Trevor Wilson, 490 was the average casualty rate of the 29 battalions that attacked on 1 July with the worst affected formation, the Newfoundlanders, suffering 710 casualties of which 272 were killed.[19] Whilst not wishing to trivialise the slaughter of the Somme battle, reality of life in a mining community in South Wales and regional reactions to the war are best understood in this context.

For example, the area around town of Llanelli[20] in west Wales had a number of ports, coal mines (mainly at nearby Pwll[21]) and it also had heavy and light industry. The surrounding countryside was and remains agricultural land. In common with many other towns in the region, Llanelli had a strong non-conformist tradition, both religiously and politically. There was a strong trade unionist presence as befitted an industrial town. But this had brought conflict with the military when in 1911 troops were deployed against strikers during the railway dispute. This had resulted in two strikers being shot dead and others injured when the troops opened fire. There is no real evidence of an anti-military stance resulting from this incident – and a Territorial Force battalion (1/4 Welsh Regiment) was based in the town – but tradition and recent history dictated that Llanelli was not a place where the war would be unequivocally embraced.[22]

The main industry before the war had been tinplate. But this altered after 1914, mainly because of the lost export markets of Germany, Austria and Russia. This, though, freed up industrial plants to focus on war work and soon new furnaces were

Four British soldiers posing with one of the earliest of individual British gas protections: respirator veils existing of mouth pads and goggles, 1915 respirator. (In Flanders Fields Museum, Ypres)

built in the Bynea and Trostre districts to meet the extra demand for steel. Workers could do well in this new environment and in March 1915 moulders, pattern makers and boiler makers successfully negotiated war bonuses that could raise their pay up to 52s per week, many times what a soldier earned.[23] Clearly, commitment to the war effort – the civilian context for morale – came at a price.

But perhaps the most important consequence of local tradition was that its strong religious observance had created an atmosphere of moral engagement and tolerance whereby important matters were openly discussed and dissenters' views respected. This is evident in the 18 February 1915 edition of the local newspaper. An editorial innocuously entitled '*Babes with German Fathers*' drew attention to cases whereby women had become pregnant after being raped by invading German troops in Belgium, including at least one British woman of 18 years of age and as many as 29 Belgian nuns.[24] Whatever the veracity of the story, the point here is that the focus of the article is a moral one because it engages with the idea of abortion and calls upon the church to take a lead in the debate. Abortion, of course, was not legally possible in Britain until 1967 and so this article demonstrates how even such an uncomfortable question of morality was not avoided.

This, in fact, typified local coverage of the war with moral issues given primacy over conventional war news. On the face of it Llanelli had adopted a position of neutrality, which fluctuated between passive (as in the rape story) and active neutrality. A useful example of the latter position was the coverage given to a pacifist meeting. Entitled '*Peace at Any Price*', the article reported in a highly positive manner on a meeting held by the Llanelly Labour

Association. In a curious mix of religious and Marxist rhetoric that reflected the twin non-conformity (religious and political) of the area, the speaker claimed:

> this war would never have happened if the teachings of the international Socialist were accepted,

adding:

> The more powers a nation had to kill and destroy the greater was the proportion of poor children in that nation. […] The greatest nation was that with the largest number of bright and happy children with the opportunity to develop their powers which God had given them.[25]

Beneath the article and given relatively little space on the page is another war-related item 'Llanelly Guardsman. Wounded, but going back'.

But mostly the Llanelli press remained in a passively neutral position. For example, recruitment campaigns were covered, but were hardly given prominent copy, often being relegated to a single sentence at the end of other war-related items and rarely as visible on the page as mundane local stories. Opposite the 'Babes with German fathers' article of 18 February 1915 there appeared a very small item about recruiting at nearby Pontardulais and Burry Port. Not only was this item dwarfed by the 'rape' story, but also by local ones such as the winners of awards at the Pontardulais Eisteddfod (Welsh cultural festival).[26] Most intriguing, though, was another brief article about a recruiting campaign for the Welsh Regiment that grants us a candid insight into local feelings about the war and emphasising how dearly guarded was that neutrality:

> It must be confessed that a certain deficiency of tact, and use of opprobrious remarks by some of the recruits did not tend to stimulate recruiting, as it only embittered those on whom these remarks were cast. Some persons were under the impression that the ancient press gang had been revived. It is to be hoped that the canvassers will bear in mind in future that persuasion should be their keynote.[27]

The war, it seems, remained somewhat distant for Llanelli. One might argue that the commitment of the town to the war effort – its morale – was not what the government would have hoped. There is ample evidence to suggest that this neutral position was not merely an editorial stance but had deep roots in the history and culture of the town. In the 1830s a furore broke out over the use of a Church Court to enforce religious conformity. Similarly, in the 1840s a large-scale 'Druidic-procession' in the nearby village of Pembrey was widely celebrated.[28] Alternative ideas and ways of life thrived in the cultural climate of the area. Certainly, the maintenance of a balanced view – a position of neutrality – was highly valued. It would take something quite remarkable to rout the people of Llanelli from their positions on the moral high ground.

In fact it would take more than the gas attack on 22 April 1915 to shake Llanelli out of this position of apparent neutrality. By the time of the next edition of the newspaper (29 April), the news of the gas attack was a week old. Perhaps this was the reason that the paper did not report it. More likely, though, this factor had combined with the more general lack of enthusiasm for the war. Unlike most other parts of the country, moral indignation did not immediately take hold here. Morale – bolstered elsewhere by a greater commitment to the war on terror – was unaffected. Of course, there were no local units directly involved and this might have influenced the reaction. But as details emerged later on about the wounding or death as a result of the attack of local men serving in formations such as the medical corps or the artillery, this position did not alter. In fact, the death of a local man, Sergeant D. Jones, who had migrated to Canada and had been serving with the Canadian force that withstood the gas attack, was reported in an entirely dispassionate manner. Almost a month after the gas attack, the local press reported bluntly: 'In the last fight he [Jones] was gassed and both feet were shattered'.[29]

Some other Welsh newspapers were less detached. The Welsh language weekly newspaper of the Welsh Calvinistic Methodists, *Y Goleuad*, immediately denounced German actions:

> CRUELTIES [CREULONDERAU]
> Last week there were serious revelations about the uncivilised behaviour of the Germans towards their British prisoners. [...] But now it seems that Germany has lost all humane feeling in this war. They are now, in contradiction to their own commitments and contrary to all international law, using poisonous gases as they wage war. They [the gases] were very effective as they attacked Ypres and it is a lie to say, as the enemy do, that they cause a painless death.[30]

The *Abergavenny Chronicle and Monmouthshire Advertiser* closely reflected the national daily newspaper line in reporting the halting of the German advance in triumphalist tone. British troops, it said, had: 'annihilated the advancing German columns at point-blank range'.[31] One week later the same newspaper added German deviousness to savagery when it declared in a headline: 'CONTINUED USE OF GAS. GERMANS IN BRITISH UNIFORM'.[32] Then one week later it ramped up the indignation further still in an article headed 'POISON GAS AGAIN'. Citing as its main source a correspondent from *The Daily Telegraph* the article relayed an account of the battle:

> Never, however, have men shown such courage as they did then. Around us for a radius of ten yards lay wounded or killed brother officers, and almost next to me the regimental doctor had fallen dead, hit by a shot as he was attending to an officer. Next day we called for volunteers to go into the village of Neuville to bring out the wounded. As we were crossing the open fields under fire we saw a German soldier badly hurt. We waited and picked the man up, and roughly

dressed his wound. The Germans were but a short distance on, and were able to see what we were doing, and as a reward for our pains they started to fire at us. The only man to be killed by this bombardment was the wounded German.[33]

For most of the Welsh press the ethical dilemma did not so easily conform to the simple polarised narrative of a morality tale. *Llais Llafur – Labour Voice* dispassionately reported the widespread call for reprisal attacks in its edition of 8 May 1915.[34] One month later, the same newspaper reported on a meeting of the County of Pembroke Baptists Association in which a plea for restraint was made by Reverend Campbell of Haverfordwest that: 'if England [Britain] was to go down, let her go down because she was true to her pledges [Hague IV], true to her friends, and because she stood for honour among the nations and against barbarous and merciless cruelty even in war'.[35] Nevertheless, the meeting still passed a motion pledging full support to Lord Kitchener's position on the matter.[36]

Despite the restrictions imposed by DORA, local news continued to carry accounts of battle. *The Merthyr Pioneer* was a newspaper closely associated with the local Labour MP, Keir Hardie.[37] A former leader of the Labour Party, a socialist and a pacifist, Hardie had also been openly critical of the deployment of the military at industrial disputes.[38] On 31 July 1915, the paper reported German use of gas under the following eye-catching headline:

Under Gas in the Trenches.
MERTHYR MAN'S FOUR HOURS OF HORROR

Private T. Blasby, of 43 Mount Pleasant, Merthyr Vale, has communicated his experiences under a German gas attack, lasting over four hours. 'I am alive', he says, 'but how I got over it I do not know, for last night, at half past eleven, the Germans made an attack with gas till a quarter to four in the morning. I was overpowered and fell down three times, but with pluck enough to get up again. If ever a man prayed in earnest, I did. I thought I was done, and every one man among us thought the same.

Hell and All the Devils Let Loose!

They sent us such an inferno of high explosive shells that you would have thought that hell and all the devils had been let loose, and were shrieking at us. You never heard such a roar amidst the bursting of shells and with the gas still playing upon us. But they didn't break through our lines, and our losses, thanks to the respirators, were very slight. I expect the Germans lost a few, for we kept up a continuous rifle fire.[39]

There is much that is notable in that account. But interestingly the soldier himself plays down the effect of the gas, whereas the newspaper appears to have emphasised it in its headlining.

The use of poison gas, it seems, quickly assumed symbolic significance; a continuation of the anti-German narrative established at the outset of the war that was focused mainly on ideas about militarism and warlike culture. A letter from an anonymous British officer published in Welsh language newspaper *Y Dinesydd Cymreig*, published in Caernarfon with a circulation mainly in North Wales, claimed: 'Of all the devilish crimes the Germans are guilty of since the start of the war, this [gas] is the most evil by far [...]'.[40] Similar views were expressed in another Welsh language paper *Baner ac Amserau Cymru*, which accused the Germans of 'trampling so evilly the laws and practices of war' in its use of gas on 22 April.[41] The theme was continued in a letter from Private F. M. Hook, 1/4 Gloucestershire Regiment, published in the *Barry Dock News* on 4 June 1915 under the heading:

> FIGHTING GERMAN 'KULTUR'. BARRY SOLDIER'S LURID DESCRIPTION. EARNEST APPEAL TO THE 'SLACKERS'.

Hook's published view showed no restraint:

> Hoist the Germans by their own petards and wipe them out quickly, or by [unreadable] it may be too late. Some time ago a German fell in front of our trench, and kneeling began saying his prayers. Well, we let him finish praying, someone drew a trigger and the Hun went to see if he had drawn a blank, notwithstanding his prayers. We are not fighting heathen now or we should be more severe. What a savage hasn't enough *kultur* to behave like these ravenous wolves, and men are urgently wanted to finish off the [unreadable]. It takes about six months to make one a member of this noble crowd at the front, and it is much better that men should volunteer for service than be 'roped in' as conscripts sooner, or later. How the eligible young men in Barry have the face to be seen in a soldier's presence I can't understand. Dark holes and corners should be reserved for them till they are drawn out by conscription.[42]

The moral imperative as a motivation for recruitment appears to be a constant element in British reporting.

Even in Llanelli the press eventually came off the fence. But it was not the use of gas on the battlefield that brought about its *volte face*. The event that appears to have brought home to Llanelli the nature of total war came soon after. On 13 May the local press reported in very large bold type:

> LOSS OF THE LUSITANIA.
> WHOLESALE MURDER.
> DEATH ROLL OF 1,500.

Two early types of British individual gas protection: the hypo helmet and the black veil respirator.
(In Flanders Fields Museum, Ypres)

The article represented an abandonment of any semblance of neutrality with emotive and at times jingoistic language that would have been startlingly out of place in earlier editions. According to the article, the sinking 'will stain for ever the German, and places the race outside the pale of civilised communities'. The survivors, it was claimed, 'stood firm and sang 'Rule Britannia' [...] They were wonderfully calm and collected'. Significantly, the newspaper proudly pointed out that the singing was 'led by a Welsh male choir who were among the passengers, they sang as the ship went down'.[43]

This was a pivotal moment in the morale of the town. The moral outrage, so obviously absent following the gas attack almost a month earlier, now infiltrated other news reporting. Neutrality was from this moment regarded as treacherous. A pacifist meeting did not attract the positive reporting of earlier editions. Instead, the article detailing the prohibition by the police of the meeting organised again by the Llanelly Labour association was entitled 'Alleged Pro-German'. In a bid to limit the damage to the reputation of the Labour Association its secretary 'moved a vote of condolence with the relatives of the persons drowned with the sinking of the Lusitania'. The motion, which was passed unanimously, was unprecedented. Elsewhere, the people of Llanelli turned on German nationals and other aliens. Protests were organised and riots threatened. At a meeting of the Town Council the sinking of the Lusitania was cited as justification for internment of German nationals. The press reported that:

Alderman Griffith said it gave him the greatest pleasure in the world to support the motion. There were a few of the alien enemy in Llanelly, and the sooner they got rid of them the better. It was a scandalous shame that Germans should be allowed to remain in this country. If he had his way he would hang every German instead of having them interned.[44]

Just one week later a full-page recruitment poster appeared in the local newspaper together with photographs of six local soldiers, their personal details and those of their families. In this way this bold and strikingly graphic appeal was subtly backed up with local references.[45] By early June, recruitment into the Welsh Territorial Force units showed a remarkable increase (it actually doubled at one point) that far outstripped rises in English and Scottish units for the same period.[46]

This heralded a new phase in the reporting of the war. Stories about the commitment to the war effort displaced those of a neutral position. A headmaster and two teachers who refused to co-operate with the National Registration Act might previously have expected local support, but in August 1915 they were castigated as 'unpatriotic teachers'.[47] The old style neutrality – something that had inspired a local pride in earlier editions – was no longer tolerated. The reluctance of the Carmarthenshire Police to guarantee the jobs of any officers who wished to join the armed forces attracted an unfavourable comparison with police forces in other parts of the country. 'Why is it that the Carmarthenshire Committee do not follow suit?', the paper asked. But most important was the increasing commitment to war work such as munitions. West Wales was a major steel producing area and the increased work on behalf of the military received favourable editorial comments.[48]

Old war items were now more newsworthy and the gas attack in April featured prominently amongst those stories revisited. The return to his home in Burry Port of a soldier gassed at Saint Julien whilst serving alongside the Canadians was extensively reported on 3 June 1915. According to Private David Griffiths:

> it was an awful sensation to get gassed. He could scarcely breath, whilst his eyes were burning terribly. He was one of the 300 men rendered unconscious, and 200 of the cases proved fatal.[49]

As 1915 drew on and the impact of the Lusitania sinking faded, so too did the reporting style alter once again. Recruiting campaigns no longer attracted the bold graphic style that followed the sinking. But this might owe more to the increasing sense that conscription was unavoidable, thereby rendering such campaigns obsolete. Gone, though, were the pacifist meetings. Gone, also, was criticism of recruitment with its emotive reference to press gangs. The war occupied an increasingly large proportion of the news. In truth, this partly reflected the broadening of the war itself. But it also represented an increased local involvement in events at Loos or Gallipoli where Welsh units were serving. Whether or not Llanelli had attempted to avoid the war is unclear. What is clear though is that by the middle of 1915 the town had lost its innocence. The process was irreversible and by September the war was the main news item. With its lost innocence came an increased commitment to the war effort – a greater resolve. The edition of 21 October 1915, whilst carrying several accounts of the deaths in action of local men, often accompanied by photographs, also detailed news of promotions. It also contained numerous letters from men at the front such as the following from Private W. John, 9 Welsh Regiment (written to a former work colleague in Llanelli):

> I am in good health, but poor Tom Rees, who used to work furnace with me at the Ashburnham, has been killed. I had a narrow escape too. A shell dropped about a yard from me, and our officer was killed on the spot. He was the third man from me. The 25th September [Battle of Loos] was an awful day. I will never forget it so long as I live. I saw in the paper that the works have started. I should like to be there working too, but somebody must do the fighting out here, and I am doing my little bit. We are now out of the trenches, after being there for five weeks at a stretch. The snipers are very busy here, especially in the night. The Germans do not like cold steel. Give my best respects to all the chaps. Send me a few cigarettes if you can get them.[50]

Conclusion

Gas was a terror weapon. It had the potential to destroy troop morale. But on the battlefield its success was limited. As Rolf-Dieter Müller points out: 'gas brought only tactical victories [and] remained of limited military usefulness'.[51] However, its impact on civilian morale was great. Paradoxically, this was not as originally envisaged and if anything, it had the reverse effect. Rather than undermining morale, the use of gas appeared to confirm the widespread view of German savagery that had been the cornerstone of British government propaganda since August 1914 – and we should recall that gas was not the only terror weapon deployed by the German military in 1915. To most communities in Britain, gas represented an unwelcome escalation of this savagery, but to other ones its impact is less obvious. One such region was in the Welsh mining communities and, in particular, the town of Llanelli where the familiarity of industrialised death combined with a long tradition of non-conformity, tolerance of dissent, respect for alternative viewpoints and moral engagement. There might also have been a slight antipathy to the military as a consequence of the Railway Strike in 1911. Perhaps, then, the civilian deaths of the Lusitania 'atrocity' found a resonance with local people that the military victims of the gas attacks did not. If that was so, then it also served to re-focus attention on the events of April 1915. The gas attack had achieved a limited military victory; it had temporarily undermined the morale of the men at the front. But when viewed in the context of other atrocities, the gas attack actually improved civilian morale by sweeping aside dissenting voices and unifying most of the British people in their commitment to the war effort. That the same effect can be detected in Llanelli – albeit belatedly – with its strong tradition of tolerance and neutrality proves the extent of the moral victory that the Germans handed to the British propagandists.

Pacifism remained a feature of life in Wales. For example, in July 1915 *The Merthyr Pioneer*, reflecting its socialist leaning, carried a prominently displayed advertisement for:

> A SERIES OF PEACE MEETINGS Under the auspices of the Merthyr and District Peace Council [which] will be addressed by THE HON. Bertrand Russell [...][52]

Such meetings were increasingly confined to a few areas, mostly coal producing areas such as Merthyr Tydfil, where trade unionism was strongest. Some trade unions and religious groups declared their opposition to conscription when it was introduced in 1916. At a public meeting in Briton Ferry, a small industrial town and dock situated at the mouth of the River Neath, some 32 kilometres from Merthyr, the local Trades and Labour Council carried a motion declaring against conscription with only four dissentients out of several hundred people present. At the Jerusalem Baptist Chapel, also in Briton Ferry, a vote against conscription was carried at a Sunday evening service.[53] The Jerusalem chapel became a focal point for such opposition and *The Merthyr Pioneer* reported further peace meetings held there throughout 1917 and 1918.[54]

In reality this reflected the growing marginalisation of both the chapel and the newspaper from the general mood of the local population. Despite the best efforts of pacifist groups and non-conformist religious organisations, together with the local newspaper's continued reporting of peace meetings, the people of Merthyr were otherwise persuaded. Fuelled by a growing sense of outrage at German atrocities a wind of change was blowing through the Welsh valleys and at the end of 1915, following the death of Keir Hardie, Merthyr Tydfil elected a new Member of Parliament. The election campaign and its outcome marked a genuine watershed in the attitudes of the majority in the region towards the war. The new MP, Charles Stanton, stood as an Independent Labour Party candidate. He had the backing of the Conservative and Liberal parties and also the anti-socialist British Workers League, an organisation that presented itself as an alternative to the trade unions. Stanton conducted a conspicuously 'patriotic', almost jingoistic, pro-war campaign. The measure of his success and of how far attitudes had moved in Merthyr can only be appreciated fully when we consider that the defeated Labour Party candidate, James Winstone, was himself a trade unionist and former collier. He was also closely associated with Keir Hardie.

There remained one constant, though, in the newspapers in South Wales. Industrial and mining accidents continued to dominate the pages even during the war years. War news, even when there was a local connection, was subordinate to these tragedies that took place within the community. Men were crushed to death in machinery, trapped by collapses in coal mines. They fell into vats of acid, were burned by chemicals or were killed by explosions underground. In June 1915, the death of a steelworker crushed by machinery received more copy than the entire war news.[55] For people on this particular home front the reality was every bit as shocking as that of the Western Front. Although not exactly an everyday occurrence, hideous death by poisonous gas or explosions was a regular part of life in the South Wales valleys. It is not altogether surprising, therefore, that the gas attack in April 1915 did not universally attract the derision and outrage that characterised the media response in other British newspapers. But such news certainly contributed to a gradual erosion of opposition to the war. Exactly one year after the outbreak of war, Welsh language newspaper, *Y Cymro*, established in 1914 and with a circulation throughout Wales, listed the crimes of Prussian militarism [*militariaeth Prwsia*]:

> a) killing and raping French and Belgian women; b) Zeppelin attacks on defenceless English coastal towns; c) warships killing the innocent inhabitants of Scarborough; d) submarines sinking fishing boats and merchant ships, and drowning over a 1000 on the Lusitania; e) using poison gas to kill the British in France; f) shooting British and French soldiers by the hundred after they'd been taken prisoner.[56]

Further evidence from newspapers across Wales suggests that even in areas notable for pacifism and socialism there was by the end of 1915 a marginalisation of dissent. But it is important to note that dissent was never eradicated.

By 1917 new regulations introduced into DORA required pacifist leaflets to be submitted to the censor. Local newspapers were increasingly brought into line with national policy (and news reporting). The unfolding events of 1915 appeared to confirm the general narrative with which Britain had entered the war the previous year. Tales of German barbarity and atrocity reinforced these views. Arguably, the sinking of the Lusitania was the most significant of these but the use of gas also played its part. As dissent gradually evaporated a mood of determination and resolve to continue the war effort – to defeat what was viewed as terror tactics – can be detected in the way that war news was reported in the Welsh press. A clearly presented moral cause, it seemed, led to a strengthening of morale.

APPENDIX 1:
Gas casualties

Year	Admission	Deaths	Admissions per 1,000	Deaths per 1,000	% of total wounded
1915	12,792	307	21.64	0.52	5.79
1916	6,698	1,123	5.01	0.84	1.34
1917	52,452	1,796	26.64	0.91	9.29
1918	113,764	2,673	57.19	1.34	18.22
1915–18	185,708	5,889	31.55	1.00	9.72

Source: *Official History of the War, Medical Services, Casualties and Medical Statistics* (HMSO: London, 1931), p. 111.

Two fatalities of the chemical attack on 22 April 1915, photographed the day after by a German officer. (In Flanders Fields Museum, Ypres – von Kanne collection)

Notes

1 G. F. R. Henderson, *The Science of War* (Longmans, Green and Co.: London, 1919), p. 101. Taken from a collection of Henderson's essays written between 1891 and 1903 and later edited by Colonel Neill Malcolm.

2 For a more rounded discussion of my views on morale, see: G. Oram, *Military Executions during World War One* (Palgrave: Basingstoke, 2003), especially Chapter 2, and G. Oram, 'Pious Perjury: Discipline and Morale in the British Force in Italy 1917–1918', *War in History*, vol. 9, no. 4 (2002), pp. 412–30.

3 Brigadier-General F. P. Crozier, *A Brass Hat in No-Man's Land* (Jonathan Cape: London, 1930).

4 See, for example, L. Smith, *Between Mutiny and Obedience* (Princeton University Press: Princeton, NJ, 1994); J. G. Fuller, *Troop Morale and Popular Culture in the British and Dominion Armies 1914–1918* (Clarendon Press: Oxford, 1990); and G. Sheffield, *Leadership in the Trenches: Officer-Man Relations, Morale and Discipline in the British Army in the Era of the First World War* (Palgrave: Basingstoke, 2000).

5 Telegram of Field Marshal Sir John French sent to War Office on 23 April 1915, National Archives WO142/241.

6 R. Blake (ed.), *The Private Papers of Douglas Haig, 1914–1919* (Eyre and Spottiswoode: London, 1952), p. 91.

7 M. Gilbert, *The First World War* (Weidenfeld and Nicolson: London, 1994), p. 145.

8 W. St. Clair (ed. J. St. Clair), *The Road to St. Julien: The Letters of a Stretcher-Bearer from the Great War* (Leo Cooper: Barnsley, 2004), p. 23.

9 Even the inflated figures of the War Office (for propaganda purposes) reflected the relative ineffectiveness of gas. But the psychological and moral impact cannot be over-estimated. See Appendix 1.

10 B. Shephard, *A War of Nerves: Soldiers and Psychiatrists 1914–1994* (Jonathan Cape: London, 2000), p. 62.

11 Thousands of unarmed Belgian and French civilians were executed or used as human shields by the invading German Army in 1914. Cultural artefacts and buildings were also systematically destroyed. For a complete account of these events see the excellent book by J. Horne and A. Kramer, *German Atrocities 1914: A History of Denial* (Yale University Press: Yale, 2001).

12 R. J. Kentish, *The Maxims of the Late Field-Marshal Viscount Wolesley, KP, GCB, GCMG, and the Addresses on Leadership, esprit de Corps and Moral* (Gale and Polden Ltd: London, 1918), pp. 66–67. This address was given to officers attending the Third Army training course in France on 1 December 1915.

13 H. G. Wells, 'Why Britain Went to War' first published in *The War Illustrated*, 22 August 1914, cited in J. A. Hammerton, *World War*, vol. 1 (Amalgamated Press Ltd: London, 1925), p. 7.

14 *Statistics of the Military Effort of the British Empire During the Great War 1914–1920* (War Office, HMSO: London, 1921), p. 364.

15 Gilbert, *The First World War*, p. 162.

16 *The Times*, 9 April 1915.

17 David Lloyd George, speech at Queen's Hall, 19 September 1914.

18 11 (S) East Lancashire Regiment, Battalion War Diary, National Archives WO95/2366.

19 R. Prior and T. Wilson, *The Somme* (Yale University Press: New Haven and London, 2005), pp. 78–80.

20 The name for the town of Llanelli in west Wales was more commonly spelt as Llanelly' in 1915.

21 The word *pwll* is Welsh for 'pit'.

22 It should also be noted that the 1/4 Welsh Regiment was attached to the 53rd (T/F) Division and served in 'Eastern' theatres rather than on the Western Front. Therefore, gas attacks were less relevant in a local context.

23 *Llanelly and County Guardian*, 25 March 1915. The bonuses were calculated as follows: men on 24s per week – 4s bonus; men on 24–30s per week – 3s bonus; and men on 30–50s per week – 2s bonus. Conceivably, then, a man on top pay could earn over £100 per annum. Admittedly, these were skilled men who were highly valued, but the pay for an infantry soldier was comparatively meagre: 1s per day.

24 *Llanelly and County Guardian*, 18 February 1915.

25 *Llanelly and County Guardian*, 1 April 1915.

26 *Llanelly and County Guardian*, 18 February 1915.

27 *Ibid*.

28 *A Llanelli Chronicle* (Llanelli Borough Council, 1984).

29 *Llanelly and County Guardian*, 20 May 1915.

30 *Y Goleuad*, 7 May 1915, translated from Welsh by Dr Gethin Matthews.

31 *Abergavenny Chronicle and Monmouthshire Advertiser*, 14 May 1915.

32 *Abergavenny Chronicle and Monmouthshire Advertiser*, 21 May 1915.

33 *Abergavenny Chronicle and Monmouthshire Advertiser*, 28 May 1915.

34 *Llais Llafur – Labour Voice*, 8 May 1915.

35 *Llais Llafur – Labour Voice*, 5 June 1915.

36 *Ibid.*

37 In its earlier form it had endorsed Hardie during the 1906 general election. *The Merthyr Borough Labour Pioneer*, January 1906.

38 Oram, *Military Executions*, p. 26.

39 *The Merthyr Pioneer*, 31 July 1915.

40 *Y Dinesydd Gymreig*, 12 May 1915. Translated from Welsh by Dr Gethin Matthews.

41 *Baner ac Amserau Cymru*, 15 May 1915. Translated from Welsh by Dr Gethin Matthews.

42 *Barry Dock News*, 4 June 1915.

43 *Llanelly and County Guardian*, 13 May 1915.

44 *Llanelly and County Guardian*, 20 May 1915.

45 *Llanelly and County Guardian*, 27 May 1915.

46 The strength of the Welsh units of the Territorial Force was relatively small when compared to English and Scottish units. Generally, rises in unit strength were mirrored by similar ones in England and Scotland, but the rise in the first week in June was far greater in relative terms than elsewhere in Britain. See *Statistics of the Military Effort*, p. 366.

47 *Llanelly and County Guardian*, 5 August 1915.

48 *Llanelly and County Guardian*, 3 June 1915.

49 Private David Griffiths, cited in *Llanelly and County Guardian*, 3 June 1915.

50 *Llanelly and County Guardian*, 21 October 1915.

51 R.-D. Müller, 'The Use of Chemical Agents', in R. Chickering and S. Förster (eds), *Great War, Total War: Combat and Mobilization on the Western Front, 1914–1918* (German Historical Institute, Washington DC and Cambridge University Press, Cambridge, 2000), pp. 101–03.

52 *The Merthyr Pioneer*, 8 July 1915.

53 *South Wales Weekly Post*, 22 January 1916, p. 3.

54 Peace meetings and sermons held at the Jerusalem Baptist Chapel, Briton Ferry were reported in the *Merthyr Pioneer* in the editions dated: 18 August 1917, p. 4; 17 November 1917, p. 2; 13 March 1918, p. 4; 30 March 1918, p. 4.

55 *Llanelly and County Guardian*, 3 June 1915.

56 *Y Cymro*, 4 August 1915, p. 3. Translated from Welsh by Dr Gethin Matthews.

GAS WARFARE IN 1915 AND THE GERMAN PRESS

WOLFGANG WIETZKER

The amount of ammunition used had already reached enormous proportions in the first year of the First World War. In spite of this the soldiers survived in their trenches. The ground had been turned into a wilderness, but the trenches effectively prevented any offensive operations. Something new had to be invented to drive the soldiers out of their earthen surroundings in order to break the stalemate and to allow their commanders to restore some action to the war. Poison gas seemed to offer certain success. Of course, the development of poison gas had to be concealed from the enemy as well as from the nation's own population, but once used, it was no longer necessary to keep it secret. Many people had been involved in the development and production of both poison gas and protective gear and other defensive measures that their own troops would need should they themselves become the target of a gas attack. Naturally, as soon as the gas mask became an item of equipment for the soldiers, everybody was well aware that a new means of warfare was about to be introduced. Yet, news of German gas deployment did not reach the German public through official channels. Instead, it had to rely on enemy newspapers and reports for information on this subject. Their foes, as might have been expected, made the most of poison gas propaganda, something the *Oberste Heeresleitung* (OHL) had completely failed to take into account.

These facts raise the question about the amount and nature of the information about gas warfare available to German newspaper readers during the war. One cannot trace what they actually knew, as this would have depended on their willingness to interpret available information.

Press, censorship and propaganda: a general introduction

The German press had enjoyed a certain degree of freedom thanks to a law of 1874. This changed when war became imminent. Journalists could longer publish special military issues after hostilities had broken out; the press had to accept certain restrictions. From then on only army press releases, issued by the *Große Hauptquartier* and later by the OHL could be printed. The newspapers were not allowed to make any changes to the press releases or to comment on them.

Newspapers could also take over Allied reports. At first glance this may have seemed bizarre, but it made sense: newspapers from neutral countries, which carried reports from all fronts, could be purchased in Germany. They contained war news. Branch

Officers and men of German Infanterie-Regiment 27 wearing their "Riechpäckchen", early versions of gas masks, 1915. (Imperial War Museum, London)

III B of the OHL, responsible for German as well as enemy reports, justified the takeover by declaring that they had nothing to hide. Whenever foreign reports differed from German ones, people were supposed to consider the German reports to be truly reliable. Usually, the OHL did not comment on Allied reports.

Nevertheless, the German press was also forbidden to change official foreign press releases, and negative comments concerning Germany were not to be suppressed. However, the newspapers were asked to call for additional support from OHL should any misunderstandings arise. The official Allied reports were published up to four times a day. It was left to the German editors to decide which ones they would publish. It was therefore possible to compare German and Allied information. As far as non-official foreign reports were concerned, the latter could be re-printed as long as they shed a positive light on Germany. Negative reports were subject to censorship. Naturally, few foreign reports showed goodwill towards Germany, and therefore only few passed censorship.

Censorship and propaganda were the essential instruments for influencing the public. All military news in the German press had to pass the censor. The OHL decided which news fell into a military category. From 1915 on political news became increasingly viewed as military news. As such it also became subject to restrictions. The institutions responsible for censorship were not allowed to change information edited by the OHL. Due to the enormous number of newspapers, censorship was carried out by the Deputy General Commands. In case of violation, the newspapers were threatened with different sorts of consequences, including a prohibition to publish.

Supposedly a photograph of a gas cloud on the Flanders' front.
(In Flanders Fields Museum, Ypres)

This was by no means an empty threat and the penalty was enforced in some cases. In 1915, the newspaper *Vorwärts* of the social democratic party was punished for its essentially pacifistic attitude. An article entitled 'Prevention of the Chemical War', informing its readers about a conference at Rouen attended by members of the French and Belgian government, resulted in a temporary publishing ban.

Censorship took on different forms. Newspaper editors therefore called for an overarching censorship institution, which was established in 1915. Its purpose was to provide practical and coherent press control by supervising the censorship institutions. The OHL retained exclusive control as it determined censorship and managed the overarching censorship institution. OHL could impose certain topics on the press or prevent other ones from being discussed, as was the case with gas warfare.

While censorship was a passive way of gagging the press, journalism could also be actively used for propaganda. Propaganda placed the war in a brighter light, spread patriotic optimism or strengthened determination when enthusiasm was dwindling fast. Propaganda and censorship complement each other. Censorship was usually decentralised; propaganda should be the preserve of a single institution. In Germany, however, there was no institutional propaganda. In 1917, General Ludendorff, Chief of Staff (COS) of the OHL, confessed that the country had underestimated the influence of propaganda. The German military command was convinced it was capable of winning the war by military means alone. It turned out to be a fatal error. Even III B's strong recommendation to institute propaganda was not followed up. Whenever OHL got a proper chance to turn the propaganda war against the allies, it failed. It simply did not take place. Internal propaganda resulted in misleading war reports, which in 1918 caused widespread surprise that the war had been lost.

In Great Britain the exact opposite happened. From the outset it institutionalised propaganda and disseminated it in a highly professional manner. By the end of the war the Allies spread their propaganda not only along the front lines, but also throughout the whole of Germany. This contributed significantly to destabilising the morale of German soldiers.

Gas reporting in German newspapers before 22 April 1915

Newspaper articles on the gas discharge can be grouped in three phases: the period before the first major German attack, 22 April and the Second Battle of Ypres, and the reports through the end of 1915.

An official army press release mentioned gas for the first time on 1 March 1915. German gas attacks had taken place in Russia without becoming common knowledge. Instead, the OHL informed the public that French troops had again used gas against German forces. The notice was concealed in the army press release without emphasising that gas deployment meant the introduction of a new mode of warfare. Rather it suggested that the French action had been recurrent, but not worth mentioning before. The French tear gas had been wholly ineffective. Germany did not accuse the French side of chemical warfare. The only explanation for Germany's silence was that it was about to deliver gas much more effectively. To the German public the escalation would appear as a measure to counteract illegal French operations.

We can be certain that any mention of poison gas in the army's press releases was deliberate. Between 9 and 22 April the OHL mentioned poison gas in nine additional reports. The sequence indicated that the day for a German gas attack was imminent. A press release on 12 April reported a Russian gas operation for the first time and one on 17 April mentioned a British chemical attack. Poison gas was not available to the Russian Army or the British Expeditionary Force (BEF) at the time. Up to 21 April official German press releases referred several times to incidents involving enemy gas, whereas Allied accounts taken over by the German press never mentioned them. On 22 April the OHL gave its opinion on the own gas deployment for the first time in response to an accusation by Field Marshall Sir John French. The OHL stated that German troops were not using grenades with the sole purpose of dispersing suffocating or poisonous gases. German grenades were said to be less dangerous than those of the French, Russians or British. The smoke was supposedly perceptible even in the darkness of night, thus allowing everyone to retreat.

German troops waited for proper wind conditions and seized their chance in the evening of 22 April. One might have expected the OHL to report on the gas use by its own forces, but instead it presented military success as the result of the braveness and the competence of German leadership. After 22 April, gas was not mentioned again except for two instances in April and June 1915. The first article appeared in the *Frankfurter Zeitung* on 25 April and admitted to possible release of gas. Even though it claimed retaliatory action against the Allies, it also boasted greater effectiveness of its own gas. While not an official OHL statement, it had definitely authorised the piece.

Foreign newspapers took up gas warfare and blamed Germany for its initial deployment. The Allies retained the propaganda advantage. In Germany, the publication of Allied reports peaked in the first days of May.

Whereas a German reader would come across official Allied press releases each day, only few non-official war reports passed the German censor. Furthermore, reprints of non-official articles would have been abbreviated and supplemented with German statements. Only these reports informed the German readership about German gas warfare. The following articles, dated from 25 April to 8 May were taken over by the *Frankfurter Zeitung* and *Vorwärts*.

Haag, 25 April. According to a Reuter news report, Marshal French announced that the French, who were threatened by the asphyxiating gases of the German smoke bombs, have retreated towards the Yser Canal in the vicinity of Boesinghe, 2½ kilometres from Steenstraete and 5 kilometres from Ypres. Only the left flank of the British front has been dented. Battle continues to the north of Ypres.

Furthermore, according to the evening dispatches of the Daily News from Dunkirk: [...] That is why it was such a great surprise, when after heavy gunfire a number of bomb throwers jumped out of the trenches and threw smoke bombs in spite of heavy firing. Their gases filled the English trenches. The available smoke hoods and nose shields, that had already been used against the German smoke bombs on the Meuse, arrived too late to be of any use. If

German photograph of British casualties in a trench near Frezenberg, May 1915.
(In Flanders Fields Museum, Ypres)

you didn't want to choke you had to get out of the trenches. The English and French, whose contact was interrupted, incurred heavy losses [...][1]

The Battle for Hill 60

WTB London, 26 April. As opposed to the statement of General Field Marshal French, who claimed that the English did not use any bombs with asphyxiating gases during the battle for Hill 60, an eye witness in the British headquarters reports the following about the last phase of the battle:

On Wednesday afternoon only a few German bomb throwers remained on the hill, where they were they stood firm on its north-eastern edge. A hail of rapidly exploding shells, filled with asphyxiating gases, rained down on the defenders from three directions. The German fire mowed down entire sections of the British infantry, filling the trenches with bodies, and often making it difficult to reach enemy lines. Reinforcement troops had to climb over the bodies of their fallen comrades.

Obviously our losses were severe, but the battle for the hill cost the Germans far more than it did us.

A panel displaying German rocket color signal codes: two red flares = enemy attack, two green flares: own artilley too short, a red and a green flare = enemy gas attack.
(In Flanders Fields Museum, Ypres)

The following articles were printed consecutively in the *Frankfurter Zeitung*. As they were non-official reports some comments had been added to them. It is interesting to note that barely a few days after the first gas release the editors gave their own opinion about gas in a way that seemed to imply that gas warfare had always been a part of military ritual.

Marshal French on the Defeat of the Allies

London, 26 April. (Priv.-Tel. Indirect. Ctr. Frkft.) Reuter reports: Field Marshal French reports that heavy fighting continues, while the general situation has remained unchanged. 'Our left flank, which had to reassemble in order to join the changed positions created by the forced retreat of the French had to take up position against the enemy in the north, and spread out in the west down to below St. Julien. This extension weakened our line and St. Julien was taken by the enemy after the Canadians had opposed very valiant resistance against their superior strength. The German attacks launched yesterday to the east of Ypres were unsuccessful in spite of the asphyxiating gases used. German officers and troops were taken prisoner. During the past three days we inflicted heavy losses on the Germans but our losses are heavy too. The wireless German report claiming that four English cannons had been seized by the Germans is not true. *(Maybe the catch is in the word 'English' cannons? Editor's note.)* This afternoon one of our pilots dropped bombs on the railway station of Combres destroying the railway line.

Mr. Repington's Opinion

Reuter further states the report of the military correspondent of 'The Times'. It states: 'The strike against the left flank of French's Army yesterday evening to the north of Ypres cannot have come unexpectedly. What was unexpected, however, was the German use of asphyxiating gases, produced by means of a special installation in the German trenches and driven by a north-westerly wind towards the French lines. The use of projectiles with the sole purpose of dispersing asphyxiating or deadly gases is prohibited by the International Treaty of 29 July 1899 and Germany signed that treaty. The German justification for the use of these gases is based on the words 'sole purpose'. It is claimed that the German projectiles were solely intended to cause asphyxiation. With specific regard to the attack to the north of Ypres, it is not as yet certain that such projectiles were used, however, we are quite certain that asphyxiation was the sole purpose, that the Germans did not observe the spirit of the treaty and that they have added one more crime to their long list of abominable deeds.' *(Maybe Mr. Repington could also share his opinion on the bombs and stinkpots that the French and English have been dropping from planes and have been using as weapons in other ways for a long time. Moreover, it would appear that there has been a gradual realisation of the representation that should be used to pillory the use of asphyxiating gases by the Germans in a most horrific manner. In his first reports French claimed that the German attack had been preceded by heavy gunfire, for which the Germans had used this type of equipment, and the French bulletin only made mention of German bombs. Now, they are retrospectively trying to twist things by claiming that clouds of smoke were literally projected from the German trenches. War as such is terrible enough; we should be wary of defiling it even further with lies and calumniations about the objective of the battle. Editor's Note.)*[2]

In Germany not a single commentary, not a single letter to the editor on poison gas was ever published. The reader was informed about the German gas discharge only through Allied reports as reprinted in German newspapers. In the aftermath of every important battle the OHL edited official summaries. There was no mention of poison gas in the account of the Second Battle of Ypres, dated 8 May. However, in line with general policy on non-official foreign reports, the numerous comments and letters to the editors in the British press, especially after 22 April, also did not appear in the German press.

The newspapers nevertheless developed their own style, as can be demonstrated by focussing on gas reporting in four German dailies, selected out of roughly 4,000 newspapers. The *Kriegszeitung der 4. Armee* was a front newspaper. It has been included here, because the soldiers of the Fourth Army were involved in the events of 22 April. The *Neuss-Grevenbroicher Zeitung* (NGZ), a small regional newspaper, was issued at Neuss, near Düsseldorf. The *Vorwärts* newspaper of the social democratic party was printed in Berlin. The nationwide *Frankfurter Zeitung* was known to be left-liberal. It was issued three times a day, four times on Sundays and twice on Mondays. The other newspapers were published once per day, and the *Kriegszeitung der 4. Armee* twice a week.

The *Frankfurter Zeitung* took over the OHL statements on a daily basis. In general, each report was published on the day of issue. Statements printed in the evening edition were repeated in the first edition of the next day. As a rule, the Allied reports reprinted in the *Frankfurter Zeitung* never made front page news and were usually printed with some delay. This made direct comparison virtually impossible.

In the *Kriegszeitung der 4. Armee* the soldiers read for the first time about gas a year after its first use. The soldiers of the Fourth Army, who had taken part in the actual battle, thus received the poorest information on the topic. As noted before, the military success of 22 April was reportedly due only to the bravery of the soldiers and the competence of their superiors. Enemy reports were not reprinted.

The *NGZ* took over the OHL reports erratically, Allied reports were never printed. So *NGZ* readers on the whole were poorly informed about gas warfare.

In 1915 *Vorwärts* generally printed OHL reports on the front page, perhaps in order to indicate their willingness to stick to the so-called *Burgfrieden*. *Vorwärts* also took over the official Allied reports on the front page without any delay. In 1915 *Vorwärts* readers therefore had the best opportunity to compare German and Allied reports of the same day regarding the same event. The number of reports mentioning poison in *Vorwärts* articles equalled that in the *Frankfurter Zeitung*. Bearing in mind that the *Frankfurter Zeitung* was published up to four times a day, *Vorwärts* readers were still better informed about gas warfare.

The newspapers found ways of giving their reports a distinctive character without

German soldiers waiting to undergo gas training.
(Militärhistorisches Museum der Bundeswehr, Dresden)

circumventing the official rules. Such divergences certainly did not come about by chance, but were the result of deliberate editorial policies. The *Kriegszeitung* set out to strengthen the soldiers' morale. The *NGZ* took care of regional items, whereas *Vorwärts* was reluctant to support German policy: it seized every opportunity to present its own and Allied information in a comparative manner. The *Frankfurter Zeitung*, in contrast, was more supportive of the German government. Reporting methods changed during the war, but this is an altogether different topic.

The following foreign non-official articles passed the censor and could therefore be reprinted. They illustrate how the Allies reported German gas deployment.

The Poisonous Gases

London, 27 April. (W.T.B. Unofficial.) The 'Daily Chronicle' reports the following details from Northern France about the use of poisonous gases by the Germans: On 22 April at five o'clock in the afternoon French soldiers in the front trenches between Langemarck and Knocke noticed how thick yellow smoke was rising from the German trenches and was gradually advancing towards the French positions. The north-easterly wind allowed the smoke to spread over the soil like a carpet, which it covered up to a height of 16 feet. The Germans used large cylinders of compressed gas, which were fitted with valves.

These valves were opened as soon as the wind blew towards the enemy trenches. The French were surprised by the use of gases. Many were poisoned and died; some managed to escape but shortly later their faces turned black, coughed up blood and collapsed. At the front the effects of the gas were noticeable over a width of six kilometres and a depth of two kilometres. Fifteen minutes later the Germans advanced from their trenches. At the front the soldiers wore safety helmets to make sure they could breathe the air. As the gas was no longer being dispersed hordes of Germans advanced.[3]

General French's report

London, 27.April. (W.T.B.) Report of Reuters Bureau. General French reports: Heavy fighting continues, the general situation remains unchanged. As the front line had changed because of the retreat of the French, our left flank had to resist attacks from the north, while simultaneously spreading out in a westerly direction past St. Julien. This weakened the line. After having bravely resisted their superior strength St. Julien was captured by the enemy. The German attacks to the east of Ypres failed yesterday in spite of the use of asphyxiating gases. German officers and troops were taken prisoner. In the last three days we inflicted severe losses on the Germans. Our losses are heavy too. The German report that four heavy English guns were captured is incorrect [...].[4]

Protection against the gases

London, 8 May. (W.T.B. Unofficial.) In the House of Commons, the Deputy State Secretary Tennant answering a question: When the Germans first used

A German medical officer is administering oxygen to a gas casualty at a German *Sanitätsunterstand*, 1916–17. (Militärhistorisches Museum der Bundeswehr, Dresden)

poisonous gases, the War Ministry supplied one million respirators, which did not prove to be fully effective. Therefore they were replaced with a different model, consisting of cotton waste drenched in sodium carbonate and sodium hydrosulphite held in place by a veil. We are investigating whether woollen helmets would not be a better option.[5]

The following comparison demonstrates how the same foreign report could differ when reprinted in two German newspapers.

FZ[6]

A report by French

† *London, 6 May. (Priv.-Tel. Indir. Ctr. Fkft.) A report of Marshal French states: The general situation remains unchanged. In the morning the Germans took hold of Hill 60 to the south of Ypres by using large amounts of asphyxiating gases under favourable weather conditions. The battle, which is still raging, was preceded by a minor attack to the east of Ypres, in which large amounts of asphyxiating gases were used. This attack was easily countered by our artillery that inflicted heavy losses on the enemy. In the region of Givenchy the Germans exploded mines and also used asphyxiating gases. Four men were poisoned. Apart from this the German attacks on this side proved entirely unsuccessful. (!)*

Vorwärts[7]

French's report

London, 6 May. (W.T.B.) Field Marshal French reports: The general situation remains unchanged.

A battle is still raging near Hill 60, which the enemy has taken hold of with the help of poisonous gases. A minor attack to the east of Ypres, in which poisonous gases were used, was easily countered. Our artillery inflicted heavy losses on the enemy.

The Germans exploded a mine near Givenchy; four men were poisoned by the gas.

These articles were reprinted in the same or at least in a similar style in many German newspapers. Other articles printed in the British press did not pass censorship.

The presentation of German newspapers shall be completed with two additional excerpts from newspapers published all over Germany. The satiric journal *Simplicissimus* made two contributions and mocked Great Britain:

Ypres

I

The Success of the English Strategy

In a portrayal of the events near Ypres, in which he demonstrates surprising military insight, the famous English author Sir Algernon Puzzle reaches the following sensational conclusion:

'Even though the actions of the Germans completely baffled our High Command, the genial perspicacity of the subsequent realisation that the German attack had been carefully planned for weeks fully demonstrates the superiority of the English strategy.'

II

The Evil Vapours

Puzzle refers to the performances of the Allies in bitter words:

While our valiant troops were selflessly engaged in trying to determine the composition of the poisonous vapours used by the Germans and were lamenting their use with indignation, the French regrettably showed a lack of fighting spirit.– With regard to the vapours it would appear that they merely had an anaesthetising effect; however, the fact that instead of dispersing a mist of Eau-de-Cologne they spread gas smells, can indeed be considered as flagrant evidence of an intentional breach of international law. In any case the obviously pro-German view that these vapours were caused by cheap charitable gift cigars, is hardly credible as our soldiers, who receive much cheaper charitable gifts, should have made many more Germans unfit for battle than the other way round.

Emanuel[8]

The journal *Jugend* was especially intended for young German soldiers. Like the *Kriegszeitung der 4. Armee*, *Jugend* did not bring poison gas to the public's attention. Yet the cartoons published in Numbers 19 and 26 in 1915 indicate that the journalists knew about gas warfare, but that they had not received permission to broadcast that knowledge.

Jugend, 1915, Nr. 19, 1.5.1915

The inscription reads:

The dreadful vapours in Flanders
'Gosh, Michael is smoking the cheap stuff again!'

Jugend, 1915, Nr. 26, 19.6.1915

The inscription reads:

Parisian Comfort
'Come what may – our trusted cultural fragrance withstands even the most pungent chlorine gases of the German barbarians!'

Great Britain was the main target for *Jugend* and the traditional journals. Most of the cartoons were aimed at John Bull.

Jugend, 1915, Nr. 23, 28.5.1915

The inscription reads:

John Bull
'General conscription? ? Nonsense! There will always be fools willing to risk their neck for me and scoundrels, who can be bribed!'

When the British discharged gas at Loos in September 1915, the OHL failed to lead in informing the public. That was left to a correspondent reporting directly from the theatre of war. Such correspondents were embedded with headquarters and seconded to active officers. The army commands released the articles.

Generally speaking, German readers did not receive the opportunity to discuss either gas warfare or deployment. Gas warfare must have appeared as common procedure to them. At the same time the accounts remained mute on casualties.

Gas warfare in *The Times*

The German reader had no idea of the extent to which British newspapers reported on gas. In early May 1915 the British press claimed Germany was poisoning wells. Yet, the South African *Cape Times* had already accused the German forces in German Southwest Africa of such crimes since February 1915. My research has led me to conclude that the German troops in southern Africa did indeed poison wells to delay the South African forces.[9]

British propaganda seized on the accusation reached at the right time. Onwards this topic became an important propagandistic tool. *The Times* headline (6 May 1915) read:

POISONED WELLS
GERMAN WARFARE IN AFRICA
REPRISALS THREATENED

British propaganda could now link the poisoning of wells to gas deployment. A nation contaminating water holes is capable of using gas too, for, so it was argued, a country prepared to violate one article of The Hague Convention would not hesitate to violate another one. Gas warfare became a major topic in *The Times*. An inventory of poison gas articles for May 1915 indicates the density of coverage in British newspapers.

Date	Headline	Page
105	The Poison Gas. After Effects of the Fumes: Victims in Hospital	7
	The Canadians At Ypres. How They Saved the Situation. The Poisonous Gases	7
	Effect of the Gases	7
	Complete Diary of the War	17
305	Saving the Line at Ypres. A Match for German Chemicals	7
405	Poisonous Gases used at Hill 60	8
505	Soldier's Story of Ypres. Retirement of the French	9
	The Next Phase at Ypres. Preparing for Battle	10
	War by Poisoned Gases	10
	The Budget and the War. Asphyxiants in War	14
605	The Ultimate Victory	7
	Poisoned Wells. German Warfare in Africa	7
	Fighting with Poison Gas	8
	'Kultur' and Poison	9
	Sufferings of the Victims	10
	Effect of Poison Gas	10
	A Victim of Gases	10
	The Disregard of Conventions	12
705	What Gas Means. A Visit to A French Hospital. Incredible Tortures	9
	'Kultur' and Poison	9
	Parliament. Respirators	10
805	'The Most Damnable Invention'	5
	Christianity and Poison	5
1005	The New Phase. 'Incredible Spirit of Savagery'	6
	Kultur and Poison	6
	German Batteries of Poison Gas	7
	German Poison-Shells	7
1105	Poison Gas. Why Retaliation is Necessary	5
	To Fight German Gases	5
1205	The Poisoners. Reprisals Demanded by the Army	7
	Gas and Retaliation	12
1305	Fact and Fiction	7
1405	100.000 Respirators Wanted. Miss Haldane's Appeal for Belgian Soldiers	5

Date	Headline	Page
	The Passage of the Poison Cloud	6
	Formidable Defences	8
	German Losses, 30,000	8
1505	British Troops and Poison Gas	8
1705	Gas Attacks Foiled	7
	A Hopeless Assault	7
1905	Poison in the Air	5
	War Secretary's Statement	9
	Shells and Men. Allies to Use Gases	9
	Tribute to Canadians	9
2105	A French Bomb Factory. Chemistry As An Ally	6
2205	Neutrals and Gas	6
2405	Poisonous Gas on Eastern Front	5
2505	Germans Again Use Poison Gas	6
	Mobilize the Nation. The Only Way. Soldier's Question	7
2605	Poison Cloud 40 Feet High	8
2705	William the Poisoner	11
2805	Poison Gas Torments. Victims of Uncivilized Warfare	7
2905	The March to Windhuk. Polluted Wells and Mined Roads	5
3105	The Gas Poisoners. How the Attack Was Planned	5

The Times, headlines in May 1915

Many opinions were published. They accused Germany of having overstepped the mark and regressed to barbarism. It was pointed out that it would take a long time to re-educate Germany. Germany was regarded as the living example of the mutual exclusion of 'Kultur and poison'. The very nation that had always professed to value culture above all now stood accused of dwelling in a state of primitivism. Kaiser Wilhelm was renamed 'William the Poisoner' and there were calls for retaliation. At the very least Germany was accused of discharging poison gas and of poisoning wells, but ironically, in the articles the Allies also blamed themselves for not having implemented poison gas in time.

The German government and OHL, however, had misread the situation completely. Instead of ending the war, gas warfare resulted in more money and mobilisation propaganda for the BEF (see illustrations on the next page). Solidarity grew. Moreover, British propaganda enabled the United States to overcome resistance to joining the Entente.

Insufficient German propaganda

In Germany gas reporting did not change until the end of 1915: national reports did not mention gas and official foreign reports were reprinted. An exception was the publication of a rather remarkable press release by the OHL, dated 25 June 1915. Its length – almost 400 lines – and contents were unusual. Only the *Frankfurter Zeitung* reproduced it entirely, while the *Militärwochenblatt* split it into two parts. Certain sections were printed in a smaller font, making it barely readable for the average reader.

In it the OHL expressed its opinion on gas warfare for the second time. The article opened with a verbatim repetition of the statement on 22 April. It continued by blaming the French military command for having used gas since February 1915. The article then turned to the Lusitania affair. The ship was said to have carried a cargo that, according to US newspapers, consisted of 250,000 pounds of tin tetrachloride, a basic ingredient for deafening bombs. The statement claimed that the smoke produced by this material had spread throughout the ship causing passengers to collapse. It recounted the standpoint of the United States on chemical weapons at the 1899 Hague Peace Conference. The US representative had argued the humaneness of these weapons humane and consequently refused to sign The Hague Declaration (IV,2). The OHL pointed out that poisonous gas as used by Germany did not violate The Hague Declaration, because it only forced the enemy to abandon their trenches. Different methods of waging war justified resorting to new means. The French and British would most certainly have used similar arguments had they been able to forestall the Germans. The piece further quoted an advertisement in the *Cleveland Automatic Machine Company*.

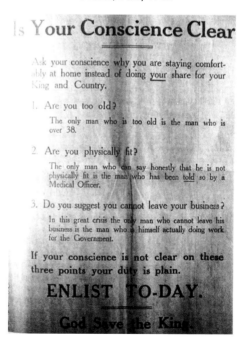

LEFT: From *The Times*, 30 April 1915.

BELOW: From *The Times*, 5 May 1915.

Because of its length, the article was not a propagandistic highlight. For many years it was the last attempt by the OHL to counter Allied propaganda. While the OHL mentioned the advertisement of the Cleveland Company, it missed the opportunity to exploit it and left this to the *Frankfurter Zeitung*. The next day, 26 June, it reproduced the advertisement of *Cleveland Automatic Machine Company* on its front page. It had been published in the *American Machinist* on 6 May 1915.

FZ, 26. Juni 1915, 3. Morgenblatt

Worth Knowing

On the opposite page we show two slices of high explosive shells which can be produced from the bar on our 4½" PEDESTAL BASE MACHINE (see cut on opposite page).

On this machine we can finish a complete 13-lb. shell, in 24 minutes if it is made from very tough material from which shells are made, and in 17 minutes if it is made from ordinary machine steel.

The 18-lb. shell in 30 minutes, or from regular machine steel in 22 minutes.

When you figure about $1.00 per day for operating this machine, you can then arrive at the actual labour cost for producing the piece.

We are going to tell you something else which might be of interest to you. The following is a description of the 13 and the 18-lb. high explosive shells which are now being used so extensively in the war to replace common shrapnel.

The material is high in tonalle strength [sic] and VERY SPECIAL and has a tendency to fracture into small pieces upon the explosion of the shell. The timing of the fuse for this shell is similar to the shrapnel shell, but it differs in that two explosive acids are used to explode the shell in the large cavity. The combination of these two acids causes a terrific explosion, having more power than anything of its kind yet used. Fragments become coated with these acids in exploding and wounds caused by them mean death in terrible agony within four hours if not attended to immediately.

From what we are able to learn of conditions in the trenches, it is not possible to get medical assistance to anyone in time to prevent fatal results. It is necessary to immediately cauterise any body or head wound, or to amputate the affected limbs, as there seems to be no antidote that will counteract the poison.

This clearly shows that this shell is more effective than the regular shrapnel, since the wounds caused by shrapnel balls and fragments in the muscles are not as dangerous because they do not have a poisonous element making prompt attention necessary.

CLEVELAND AUTOMATIC MACHINE COMPANY
Cleveland, Ohio, U.S.A.

A propaganda staff would have taken advantage of this advertisement. The authors of the OHL press release of the previous day were clearly cognisant of the advertisement's contents, but failed to draw the German public's attention to it. Indignation in the USA can be deduced from reactions by the Machine Company and the US government. The company declared that the advertisement had been misinterpreted. The US government accused the company of unpatriotic behaviour.

Perhaps the lack of an official reaction on the German side is linked to the Lusitania affair and submarine warfare. Or possibly, the OHL did not want to annoy the US government any further. Yet the real reason seems simpler: no official reaction came because of the lack of a propaganda institution.

Influence by other means

The German public could be reached by other means as well. These included letters to and from the military forces. Nearly 30 billion cards, letters and parcels were delivered to the trenches and vice versa. On their postcards the soldiers described matters of no importance. The letters from the front were subject to censorship and regulations. Topics of military interest could not be disclosed. Military activities were seldom mentioned. Letters of privates and NCOs were unsealed, so superiors were able to read their contents. After a great deal of protest this regulation was changed. At home only a limited number of persons got hold of the letters. Even if there had been a breach, whatever written would have caused little damage.

In the first six months of the war no letters could be published in newspapers. Later they became very popular and letters from the front were printed in almost every issue. The intention was to provide genuine information. Since these letters had to pass the censor, reduced authenticity had to be accepted.

Belletrist contemporary literature discovered the First World War in due course. In Germany, many books on the subject of warfare were published during the war, but gas was hardly mentioned. Was it impossible to create heroes in gas warfare? Instead, heroic deeds were attributed to pilots, U-boat commanders or soldiers on foreign battlefields.

Exhibitions also served to make the war more accessible to the public. The first of these opened in 1915, when everybody wanted to be informed about what was happening in the theatre of war. Due to their success, five of them toured the towns of Germany presenting the same items. Especially captured weapons, ammunition and items of equipment were displayed, but nothing relating to gas warfare.

Conclusion

The German public knew little about gas warfare. What information the reader got was derived mainly from reprinted enemy reports and some accounts by war correspondents. The legality of gas warfare was never discussed. The OHL could censor any article. Persons of influence – members of parliament or preachers – were unwilling to shoulder the responsibility and instead relied on military leadership. In England, German gas deployment created considerable outrage. British propaganda seized the opportunity to accuse Germany of barbarism and of having violated international laws of warfare. German gas deployment therefore proved to have been a fatal mistake. It might have been prevented not by the public or the press, but by men of science and those who held important military positions. The German public certainly had limited access to information concerning gas warfare, but never got the opportunity to engage in an open debate on the issue.

Notes

1 *Neuss-Grevenbroicher Zeitung*, 27 April 1915.

2 *Frankfurter Zeitung*, 27. April 1915, Abendblatt, p. 2.

3 *Frankfurter Zeitung*, 28 April 1915, 2. Morgenblatt, p. 2.

4 *Vorwärts*, 28 April 1915.

5 *Frankfurter Zeitung*, 9 May 1915, 2. Morgenblatt, p. 3.

6 *Frankfurter Zeitung*, 7 May 1915, 2. Morgenblatt, p. 2.

7 *Vorwärts*, 7 May 1915.

8 *Simplicissimus*, 20. Jahrgang, Nr. 6, München, 11 May 1915

9 W. Wietzker, *Giftgas im Ersten Weltkrieg. Was konnte die deutsche Öffentlichkeit wissen?*, Inaugural-Dissertation zur Erlangung des akademischen Grades eines Doktors der Philosophie (Dr. phil.) durch die Philosophische Fakultät der Heinrich-Heine-Universität Düsseldorf, Düsseldorf, 2006, pp. 125–34, available from URL <http://docserv.uni-duesseldorf.de/servlets/DerivateServlet/Derivate-3462/1462.pdf>.

CIVIL RESISTANCE TO CHEMICAL WARFARE IN THE FIRST WORLD WAR

PETER VAN DEN DUNGEN

It is difficult to speak of 'civil resistance' to chemical warfare during the First World War. The notion of 'civil resistance' suggests some kind of deliberate, purposeful, organised activity on the part of a group of citizens with the aim of bringing about a change in actual or intended government policy. Whereas it is possible to identify several issues around which 'civil resistance' became mobilised in various countries during the war, this does not seem to have been the case with chemical warfare. Among the several thousand entries in Eric Croddy's annotated bibliography on chemical and biological warfare there is not a single reference to 'civil resistance', nor is this expression to be found in the subject index.[1] In the UK, for instance, resistance to conscription arose when introduced. The No-Conscription Fellowship with Fenner Brockway emerged as an organisation working for the right of conscientious objectors to resist enlistment and to assist them. In a similar vein, a small number of Christians believed that their faith did not allow them to kill fellow Christians, which resulted in the formation of the Fellowship of Reconciliation (FOR) – another instance of civilians resisting the power of the state over the individual. This organisation also included men beyond the age of conscription. As such it became an instance of civilians who proclaimed their fellowship with citizens abroad, including those in enemy countries.[2] Yet another organisation was the Union of Democratic Control (UDC), which blamed the war on the secret machinations of cabinets and aristocratic and military elites. It agitated for the democratisation of foreign policy in the belief that a transparent one under control by a majority of citizens would far less likely lead to war.

A few instances of civilian and military 'resistance'

It is of course true that there was *individual* resistance, both civilian and military, to chemical warfare. In fact, it hit Fritz Haber directly when fighting in the Ypres Salient was still raging. His wife, Dr Clara Immerwahr, took her life – in all likelihood, an act of anguished protest – when he was about to return to the front to direct operations, this time in Galicia. Earlier in her life, she had had to struggle hard to become a scientist herself. The culmination of this was the award in 1900 of her doctoral degree in chemistry by the University of Breslau, whose first female academic doctor she became. Immerwahr witnessed several experiments, involving her husband, including the testing of gases on animals. In her view, such activities constituted a perversion of the science she loved. Haber, in contrast, accused her of failing to support Germany in its hour of need. Before shooting herself through the heart with her husband's army pistol on 2 May 1915, she had spent some hours writing letters justifying her dramatic act to friends. Yet, when the local newspaper published an obituary, it merely stated: 'The reasons for the act of the unfortunate woman are unknown.' Her letters were apparently destroyed at the time. It appears, furthermore, that her husband, family, and society at large undertook everything to cover up the drama.[3]

Few scientists resisted Haber's invitation to set up the chemical warfare programme. Max Born rejected participation in the development of what he viewed as barbaric weapons. Forty years later, his objections to nuclear weapons made him one of the 11 signatories of the Russell-Einstein Manifesto (1955) and even, in some ways, its initiator.[4] Another example was Hermann Staudinger, Haber's one-time close friend and colleague at the University of Karlsruhe. He was one of the first to criticise the new form of warfare both in private and in public from within the scientific community. In 1912, Staudinger was appointed professor at the *Eidgenössische Technische Hochschule* (ETH) in Zürich, one of the most prestigious universities in Europe (where at the same time Albert Einstein accepted a professorship in physics). In neutral Switzerland, Staudinger's concerns grew about industrialised warfare in which science and technology made war increasingly resemble mass slaughter. He joined the growing anti-war movement in Switzerland and in July 1917 published an article entitled 'Technik und Krieg' in the leading peace journal, *Die Friedens-Warte* (which, with its editor, Alfred Hermann Fried, had moved from Vienna to Zürich).[5] Later that year he wrote to General Erich Ludendorff, head of the German military, in the hope of encouraging peace negotiations. Instead, he was invited to join the reportedly 2,000 German scientists already engaged in chemical warfare research and development. Fearing its future expansion, Staudinger conceived of a broader appeal to the warring powers to stop the use of poison gas. Through an intermediary, he approached the International Committee of the Red Cross (ICRC) in Geneva. Following a visit to Staudinger by Frédéric Ferrière, Vice President of the Committee, the ICRC issued an appeal on 8 February 1918 calling for the renunciation of all chemical warfare.[6] Staudinger also submitted an article on modern warfare to Ferrière, which eventually was published in May 1919 in the *Revue Internationale de la Croix-Rouge* under the title 'La technique moderne et la guerre'.[7] He was concerned that the Red Cross appeal, which had condemned gas warfare as a 'barbarous innovation', had been ignored when it was issued, and was now largely forgotten by those who had read it. He concluded his article by an appeal to the Red Cross to draw attention again to the danger of the use of poison gas and to somehow assist in saving humanity 'from a new catastrophe whose effects would be infinitely more terrible'. When, later that year, the author sent an offprint of his article to his former colleague and friend, Haber accused him of having 'betrayed Germany at the time of her greatest crisis and helplessness' and announced an end to their friendship.[8]

Talk of 'resistance' to gas warfare among the German military would be an exaggeration. However, 'distrust and displeasure' were in evidence, as Colonel Otto Peterson's newly trained units experienced when in February 1915 they began with the placement of heavy steel cylinders with chlorine (codenamed 'F batteries') in General von Deimling's corps area near the village of Gheluvelt in the Ypres Salient. Crown Prince Rupprecht of Bavaria, who commanded the Sixth Army, told both General Erich von Falkenhayn and Haber that the impending cloud gas attack seemed to him not only distasteful, but also militarily unsound. If the technique proved effective, he argued, the enemy would certainly adopt it too, and since the prevailing winds on the Western front came from the west, the Allies would be able to blow off gas 'against us ten times more often than we could'. Rupprecht's concern proved justified: by September the British staged a major cloud gas attack of their own, as it turned out against the army under his command. While some criticism to the introduction of gas warfare was based on pragmatic and technical considerations, other objections were ethical in nature. For instance, General Karl von Einem, who commanded the Third Army in Champagne, wrote to his wife shortly after he had heard about the first gas attack at Ypres: 'I fear it will produce a tremendous scandal in the world. [...] War has nothing to do with chivalry any more. The higher civilisation rises, the viler man becomes.' Two years later, after both sides had introduced ever more toxic gases on the battlefield, von Einem would express himself even more strongly about von Falkenhayn's initiative to use such an 'unchivalrous' weapon: it 'was repugnant to me from the very start'.[9]

Resistance to chemical warfare in the 1920s

It seems that only after the war a popular movement for the abolition of new types of warfare emerged. First and foremost it concerned chemical warfare, but also aerial warfare. Both modes of combat often featured in future apocalyptic scenarios. Women played a leading role in the rising resistance. A key event in the development of the movement against gas warfare was the visit by two women scientists to the American chemical armaments centre, Edgewood Arsenal in Maryland, in 1924. The centre had been established in November 1917 as a facility for chemical weapons research, development, and testing. Their visit followed an invitation to be guests of the Conference of the American Chemical Society held in Washington, DC at the end of April. The two scientists were Dr Gertrud Woker (1878–1968), professor at the University of Berne, where in 1911 she had been appointed head of the Institute of Physico-Chemical Biology, and Dr Naima Sahlbom (1871–1957), Professor of Minerology in Stockholm.[10] Both were active members of the Women's International League for Peace and Freedom (WILPF). This organisation goes back to the famous international congress of women in The Hague in April 1915, which led to the foundation of the International Committee of Women for Permanent Peace. WILPF was formally constituted at a second conference in Zürich in May 1919. Today, it is still the leading global women's peace organisation.

LEFT: Gertrud Woker (1878–1968).

The women's congress opened in The Hague on 27 April 1915 – less than a week after the first use of gas near Ypres. However, the delegates did not discuss the issue. A most unusual and highly significant aspect of the meeting was the decision to appoint two delegations to present its resolutions to the prime ministers and foreign ministers of many countries, both belligerents and neutrals. In Switzerland President Giuseppe Motta and Minister of Foreign Affairs Arthur Hoffmann received the delegates, Aletta Jacobs and Jane Addams, thanks to Woker's intervention.[11]

Both Woker and Sahlbom were dismayed and horrified by the large-scale poison gas manoeuvres, which also involved release from aircraft, at the Edgewood Arsenal. The exercise resulted in serious injury for many of the participating soldiers (as they learnt later). Woker reported on their visit in graphic detail in her account *The Next War, a War of Poison Gas*. She was horrified by the huge development of the US military site which 'before 1918 [...] was only an unimportant affair. It can only awake painful feelings in Americans of high ideals to know that it is today an arsenal of 1000 acres [...]'.[12]

The Conference of the American Chemical Society was followed in May by a WILPF conference in the same city. Unsurprisingly, it established an International Committee on Chemical Warfare, with Sahlbom as chairperson, and Woker as secretary. The Committee was urged to recruit collaborators, both experts and propagandists, in all countries with WILPF sections. On her return from the USA, Woker consulted members of the French section of WILPF in Paris and succeeded in enlisting the support of eminent scientists, including Dr Paul Langevin. Following a

Gertrud Woker: *Der kommende Gift- und Brandkrieg* (Leipzig: 1932). The cover of Gertrud Woker's *The Coming Poison and Fire War* had a telling cover reminiscent of the horrors she predicted.

similar meeting in Berlin in October 1924, a campaign was launched throughout the national WILPF sections appealing to scientists to condemn the misuse of scientific research for war purposes and to refuse to serve war with their knowledge. The Conference on the Control of Traffic in Arms organised by the League of Nations in Geneva in May 1925 brought fresh opportunities to publicise the WILPF campaign. The WILPF Committee on Chemical Warfare sent a memorandum on the dangers of modern armaments to all delegations. It is uncertain to what extent the Geneva Protocol (1925) was influenced by the WILPF campaign.[13]

Following her return from the USA, Woker decided to publish her findings; she had been further encouraged to write a popular book about and against chemical warfare by a letter she had received from Prince Alexander von Hohenlohe-Schillingsfürst shortly before his death in May 1924.[14] The following year her famous book, *Der Kommende Gift- und Brandkrieg und seine Auswirkungen gegenüber der Zivilbevölkerung* (The coming poison and fire war and its effects upon the civilian population) was published.[15] It established her as the world's leading authority on and campaigner against chemical warfare. Her prominence in the field was also underscored by the invitation to write the chapter on chemical and bacteriological warfare for the equally famous book, *What Would Be the Character of a New War?*[16] It was the only contribution by a woman whose fellow authors were leading generals and other military professionals, senior politicians and professors. The perceived importance of Woker's book is well described by her friend and fellow campaigner, Frida Perlen (1870–1933), who wrote: 'Dieses Werk ist uns in unserem Kampf so unendlich wertvoll und wird Gertrude Woker's Name unsterblich machen. Sie wird neben einer Beecher-Stowe stehen, die mit ihrem Werk 'Onkel Toms Hütte' den Auftakt zur Sklavenbefreidung gegeben hat' ('This work is immensely useful in our struggle and will render Gertrude Woker's name immortal. She will be like a Beecher-Stowe who, with her work "Uncle Tom's Cabin", initiated the liberation of the slaves'). In fact, in August 1924, Perlen had visited Woker and received the manuscript of the book to use as she saw fit. Perlen's proposal that the book be published by the German section of WILPF (a proposal made during the section's annual conference in Hamburg later that year) was unanimously accepted. Albert Einstein congratulated the section after its publication.

Perlen was already involved in the campaign for women suffrage, and opposed the First World War.[17] She was a strong supporter of WILPF from the beginning, having participated in the preparatory conference in Amsterdam in February 1915. Because the German military authorities refused to give her a passport, she was unable to attend the conference itself in The Hague in April. Although not a scientist, she was an early and fervent campaigner against chemical warfare, and pursued her work through the Württemberg/Stuttgart section of WILPF. Already in 1921, at the congress of the German peace movement in Essen, she, together with Lida Gustava Heymann, warned against the dangers of a future poison gas war. Perlen detailed the WILPF campaign in a valuable booklet entitled *Der Kampf der Frauen gegen die Hölle von Gift und Feuer* (The struggle of women against the hell of poison and fire).[18] The opening lines of

Internationale Frauenliga für Frieden und Freiheit G. W.

Der Kampf der Frauen
gegen die Hölle
von Gift und Feuer

Frida Perlen: *Der Kampf der Frauen gegen die Hölle von Gift und Feuer* (Stuttgart: 1927).
The Struggle of Women against Hell of Poison and Fire, published by the International Women's
League for Peace and Freedom in 1927 had a cover image by the famous Berlin artist Käthe
Kollwitz who herself had lost a son during the Battle of the Yser in 1914.

this passionate protest deserve to be quoted: 'Es sollte einmal in der Weltgeschichte
eingehen, daß es Frauen waren, international organisierte Frauen, die versuchten,
systematisch den Kampf gegen die chemisch-bakteriologischen Kriegsmethoden
aufzunehmen' ('One day, world history will record that it was women, internationally
organised women, who tried to undertake a systematic campaign against chemical-
bacteriological methods of warfare').[19] Together with Woker and Sahlbom, Perlen was
most definitely in the forefront of this campaign.

The efforts culminated in the international WILPF conference on 'Modern methods of war and the protection of the civilian population'. Held in Frankfurt in early January 1929, it became popularly known as the anti-poison gas conference and was one of the most famous and important events of the organised peace movement during the interwar period. Some three hundred scientists and others participated, and representatives of almost seventy newspapers followed the discussions. The conference was sponsored by a distinguished international committee which included, for instance, Albert Einstein, Bertrand Russell, Viscount Cecil, Aletta Jacobs, Käthe Kollwitz, Romain Rolland, Charles Richet, Auguste Forel, Selma Lagerlöf, and Ludwig Quidde. Others, such as Marie Curie, sent expressions of gratitude and support to the meeting. Likewise, some seventy national and international organisations expressed their support in one way or another. All this is detailed in a comprehensive report that was published by the Working Party of the Stuttgart section of WILPF. It was prepared by Clara Ragaz, Hortense Rathgeber and Frida Perlen, who also wrote a preface.[20] It included the texts of a dozen presentations grouped under the following three headings: 'The character of modern war'; 'The problem of the protection of the civilian population'; and 'The problem of disarmament from economic and technical points of view'. Woker's presentation critically evaluated the statistical data concerning the victims of gas warfare.[21] She took issue with the argument, widely used by advocates of chemical warfare, that it was more humane than conventional warfare. Using figures (including from the gas attacks near Ypres), she argued that the official mortality and invalidity statistics of gas warfare under-estimated the damage done.[22] Even Dante's inferno, she concluded, would be no match for the horrors that a future chemical war waged from the sky would bring. Dieter Riesenberger has rightly argued that it is impossible to indicate precisely the strength of the popular movement against chemical warfare. Notwithstanding, the German section of WILPF, with some 1,000 members, was its driving force.[23]

Comments on the first use of gas in some British newspapers

In the absence of evidence for civil resistance to the introduction of gas warfare in 1915 on any scale, we will consider public opinion and the nature of the debate in the UK immediately following the first German chlorine attack. In order to gauge early public reactions, we have used editorials and letter columns in national and regional newspapers. However, in view of the small number of papers and limited time frame covered, we cannot offer general conclusions. Given those limitations, 'resistance' has to be interpreted as a refusal by Britain to countenance the introduction of gas warfare, i.e., the unwillingness to contemplate using the same instruments introduced by the German Army. Those who were minded to adopt the moral high ground, which excluded retaliation in kind, had to face up to one possible consequence of their position: contribution to defeat in war of one's own country. However, those who pleaded to keep their hands clean and conscience clear countered such criticisms with the argument that they were not remaining passive in the face of evil. Some advocated defensive or other countermeasures that neither infringed the moral scruples, nor violated international law. The use of protective masks and an appeal to the neutral powers to pressure Germany to abandon its errant ways were the two most commonly suggested approaches by those who opposed Britain following Germany's example.

From the outset the approach apparently rejected retaliation against the Germans by means of similar or other, but equally barbarous and illegal methods of warfare. Instead the opponents of chemical warfare proposed defensive and protective means to counter the use of gas. This was, for instance, the line taken by an editorial in *The Yorkshire Observer* of 26 April:

> We hope the Government will be able to meet this new form of savagery without departing from their decision not to set back the clock. There are, it would seem, such expedients as the use of respirators by which the latest form of barbarism favoured by the enemy can be counteracted. It is better that we should devote our science to safeguarding the lives of soldiers against the methods of savagery than that we should begin to try to surpass the enemy in these diabolical contrivances. We have had in the past to fight Red Indians who scalped their prisoners and Hottentots who burned them over a slow fire. But we never, of course, retaliated by stooping to that kind of barbarism, and we shall doubtless have to be content to leave the Germans supreme in the field of inhumanity. Most people will agree with what is written on this subject by a correspondent of 'The Spectator', who deals with 'criminal warfare and retaliation'. 'It is sincerely to be hoped', he says, 'that the demand for retaliation against German prisoners will be disregarded. For if it comes to a game of mutual retaliation English people can never go as far as Germans. In view of German methods we can have little doubt that the German authorities would not shrink from any crime in the name of retaliation, and that they would not hesitate to starve or kill their prisoners.' The argument may be extended from the comparatively narrow field of the treatment of prisoners to that of methods of making war. From the diffusion of asphyxiating gases it is not a long step to the poisoning of wells. It is impossible to conceive of Englishmen engaging in that abomination. There are limits beyond which we cannot go, and the stricter those limits are made the better for the success of our appeal to the hitherto neutral part of the world.

The editorial continued with another quotation from the Spectator article:

> The logic of history will punish Germany more severely than can the Governments of the Allies. If the allied Governments continue to fight a clean fight it will redound to their credit for generations and generations. [...] If [...] Germany stands branded as a nation which has conducted a criminal war with criminal means, a war of revenge on the part of Germany need not much be feared, for that country would remain isolated.

The editorialist agreed, and concluded his article as follows:

> There is, of course, a distinction to be made between retaliation from motives
> of mere revenge and the adoption of unwelcome measures to which a nation
> may perhaps be driven in sheer self-preservation. If Germany, by resort to
> inhuman methods of warfare, could threaten humaner nations with a real peril
> of extinction it is not to be supposed that those nations could consent to see
> themselves submerged rather than adopt the means of self-protection that were
> open to them. But it remains to be proved that the German use of asphyxiating
> gases is either so potent or so incapable of being counteracted in other ways
> than by a resort to the same proscribed methods of making war.[24]

An editorial in the *Bradford Daily Argus* the next day expressed similar sentiments:

> It is satisfactory to learn, from the official statement issued in Paris last night,
> that a means of protection against the asphyxiating gases used by the Germans
> has been brought into service with good results among the French and Belgian
> soldiers. The announcement that the Germans had resorted to this unlawful
> method of disabling their foes did not come as a surprise, though it naturally
> caused deep indignation in the Allied Nations. We were told months ago that
> the scientists of Germany were thinking how best they could help their country
> and we know from past experience that no Hague Convention and no law of
> humanity would hamper them in their investigations and recommendations.
> The Germans are experts in criminal warfare.

The writer went on to quote chapter and verse from the Hague Declaration (IV, 2) in
order to demonstrate the illegality and, therefore, criminality of the German Army's
latest action:

> The use of asphyxiating gases received consideration at the first Conference in
> 1899, and the resolution adopted runs as follows: – 'The contracting Powers
> agree to abstain from the use of projectiles the object of which is the diffusion
> of asphyxiating or deleterious gases. – The present Declaration is binding on
> the contracting Powers in the case of a war between two or more of them. – It
> shall cease to be binding from the time when, in a war between the contracting
> Powers, one of the belligerents shall be joined by a non-contracting Power.'[25]
> This was signed by all the present belligerents and one neutral, Italy. Therefore
> Germany can put forth no defence of her latest violation of international law.
> Naturally the question of retaliation and reprisals arises. [...] Now, according
> to the German handbook on the customs of war, issued by the General Staff
> in 1902, a nation can be forced to observe the laws of war only by retaliation.
> Ought the Allies to retaliate? A military correspondent suggests today that in

Photographer 2nd Lt Thomas Keith Aitken: A line of British troops blinded by mustard gas at an Advanced Dressing Station near Bethune, 10 April 1918. (Imperial War Museum, London)

this instance, as in other cases of the application of scientific inventions to the purposes of war, the Allies might legitimately follow the German lead. 'We have allowed ourselves to be tied too much', he says, 'by artificial restrictions which the enemy ignores. It is mere foolishness to elect to fight at a disadvantage when it is possible to meet the enemy on equal terms.' That is one aspect of the situation. But the English people naturally shrink from lowering their high military and naval standard of warfare.

The writer went on to quote approvingly from the *Spectator* article mentioned above.[26] The same sentiments, calling for restraint rather than retaliation, were also expressed the following day in the *Bradford Daily Telegraph*.[27] Referring to the debates the previous night in Parliament, the editorialist wrote:

The only consideration is – ought we to retaliate? Our enemy is so inhuman in his expedients that it becomes a question whether we can afford to leave him alone with the advantages of science applied to war amounting to criminality. We are glad, however, to find that this notion of retaliation in kind was rejected by both Houses of Parliament. We are going to keep our hands clean. We may suffer from the barbarities of an enemy who has thrown civilised conventions to the winds, but we can beat him without staining our honour. The punishment must come hereafter. [...] That is the right course to take and we must not, we cannot forget the duty we owe to humanity at the end of the war. There may be wars after this, but we can ensure that they shall be conducted with decency and within the recognised rules, even though one of the combatants be Germans. [...] We shall not forget and we cannot forgive.

Barely a week later, with the German gas attacks continuing, the same newspaper adopted a more hesitant tone:

There is fresh evidence daily of the progress of the policy of German frightfulness. The British chiefly are reaping the consequences of the attempt to force this devilish civilisation upon the world, and the time has come to ask whether the enemy should be allowed to gain successes without some form of retaliation. We know how desirous the Allies are of keeping to the Hague Convention, or, as we prefer to put it, keeping their hands clean. But it is intolerable to think that the Germans should be able to go on winning battles by unclean and atrocious means. Sir John French's despatches certainly seem to convey the hint that some effective reply or protest ought to be made to the use of poisonous gases. The Germans gained ground before Ypres by the systematic use of asphyxiating gases, and they seem so enamoured of the practice that they now employ it on any day that the conditions are favourable. Thus they gained a footing on Hill 60 yesterday by the use of these gases. They also poisoned a number of our soldiers at Givenchy. We may hesitate long before resorting to such weapons. We must, however, ask the signatories of the Hague Convention whether they do not feel sufficiently outraged to make some effective protest.[28]

The writer drew attention to other reports of the German violations of the laws of war, including poisoning of wells and piracy at sea. The rather confident tone adopted earlier by the *Bradford Daily Argus* ruling out retaliation in kind, and advocating defensive measures, came under some strain shortly afterwards when it transpired that they were rather ineffective. In an article headed '"Kulture" [sic] and Poison', the editorial in the *Bradford Daily Argus* commented:[29]

Last night the Under Secretary for War was asked what steps the military authorities had taken to protect our soldiers against Germany's diabolical methods of warfare. It seems that when the ruthless enemy first used gas a million respirators were sent to the front, but they were not so efficacious as was desired. Another form of respirator has since been tried, and Dr. Haldane is now conducting experiments with various materials and methods. No doubt his report will be available in a few days. There is a growing feeling that Great Britain and her Allies will have to resort to the use of gas in self-defence. One authority says, 'It is clear that if one side deliberately employs prohibited weapons the other side are free[d] ipso facto from the prohibition to use them.'[30] If the rules prohibit the use of a certain weapon, be it gas or crossbow, and if our opponents deliberately and persistently use that weapon against us, shall we, asks a correspondent in the 'Times' today, sacrifice men and time and treasure and observe the rule, or shall we ourselves take into our hands the forbidden weapon so shamelessly used against us if it be shown to be to the advantage of our armies to do so?[31]

The *Bradford Daily Argus* writer continued:

> The exponents of 'Kultur', by their latest crime in the field, have forced us to face this question. One thing is certain: we cannot agree to use a weapon which will inflict upon any human being the tortures which follow the use of the German gases. [...] We must find a less barbarous method of retaliation. Sir John French reports that the poisonous fumes from the German trenches do not merely incapacitate the victims for a time, but often destroy the lungs, and subject to a painful and lingering death those who breathe them. The 'Yorkshire Post' expresses the hope that the Allies may be able to devise and manufacture, or to procure, other gas bombs, not less effective to the immediate purpose, but more humane.

It is unclear whether the latter proposal would have received the approval of the Bishop of Pretoria, Michael Furse, whose letter to the editor of *The Times* the following day was full of condemnation of what he called 'this latest and most damnable invention of the German Imperial Staff' whose effects he had just witnessed in a clearing hospital at the front and went on to describe in vivid detail.[32] He wrote,

> A more cruel and diabolical method of conducting war it would, I believe, be impossible to conceive. If the gas used merely knocked the men out for the time being, so that the Germans could walk over their unconscious bodies with impunity, it would be a sufficiently cowardly method of making war; but when as a fact, in a large percentage of cases, it kills men by a slow and torturing death, no language that I am master of can express what I [felt].

The bishop concluded his letter, which nowhere as much as hinted at retaliation in kind, as follows: 'There is only one way to counter this sort of devilry and avenge the lives of the men who have thus been murdered, and that is for the Empire to concentrate its whole energies to supply every man and every *legitimate* [emphasis added] munition of war that is necessary to smash this enemy; and that, too, right away, without one week's unnecessary delay.'

A correspondent for the *Manchester Guardian*, Henry W. Nevinson, writing from the National Liberal Club in London, added his voice to those who asserted that, with the use of poison gas, war had sunk to an unprecedented level of barbarity. He wrote:

> [...] the present war is being conducted with horrors that no Englishman, and, I think, very few Germans, would have thought possible a year ago. I need not speak of the destruction of beautiful cities, the slaughter of civilian populations, and the outrages upon women. For such actions war has always supplied precedents. The sinking of unarmed and even neutral ships, with crews and passengers and all, is new and horrible beyond words. But of all new horrors the use of poisonous and painful gas and the poisoning of wells seem to me the worst, and I think most people would agree.[33]

He found confirmation for his belief in letters such as those by the Bishop of Pretoria (quoted above), and by a British Officer whose description of the effects of the gas upon the victims on Hill 60 the *Manchester Guardian* had published. The officer had written that gas warfare 'is without doubt the most awful form of torture'. Yet, Nevinson wrote,

> in spite of all such expressions of horror and indignation, which I believe utter the common sentiment of the whole country, we are told on the highest authority – we are told by Mr. Tennant himself – that the question of resorting to 'similar expedients' on our part is now under the consideration of the Government. It seems strange to me that such a question should need the consideration of any British Government or of any Briton. In yesterday's 'Daily Chronicle' Professor Vivian Lewes, professor of chemistry at the Royal Naval College, Greenwich, is reported to have said: 'The attitude of the British Government has been throughout that clean hands are worth more than any temporary advantage that the use of asphyxiants in warfare could give.' I should have expected this attitude to be maintained without any consideration at all, and yet one finds certain people inciting the Government to resort to these 'similar expedients'.

Among those 'certain people' were M.B.R. in *The Times*, as well as its editorialist, both of whose views were disapprovingly quoted by the writer. He also criticised the editorialist of the *Daily Chronicle* who, in the very same issue which reported the view of Professor Lewes, cried, 'We must fight gases with gases, and do so with the least possible delay.' Nevinson concluded:

> I should have thought myself that the attitude described by Professor Lewes was the natural one for England or any other decent country that values the gradually acquired traditions of manliness and honour. I should have thought that our Government, now as in the past, would have resolved without debate that 'clean hands are worth more than any temporary advantage'. [...] If we

resort to [Germany's] methods England will be held to have authorised them, and their imitation will be considered justified among other nations which, in spite of all our errors, do still regard us as maintaining a high standard of humanity and decent behaviour. The crisis of all standards of civilization may be involved in this war, and it is our part, as it seems to me, to abide true to the highest we know, in the certain belief that only then can we save them from perishing out of the world.

It seems that the writer's principled and high-minded stance, admitting no compromise, was implicitly based on a belief that England would be victorious, come what may. In any case, his lofty position did not address the urgent and vital question of how the new German method of warfare could be countered, or how, in the absence of effective countermeasures, the advantages it brought the German side could be neutralised. Rather surprisingly, it may be thought, these latter issues were not raised either by the newspaper editorialist in his lengthy and wholly approving comment on Nevinson's letter and the argument put forward there. Germany's latest weapon of war, he wrote:

is, in fact, by far the most cruel instrument of war yet invented, and compared to it the explosive, or 'dum-dum' bullet, which shatters the bone and rends the flesh, is almost merciful. These accounts may be exaggerated, but if they are true what are we to say of those who make use of such weapons? And yet we are told, and told in quite reputable quarters, that there is nothing for it but that we ourselves should do likewise – in other words, that we should emulate the crimes which we condemn. If that indeed were so, then it would be idle to pretend that we can henceforth place any limit to the atrocities of war. War, it is true, must always be atrocious, but there are degrees of atrocity, and it is worth something – it is worth very much – to maintain such poor restrictions as the conscience and pity of mankind have sought to build up. Mr. Nevinson is no sentimentalist. He has seen much of war and has played his part bravely in it. His protest is that of a man who knows of what he speaks.[34] If we are driven to emulate this latest German atrocity, and thus to give to it the sanction of the fair fame of our country, it will mean that we abandon henceforth – so far at least as this war is concerned, and it may be permanently – every restraint on the conduct of war which the slow progress of mankind has imposed. Is it not worth some effort and even some loss to avoid that?[35]

The reference in the concluding words of the editorial to 'some loss' that might have to be borne as the possible price of such rectitude by the British people suggests, as in Nevinson's letter, a remarkable degree of complacency or insouciance about the potential consequences of such a stance, or at least a sanguine belief that the offending side would benefit only marginally on the field of battle from its devilish new invention.[36] It seems that at this early stage the initial reactions of some commentators to the German initiation of gas warfare on the Western front were momentarily dominated by feelings of utter horror and total rejection that did not permit any consideration of following suit. Much clearer, in contrast, was the position adopted by W. P. Byles, MP, who wrote to the *Manchester Guardian*, 'rejoiced' to have read Nevinson's letter. He added, 'Cruel and diabolical is that method of warfare, as the Bishop of Pretoria says, but that is the very reason why Britain cannot soil her hands by imitation. I shuddered at the Government's suggestion of "similar expedients". As well might we imitate the Lusitania crime. Whether we win or lose in this world-war, let us come out of it with clean hands. Honour and chivalry are even more worth preserving than human life. I would rather England were conquered than disgraced.'[37]

Another letter writer in the same issue of the *Manchester Guardian* shared the MP's principled stance, but at the same time indicated that he did not expect his country to suffer defeat as a consequence of refusing to retaliate in kind. J. Stuart Bogg wrote, 'One thing could be more injurious than the poison gas fumes in Flanders, and that is that England should stoop to imitate a practice condemned alike by Christian and heathen nations. We have not sunk so low as to copy methods so wicked and so abhorrent. I have confidence that the skill of our English chemists will yet devise an innocent method of rendering the fumes innocuous to those whom they are intended to injure. But in any case our hands should remain clean.'[38] Two days later, a contributor writing under the name 'Artifex' wrote a long column expressing the same sentiments as those quoted already. He found it very difficult, he admitted, to be very angry and at the same time, following the Bible commandment, not to sin. 'It is certainly strange,' he wrote,

> to read in the newspapers letters full of reprobation for the atrocious and dastardly methods, which close with a fervid appeal that we should immediately adopt similar tactics. Personally, I will confess that no misfortune that could befall us would seem greater to me than that England should fall from her high position among the nations and sink to the level of Germany in this matter. [...] who is there who would not rather that anyone he loved should die with clean hands than live disgraced? And what is true of individuals, who can die and be forgotten, is doubly true of nations which remain. When the British name ceases to stand for clean methods of warfare, and for honour between man and man, let the end come. – Nor is it in any sense a matter merely between us and the German nation. Once again, as so often in our national history, we are trustees of the moral wealth of the world, for all nations and for generations yet unborn. If we use tainted methods we can, of course, say, 'Germany began it; she used these methods before we did'. But suppose twenty years hence we are at war, let us say, with Patagonia, and they adopt these methods. If we complain and say 'We did not use them till the Germans had', our foes can reply, 'We did not use them till twenty years after you did'. To do as some people suggest and copy German methods would be to launch not only England but the civilised world on an inclined plain whose lower edge is in – who knows what hell? No!

when the war is over let Germany have no one to share with her the infamy which will be hers. That is the way in which we can best punish her, by leaving her no companion to share her shame.[39]

Anti-German Riots

The German gas attacks in late April, together with the sinking of the Lusitania on 7 May and the Zeppelin raids in the south of England, caused anti-German riots in several cities. Germans permanently living in England, whether naturalised or not, expressed their protest against these methods of warfare. They condemned the German Army and navy, and their leader, the Kaiser, and conveyed their wholehearted support and pledges of loyalty to their adopted country. Under the heading, 'Germans in Bradford. Protest Against Barbarism. Some Striking Letters', the *Bradford Daily Telegraph* introduced the reactions of a number of German-born readers who had written to the paper as follows:

> The action of German residents in Bradford, naturalised or otherwise, against barbarism in war, with special reference to the sinking of the Lusitania, is being followed up effectively. – It is to be hoped that this action will prevent a repetition of what is happening in London and elsewhere – anti-German riots and attacks on persons and property. It will be remembered that the Bradford Germans began their protest against infractions of the Hague Convention last Tuesday, when they sent a deputation to the Lord Mayor. They are following this up by signing a memorial expressing abhorrence of the methods of inhuman warfare.[40]

Among the letters that followed was one from Rev. Joseph Strauss, pastor of the Jewish Church in Bradford who described himself as a naturalised German of some 36 years standing;[41] one from Oscar Müller who referred to his large number of German friends and acquaintances who had made their home in the city for 20 or 50 years; and one from R. Sackur. The latter wrote from Southampton, having left Bradford 21 years ago. Aware of the large German community in the city, and no doubt in an attempt to vouchsafe for its members' trustworthiness and loyalty, he wrote, 'I wish to express my extreme disgust with the barbarous methods adopted by Germany in this war. Every right-minded German in England must be horror-stricken by their latest outrage. I, for one, am thoroughly ashamed of the country of my birth.'

His letter was followed by a short article entitled 'A Leeds Protest. Men of German Birth Indignant.' It read: 'Following the example set in Bradford a number of naturalised British subjects of German birth, resident in Leeds, have signed a protest against the German Government's mode of warfare. The document has been sent to the Lord Mayor, who has been asked to allow others to add their names.' It also reported on a suggestion by the person who forwarded the document to the Lord Mayor 'that a meeting might be held to consider whether naturalised Germans residing in Leeds will

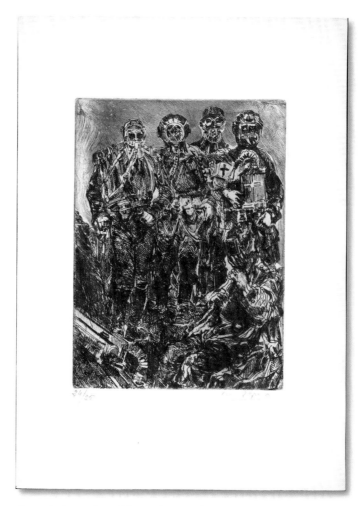

Henry de Groux: Five soldiers with types of gas masks. Belgian artist Henry de Groux was much impressed by the horrors of war which he depicted in a series of etchings entitled "The faces of victory". One soldier is manning a machine gun, another one carries a flame thrower and a third one carries a Red Cross armband.

forward an address of loyalty to the King, independently of or in conjunction with the Bradford Germans.'

The next day, the same paper welcomed the Government's 'far-reaching' decision on the treatment of alien enemies in the country. This was to intern all the men of military age and to send back to their country those Germans who were above military age. According to official estimates, some 40,000 Germans and Austrians (60 per cent of whom were men, and 40 per cent women) were still living freely in the country. As regards the 8,000 naturalised persons of German origin, individuals would be interned in case of proven necessity or danger. The editorialist agreed with Prime Minister Herbert Asquith's statement in the House the previous day that no people ever had greater provocation for reprisals than the people of Britain, but this did not warrant the confounding of the innocent with the guilty. He continued, 'Let Englishmen rise to a higher conception of civilisation [...] we should set the Germans an example of higher conduct even under the greatest possible provocation. Therefore we welcome the Government measures as effective without being vindictive or injurious to the innocent.' There was no longer any excuse for mob rule and people taking the law into their own hands.[42] The neighbouring column reported an instance of this when the big plate-glass window of a butcher shop – 'the proprietor of which, though of German descent, was born in Bradford, and has remained here all his life' – was smashed the previous day. It seems that the notice which was published on the same page by Charles Schulz and his wife Ethel Mary Schulz (formerly Robinson), who described themselves as pork butchers from Keighley (near Bradford), concerned the same incident. They wrote:

> That it having come to our knowledge that certain statements have been made and rumours are current that we are of German nationality, we hereby declare that such statements are entirely untrue. The father and mother of me, Charles Schulz, resided in England from Childhood. I was born at Heckmondwike [near Bradford] and my wife at King's Lynn. We have lived in the Keighley and Bradford Districts for the last 25 years and in Yorkshire practically all our lives. – We have never been to Germany and do not know the language, nor do we employ anyone of German nationality. – Our interests and sympathies are, always have been and always will be with the land of our birth and the people among whom we live.

A letter containing a variation on the same theme had appeared the day before in the *Bradford Daily Argus*. Alfred W. Hoffmann, of the firm A. Hoffmann & Co., wrote:

> In order to remove any possible misconception as to the nationality of our family I beg for the hospitality of your columns. – My father, who was of Swiss birth, settled in Bradford in 1844, and became a naturalised British subject a few years later. My mother was Belgian, and we, their children, yield to nobody in devotion to England and the British flag. – The desire to dissociate ourselves from any relationship to the perpetrators of the infernal horrors committed upon our Allies' armies, and non-combatants of our and their nations, must be my excuse for taking up your valuable space.[43]

This letter was preceded by other ones and some appeared simultaneously in the other Bradford daily, as referred to above.[44]

To return to the larger question of popular opinion as regards the new threat posed by the German use of gas warfare, it would not be long before the demands of 'realpolitik' led Britain to follow suit. Major C. H. Foulkes, who had been put in charge of British gas reprisals, was tireless in his efforts to promote gas warfare. The large public relations exercise that he conducted was useful 'but in the end Foulkes won the battle against the critics of gas warfare through simple military expediency. A chemical arms race developed, which left little room for ethical considerations. Soon, virtually every leading chemist in Britain was at work on some aspect of gas warfare'.[45] In his fascinating and wide-ranging survey of the use of chemistry in the First World War (of which the subject of chemical warfare is only one aspect), Michael Freemantle has observed: 'Although widespread public indignation and revilement at the ghastly, frightening, and insidious nature of chemical weapons continued throughout the war and afterwards, there were many influential figures on both sides [...] who encouraged their use wholeheartedly'.[46] Another student of the matter has commented, 'Contrary to the currently held common perception of public attitude to chemical warfare in the immediate aftermath of the First World War, there seems to have been little immediate public outcry against it [...] gas warfare [...] had become accepted as just another weapon in the arsenals'.[47] It is interesting to note that in her autobiography, *Testament of Youth* (1933), which is one long criticism of the war and prevailing social attitudes, and which has been called 'the most popular anti-war book written by a woman between the wars',[48] Vera Brittain refers to gas warfare only in two small paragraphs. Likewise, there is only a single passage on the subject in Erich Maria Remarque's *All Quiet on the Western Front* (1929). To the soldiers in the trenches, gas was one nuisance among many they had to endure, and this helps to explain the limited resistance at the time as well as the fact that protests were usually by outsiders (including women, as documented above).[49]

The author wishes to acknowledge the preliminary research by Gary Walker on which large parts of this chapter are based.

Notes

1 E. Croddy, *Chemical and Biological Warfare: An Annotated Bibliography* (Lanham, Md. and London, 1997). It is surprising, however, that such leading experts and writers on, and campaigners against, gas warfare in the 1920s as Gertrude Woker, Frida Perlen, and Naima Sahlbom are also absent. See below.

2 For a recent account, see C. Barrett, *Subversive Peacemakers: War Resistance 1914–1918. An Anglican Perspective* (Cambridge, 2014).

3 G. von Leitner, *Der Fall Clara Immerwahr. Leben für eine humane Wissenschaft* (Munich, 1993). After years of oblivion, her name and sacrifice are now commemorated in the prize for whistleblowers, instituted by the German chapter of International Physicians for the Prevention of Nuclear War. The *Clara Immerwahr Auszeichnung der IPPNW* was first awarded in 1991; the most recent award was made in 2007. Von Leitner's book has not been without criticism. See especially, M. Szöllösi-Janze, *Fritz Haber 1868–1934. Eine Biographie* (Munich, 1998), who highlighted the lack of documentary evidence, including for the reasons for Immerwahr's suicide (pp. 393–405).

4 von Leitner, *Der Fall Clara Immerwahr*, p. 203; S. Ionno Butcher, 'The Origins of the Russell-Einstein Manifesto', *Pugwash History Series*, no. 1 (May 2005), esp. at pp. 8–10.

5 *Die Friedens-Warte*, vol. 19, pp. 196–202. The issue of chemical warfare is only briefly dealt with at the end of the article.

6 Appeal to the belligerents, issued by the International Committee on 8 February 1918, full text available from URL <https://www.icrc.org/eng/resources/documents/statement/57jnqh.htm>.

7 *Revue Internationale de la Croix-Rouge*, vol. 1, no. 5 (1919), pp. 508–15.

8 For further details, see Y. Furukawa, *Inventing Polymer Science: Staudinger, Carothers, and the Emergence of Macromolecular Chemistry* (Philadelphia, 1998), esp. the section 'World War I and Staudinger as a Pacifist', pp. 54–59. In 1953 Staudinger received the Nobel Prize in Chemistry. The next year the prize was awarded to Linus Pauling, who nine years later, in 1963, also received the Nobel Peace Prize for his efforts to stop nuclear testing in the atmosphere. It seems that Staudinger, too, might have been a deserving candidate for the Peace Prize (early on in his career). However, during the First World War no Nobel Peace Prizes were awarded with the exception of the one to the Red Cross in 1917.

9 I have borrowed heavily from U. Trumpener, 'The Road to Ypres: The Beginnings of Gas Warfare in World War I', *Journal of Modern History*, vol. 47 (September 1975), pp. 460–80, esp. pp. 471–73.

10 For a concise biography of Woker, cf. the entry by Dieter Riesenberger in H. Donat and K. Holl (eds.), *Die Friedensbewegung: Organisierter Pazifismus in Deutschland, Österreich und in der Schweiz* (Düsseldorf, 1983), pp. 422–23. See also her memoir, 'Aus meinem Leben/Kinderjahre', in Elga Kern (ed.), *Führende Frauen Europas* (Munich, 1928), pp. 138–69. Woker was one of sixteen women selected for inclusion in this book on leading women in Europe. For a concise biography of Sahlbom, cf. the entry by Elisabeth Stahle in H. Josephson (ed.), *Biographical Dictionary of Modern Peace Leaders* (Westport, Conn., 1985), pp. 831–32.

11 Cf. M. Bosch, *Een onwrikbaar geloof in rechtvaardigheid: Aletta Jacobs 1854–1929* (Amsterdam, 2005), p. 555.

12 This 7-page pamphlet was no. 8 in *Pax*, a series of publications by WILPF (Geneva).

13 For further details, cf. G. Bussey and M. Tims, *Women's International League for Peace and Freedom 1915–1965. A Record of Fifty Years' Work* (London, 1965), pp. 65–67. The International Committee of the Red Cross was also actively involved in those debates.

14 A concise biography of this enlightened aristocrat by Helmut Donat is in Josephson (ed.), *Biographical Dictionary of Modern Peace Leaders*, pp. 418–21, and by the same author in Donat and Holl, (eds.), *Die Friedensbewegung: Organisierter Pazifismus in Deutschland, Österreich und in der Schweiz*, pp. 190–92.

15 Later editions appeared as *Der kommende Giftgaskrieg* (The coming poison gas war). The success of the book is shown by the publication of a 9th edition in 1932. The book was published in Leipzig by Ernst Oldenburg Verlag, on behalf of the German section of WILPF. In the intervening years, Woker published several articles and comments on the subject in the leading peace journal, *Die Friedens-Warte*.

16 Cf. N. Angell *et al*, *What Would Be the Character of a New War?*, Enquiry organised by the Inter-Parliamentary Union, Geneva (London, 1933), pp. 354–91. The book had originally been published on behalf of the Inter-Parliamentary Union in Geneva in a small edition two years before. Attracting little attention, and believing its wide circulation to be of 'great and immediate importance', Victor Gollancz brought out this inexpensive edition. In his publisher's foreword, he singled out Woker's contribution (p. III).

17 For a concise biography, see the entry by G. Brinker-Gabler in Donat and Holl, (eds.), *Die Friedensbewegung: Organisierter Pazifismus in Deutschland, Österreich und in der Schweiz*, p. 302.

18 Published in Stuttgart in 1927 by the Württemberg section of WILPF, p. 51. The cover features a drawing by Käthe Kollwitz.

19 *Ibid.*, p. 3.

20 *Die modernen Kriegsmethoden und der Schutz der Zivilbevölkerung,* Dokumente der Internationalen Konferenz in Frankfurt a. M., am 4., 5. und 6. Januar 1929 (Stuttgart, 1929). The cover shows the same drawing by Kollwitz mentioned earlier.

21 G. Woker, 'Der chemische Krieg unter besonderer Berücksichtigung der Ergebnisse der Kampfgasstatistiken', in *Die modernen Kriegsmethoden und der Schutz der Zivilbevölkerung,* pp. 35–46.

22 Since there was no triage in Ypres, the figures used must be treated with caution.

23 D. Riesenberger, 'Der Kampf gegen den Gaskrieg', in R. Steinweg (ed.), *Lernen aus der Geschichte? Historische Friedensforschung* (Frankfurt a. M., 1990), at p. 257. It is surprising that the intensive WILPF campaign of the 1920s, with its prominent women leaders, is not mentioned at all in the excellent, pioneering study on 'women fighting for peace' by W. H. Posthumus-van der Goot, *Vrouwen vochten voor de vrede* (Arnhem, 1961).

24 'Savagery and Slander', *Yorkshire Observer* [Leeds], 26 April 1915, p. 6.

25 This Declaration is also reproduced, for instance, in the *Manual of Military Law*, published by the War Office in London in 1914, pp. 317–18: 'International Declaration Respecting Asphyxiating Gases Signed at The Hague, 29 July 1899'. The first edition of this Manual appeared in 1884; its 6th edition in February 1914. (The text as quoted in the press article was the British translation from French, which omitted the word 'sole' as qualifier of 'object'. The US translation remained faithful to the original and only authentic French text. This omission enabled British commentators to be more sweeping in their condemnation of the gas attack.)

26 'Criminal Warfare', *Bradford Daily Argus*, 27 April 1915, p. 2.

27 *Bradford Daily Telegraph*, 28 April 1915, p. 4.

28 *Bradford Daily Telegraph*, 6 May 1915, p. 4.

29 *Bradford Daily Argus*, 7 May 1915, p. 3.

30 The authority quoted here is the editorial in *The Times*, 6 May 1915, headed '"Kultur" and Poison'. *The Times* editorial continued, and concluded: 'The obligation is reciprocal. The question is no longer a question of right, but merely a question of expediency. Even in peace homicide is justifiable in self-defense.'

31 Cf. M.B.R., '"Kultur" and Poison. To the Editor of *The Times*', *The Times*, 7 May 1915. This correspondent clearly wanted his last question answered in the affirmative. Earlier in his letter he had written, 'We have heard so much in the last six months or so of the rules of war, rules human and divine, rules which have been broken, deliberately broken, by our foes, that some of us are perhaps in danger of beginning to think that the rules of war are more important than war itself. Is it more important that we should be able to say to ourselves and to the great neutral America, "Our hands are clean, search the book of rules, we have broken none of them," or that we should take every step in our power to secure victory and peace?'

32 M. Furse, '"The Most Damnable Invention." The Only Answer. To The Editor of *The Times*', *The Times*, 8 May 1915. Below this letter was that of another reader, who signed himself Anti-Cant. Headed 'Christianity and Poison', it appealed to the eminent German Christians (who at the start of the war had proclaimed that it ought to be the concern of all Christians to ensure that the war be fought with honourable weapons) to denounce the use of lethal gases and of poisoned wells.

33 'Correspondence. Germany's Use of Poison. The Question of "Similar Expedients".' To the Editor of the Manchester Guardian', *Manchester Guardian*, 10 May 1915.

34 Henry Wood Nevinson (1856–1941) was a war correspondent.

35 'Poison as a Weapon', *Manchester Guardian*, 10 May 1915.

36 Perhaps part of the explanation can be found in a report titled 'Lusitania Recruits' in a column one removed from 'Poison as a Weapon'. It opened, 'One of the healthiest signs of the war spirit of London all along has been the fact – verifiable by statistics – that every setback or disaster has meant good business at the recruiting offices. The effect of bad news upon recruiting is always most immediate when, as in the case of the Scarborough raid and now the outrage on the Lusitania, the German 'success' has been gained at the expense of the lives of innocent non-combatants. It is then that the blood heat of our young men, marked in recruiting figures, rises highest. It is certain that the Lusitania news just turned the scale in many a hesitating mind.' The report provided evidence of this, and

concluded, 'The officials expect a rush of recruits during the early part of this week, and their opinion is that the sinking of the Lusitania ought to be worth one new London regiment at least.' We have so far not had an opportunity to discover whether the news of the German use of gas resulted in a similar boost to recruitment. It is also conceivable that it had the opposite effect.

37 W. F, Byrnes, '"Similar Methods to Germany's." To the Editor of the Manchester Guardian', *Manchester Guardian*, 11 May 1915.

38 J. S. Bogg, 'To the Editor of the Manchester Guardian,' *Manchester Guardian*, 11 May 1915.

39 Artifex, 'Clean Hands', *Manchester Guardian*, 13 May 1915.

40 'Germans in Bradford. Protest Against Barbarism. Some Striking Letters,' *Bradford Daily Telegraph*, 13 May 1915, p. 3.

41 The curious fact that Strauss did not refer to himself as Rabbi of a Synagogue may be related to the apparent 'indifference' towards their faith that had been a characteristic of the city's Jewish community and the wish not to stand apart.

42 *Bradford Daily Telegraph*, 14 May 1915, p. 4.

43 'Perpetrators of Horrors. To the Editor of The Bradford Daily Argus', *Bradford Daily Argus*, 13 May 1915, p. 3.

44 'Germans in Bradford. The Protest Against Inhuman Warfare. Views of Naturalised Subjects,' *Bradford Daily Argus*, 13 May 1915, p. 3. The column next to it and headed, 'Internment of Aliens. Result of Wild Rioting in London and the Provinces,' gave details of the extensive and serious rioting in various parts of the country. It said that 'Thirty thousand special constables were called out to deal with the situation, and the military were confined to barracks ready for emergencies.'

45 Cf. R. Harris and J. Paxman, *A Higher Form of Killing: The Secret Story of Gas and Germ Warfare* (London, 1982), p. 21. We should of course not forget the protests of the poets, notably Wilfred Owen (pp. 20–21).

46 M. Freemantle, *The Chemists' War 1914–1918* (Cambridge, 2015). The book, published by the Royal Society of Chemistry, contains a chapter entitled 'Women's Contributions'. No mention is made of the WILPF women involved in the early campaign against chemical warfare. In all fairness to the author, this concerns the post-War period; moreover, his was not meant to be a critical approach to the subject.

47 N. J. McCamley, *The Secret History of Chemical Warfare* (Barnsley, South Yorkshire, 2006), p. 40.

48 Cf. S. Oldfield, *Women Humanitarians: A Biographical Dictionary of British Women Active between 1900 and 1950* (London, 2001), p. 30.

49 Private discussion with J. P. Zanders, 13 April 2015.

MAN-MONKEY, MONKEY-MAN: NEUTRALITY AND THE DISCUSSIONS ABOUT THE 'INHUMANITY' OF POISON GAS IN THE NETHERLANDS AND INTERNATIONAL COMMITTEE OF THE RED CROSS

Leo van Bergen and Maartje Abbenhuis

Introduction

Of the many enduring images the Western Front of the First World War has left to posterity, those of soldiers wearing primitive masks to combat waves of deadly and debilitating gases and poisons remain some of the most arresting. Such imagery has helped to define the trench experience – if not the wider war experience – as a symbol of an industrial-military complex run amok. Unsurprisingly, the news of the first large-scale gas attacks initiated by the German armies somewhat north of the Belgian town of Ypres on 22 April 1915 shocked and dismayed the newspaper-reading public around the world, including in the Netherlands, a neutral country precariously positioned between the might of Germany and Great Britain and within ear shot of the fighting front in Belgium. For the Dutch, and particularly those living in the southern provinces bordering Belgium, Ypres (Ieper or Ypern) was not a far-off imagined place, but a familiar place within a day's travel – pre-war cross-border relations between the Dutch and Belgians were uninhibited and dynamic – where people spoke the same language, lived similar lives, and if not related to them, were distant relatives.[1] In many respects, it was the familiarity of Flanders as well as the daily reminders of the proximity of the war – hundreds of thousands of Belgian refugees had fled for the relative safety of the Netherlands along with tens of thousands of foreign soldiers, the country was on full military alert, its armed forces mobilised, its borders guarded, its merchants and fishermen risked their lives to mines and blockades at sea, and Dutch families everywhere felt the pinch of limited foodstuffs and goods – that made war news all the more relevant.[2] By April 1915, the fear of invasion by either the Germans or the British had not left the Dutch, nor were they unaware of the vulnerability of their neutrality. Within this context, the poisonous news from Ypres spread genuine shock and concern around the country.

This chapter investigates the different discourses that surrounded the use of gas as a weapon of war in the Netherlands during and after the First World War: among the public, within military and medical circles, among pacifists and Red Cross workers and among the political leaders of this neutral nation.[3] Importantly, there was no consensus view on the potential impact of chemical warfare although there was also very little open debate on the topic during the war years. Where the military and government leadership concerned itself mostly with the strategic and logistical consequences as well as possible opportunities presented by gas weaponry, some medical professionals grappled with the ethical dilemmas posed by the impact of gas attacks on human bodies, while the wider public struggled to come to terms with the inhumanity of chemical warfare more generally. Gas, for the latter two groups at least, symbolised the horror of what was a horrible war, and the wider public's revulsion became the mainstream media view. It was not until the middle of the 1920s and going into the 1930s that the Dutch – spurred by the ambivalent position of the Dutch Red Cross and International Committee of the Red Cross (ICRC) on the matter – debated the value of chemical warfare publicly in a variety of media.

That there was no newspaper discussion of substance on the topic of gas warfare during the war and early post-war years is significant particularly as the nature of reporting in the Netherlands was quite different from that which occurred in belligerent newspapers.[4] This article advances several possible explanations for this lack of investigation, reflecting both on the politics of neutrality as well as the relative isolation of the various groups who had a particular interest in the topic. It would be wrong to suggest, however, that gas warfare did not catch the public's imagination or that chemical warfare was not thought about and discussed outside the very public gaze of the daily news media. Above all, the lack of public wartime debate does not take away from the fact that there were distinct and markedly divergent views on poison gas use in the Netherlands during the war, which, ultimately, contributed to a vibrant and very public debate on the topic in the late 1920s. At that stage, the perceived public image that gas was an inhumane weapon of industrial war came under attack and revision.

Wartime reporting on poison gas

In contrast to interwar newspaper coverage on topics of poison and gas as weapons of war, wartime reporting in the Netherlands tended to focus on the factual – what happened, when and where. Across the spectrum of political and editorial publications, a moral judgement, let alone a deeply felt indignation, about gas warfare was noticeably absent, although certain pro-German and pro-Allied biases were apparent. While most Netherlanders were firmly committed to neutrality, preferring to stay out of the war at almost any cost above an alliance with either the Entente or Central Powers, there were obvious pro-British and pro-German biases in newspaper reporting, depending on a newspaper's audience and editorial preferences.[5] These leanings did impact on the interpretation of the events of the war and were, also, carefully monitored and promoted by the belligerents where they were able. Still, the relative moral or strategic merits of the use of gas on the Belgian and French fronts from 1915 on were rarely commented upon in mainstream newspaper reports, which may reflect an adherence to the international legal requirement that neutral countries do nothing to jeopardise their country's impartial position, or suggest that gas was one of a string of major and deadly war events that all deserved mention in the news but warranted no special attention in and of themselves, particularly since the risk they posed to the Netherlands was not immediately obvious.

In the leading liberal newspaper, *Het Algemeen Handelsblad* (The General Economist), for example, the use of gas was first mentioned on 24 April 1915 in a purely matter-of-fact way.[6] Another liberal newspaper, the *Nieuwe Rotterdamse Courant* (New Rotterdam Paper, NRC) mentioned the use of 'poisonous fumes' at Ypres that day in the same factual manner,[7] although it did reflect on the belligerents' perspectives on the development by stating that 'according to General French' the use of poison gas was a violation of the The Hague Convention (1907), while the Germans had remarked a week earlier that the Allied forces had started using chemicals, which the *NRC* commented was 'a clear attempt [by Germany] to nip criticism from neutral countries in the bud'.[8] The *NRC* clearly understood that the use of gas was contentious and was understood as contentious by all parties, but held firm to its duty as a leading newspaper of a neutral country not to pass comment on the relative merits of either belligerent cause. Importantly, it signalled as much to its readers when it commented that 'as a consequence of a lack of information, we will not pass judgment' except to state that 'using gas [the actual word used was 'rook' which translates to 'smoke'] in battle to force the enemy either to suffocate or flee' was horrible, but as old as warfare itself, and no more or less horrible than 'the use of flooding to force the enemy either to drown or flee', a likely reference to the Allies earlier inundation of the Yser or to the Dutch defence plans for the protection of Fortress Holland by flooding the countryside around it.[9] In other words, passing judgement on Germany for its use of gas required, according to the NRC editors, equal judgement of other acts of war that were used and adopted by the Allies and the Dutch themselves. The comparison was clearly intended to protect the politics of neutrality, while still highlighting the general dreadfulness of war.

Like the liberal newspapers, the Protestant and pro-German publication, *De Standaard* (The Standard), founded and edited by the former Minister President of the Netherlands, Dr Abraham Kuyper, also attempted to situate the German use of gas within a wider argument about the nature of this war, albeit with a marked anti-Entente leaning. On 24 April 1915 it published the German plea that it was only because Germany was ahead in chemical science that its weapons were more effective. Furthermore, the newspaper cited that the Germans had not breached international law at Ypres because the poison had not been released from projectiles.[10] In so doing the paper at least insinuated that the Germans should not be blamed for trialling new weaponry. Besides, it explained that as far as inhumanity was concerned in waging this war, both sides were guilty.[11] This would remain *De Standaard*'s position: gas is horrible, but war is horrible and both sides were committing horrible deeds.[12]

Popular representations of gas warfare

While there was little real debate or engagement with the morality of the use of chemical weapons in the daily newspapers, the idea of gas warfare did capture the public's imagination in other popular media, such as songs, poems, fictional stories and drawings and cartoons. Moral judgement was always at the heart of these representations. Gas, all of them stated, was a terrible weapon that made war more inhumane and impersonal. For example, shortly after the first gas attack in April 1915, the bookseller and author F. Rombouts, who lived in Roosendaal, a town close to the Belgian border, wrote a lyrical poem on his impressions. As all his around and about thirty 'war-songs' it could be sung, this one to the tune of a popular Dutch lullaby *Zachtkens klinkt het avondklokje* (Softly the nightbell rings). The soft somnolent music was intended to stand in contradiction to the lyrics and thereby put extra emphasis on them:

> *Their eyes are opened wide*
> *And stare into nothingness*
> *No power to walk on*
> *They must face death like this.*
>
> *With opened mouths and distorted faces,*
> *Claustrophobic, breathless*
> *Their lungs rip, and rouse*
> *The death for hundreds there.*
>
> *The cold northern wind was favourable*
> *They had waited for it*
> *Because those winds would bring*
> *The poisonous gases to their enemy.*
>
> *Gas designed like dew*
> *Brought forth by the wind*
> *Over trenches, countryside, villages*
> *Saved not woman, man nor child.*
>
> *Does the whole world not speak of shame*
> *About this atrocity?*
> *The pinnacle of civilised nations?*
> *Who attacks humanity like this?[13]*

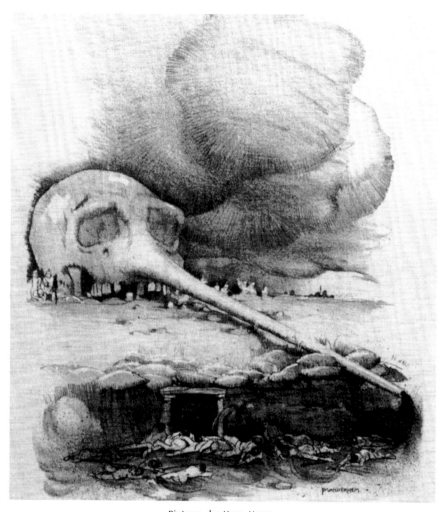

Piet van der Hem: Ypres.

Another author, J. Bleeker, used many of the heroic ideas about war prevalent in most belligerent societies of the time in a fictional story about a mutilated soldier who had 'murdered and maimed for freedom and fatherland', who had gone into war with grand hopes for military life and warfare, but soon lost these when he faced the reality of the Western front: a war 'of shells and grenades, of liquid fire and poisonous gases, of invisible enemies on distant places, has no romance in it'.[14]

The Dutch cartoonist Albert Hahn (1877–1918), furthermore, published his work in the socialist, satirical *De Notenkraker* (The Nutcracker). A convinced pacifist and not eager to limit his anti-war opinions, he used the image of gas and gasmasks to illustrate his opinion that the war had taken a turn for the worst on 22 April 1915. Shortly thereafter he published two cartoons on chlorine called 'The new death' and 'The blessing of weapons', at the same time attacking the role of religion in modern warfare. His most effective depiction, however, came a few months later, when he critiqued the effects of industrial warfare by linking a soldier wearing a gas mask with a monkey in the cartoon 'The evolution of mankind' (see page 219). The depiction summed up his view that this war was inhumane, regressive and bestial. Many of Hahn's readers shared his view: the war was turning soldiers into animals, more 'monkey' than 'man'.

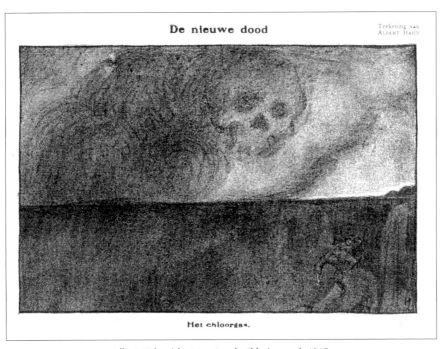

Albert Hahn: 'The New Death. Chlorine gas', 1915.

Dutch cartoonists like Hahn, Louis Raemaekers (1869–1956, 'The Gas Fiend' (see page 220) and 'Slow Asphyxiation' (see page 17). 'Gradual asphyxiation', some of which were published in the pro-Entente *Telegraaf* newspaper) and P. van der Hem (1885–1961, 'Ypres') brought to life the agony of gas warfare for the Dutch public. According to the journalist H. S. Villard, Raemaekers's cartoons, such as 'The Gas Fiend', which identified gas as devil's work, 'did as much as anything else, perhaps, to stir up the most intense kind of feeling' about the repulsiveness of chemical warfare.[15] It epitomised the pointlessness and inhumanity of the war, which was itself often depicted as a bestial and mythical if industrial creature requiring taming by the civilising ministrations of the angel of peace. In pictorial weeklies, such depictions helped to entrench the image of gas as a dreadful element of modern warfare. One important side effect was that the use of gas helped to underline the value of neutrality. The war was something that most

Netherlanders wished to avoid at all costs. It has been said that the absence of war made 'time stand still'.[16] Poisonous gas, the 'dew of death', was one of the reasons most Dutch were not eager to wind up the clock.

Gas and the Dutch military and political leadership

While the Dutch public's engagement with the concept of gas warfare was generally an intellectual one – gas was part of a war that they wished to stay out of – the most pressing concern for the Dutch authorities during the war was how to combat chemical warfare if the country was forced into it. Their response in first instance was pragmatic and realistic. The expectation that the Netherlands might still be invaded by Germany or Britain was always in the forefront of the minds of the military and political leadership.

General C. J. Snijders, the Commander-in-Chief of the Dutch Armed Forces, for example, was heedful of the need to keep up with the technological advances made by the warring armies in order to avoid obsolescing his defence forces. With the gas attacks on Ypres, Snijders recognised that masks became an urgent priority for all troops as were developing appropriate strategies for combating the impact of chemical warfare.[17] But obtaining enough to outfit an army of 200,000 soldiers as well as a growing number of reserves (which by 1918

Het zegenen der wapenen.

Albert Hahn: 'The Blessing of the Weapons', published on 29 May 1915.

The drawings of Dutch cartoonist Albert Hahn express the socialist and anti-militarist view on the war and its horrors.

consisted of another 200,000 troops) proved highly problematic. The Dutch military production facilities were not up to this task and importing the rest was extremely difficult when the belligerents placed their mask supply needs first. By April 1918, three years after chemical warfare became a common weapon on many fighting fronts, the Dutch Army had only one respiratory mask in stock for every eighty mobilised soldiers. By November of that year, thanks to some generous support from Britain's Northern Neutrals' Committee, the army could outfit all its mobilised troops with their own masks, although it only had 50,000 obsolete examples available for the 200,000 reserves that would be called up if the country were invaded.[18] This highly inadequate level of

De ontwikkelings‑gang der menschheid

(Naar aanleiding der nieuwe uitmonstering van de Fransche troepen).

Teekening van
ALBERT HAHN

Van mênschaap tot aapmensch.

RIGHT: Albert Hahn: 'The Evolution of Mankind (on the occasion of the new uniform of the French troops) – From Man Monkey to Monkey Man', published 2 October 1915.

outfitting was understandably concerning and made it all the more imperative that the country stayed neutral and out of the conflict.

Aside from the pragmatic concerns about combating the impact of chemical warfare, the government and military authorities also saw in gas weaponry an important opportunity. Snijders recognised that gas could strengthen existing defences,[19] which focused on keeping potential invaders away from the strategic heartland of the country, the provinces of North and South Holland, as said, by inundating the landscape around Fortress Holland with water. The government agreed with Snijders that gas might offer a relatively cheap and effective way of heightening the defensive capacity of the fortified position, particularly since advances in the range and effectiveness of the belligerents' artillery had made it increasingly obsolete. Shortly after the Ypres attack, a Dutch chemical warfare experimentation programme was started.[20] Part of it was paying the princely sum of 400,000 guilders in May 1916 to the Vereenigde Chemische Fabrieken (Association of Chemical Factories) to develop and produce gas receptacles to carry the poison and weapons to distribute it.

Louis Raemaekers: The Gas Fiend, 1916.
This print was published in The Great War: A Neutral's Indictment by Dutch graphic artist Louis
Raemaekers, well known for his fiercely anti-German cartoons.

The production of chemical weaponry was an important part of the government's
wartime strategy, so much so that the Minister of War, Nicolaas Bosboom, asked
the Commander-in-Chief to pass on his personal thanks to the management of the
chemical factories for the 'great effort and risk they are willingly undertaking in aid
of the country's defence'.[21] By the end of the war, the country had 380 tonnes of

asphyxiating gases in stock and had experimented with numerous ways of projecting and distributing the poison over as wide a distance as possible.[22] That their own forces barely had enough gas masks to protect themselves from the deadly vapours was secondary to the potential advantages of gas to defend a country with a declining defensive capacity. The potentials of gas warfare were, therefore, obvious to the Dutch military and government leadership. It is telling of the nature of the war as well as the desperate defensive position the country was in, that, between 1915 and 1918, there was no official discussion or debate about whether the army should use gas, let alone whether the country should produce chemical weaponry. In this way, gas was not seen as an ethical concern but rather as a pragmatic reality.

The Dutch pacifists' view of chemical warfare

Where the Dutch armed forces were actively involved in utilising the potential of chemical warfare, the army's most critical and vocal detractors, the Dutch anti-military movement, did not posit a strong anti-gas campaign during the war. In line with the general public's position, activists, like those from the popular *De Wapens Neder* (Down with Arms) group, despised war in all its forms and gas was only another example of the inhumanity of war. In other words, gas was a small part of a much larger anti-war campaign. While many anti-militarists agreed that gas was particularly loathsome, they also advocated that chemical weapons were a symptom of modern warfare that should, therefore, not be singled out. It was inappropriate to place any greater value on gas, or to engage with notions that gas was more inhumane than other weapons. It was not weaponry that had to be eradicated but human beings' drive for war.

Hence, it was not in the methods of war that the anti-militarists sought solutions but in the abolition of war and militarism. To them, war was not and never had been a 'gentlemanly' struggle, in which honour and glory were at the behest of every man-soldier. The use of gas only strengthened the anti-militarists' arguments that war and militarism were the devil's works. This point of view was particularly important to the anti-militarists' vicar, Bart de Ligt, who was repeatedly banished from 'state of siege' areas during the war out of fear he would undermine mobilised soldiers' morale. In the 1920s, De Ligt took a strong stand against the use of gas, but also held that it was impossible to separate its use from the wider concerns brought about by the mere existence of war, armies and defence preparations. Isolating gas as a particularly 'barbarous' means to wage war suggested that wars could be fought as long as this was done 'humanely'. He reiterated the famous exclamation from Dutch anarchist Ferdinand Domela Nieuwenhuis: 'to humanise war is to humanise the devil'.[23]

The anti-military position is important as it kept one of the most vocal and active voices against war in the neutral Netherlands as good as silent on the issue of the use of gas as a weapon of war. At least from this group there was no public admonishment of the belligerents' use of gas warfare, which, significantly, also helped to protect the Netherlands' neutral position. Similarly, the anti-militarist activists did not force the

Dutch armed forces to justify their production of chemical weaponry (although outside of the armed forces few Dutch may have known about it at the time). As a result, there was no driver for public debate on the issue of chemical warfare during the war.

The Dutch medical world's experiences of gas wounds

Even without public debate, however, there were other experiences and interpretations of the impact of chemical warfare around during the war. The most significant, in terms of fuelling post-war debate, was that of the Dutch medical profession, large numbers of whom spent time on the war fronts treating wounded soldiers. Importantly, however, most medical publications during the war were silent on the impact and ethics of the use of gas as a weapon. Nevertheless, it was in the medical arena that the first stirrings of a real discussion in the Netherlands for and against the use of gas warfare was forged.

Significantly, although the Dutch military health service (MHS) actively participated in the armed forces' chemical warfare trials,[24] their practitioners did not contribute to any discussion about the use of gas weapons in medical journals or magazines during the war. There were, nevertheless, a handful of references to the impact of gas on humans. In 1915, for example, the *Nederlandsche Tijdschrift voor Geneeskunde* (Dutch Magazine for Medicine) summarised the contents of the belligerents' medical publications, such as the British Medical Journal, on the topic, without passing any comment of their own. One of these pieces focused on the direct effect of inhaling chlorine and another dealt with 'some results of German gas poisoning' on victims.[25]

In 1918, the Dutch surgeon J. W. P. Fransen published his *Eerste Heelkundige Behandeling van Oorlogsgewonden* (First Surgical Treatment of War Wounded) based on his wartime experiences. One chapter of the volume dealt with the treatment of gas poisoning. Understandably, Fransen's principal focus was on offering surgical answers to gas wounds. From reading this chapter, the only conclusion one can draw is that there were few, a position that was in line with the opinions of his surgical and non-surgical medical colleagues elsewhere. Physicians 'failed to master gas weapon injuries', as the historian Marion Girard, author of *A Strange and Formidable Weapon* put it. In other words, the treatment of gas illnesses and wounds was the treatment of symptoms. The only way to get the chemicals out of the body once they had entered was to give them time and hope that the dose was small and the poisons not too strong. Symptoms differed with every kind of poison and new versions appeared regularly, which made it almost impossible to come up with effective treatments. All doctors could do was to advise victims to keep warm, drink plenty of water, say one's prayers, and with time and patience, hope things turned out for the better.[26]

In this inability to combat gas poisoning, Fransen acknowledged his underlying helplessness as a doctor. Perhaps one of the reasons for the lack of reporting on gas weaponry within the Dutch medical world during the war was that gas wounds offered no genuine medical or scientific challenge. Furthermore, due to the nature of their profession, many doctors would not be drawn into any ethical debates about the wider significance of gas weaponry. They would describe symptoms and offer solutions where possible, but they did so without passing judgement on the use of the weapons in the first place. Their presence on the war fronts as representatives of a neutral country may have influenced, at least in part, this position. While undoubtedly many Dutch doctors and nurses developed sympathies for the cause of the side of the frontline they were working on, they, more than their counterparts from warring countries, tended to see in their patients pitiable victims of war before military and scientific opportunities. As a result, they tended not to treat their patients with the same 'objective' and 'controlled approach' that characterised German and Allied physicians' behaviour, at least according to Girard.[27]

Some Dutch doctors and, particularly, nurses, however, stepped outside the restraints that their profession and their neutral nationality seemed to demand of them. In some of their writings, they mentioned the horrors of war and the moralities and 'inhumanity' behind the use of gas were often subsumed in their comments.[28] To many of them, gas warfare had gone where they, as medical men and women, could not follow. It overstepped the boundaries of what was 'humane'. It is in this light not surprising that during the inter-war years many in the Dutch medical profession joined Dutch peace movements or set up their own medically focused equivalents. They voiced the argument that in their helplessness to deal effectively with gas injuries – where they could do little more than ease the symptoms of exposure – it was not in healing but in the prevention of war that health professionals should seek answers to the concerns created by modern military conflict.[29]

A Dutch nurse who voiced her repulsion towards gas during the war was Adrie Schipper. She worked in a hospital in France on the Allied side of the front in 1915 and 1916 and wrote about her experiences in the *Tijdschrift voor Ziekenverpleging* (Nursing Magazine). In general, when speaking of the sick and wounded, she was modest and caring, but her tone changed on referring to gas patients. In February 1916, she wrote:

> The more one thinks about it, the more one asks oneself how the staff of an army in our days can sanction and use such a weapon of assassination! The poor soldiers brought in resembled in their sultriness last-stage tuberculosis patients.[30]

As set out in 'Would it not be better just to stop?' some Dutch nurses even began to call for a strike of all medical workers in the service of the armed forces,[31] a notion certainly not subscribed by all nurses. But most of them did despise war and saw absolutely no good coming out of it. Some Dutch doctors, however, working in frontline hospitals pointed out the – arguable – advantages and improvements brought by the war to the medical profession.[32] For example, shortly after returning from a stint at a front-line hospital to his home in Utrecht in 1917, neurophysiologist and pharmacist professor Rudolf Magnus held a lecture about the relationship between war and medicine pointing out how war was an ideal training ground even for experienced doctors and surgeons, and one that would benefit medicine in the long-term and their non-soldier patients as well. According to Magnus, the war proved an ideal way to experiment and learn about all manner of medical ailments and wounds. Magnus also focused on the advantages brought about by gas warfare, which made the invention of better equipment a necessity and would therefore ensure safer gas masks and other safety devices in case of accidents in chemical industries.[33] The divergence in opinion among Dutch medical experts and practitioners during the war were an important driver of the post-war debate on the value of gas warfare more generally.

A real debate – the 1920s

It was not until the 1920s that a real debate about chemical warfare became a subject of public discourse in the Netherlands sparked initially by the position taken by the ICRC from 1918 onwards.[34] The ICRC's stand fuelled arguments across the Western world and like the international debates during the 1920s, in the Netherlands the clash between those who were repulsed by the use of gas as a weapon of war and those who saw the potential military advantages thereof was heated.[35] On the one side, several Dutch chemists, politicians and military men portrayed gas as a humane weapon and more useful and less lethal form of combat than the more traditional artillery, machine-gun and rifle machinery. They based their arguments on the experiences of the First World War both in the production of chemical weaponry, their medical and non-lethal impact, as well as in the military strategising around their use in aid of military defence. In direct opposition, pacifist groups, socialists and left-wing liberals, argued that the experiences of the First World War proved that gas was inhumane and even more so than conventional weaponry. Quite in contrast to the relative silence on the issue during the war, in the post-war years, this debate was public and fierce and revolved around the question of whether it was warranted for 'civilised' nations to use chemical warfare.

Both sides on the gas debate in the Netherlands during the 1920s invoked the opinions of belligerents as well as those of Dutch medical professionals who had witnessed the impact of gas attacks first hand. There was plenty of opinion available for both views, since the debate was not typically Dutch. In the international arena as well, it was defined by acceptance as well as hatred of gas. It split up German chemists, with Fritz Haber coming out in defence of chemical weapons, on the one hand, and Hermann Staudinger, a chemist who urged the Red Cross not to stop speaking out against chemical warfare, on the other hand.[36] But it is perhaps best shown by the British example. Most British soldiers condemned gas and so did their relatives on the home front. Nevertheless at the end of the war Britain was a leading nation in the production of chemical weaponry. As the chemist Julian Robinson explained: 'By the end of the war gas had become a standard weapon, if not a universally popular one.'[37]

As part of a broader conviction, shared by many scientists and only attacked by some, that eventually science (and medicine) would humanise and civilise warfare, in this debate several commentators focused on the observation that gas limited the numbers of deaths in combat and the severity of wounds when compared with other weapons. Cambridge biochemist J.B.S. Haldane, for example, defended the weapon by hailing its efficiency in trench warfare, although especially referring to those with arsenic compounds, which by the way had seen less wartime use than some other agents, and by pointing out that it caused much less harm than guns and shells. According to him, opponents to such chemical weaponry were either radical pacifists or ignorant politicians led by fear of the unknown, but an unknown weapon is not by definition more inhumane than an old one. In his view, to forbid its use was 'a piece of sentimentalism as cruel as it [was] ridiculous'. If it was right to fight 'with a sword', it was right to fight 'with mustard gas'.[38]

Ex-soldier Norman Gladden waded into the British debate by remarking that poison gas caused widespread fear 'out of all proportion to the damage done'.[39] Going even further, both Otto Muntsch, German author of *Leitfaden der Pathologie und Therapie der Kampfgaserkrankungen* (Guide into Pathology and Therapy of Poison Gas Illnesses, 1932), and J. F. C. Fuller, British author of *the Army in My Time* (1935), used their experiences of the First World War to justify that gas was a humane weapon, because it stunned soldiers into inactivity and made it possible to capture and imprison them. Others argued that the long-term side effects of gas were negligible and the immediate effects were more psychological than physical,[40] an argument perhaps most fiercely advocated by Amos Fries, head of the United States Chemical Warfare Service during the war (in trying to secure the job). According to Fries, gas was a humane weapon because it had helped to defeat 'barbarous' Germans, but more importantly because it was a very powerful weapon that rarely killed its victims. Such positions reiterated that war was always nasty, but chemical warfare came closest to offering a civilised way of waging it.[41]

In contrast to these pro-gas arguments, the war experiences, memoirs and stories told by men and women like Vera Brittain, Erich Maria Remarque and Wilfred Owen presented gas as a horrible weapon because of the fear it spread and the way it killed or wounded. Even Ernst Jünger did not disagree with them on this point.[42] Belgian soldier-poet Daan Boens expressed similar sentiments in his poem 'Gas' (1918):

> The stench is unbearable, while death mocks back.
> The masks around the cheeks cut the look of bestial snouts,
> the masks with wild eyes, crazy or absurd,
> their bodies drift on until they stumble upon steel.
> The men know nothing, they breathe in fear.
> Their hands clench on weapons like a buoy for the drowning,
> they do not see the enemy, who, also masked, loom forth,
> and storm them, hidden in the rings of gas.
> Thus in the dirty mist, the biggest murder happens. [...][43]

When released – either by cylinders or grenades – gas was uncontrollable, mastered only by the wind, and was indiscriminately breathed in by or dripped onto soldiers and non-combatants alike. Indeed, it spread a fear unexplained just by its actual casualty rate, probably because of the way it killed: silently, through suffocation and without leaving any battle wound (although this does not apply to mustard gas, which could rip off your entire skin).[44] Gas masks were always in competition with new chemicals. While, in time, the masks were more effective, they could not eradicate the fear of gas, most importantly because soldiers often believed them to be ineffective; which was only partly true.[45] Furthermore the masks proved cumbersome and 'dehumanising' to wear and, as such, were a cause of psychological problems among soldiers. Besides, gas was always used in combination with bullets, shells and grenades. Usually it was not unconsciousness and imprisonment that determined the fate of a gas victim, but artillery or machine-gun fire. Therefore, even if gas was by itself a largely non-lethal weapon, soldiers knew that it was a weapon that often proved fatal. In other words, while military leaders might advocate that 'it was better to recover from a gas poisoning than to die of a non-poisoned bullet', many soldiers had an opposite opinion. For those who did recover, gas often left long-lasting legacies, among which blindness and respiratory ailments were common.[46] It was this experience that bolstered the anti-gas campaign in Britain and abroad during the 1920s.

The International Red Cross

Professor Magnus' opinion on the medical advantages of (chemical) warfare was respected by many of his Dutch colleagues, even if they despised war itself.[47] The majority of physicians in the warring countries took a more opportunistic than pacifist point of view on war and the use of gas as well. They welcomed the chance to experiment on and with the vast number of war wounded, and saw in war a means of strengthening the physical and psychological health of their people, nation or race. From this position, war was not an enemy of medicine, but rather its colleague or even teacher.[48] In how far such opinions aligned with those of International Red Cross doctors, most of whom came from military backgrounds, is uncertain. Importantly, however, the ICRC, a neutral organisation when it came to the politics of war, took a very strong stand against gas warfare in the last year of the war.

On 6 February 1918, the ICRC, which just had been awarded the Nobel Peace Prize, protested against the use of poison gas and other modern weaponry.[49] According to the committee, such weapons ended any illusion that war was a 'struggle between gentlemen' and highlighted the realities of modern industrial conflict killing and maiming indiscriminately. The protest was unique in the ICRC's history since it, certainly up until the Cold War, usually hid behind the principle of impartiality and non-interference in the politics and military decisions of warring countries, focussing instead on aiding all victims of war and crisis regardless of background and circumstance. However, in the case of gas attacks, the institution felt compelled to report on the general inhumanity of the use of gas on soldiers and civilians alike especially since the use of 'poison or poisonous weapons' and 'projectiles causing unnecessary harm' were

Albert Hahn: Ecce Homo, published on 13 April 1918.

prohibited by the Hague Conventions.[50] The ICRC felt that the continued use of such weaponry would lead to a situation in which 'warfare would be nothing else but a work of general destruction without any mercy'.[51] The 'horrible suffering, these gases caused – to look at it is even more cruel than the most dreadful wounds' proved the criminal character of their use. If continued, the ICRC foresaw a 'struggle that would top everything in cruelty, history has seen up until this moment'.[52] According to the ICRC at least, poison gas was anything but a humane weapon of war.

Official reactions to the ICRC announcement were mixed. The appeal was seen

Henry de Groux: Amidst smoke and barbed wire, a soldier with a mouth pad is emerging,
carrying hand grenades. A print from the Belgian artist's series of etchings
'The faces of victory'.

as controversial, because each side accused the adversary of being the instigator. The Allied forces wrote that they were prepared to sign an agreement on the ban on chemical weaponry if Germany would do the same. Germany accused the Entente of barbarism, because of their use of 'primitive peoples' as soldiers, before acknowledging they were willing to look at the proposition. Nevertheless, no progress was made and, in general, the belligerents attacked the ICRC for its public and 'anti-neutral' stand. For the ICRC, the backlash to its public declaration confirmed its need to stay out of ethical and moral debates about war and weaponry in the future, and instead focus on its primary task of aiding victims.[53] This decision would be decisive and ensured the ICRC stayed out of publicising to the world news about the impact of war as it happened. For example, when in the 1930s, the ICRC collected data on the use of mustard gas by the Italian armies in Abyssinia, it refused to hand over its findings to the League of Nations fearing claims of partiality again. During the Second World War, similar fears influenced the Committee's decision to withhold from protesting against the Nazi persecution of European Jews.[54]

Nevertheless, once peace returned and the neutrality of the ICRC was less at threat, the Committee did actively involve itself in many of the general international peace appeals that were made during the inter-war years, when it was safe from being seen as anything but impartial. For example, on 19 July 1921, together with the League of Red Cross Societies, the Committee signed a statement saying:

> It now is the task to blossom anew the foundations of internationalism in the spirit of man, who respects the love of each citizen for his city, of each patriot for his fatherland, but who also learns each man to respect the rights of his fellow men, by enlightening everyday life of the individual through the light of universal and eternal justice.[55]

It also asked the League of Nations to prohibit the use of poison gas in 1920 and in 1921 it appealed to all nations to ratify such a prohibition.[56]

The 1920s did see important changes to the protocols and laws dictating the use of chemical (and bacteriological) weaponry, most of which received ICRC support. In June 1925, for example, the Netherlands and many other states signed the Geneva protocol prohibiting their use, with the proviso that if they were attacked with chemical weapons they would reserve the right to defend themselves using similar weaponry. This was an important achievement of the anti-gas movement locally and internationally,[57] and was strongly supported by the ICRC, which urged all its committees to make the abolition of gas weapons one of their primary tasks.[58] According to ICRC historian André Durand, the Protocol would never have come into being without the exertions of the Red Cross organisations, even if it was more a 'The Hague law' than 'Geneva law'.[59] At the 1928 ICRC conference, held in The Hague, both chemical and biological warfare were repeatedly condemned.[60]

However, at the 1928 Hague conference a key change in approach to chemical warfare was also signalled, when the ICRC recommended that each national Red Cross organisation establish their own national gas committee, in accordance with the recommendation made by a panel of chemical, military and medical experts, who had gathered together for the first time in January 1928.[61] Two years later, during the ICRC conference in Brussels the organisation's blanket rejection of chemical and biological weapons on the grounds of their 'inhumane' effects on victims further changed in a subtle, but key respect. At this conference, the organisation acknowledged that it was not enough to advocate for a ban on such weapons, it also needed to prepare for dealing with the impact of chemical warfare as well as finding ways to combat it effectively. It offered a prize for the best ideas to protect against gas attack and then implemented the innovations, which included improving gas masks, gas-locking and air-conditioning units for underground shelters, and developing reactants to mustard gas.[62] In other words, the ICRC waged war against gas warfare as best it was able, firstly by attempting to make this method of fighting illegal and then on making it impractical, because who would need to use the weapon if its uses could be neutralised?

The changing position of the Dutch Red Cross

The change in focus of the ICRC on combatting the effects of gas warfare, rather than continuing its protests against the 'inhumanity' of its use, caused the Committee to receive intense criticism from pacifists and peace movements alike. For the staunchly anti-gas campaigners, the ICRC had deserted their cause and had as good as joined the pro-gas camp. In the Netherlands, the change of focus from abolishing chemical warfare to combating was already clear in 1928 when the Dutch Red Cross (DRC), following the ICRC recommendation, created the National Gas Committee (NGC), whose task was to investigate the best way to protect the civilian population from aero-chemical attack. At this point, several Dutch chemical engineers refused to co-operate with any science leading to the possible development of chemical weaponry and were critical of the DRC's (and later ICRC's) position on gas use, which became part of the wider political debate on the issue in the Netherlands.[63] The anti-militarist vicar J. B. Th. Hugenholtz, for example, upheld that the DRC was haphazard and hypocritical in its creation of the NGC. In his eyes, combatting the effects of gas instead of condemning it completely reeked of compromise and collusion with the military establishment:

> Now that the military, present also in the Red Cross, is out of answers, now that at last our warnings are dripping through, now that at last it becomes clear that humanity is hopelessly lost against one of the most infernal weapons of our Christian governments, the Netherlands anything but excluded, now we have to solve a prize question…!! A fool is he who still co-operates with such (war) work. We tear off the Red Cross's mask, so the world can see that this organisation is nothing but an accessory of militarism existing under the pretence of goodness.[64]

A.R.P.   E.P.S.

The New Zealand Red
Cross Society

FIRST AID IN

CHEMICAL

WARFARE

Including Collective and
Individual Protection

Outside cover and title page of *The
New Zealand Red Cross Society: First
Aid in Chemical Warfare Including
Collective and Individual Protection.*
(Christchurch: 1940)

The New Zealand Red Cross
Society

FIRST AID IN
CHEMICAL WARFARE

INCLUDING COLLECTIVE AND PERSONAL PROTECTION

BY

G. THACKER PATERSON

*Instructor Air Raid Precautions School, Falfield, England
Chairman Auckland Centre N.Z. Red Cross Society*

WHITCOMBE & TOMBS LIMITED
Christchurch, Auckland, Wellington, Dunedin, Invercargill,
London, Melbourne, Sydney.

Hugenholtz's views were further developed by his Christian anti-militarist friend G. J. Heering, author of *De Zondeval van het Christendom* (The Fall of Christianity, 1927), the 'bible' of Dutch Christian pacifists of the time. According to both men, poison gas was a key step in the ongoing brutalisation of warfare. Warfare could not be humanised but was destined to get worse every time it was waged, and chemical warfare proved it. Heering argued that by focusing on alleviating gas warfare the ICRC, DRC and NGC were perpetuating its use and were, therefore, guilty of acting in the 'comedy' of warfare humanisation.[65]

As said, the DRC's NGC was set up to prepare the Dutch people for the possible impact of widespread gas warfare. While Dutch pacifists agitated against the Committee for this stand, NGC members voiced rather more muted opinions on gas, some of which clearly justified its use. For example, the Inspector of the MHS, J. C. Diehl, also a long-serving member of the DRC board,[66] was an ardent supporter of the possible military applications of gas warfare. In 1926, he had already publicly published a piece that stated that in wars a civilised country could be expected to cause 'as less death, suffering and perpetual disability as possible'. However, 'this naturally should not hinder reaching the military targets'.[67] Therefore, gas was a legitimate weapon since it helped armed forces attain these targets.[68] Diehl also held that gas was a humane weapon and that pacifist propaganda was overstating the case of its 'inhumanity'.[69] Other members of the NGC expressed similar opinions. For instance, J. T. H. van Weeren, wrote a book in 1929 entitled *Lucht- en Gasoorlog* (Air- and Gas Warfare) in which he analysed the use of gas in World War I and advocated that, although gas had not ended the war, it had served an important role. According to Van Weeren gas had demonstrated that warfare had no rules and could not be limited, not even against civilians.[70] Therefore, the focus of the Committee lay on training its staff, on avoiding exposure to gas and on treating gas victims.[71] As a result, the DRC gave gas courses and purchased 'hospital gas masks' for its staff.[72] It tested gas masks and shared its information with other Red Cross committees, including in 1937 the German one even though it was aware that the GRC had been completely Nazified.[73]

With such vocal supporters of the military application of chemical warfare, it seemed that even before the ICRC declaration at the 1930 Brussels' conference, the DRC had gone full circle from admonishing gas as an 'inhumane' weapon of war to supporting its use while trying to diminish its impact. Importantly, after the Dutch government's *Leidraad Luchtbeschermingsdienst* (Guideline Air Defence Service) was released in 1931, the NGC was abolished. But the Dutch Chief of Staff, General H. A. Seyffardt, explained to the DRC that he saw that the Red Cross still had a vital role to play in terms of training military personnel and informing the wider public about the potential impact of gas and air attacks.[74]

Unsurprisingly, for anti-gas campaigners throughout the Netherlands, the DRC's continued involvement with the armed forces and its inability to make a proper stand on the issue of gas was a call to action. They saw the organisation as a wolf in sheep's clothing, threatening to undermine the drive to abolish chemical warfare from within the pacifist camp. As a result, well before the ICRC conference in Brussels, a strong, vocal and non-violent propaganda campaign against the DRC, and against its parent body the ICRC, was launched in 1929 involving anti-military, pacifist groups around the country, including a large number of physicians, chemical engineers and nurses, the latter of whom united under the name *Anti-Oorlogsgroep Verplegenden* (Anti-War Group of Nurses). The impact of the ongoing campaign against the Red Cross left a long and bitter legacy that tainted the organisation.[75]

Conclusion

For several reasons the neutral Netherlands witnessed little if any debate on the use of chemical weaponry during the First World War. Firstly, even though the country was neutral, it faced the prospect of war, which restricted public discourse on military and security matters. Secondly, precisely because of the country's neutrality, the military and government leadership as well as newspaper editors were reluctant to make moral judgements about the use of gas for fear of alienating the belligerents and thereby endangering the security of the country. As a result, the armed forces focused on the challenges and opportunities presented by the very real prospect of chemical warfare and the government involved itself almost entirely in terms of the impact gas weaponry may have on the country's defences. The politics of neutrality kept mainstream newspaper editors from commenting on anything other than 'the facts' of war. Thirdly, convinced pacifists did not see the need to place extra emphasis on the use of gas because the weapon only reinforced their existing position that war was the devil's work and should be abolished at all costs. The introduction of gas warfare in 1915 did not change this opinion, only emphasised it. Fourthly, for the public at large discussion on the use of chemical warfare was largely unnecessary. Influenced more by pictures and poems rather than any informed or nuanced discussions, the Dutch in general had a reasonably 'open mind' about more traditional warfare, fought with bullets and grenades, but did not extend this to the use of gas. In their eyes, gas was not an 'honest' weapon. Choking was an inhumane way of dying. Whoever used gas had done away with 'civilisation' and had regressed humanity at the same time.

The lack of discourse between these various views on gas changed dramatically during the 1920s. The reasons behind the shift lay with the strategy of the Dutch Red Cross and by the increasing amount of available publicity that gas was a much more humane weapon of war than other more traditional weapons. The International Red Cross and its local Dutch committee played key parts. While initially, they worked with other groups and organisations within and outside the Netherlands to ban gas weaponry, from 1928 on, the DRC changed its approach, focusing instead on helping to prepare the population for the possible use of gas against civilians in a future war. For its change in tactics, the Red Cross came under attack from pacifists and other critics for legitimising chemical warfare rather than finding ways to abolish it completely. This critique became particularly damning when the National Gas Committee – a DRC creation – openly came out in support of arguments that gas was a militarily necessary and a humane means to wage war. The critique became international when the ICRC effectively gave legitimacy to the DRC's position at its international congress in 1930 and advocated that finding means to alleviate the impact of chemical warfare was a more pragmatic and effective means of handling the matter. From this point on, the divide between those in support of gas weaponry as a viable part of war and those who campaigned in favour of total abolition became decidedly entrenched. Importantly, however, the origins of the divide appeared in the immediate aftermath of that first fateful attack near Ypres at the end of April 1915.

Acknowledgement

This chapter was originally published as Leo van Bergen and Maartje Abbenhuis, 'Man-monkey, monkey-man: neutrality and the discussions about the "inhumanity" of poison gas in the Netherlands and International Committee of the Red Cross', *First World War Studies*, Volume 3, Issue 1 (2012), pp. 1–23.

The article is reproduced by permission of Taylor & Francis Ltd, www.tandfonline.com.

Notes

1 M. Abbenhuis, 'Where war met peace: The borders of the neutral Netherlands with Belgium and Germany in the First World War, 1914 – 1918', *Journal of Borderlands Studies*, vol. 22, no. 1 (2007), pp. 53–77.

2 Standard histories of the Netherlands in the First World War: M. Abbenhuis, *The Art of Staying Neutral. The Netherlands in the First World War, 1914 – 1918* (Amsterdam, 2006); H. P. van Tuyll-van Serooskerken, *The Netherlands and World War I. Espionage, Diplomacy and Survival* (Leiden, 2001); P. Moeyes, *Buiten schot. Nederland tijdens de Eerste Wereldoorlog 1914–1918* (Amsterdam, 2001); C. Smit, *Nederland in de Eerste Wereldoorlog (1899–1919)*, 3 volumes, 1971–73.

3 The Dutch tended to use the descriptor 'gas' to cover all kinds of chemical weaponry, including those, like mustard gas, that were not actually gases.

4 For example, T. Cook, '"Against God-Inspired Conscience": The Perception of Gas Warfare as a Weapon of Mass Destruction, 1915 – 1939', *War and Society*, vol. 18, no. 1 (2000), pp. 55–57.

5 Cesorship practices did operate in the Netherlands during the war, although they were haphazard, see: Abbenhuis, *The Art of Staying Neutral*, pp. 169–173.

6 *Het Algemeen Handelsblad*, 24 April 1915, p. 1.

7 *Nieuwe Rotterdamse Courant*, 24 April 1915, Ochtendblad, p. B 3.

8 *Nieuwe Rotterdamse Courant*, 24 April 1915, Avondblad, p. C 2.

9 *NRC*, 24 April 1915, Avondblad, p. B 1.

10 Declaration (IV, 2) concerning asphyxiating gases, The Hague, 29 July 1899, URL http://bit.ly/18Qn1xq.

11 *De Standaard*, 24 April 1915, Eerste blad, p. 1; J. Hemels, *Een Journalistiek Geheim Ontsluierd. De Dubbelmonarchie en een geval van dubbele moraal in de Nederlandse pers tijdens de Eerste Wereldoorlog* (Apeldoorn-Antwerpen, 2010), p. 69.

12 *De Standaard*, 28 April 1915, p. 1.

13 'Oorlogspoezie onder het volk', *De Groene Amsterdammer*, 30 December 1916, p. 9.

14 J. Bleeker, 'Het Spookhuis', *De Groene Amsterdammer*, 9 November 1918, p. 3.

15 E. Russell, *War and Nature. Fighting humans and insects with chemicals from World War I to Silent Spring* (Cambridge, 2001); For an essay on British cartoonists and gas warfare see: M. Girard, *A Strange and Formidable Weapon. British responses to World War I poison gas*, Working Paper, 2008, chapter 5 ('Gas as a symbol').

16 Cf. M. Brands, 'The Great War die aan ons voorbijging. De blinde vlek in het historische bewustzijn van Nederland', in: M. Derman and J. H. C. Blom (eds.), *Het belang van de Tweede Wereldoorlog* (Den Haag 1997), pp. 9–20.

17 The first instructions for dealing with gas came later in the war, with the secret military publication of the *Voorschrift Stikgassen* (Instruction Suffocating Gases), n.p, c. 1917.

18 Abbenhuis, *The Art of Staying Neutral*, pp. 181, 187; H. Roozenbeek, J. van Woensel, *De Geest in de Fles. De omgang van de Nederlandse defensieorganisatie met chemische strijdmiddelen 1915–1917* (Amsterdam, 2010), pp. 25–41.

19 Correspondence to and from Snijders, 1915, in Nationaal Archief (NA), 'Archieven van de Generale Staf' inventory number 2.13.70, file number 2.

20 Abbenhuis, *The Art of Staying Neutral*, p. 49.

21 Minister of War, Nicolaas Bosboom, to Commander-in-Chief, C. J. Snijders, 16 May 1916, in NA 2.13.70, 3.

22 N. Bosboom, *In Moeilijke Omstandigheden* (Gorinchem: 1933), p. 143; Head of Munitiebureau (Munitions Bureau), 'Maandverslag van het Munitiebureau over de maanden Augustus en September 1917', 23 October 1917, in NA 2.13.70, 313.

23 B. de Ligt, *Nieuwe Vormen van Oorlog en hoe die te Bestrijden* (Huis ter Heide, 1927), pp. 42–44.

24 Roozenbeek, Van Woensel, *De Geest in de Fles*, p. 27.

25 NTvG, 1915, A II, 1285.

26 J. W. P. Fransen, *Eerste Heelkundige Behandeling van Oorlogsgewonden* (Leiden, 1918), pp. 24–28; Girard, *A Strange and Formidable Weapon,* p. 77.

27 Girard, *A Strange and Formidable Weapon,* p. 76.

28 The best example is the book by the Dutch physician A. van Tienhoven, *De Gruwelen van den Oorlog in Servië* (The horrors of war in Serbia) (Rotterdam, 1915). This book however deals with the first months of the war, so poison gas is not part of it. The pictures printed in it, make it a *Krieg dem Kriege* avant la lettre, although, contrary to Ernst Friedrich, Van Tienhoven had no pacifist intentions whatsoever.

29 Interestingly, the helplessness of the medical profession when it came to gas victims during the First World War heralded a similar medical response after the dropping of the atomic bombs on Hiroshima and Nagasaki in 1945 and a similar impetus towards joining peace movements by medical professionals post-1945. Cf., N. Lewer, *Physicians and the Peace Movement. Prescriptions for hope* (London 1992); T. M. Ruprecht, *Friedensbewegung im Gesundheitswesen. Zur Geschichte der 'Internationalen* Ärzte für die *Verhütung des Atomkrieges' und ihrer bundesdeutschen Sektion* (München, 1987); T. M. Ruprecht, C. Jenssen (eds.), Äskulap *oder Mars?* Ärzte *gegen den Krieg* (Bremen, 1991).

30 A. Schipper, 'Van het Fransche front', *Tijdschrift voor Ziekenverpleging* (1916), pp. 348–50, 349.

31 L. van Bergen, "Would it not be better just to stop?' Dutch medical aid in World War I and the medical anti-war movement in the Interwar Years', *First World War Studies* (2011).

32 For critical remarks on the goodness of war for medicine see: L. van Bergen, 'The value of war for medicine: questions and considerations concerning an often endorsed proposition', *Medicine, Conflict and Survival*, vol. 23, no. 3 (August 2007), pp. 189–97; R. Cooter, 'War and modern medicine', in: W. F. Bynum, R. Porter (eds.), *Companion Encyclopedia of the History of Medicine* (London 1993), pp. 1536–73; S. Hahn, 'How varied the image of the heart trauma has become. The development of cardiovascular surgery during the First World War', in: *War and Medicine* (London, 2008), pp. 46–55, especially, pp. 46–47.

33 'Oorlog en Geneeskunde', *Tijdschrift voor Ziekenverpleging* (1917), pp.741–42 (first published in NRC).

34 Roozenbeek, Van Woensel, *De Geest in de Fles*, pp. 37–41, 76, 79–81.

35 D. Richter, *Chemical Soldiers. British gas warfare in World War I* (London, 1994), p. 1.

36 L. F. Haber, *The Poisonous Cloud. Chemical Warfare in the First World War* (Oxford, 1986), p. 292.

37 J. P. Robinson, *The Rise of CB Weapons, The Problem of Chemical and Biological Warfare*, Vol. 1, (Stockholm/New York, 1971), p. 141. For the discussion on the (in)humanity of gas see: Girard, *A Strange and Formidable Weapon*, chapter 6; A. Becker, 'La guerre des gaz, entre tragédie, rumeur, mémoire et oubli', in Christophe Prochason, Anne Rasmussen, *Vrai et Faux dans la Grande Guerre* (Paris, 2004), pp. 257–76.

38 Richter, *Chemical soldiers*, pp. 218–19; J. B. S. Haldane, *Callinicus. A defence of chemical warfare* (London, 1925), pp. 9–10, 20–21 [quote]; 27–28, 33, 52, 81, 82 [quote]; Haber, *The Poisonous Cloud*, pp. 293–94; A. Rasmussen, 'Science and technology', in J. Horne (ed.), *A Companion to World War I* (Chichester, 2010), pp. 307–22, 319; Girard, *A Strange and Formidable Weapon*, p. 17.

39 R. Holmes, *Firing line* (London 1985), p. 212.

40 D. Winter, *Death's Men* (London, 1979), p. 123; Wolfgang U. Eckart, Christoph Gradmann (eds.), *Die Medizin und der Erste Weltkrieg* (Pfaffenweiler, 1996), p. 136.

41 Russell, *War and Nature,* pp. 39, 53–54, 60–63, 65–66. For the discussion on gas as a humane weapon, see also: L. van Bergen, 'The poison gas debate in the inter-war years', *Medicine Conflict and Survival*, vol. 24, no. 3 (July–September 2008), pp. 174–87.

42 V. Brittain, *Testament of Youth* (Glasgow, 1978) (6), p. 325; W. Owen, 'Dulce et Decorum', in P. Fussell, *The Bloody Game* (London, 1991), p. 166; E. M. Remarque, *Im Westen nichts Neues* (Frankfurt a. M./Berlin, 1983), pp. 54, 55, 96–97; E. Jünger, *In Stahlgewittern* (Berlin, 1922) (4), p. 57; J. A. Verdoorn, *Arts en Oorlog* (Amsterdam 1972), II, pp. 602–03; P. Fussell, *The Great War and Modern Memory* (London, 1977), p. 174.

43 First published in *Menschen in de Grachten* (1918); republished in R. Kammelar, J. Sicking, M. Wielinga (eds.), *Het Monster van de Oorlog. Nederlandse liedjes en gedichten over de Eerste Wereldoorlog* (Amsterdam, 2004), p. 28.

44 A. Carden-Coyne, *Reconstructing the Body. Classicism, modernism, and the First World War* (Oxford, 2009), p. 91.

45 Robinson, *The rise of CB weapons,* pp. 51–57; S. Audoin-Rouzeau, 'Combat', in Horne (ed.), *A Companion to World War I*, pp. 173–87, 181–82.

46 J. C. Diehl, 'Een en ander over chemische strijdmiddelen', *Nederlandsch Tijdschrift voor Geneeskunde*, (1926), pp. II, 1002–05, 1003; M. Eksteins, *Rites of Spring* (London, 1989), 161–62. For the fear of gas, also: Haber, *The Poisonous Cloud*, pp. 235–38.

47 Cf. P. H. van Eden, 'Oorlogs- en vredeschirurgie. De methoden der moderne oorlogschirurgie toegepast op de vredespraktijk', *Geneeskundig Tijdschrift der Rijksverzekeringsbank*, vol. 5 (1920), pp. 281–82; A. F. Rath Henricus, *Oorlogs- en vredeschirurgie. De methoden der moderne oorlogschirurgie toegepast op de vredespraktijk* (Amsterdam, 1920); O. Lanz, '*De oorlogswinst der heelkunde*', Rede uitgesproken op de Dies Natalis der Universiteit van Amsterdam, 8 January 1925.

48 Cf. J. Bleker, H.-P. Schmiedebach (eds.), *Medizin und Krieg. Vom Dilemma der Heilberufe 1865 bis 1985* (Frankfurt am Main, 1987); S. Michl, *Im Dienste des 'Volkskörpers'. Deutsche und französische Ärzte im ersten Weltkrieg* (Göttingen, 2007), L. van Bergen, *Before my Helpless Sight. Suffering, dying and military medicine on the Western Front 1914–1918* (Farnham, 2009).

49 The ICRC's appeal against the use of poisonous gases, 8 February 1918, URL <http://bit.ly/1NYzvnE>.

50 The Conventions of The Hague (1899, 1907) determined the laws of warfare, and what kind of warfare and which kind of weaponry were or were not allowed. The Geneva Conventions determine the rights of the sick and wounded soldiers as well as those of the medical personnel (1864 and 1906), the prisoners of war (1929) and the civilians (1949).

51 Quoted from W. Wolffensperger, 'Het Roode Kruis en het gebruik van vergiftige gassen', in *Het Reddingwezen*, 7 (1918), pp. 113–117, 113–114. Also: Girard, *A Strange and Formidable Weapon*, pp. 46–50; The text is almost entirely printed in: A. Durand, *De Sarajevo à Hiroshima. Histoire du Comité International de la Croix Rouge* (Genève, 1978), pp. 70–71.

52 Wolffensperger, 'Het Roode Kruis en het gebruik van vergiftige gassen', pp. 114–15; Becker, 'La guerre des gaz, entre tragédie, rumeur, mémoire et oubli', pp. 260–62.

53 D. Riesenberger, *Für Humanität in Krieg und Frieden. Das Internationale Rote Kreuz 1863–1977* (Göttingen, 1992), pp. 77–79; J.-C. Favez, *Une Mission Impossible? Le CICR, les déportations et les camps de concentration nazis* (Lausanne, 1988), p. 156; Robinson, *The rise of CB weapons*, p. 233 (fn. 3).

54 Riesenberger, *Für Humanität in Krieg und Frieden*, pp. 132–34; Favez, *Une Mission Impossible?*, pp. 156–58.

55 As cited in A. Durand, 'Das Menschenrechtsdenken der Gründer des Roten Kreuzes', *Auszüge der Revue Internationale de la Croix Rouge*, vol. 39, no. 5 (September–October 1988), p. 217.

56 Riesenberger, *Für Humanität in Krieg und Frieden*, p. 146.

57 Roozenbeek, Van Woensel, *De Geest in de Fles*, pp. 76, 83, 90; Haber, *The Poisonous Cloud*, pp. 295–96; Girard, *A Strange and Formidable Weapon*, pp. 185–97; J. Goldblat, *CB Disarmament Negotiations*

1920–1970, the Problem of Chemical and Biological Warfare, Vol. IV (Stockholm, 1971), pp. 58–71; Becker, 'La guerre des gaz, entre tragédie, rumeur, mémoire et oubli', pp. 263–64.

58 Riesenberger, *Für Humanität in Krieg und Frieden*, p. 146.

59 Durand, *De Sarajevo à Hiroshima*, pp. 76–77. See also: G. Willemin, R. Heacock, *The International Committee of the Red Cross* (The Hague, 1984), pp. 23. 'The Hague' concerns itself with the ways wars can be fought in line with The Hague Conventions of 1899 and 1907; 'Geneva' with the protection and rights of those coming into contact with it in line with the Geneva conventions, the first of which were signed in 1864.

60 'Internationale Rode Kruis-conferentie', Persdienst, 20 (28 November1928), p. 5; J. B. Th. Hugenholtz, 'Protest van Generaal-Majoor Schuurman', *Kerk en Vrede*, vol. 5, no. 3–4 (July–August 1929), p. 38.

61 L. van Bergen, *De Zwaargewonden Eerst? Het Nederlandsche Roode Kruis en het vraagstuk van oorlog en vrede 1867–1945* (Rotterdam, 1994), pp. 276–79.

62 Hoofdbestuur NRK 1867–1945, inv. nr. 175: Constitution de commissions mixtes nationales pour la protection des populations civiles contre la guerre chimique (nr. 485–28); J. B. Th. Hugenholtz, 'Het Roode Kruis ontmaskert zich', *De Nieuwe Koers*, vol. 12, no. 6 (June 1929), p. 3; A. Müller Lehning, 'De reddende prijsvraag', in: A. Müller Lehning, *Politiek en Cultuur* (The Hague, without date [1930]), pp. 111–12.

63 J. B. Th. Hugenholtz, 'Oorlogsdienst geweigerd door scheikundige', *Kerk en Vrede*, vol. 4, no. 2–3 (June–July 1928), pp. 6–7; van Bergen, *De Zwaargewonden Eerst?*, p. 279.

64 Hugenholtz, 'Het Roode Kruis ontmaskert zich', p. 3.

65 G. J. Heering, *De Zondeval van het Christendom* (Arnhem, 1928) (3), pp. 226–227 (incl 227, note 1).

66 Archives ARA, Hoofdbestuur NRK 1867–1945, inv. 190 (1): Hoofdbestuur NRK aan Diehl, 10–11–1939 (3191–39); o.c., inv. 175: Min. van defensie aan Hoofdbestuur NRK, 15–10–1930.

67 Diehl, 'Een en ander over chemische strijdmiddelen', p. 1002.

68 *Ibid.*, pp. 1003, 1005.

69 *Ibid.*, p. 1003.

70 Hoofdbestuur NRK 1867–1945, inv. nr. 175: J. T. H. van Weeren aan Beelaerts van Blokland 5–12–1929, J.T.H. van Weeren, Lucht- en Gasoorlog (1853–29); Hoofdbestuur NRK 1867–1945, inv. nr. 175: hoofdbestuur NRK aan O.C. Leeflang, 16–4–1934 (525–34). Leeflang too warned against fantasised stories tolled by non-experts. This could only lead to unilateral disarmament.

71 Nationaal Archief, Hoofdbestuur NRK 1867–1945, inv. 175, 18–10–1928: Taak der Nationale Commissies van het Roode Kruis inzake bescherming der Burgerbevolking tegen Gasaanvallen.

72 'Roode Kruis ziekenhuis te Den Haag tegen gas beschermd', *Het Ziekenhuiswezen*, vol. 9 (1936), p. 319; A. C. Nieuwenhuizen, *Van te Huis tot Ziekenhuis. Het Haagse Rode Kruis Ziekenhuis van 1899 tot 1991* (Groningen, 1992), p. 101.

73 Archives ARA, Hoofdbestuur NRK 1867–1945, inv. 175: Duitse Rode Kruis aan NRK 2–2–1937, Inlichtingen firma-Loos 18–2–1937, Loos aan RK-ziekenhuis Den Haag 20–2–1937, NRK aan DRK 23–2–1937, DRK aan NRK 26–2–1937 (172–37).

74 Hoofdbestuur NRK 1867–1945, inv. nr. 175: J.C. Diehl aan luit. Gen. De Quay (head Nat. Gascomm.), 27–11–1931; *ibid.*, H.A. Seyffardt aan hoofdbestuur NRK, 30–11–1931; H. Bakker, *Het Nederlandsche Roode Kruis*, Officieel Gedenkboek. Uitgegeven t.g.v. het 40-jarig regeeringsjubileum van koningin Wilhelmina (Amsterdam, 1938), p. 822.

75 van Bergen, *De Zwaargewonden Eerst?*, pp. 327–60; L. van Bergen, 'Internationaal zijn of niet zijn: dat is de keuze', in E. E. Meursing, *Arts Pro en Contra 'het' Rode Kruis* (Nijmegen, 1990).

THE ROAD TO THE GENEVA

Jean Pascal Zanders

Modern chemical warfare began on 22 April 1915. 'Modern', not because of the volume of toxic chlorine that rolled into the Allied trenches, but because of its expression of the total war that the First World War was to become. As no other military conflict had done previously, the First World War drew upon a nation's military, industrial, scientific and human resources. More importantly, it blended all these resources to achieve a single goal, the total destruction of the enemy's might. The First World War thus saw the maturation or introduction of novel weapons or modes of combat. Chemical warfare was one of them, as was the tank, aeroplane, submarine, reconnaissance photography, communications technology and methods to eavesdrop on enemy signals, and so forth.[1] Of all these novelties, chemical weapons attracted by far the least enthusiasm from the military community. An important difference between the development of modern chemical weapons and the other new arms was the apparent absence of military chemical warfare preparations before 1914. The development and production of new chemicals in the 19th and early 20th centuries took place in the private industry. Apart from their interest in new explosives, the military establishment had little involvement in the rapidly growing sector of industrial chemistry. Even when individuals experienced the toxic effects of some compounds, they hardly discerned any military utility, and if they did, military indifference, norms and bureaucratic politics stood in the way of further exploration and development. Nevertheless, concern, particularly in less industrialised societies, about possible future gas warfare led to the adoption of a formal prohibition on the application of asphyxiating gases at the First Hague Peace Conference in 1899 even before their utilisation on the battlefield.[2]

Aircraft, one of the other novelties, fared differently. Governments encouraged and generously funded research into dirigibles. Societies for the promotion of aeronautics, as well as dedicated magazines, had already sprung up in the second half of the 19th century. The military appreciated the great potential beyond that of the elevated observation platform, which balloons had been for more than a century. As soon as engine technology permitted higher loads, the aircraft could function as extended artillery while remaining beyond the reach of existing weapon systems. During the decade preceding the First World War German military officers retired from active service to construct Zeppelins. Training schools and other institutions sprang up in France and Germany. Active government support stimulated some sort of aeronautical arms competition on the European continent, which the smaller countries were unable to follow and Britain was slow to respond to.[3] The perceived military utility of dirigibles and heavier-than-air craft was such that at the 1899 Hague Peace Conference in a declaration to prohibit the dropping of explosives from balloons was amended to be valid for five years only. In contrast, the declaration banning asphyxiating gases had no limit on its duration. At the Second Hague Peace Conference in 1907, lagging countries such as Great Britain, Russia and some smaller continental powers successfully requested an extension of the declaration on aerial bombardments, but met with the leading powers' extreme reluctance to reopen the debate on the substance of the agreement.[4] So, contrary to developments in chemistry, the military here developed strong institutional interests from the earliest stages onwards. This occurred not only in the countries actively promoting aeronautical developments, but also in other states seeking a response to their strong sense of vulnerability. By 1910, parallel investments in aeronautics were clearly discernible in all major European countries.[5]

Of greater importance, however, was the nature of the resistance to such novelties after the war. The introduction of new types of weaponry and associated military doctrines and tactics has always created tensions within those parts of the military forces immediately affected. For example, a survey of military resistance to mechanisation in the British Army between 1919 and 1939 revealed that social determinants exerted 'a more profound effect on attitudes towards innovation than such apparently practical considerations as relative cost or efficiency'.[6] However, whatever arguments critics levelled against the tank and other vehicles, they did not question their legitimacy as war-fighting instruments. The 'key substantive issue was not the use of tanks, but whether tanks should be deployed in independent formations or disposed as auxiliaries to the traditional arms.'[7]

Chemical weapons fared differently. While their utilisation in a future war was a 'foregone conclusion' in the minds of many a military man, scientist, or politician,[8] its legitimacy as an honourable battlefield instrument remained hotly disputed. Several attempts to codify a prohibition on use finally succeeded with the adoption of the Geneva Protocol in 1925. The agreement prohibited the use in war of asphyxiating or poisonous or other gases or bacteriological methods of warfare, but this diplomatic success was not followed up by a disarmament treaty. The overall attitude towards chemical warfare was one of necessity, not one of enthusiasm. A War Office account of British chemical warfare preparations in the Second World War captured the mood during the *interbellum* well:

> No country could allow its safety to be dependent on the observance by other states of rules of war to which they were pledged. This particularly applied to gas warfare, where no agreement or conventions could stop the discovery of new gases or circumvent the ease with which any nation, bent on doing so, could evade international prohibitions or limitations on the manufacture of war chemicals in peace.
>
> Our policy from 1925 onwards, both in research and training, was primarily directed to the defensive. [...]
>
> In regard to the offensive use of gas, research continued. In so far as the

Services were concerned, Government policy, laid down in 1925, was that Service schools and commands should study the offensive employment of gas, not only because the study of offensive gas was necessary for the study of protection against it, but also in order that we might be in a position to retaliate immediately, should this course be forced upon us by our opponents. Steps were also to be taken to secure the bulk production of gas when required.

For various reasons no action was taken to implement this policy. For a time the study of offensive gas was banned, and it was not resumed until 1936. [...][9]

The United Kingdom shared this pervasive passivity regarding chemical warfare preparedness with many other leading powers. One year after the Armistice, not a single former belligerent was capable of producing chemical warfare agents on a large scale. Although they protected an indigenous chemical industry to be able to switch rapidly to wartime production of agents, governments apparently ran down preparations for offensive chemical warfare, while maintaining chemical defence on a standby basis.[10] For many other weapons or modes of warfare introduced during the First World War, technology and doctrine matured in the Second World War. None of the leading industrialised nations – with the exception of Japan in China – used chemical warfare agents despite many prewar scenarios of massive attacks against civilian population centres. In 1945, the atomic bomb eclipsed chemical weapons as the potentially most destructive arm.

That chemical weapons were not banished from the face of the Earth during the *interbellum* was very much because of intensive lobbying by small specialised institutions within the armed forces, the occasional expression of opportunistic industrial interests, and the influence of strong-willed individuals, including war-time commanders of chemical troops and leading chemists involved in chemical warfare. That chemical weapons did not become further integrated into mainstream military doctrine had just as much to do with institutional opposition and vocal opponents in academia and society at large, as with their physical limitations that allow only marginal benefits even under the best of circumstances. Caught between argument and counterargument, emotions, received wisdom and myth fuelled by the promise of improved agents and better delivery vehicles, embraced chemical warfare debates. In 1986, Lutz Haber, son of the German pioneer in chemical warfare, wrote aptly:

It is indeed remarkable to what extent between the wars a weapon of such small effectiveness cast a threatening shadow over all questions of European dis- and rearmament.[11]

The chapter describes the evolution of attitudes towards chemical warfare between 1918 and 1925 and how they affected efforts to widen and strengthen international norms against chemical weapons. The Geneva Protocol, still in force today, laid the foundation for chemical weapon disarmament negotiations in the final quarter of the 20th century.

Gas, the war crime question, and civilisational development

The opening chapter 'The road to The Hague' described the semantic bifurcation of 'poison' and 'asphyxiating gas' as a consequence of advances in chemistry the industrial application of science. At the 1899 Hague Peace Conference the diverging understanding of toxic substances produced two separate documents, one unconditionally outlawing the use of poison and poisoned weapons in warfare and one focusing on shell whose only purpose was the diffusion of asphyxiating gases. Both during and after the war, Germans and Allies alike maintained the semantic differentiation when describing the first gas attack near Ypres on 22 April 1915 and addressing questions whether and how international laws of war had been broken. However, they diverged starkly in their respective interpretations of the conditions in which the rules agreed at the 1899 and 1907 Hague Peace Conferences applied. The argument pitted the British, French and US legal positivism against German adherence to principles of natural law, of which the notion of *Kriegsraison* dominated other legal considerations if warranted by military necessity on the battlefield.

The respective viewpoints informed the accusations levelled against the opponent and their refutation both during and after the war. Those exchanges helped to set popular post-war attitudes towards chemical warfare. As Daniel Jones wrote in his doctoral dissertation on the institutionalisation of chemical warfare after the Armistice:

> Much of the early history of chemical warfare was written during and just after World War I, by men involved in chemical warfare on both sides of the conflict. Their purpose in most cases was to show that chemical warfare was not initiated during World War I as a new and terrible weapon, but had a long history of use which culminated in the development of its full potential during the war.[12]

For the Allies, the main point was that the Germans had violated time-honoured customs, and as a consequence committed serious war crimes. Research into the historical and cross-cultural antecedents of the norm against the use of poisonous substances sought to support their accusations.[13] The Germans, in contrast, maintained that chemical warfare as waged during the war was the result of recent scientific and technological achievements rather than a continuation of ancient use of poison weapons, and therefore not covered by prevailing conventional or customary law. Beyond the rhetoric, the exchanges nevertheless demonstrated that both sides shared a common semantic reference framework.

After the Armistice the Germans denied that the prohibition on the use of poison or poisoned weapons in the Annex to the 1907 Hague Convention applied to chemical warfare as conducted during the war. That rule, so Rudolf Hanslian and Fr. Bergendorff argued in their important book published in 1925, applied to 'the administration of poison in the sense of daily life, that is the poisoning of wells and food, as well as the use of poisoned weapons, for example by savage peoples'.[14] They asserted that 'poison' must be understood as the additive to food, water, etc.

This was not a new, opportunistic interpretation. Several 19th century legal writings on the prohibition of the employment of poison listed the mode of administration, including the poisoning of wells and fountains, food provisions destined for the enemy king, his officers, or other military personnel, the sending to the enemy armed forces of people infected by the pest or other contagious diseases, of animals or objects infected by diseases, or the use of poisoned weapons.[15] The enumeration captured two elements. First, it reflected the age-old understanding of poison as a naturally occurring toxic substance. This understanding also covered poisons from living organisms, including animals and plants, which are now classed as toxins. Thus, the first edition of the *Encyclopædia Britannica*, published in 1771, described poison – under the lemma 'Medicine' – as follows:

> There are three essential marks of poisons which distinguish them from other things that are noxious to human bodies. The first is, that they consist of most subtile parts, and consequently are pernicious in a small quantity. The second, that they pervert, in a short time, the regular motions of the solids and fluids throughout the body, and induce the most grievous symptoms, even death itself. And the third, that they exercise their cruelty on the most subtile fluid, and the most nervous parts.
>
> All the three kingdoms have poisons peculiar to themselves; but the animal kingdom affords the most subtile, which are communicated by the bite of mad or venomous beasts, when they are angered. The mineral kingdom produces arsenicals and mercurials; and the vegetable, herbs and plants, of a most acrid, noxious and deleterious quality, such as the most violent cathartics and narcotics.[16]

Second, those legal treatises also considered disease to be a poison. Contemporary etiology still widely believed that the breathing of air rendered infectious by particular telluric emissions caused epidemics. Such miasmic explanation of infection fit well within the prevailing understanding of poison. Bacterial propagation became a scientific fact only at the end of the 19th century. While a pathogen too small to observe under then available microscopes was already suspected in the 1880s, the existence of viruses became universally accepted only in 1928. The general concept of poison as applied in international law before the First World War thus covered biological and toxin weapons too. The Germans furthermore regarded a 'poisoned weapon' as an object that may serve as a weapon, which can kill or wound without the addition of the poison, but whose effect is augmented by the toxic substance.[17]

Such convictions not only set chemical warfare agents apart from the traditional understanding of poison, but also implied that customary laws of war as expressed in

German stormtroopers advancing through clouds of smoke towards enemy positions, 1918. (Imperial War Museum, London)

the Hague provisions on poison were not applicable to the new and advanced mode of warfare. From a legal viewpoint, German authors based this sharp distinction between poisons and chemical weapons on the different terminology in the Hague Conventions of 1899 and 1907 and the Hague Declaration (IV, 2) of 1899. Moreover, it was also consistent with the concept of *Kriegsraison*, which, as was noted in Chapter 1, permitted under conditions of extreme necessity the use of all means except those explicitly forbidden by convention or long-standing custom. Poison was one such weapon expressly prohibited. In his testimony to the special committee of the *Reichstag* investigating German breaches of international law during the First World War on 4 October 1923, Fritz Haber declared:

> I have obtained my knowledge of the origin and the first development of the gas war from documents and personal discussions, which resulted from my occupation. I have never occupied myself with the permissibility of gas weapons under international law. Also, I have found nothing on the matter in the documents from the first war years of the Ministry of War. That side of the matter was clearly investigated personally by Chief of the General Staff and Minister of War v. Falkenhayn. Even when he never asked me for my legal opinion, he never left any doubt that there existed legal limits which he wanted to be strictly observed. He would have never authorised the poisoning of food,

wells or weapons, never permitted weapons or methods of warfare that caused unnecessary suffering. He was without any doubt convinced not to contradict international law with his orders regarding gas war. If I had a contrary personal opinion, I would have baulked at collaboration. The only provision regarding gas war agreed at The Hague, which forbade shells with the sole object of diffusing asphyxiating or poisonous gases, gave me no reason whatsoever for such a divergent opinion.[18]

According to its own legal doctrine, the stalemate on the Western front had prevented Germany from achieving its war aims and thus placed it in a situation of 'extreme necessity' permitting the application of *Kriegsraison*. Gas did not fall under an absolute conventional prohibition – the Hague Declaration (IV, 2) only proscribed one specified mode of dissemination – and, being a novel technological development, no longstanding customary taboo on its use existed. The Investigative Committee followed expert opinion in its formal conclusion adopted on 12 October 1923 and declared that Germany had not breached Article 23 (a) of the Annex to the 1907 Hague Convention.[19]

German authors also classified poison and chemical weaponry separately on the basis of available protection. Poisons are usually administered secretly as an additive to food or drink and the victim is defenceless. Conversely, one can protect oneself against chemical warfare agents and usually receives ample warning of an attack. The stipulation of Article 23 (e) of the Annex to the 1907 Hague Convention, which prohibits 'arms, projectiles, or material calculated to cause unnecessary suffering', was therefore, according to German reasoning, also not applicable.[20] In other words, these authors did not question the illicitness of poison employment under international law, but instead contended that chemical warfare agents were not poisons in the traditional meaning.

Despite the often highly emotional tone, the distinction between poison and chemical warfare agents appeared to reflect a mental reality.[21] In an authoritative textbook on international law, of which the eleventh edition was published in 1918, Dr Franz von Liszt listed the prohibition of poison in war without any comment or reference to the Hague Declaration (IV, 2). His brief discussion of the latter document, again without any reference to other legal provisions, ended with a simple note that both sides had used poisonous gases.[22] The twelfth revised edition, published in 1925, replicated the passage on the Hague Declaration (IV, 2), but added in a footnote that the restrictions regarding chemical weaponry imposed on Germany by Article 171 of the 1919 Treaty of Versailles must be interpreted in function of the 'sole purpose' criterion in the Hague Declaration (IV, 2).[23] Both editions thus ignored any link between poison and chemical weapons. Moreover, the later edition discerned a direct link between the Hague Declaration (IV, 2) and the Treaty of Versailles, and consequently the other post-war international prohibitions.

That Germany tried to exonerate itself from violations of the laws of war with all means at its disposal is no cause for surprise. However, war documents and legal writings from Allied sources demonstrate a similar clear-cut distinction between the

Hague Declaration (IV, 2) and the 1907 Hague Convention. Upon returning from his investigative mission to the front after the first German attacks near Ypres, John Burdon Sanderson (J. B. S.) Haldane, Fellow of the Royal Society and an authority on causes of death in colliery and mine explosions, wrote in his report dated 27 April 1915 to Earl Horatio Herbert Kitchener, Secretary of State for War, about 'asphyxiating gas', 'irritant gas', 'gas', 'the use by the Germans of chlorine and bromine for purposes of asphyxiation', and 'other irritant substances, though in some cases at least these agents are not of the same brutally barbarous character as the gas used in the attack on the Canadians'. He did not use the word 'poison' once.[24] The XIVth Report by the Commission of Inquiry on the Violation of the Rules of the Rights of Nations, and of the Laws and Customs of War transmitted to the Belgian Minister of Justice, Henri Carton de Wiart, on 24 April 1915, was explicit in its accusation:

> M. Le Ministre:
> The Commission of Inquiry has the honour to submit to you the following report on the subject of the use by the German army of asphyxiating gases, in breach of the terms of the declaration signed at The Hague on July 29, 1899, by which the contracting Powers – including Germany – pledged themselves not to employ projectiles whose only object was to diffuse asphyxiating and noxious gases.

A German oblique aerial photograph of a gas attack near Le Bizet, 7 September 1918.

To drive forward the gases the Germans used the following means:

    (a) Fires lighted in front of their trenches; the gases which rose from them
        were swept by the wind towards the hostile positions.

    (b) Bombs thrown into the Allied trenches both by hand and by machines.

    (c) Tubes which spurted out the gases.

    (d) Shells filled with asphyxiating gas.[25]

The report further accused the German army of a 'new and long-premeditated crime'.[26] The authors evidently upheld an expansive interpretation of the key clause 'projectiles the sole object of which is the diffusion of asphyxiating or deleterious gases' in the Hague Declaration (IV, 2).[27] More important to the present discussion was that despite some imprecise or erroneous passages, they never referred to the 1907 Hague Convention.

After the war the Commission on the Responsibility of the Authors of the War and on Enforcement of Penalties, which was appointed to inquire, *inter alia*, 'the facts as to breaches of the laws and customs of war committed by the forces of the German Empire and their Allies, on land, on sea, and in the air,' charged the Central Powers with no less than thirty-two specific violations, including '(26) Use of deleterious and asphyxiating gases' and '(32) Poisoning of wells'.[28] The accusation of poisoning was highly specific and distinct from that of chemical warfare. Contemporary specialised literature on international law supported a similar differentiation. One leading French publicist specified some of the poisoning allegations against the Germans: the contamination of wells during the African campaigns and after abandoning positions in northern France in 1917 with arsenic; the repeated throwing of poisoned sweets or other mixtures behind Allied lines from planes; the poisoning of food left behind in abandoned positions, etc.[29] The leading Allied powers thus consistently adopted a distinction between poison and toxic gases similar to the German one.

The argumentation that modern chemical warfare reflected a society's scientific, technological and industrial achievements also carried not too subtle connotations of ethnic or religious prejudice. Hanslian and Bergendorff's reference to 'savage peoples' to emphasise the distinction between poison and poisoned weapons and asphyxiating gases reflected a more widespread German opinion that chemical warfare constituted a civilisational milestone.[30] Chemical warfare is such a complex weapon, wrote Dr Julius Meyer in 1925, 'that it can only be used and repulsed by an intellectually advanced nation. And if the German Army achieved such great successes in gas battles and gas defence, so this speaks only for its intellectual superiority, but has nothing whatsoever to do with customs and morals.'[31]

Even though the Allies accused the Germans of war crimes, British and American proponents of chemical warfare expressed sentiments that often paralleled German arguments. In 1925, the eminent British scientist Haldane wrote *Callinicus: A Defence of Chemical Warfare*. Titled after the Syrian inventor of Greek Fire that helped the East Roman Empire survive for a few more centuries after the demise of Rome, he echoed the prewar German military manual *Kriegsgebrauch im Landkriege* when arguing that forbidding the use of lachrymatory agents as weapons of warfare 'is a piece of sentimentalism as cruel as it is ridiculous'.[32] However, he rebutted German claim to intellectual superiority when noting that their gas masks had been bad to begin with and later on did not match up with British ones, 'because the most competent physiologist in Germany with any knowledge of breathing was a Jew', which 'prevented the military authorities from employing him'. As a consequence, he argued, German soldiers were unable to follow up their gas attacks closely, a delay that enabled the Allies to reorganise their resistance.[33] In other words, he strongly suggested that cultural prejudices neutralised German ingenuity. In doing so, however, he touched on a sore in German society that was to break open less than decade after the publication of *Callinicus*. Fritz Haber and his first wife Clara Immerwahr both had to renounce their Jewish heritage and convert to Lutheranism in order to be able to carve out their academic careers.[34] Haber's nationalist fervour was such that he might have continued to serve his country after the Nazi takeover, but the new rulers' policies accepted nothing less than 'racial' purity.

While German authors sought to deflect accusations of having violated age-old customs, Allied justifications for the use of asphyxiating gases in post-war colonial campaigns echoed their line of defence. Indigenous populations lacked both retaliatory capacities and protection. Thus in 1919 the British War Office realised that mustard or any other agent would cause a high casualty rate amongst the Afghans and hesitated to employ these weapons. However, Major-General Charles Howard Foulkes, in charge of the British chemical warfare effort since 1915, argued successfully:

> On the question of morality [...] gas has been openly accepted as a recognised weapon for the future, and there is no longer any question of stealing an unfair advantage by taking an unsuspecting enemy unawares.
>
> Apart from this, it has been pointed out that tribesmen are not bound by the Hague Convention and they do not conform to its most elementary rules [...][35]

His reference was to phraseology in the 1899 and 1907 Hague Conventions and the 1899 Hague Declaration (IV, 2) that the agreements only bind the contracting powers and reflect 'the usages established among civilised peoples'. Peoples in the colonies were consequently excluded from the rule. Such ethnic discrimination was rampant. As Julian Putkowski notes in his chapter, British and French commanders conferred about the deployment of non-colonial troops only in the organisation of the defence around Ypres in their belief of the martial inferiority of Algerians, Indians and other Natives.[36] In his contribution David Omissi describes the low morale among Indian troops as a consequence of their low standing in British formations.[37] Brigadier-General Amos Fries and Major Clarence West of the US Chemical Warfare Service went even further in their advocacy of chemical warfare against so-called lesser peoples:

[...] chemical warfare is an agency that must not only be reckoned with by every civilized nation in the future, but is one which civilized nations should not hesitate to use. When properly safe-guarded with masks and other safety devices, it gives to the most scientific and most ingenious people a great advantage over the less scientific and less ingenious. Then why should the United States or any other highly civilized country consider giving up chemical warfare? To say that its use against savages is not a fair method of fighting, because the savages are not equipped with it, is nonsense. No nation considers such things today. If they had, our American troops, when fighting the Moros in the Philippine islands, would have had to wear the breechclout and use only swords and spears.[38]

This supercilious call for the ruthless exploitation of scientific and technological prowess reflects a survival-of-the-fittest thinking that dooms less advanced societies to insignificance or extinction. In a lecture to the German parliamentary investigative committee on 1 October 1923, Fritz Haber echoed the survival-of-the-fittest theme when he argued that 'a strict selection divides the men whose gas discipline enables them to hold their position and fulfill their military tasks from the inferior mass of soldiers who crumble and abandon their positions'.[39] In contrast to Fries and West, he did not repeat the ethnic overtones.

Some conceptions of future chemical warfare were clearly informed by misunderstanding the biological notion of 'race' and physiological action of warfare agents on the human body. Haldane – scientist, Marxist, humanist and atheist – could not rise above being a subject of the British Empire. Rather than questioning experiments with warfare agents on humans in the United States, he contemplated future tactics involving mustard agent:

On the other hand, some people are naturally immune. The American Army authorities made a systematic examination of the susceptibility of large numbers of recruits. They found that there was a very resistant class, comprising 20 per cent of the white men tried, but no less than 80per cent of the negroes. This is intelligible, as the symptoms of mustard gas, blistering, and sun-burn are very similar, and negroes are pretty well immune to sunburn. It looks therefore as if, after a slight preliminary test, it should be possible to obtain coloured troops who would be all resistant to mustard gas blistering in concentrations harmful to most white men. Enough resistant whites are available to officer them.[40]

After describing an imaginary offensive with the vesicant, in which 'suddenly, behind the usual barrage of high explosive shells appears a line of tanks supported by negroes in gas masks', resulting in the occupation of hostile territory to a depth of two or three miles,[41] Haldane continued to ponder the implications of mustard gas:

[...] It would not much upset the present balance of power, Germany's chemical industry being counterpoised by French negro troops. Indians may be expected to be nearly as immune as negroes.

And clearly, the more war is complicated, the more unimportant become semi-civilized powers, such as Turkey and Russia, even as allies. The Turks were seldom capable of organizing a combined attack by any number larger than a battalion, or shoot by anything larger than a battery. Yet small groups of them fought very well, and their individual guns made very good shooting. But gas-warfare demands organization, both of attack and defence – attack, because one tries to keep up a certain concentration of vapour over a whole large area rather than to knock out given groups of men; defence, because respirators and discipline in wearing them must be perfect. [...][42]

Absent a sense of equality among peoples, the resort to a particular weapon category whose use is proscribed among belligerents of equal standing in wars against uncivilised or semi-civilised (e.g., Russians and Turks) was not viewed as problematic. Consequently, the argument became a justification for the continuation of chemical warfare preparations and a powerful countercurrent to the efforts to constrain the use of gas in war. Throughout the history of controlling poison warfare, rules applied only to members of one's own community and not to opponents considered inferior on religious, cultural or ethnic grounds.[43]

The battle behind the Versailles Treaty

Germany's signing of the Armistice with the Allied powers ended the First World War on 11 November 1918. While defeated on the battlefield, its armed forces essentially remained intact and withdrew in orderly and disciplined fashion. Without any fighting on German soil or Allied forces occupying the country, the German military-industrial complex survived unscathed under its own administrative control. The foundations for reconstituting German military power thus remained intact.[44]

The disarmament of Germany had not been an explicit Allied war aim, but it gradually emerged as a priority after the Armistice. In particular, concern about Germany's prevailing military strength arose because of its ability to fulfill the military clauses of the Armistice, which included the transfer of large amounts of major weapon systems to Allied control, more or less within the specified time frames. The worries showed up while negotiating a formal peace accord. When on 28 June 1919 the Treaty of Versailles was signed, Germany formally accepted that it and its allies were responsible for the outbreak of the war under Article 231. The treaty also made provision for territorial adjustments, demilitarisation and economic and financial compensation for the losses the Allies had incurred.[45] The German armed forces faced strict numerical restrictions: the army was reduced to 100,000 active men (there were no limitations on reservists) and the navy to 6 battleships, no submarines and a complement of maximum 15,000 men. The air arm was completely prohibited.[46]

The Versailles Treaty also imposed coercive disarmament and armament control measures through which the Allies sought to contain Germany's military resurgence. Thus Articles 169 and 170 of the treaty ordered:

Article 169

Within two months from the coming into force of the present Treaty German arms, munitions and war material, including anti-aircraft material, existing in Germany in excess of the quantities allowed, must be surrendered to the Governments of the Principal Allied and Associated Powers to be destroyed or rendered useless. This will also apply to any special plant intended for the manufacture of military material, except such as may be recognised as necessary for equipping the authorised strength of the German Army.

The surrender in question will be effected at such points in German Territory as may be selected by the said Governments.

Arms and munitions which on account of the successive reductions in the strength of the German army become in excess of the amounts authorized by Tables II and III annexed in this Section must be handed over in the manner laid down within such periods as may be decided by the Conferences referred to in Article 163 [which deals with the first reduction of German forces to 200,000 within three months of the coming into force of the Treaty].

Article 170

Importation into Germany of arms, munitions and war materials of every kind shall be strictly prohibited.

The same applies to the manufacture for, and export to, foreign countries of arms, munitions and war material of every kind.[47]

German disarmament, however, was a significant source of discord among the victorious powers. Throughout the war, Allied propaganda had held out a variety of promises to maintain support for the war effort from suffering civilians and soldiers in the trenches. Those war aims the Allied governments had never synchronised with each other, and when they met in the Paris Conference that was to produce the Versailles Treaty, the multiple domestic commitments limited their room for manoeuvre. For example, the European Allies sought harsh punishments to compensate for the suffering to which the German aggression had exposed them. British Prime Minister Lloyd George also waged an electoral campaign in December 1918 based on the abolishment of the British conscript army. In contrast, the United States had entered the war in an effort to achieve peace without retribution. As a consequence, President Woodrow Wilson opposed disarmament as a punishment for Germany. The United States would eventually sign a separate peace treaty with Germany as a consequence of the European demands for the war reparations.[48]

However, besides guaranteeing Europe against future German aggression and ensuring the stability of the new states in central and eastern Europe (not only against Germany, but also against Bolshevik Russia), the governments of the Allied powers had a third priority with respect to the peace settlement, namely reviving their economic infrastructure.[49] Power status as conveyed by the presence of a national chemical industrial base was to play an important part in those considerations. Germany's superior chemical weapon capabilities during most of the war rested on its sophisticated organic chemical industry and its virtual world monopoly in areas such as dyestuffs and pharmaceuticals. Contrary to the European Allies, the German chemical industry also had a surplus production capacity available. This it put to good use for testing new compounds and production without hampering normal war requirements too much.[50] The Allies agreed in principle on banning chemical weapon production in Germany. The Versailles Treaty included two provisions on the dismantlement of Germany's chemical warfare capacity:

Article 171

The use of asphyxiating, poisonous and other gases and all analogous liquids, materials or devices being prohibited, their manufacture and importation are strictly forbidden in Germany.

The same applies to materials specially intended for the manufacture, storage and use of the said products or devices.

The manufacture and the importation into Germany of armoured cars, tanks and all similar constructions suitable for use in war are also prohibited.

Article 172

Within a period of three months from the coming into force of the present Treaty, the German Government will disclose to the Governments of the principal Allied and Associated Powers the nature and mode of manufacture of all explosives, toxic substances and other like chemical preparations used by them in the war or prepared by them for the purpose of being so used.[51]

Chemical disarmament too divided the Allies on both sides of the Atlantic. Concerning the production ban, sharp differences arose between London and Washington. The British proposed on 28 April 1919 that Germany 'put the Allies in effective possession of all chemical processes [including drawings of plants, manufacturing instructions, and reports of research to date] used during the war [...] for the production of substances from which such things were or can be made'.[52] Under such a provision, the German industry would have been required to divulge all details, and thus the secrets, of its chemical manufacturing processes. London believed that if Germany were to retain its virtual world monopoly, it could embark on new chemical warfare programmes at short notice.[53] Whatever the real motives underlying the British proposal, the outcome would have represented one of the biggest spoils of war for the Allied countries.

President Wilson, suspecting that the Europeans were using peace negotiations to unjustifiable economic ends, opposed the idea as being excessively unfair.[54] His stance led to a campaign by the chemical industries in the Allied countries in support of the British proposal. In the United States, the Chemical Foundation acted as a powerful lobby, trying to influence President Wilson directly by shrouding its commercial interests in national-security rhetoric.[55] Yet, few references to the industry's interest in producing chemical warfare agents are on record. During the war the sector lacked enthusiasm. Important US chemical manufacturers, such as DuPont, believed that diversification into chemical weapon production would be too specialised. Moreover, the contracts offered lower profit margins than other war-related business. The Ordnance Department of the US Army, responsible for mobilising the US industrial base during the war, thus had to contract second and third rank companies to supply mustard gas and phosgene. None of the commissioned production plants are believed to have been operative by the end of the war. Faced with this indifference or lack of competence, the Ordnance Department started building a Federal arsenal at Edgewood in Maryland at the end of 1917.[56] By the summer of 1918 the agent production and weapon-filling installations were fully operational. The Ordnance Department transferred control of Edgewood Arsenal to the Chemical Warfare Service in June 1918.[57] President Wilson, sensing that the chemical industry was seeking commercial advantage when appealing to national security, remained adamant.[58]

To overcome American resistance, London tabled a new resolution amending their previous proposal. The conditions were just as demanding on the Germans, but the British cleverly associated the dismantlement of the German chemical industry with disarmament and prevention of future threats:

> The German Government will disclose to the Allied Governments the nature and mode of manufacture of all explosives, toxic substances or other like chemical preparations used both in the war or prepared by them for the purpose of being so used, including the mode of manufacture of the synthetic and nitric acids used in the making of such explosives. As part of such disclosure the Allied Governments shall have the right to inspect all plants used for the manufacture, and shall receive from the German Government full particulars of the processes of manufacture in such plants.[59]

The wording of course satisfied nobody. Initial proposals for inspection and enforcement provisions came to be dropped from Article 172, so the Allied military could never be certain of complete knowledge of the German chemical warfare secrets. The civilian industry too could never be sure whether it had obtained all critical production processes.[60] Even so, the European Allies' focus on securing German industrials secrets under the guise of disarmament likewise contributed to the US decision to conclude a separate peace treaty with Germany.

From the perspective of controlling chemical weapons, the Versailles Treaty negotiations had a fourfold outcome. First, besides the demands on Germany, Article

171 declared an unqualified ban on the use of chemical weapons. Second, in the minds of diplomats and legal scholars, the semantic bifurcation of poison and chemical weapon was complete. After the 1907 Hague Peace Conference, no further changes to the all-encompassing prohibition on the use poisons and poisoned weapons have been recorded. In 1946 the International Military Tribunal of Nüremberg declared the provisions of the 1907 Hague Convention, and therefore the prohibition on the use of poison and poisoned weapons, as universal irrespective of whether a state was party to the accord or not.[61] Today the Rome Statute of the International Criminal Court views a violation of the interdiction as a war crime in both international and non-international armed conflicts.[62] Asphyxiating gases, later re-labelled as chemical warfare agents, continued along their separate trajectory begun in 1899. As noted earlier, the German legal scholar von Liszt drew a direct line between Hague Declaration (IV, 2) and the Versailles Treaty.

Third, the Versailles Treaty intimately connected chemical warfare with scientific and industrial advances. Progress became an integral part of future threat projections in terms of novel agents, their delivery systems, or production improvements. Any restriction on chemical weapons would therefore have to take these elements into consideration. The last outcome from the way the negotiations had proceeded was the removal of verification elements from final consideration. The Allies – and by extension, the international community – thus denied themselves the opportunity to gain practical experience with the organisation of industry monitoring, inspections and compliance enforcement.

First (mis)steps to constraining chemical weapons

It is not easy to capture the mood concerning chemical weapons in the first years after the war. By 1918 chemical warfare had become so ubiquitous that soldiers in the front line lived permanently in a gas environment and were always – however slightly – exposed to the gases' harmful effects. To them, and the people living behind the front lines, gas had become one nuisance among so many, including rain, rats, disease, sniping and shelling.[63] Chemical weapons became conventionalised. The highest decision-making levels had delegated the authority to employ chemical shells to battlefield commanders. Protests against gas were limited to individuals or a gathering of eminent scientists, and emerging peace movements tended to protest the war as whole rather than as individual forms of warfare.[64] By the time the International Committee of the Red Cross (ICRC) issued its appeal against the use of poisonous gases on 8 February,[65] advanced protection and gas discipline preserved soldiers from the worst consequences of exposure, a point that post-war apologists of chemical warfare would never fail to make. Other weaponry and modes of warfare caused far higher casualty rates and exposed soldiers to intolerable levels of daily destruction, mutilation, and human suffering. In addition, on a strategic level commanders faced escalatory pressures from enemy technological development and innovative gas tactics. They needed to avoid physical and psychological degradation of fighting capacity that might be the consequence of one-sided enemy chemical weapon use. Under those circumstances, the humanitarian appeal backfired on the ICRC as both Allies and Germans questioned the organisation's motives and bias.[66] Legal writers and diplomats expressed around the same time their despondency about the inability of international humanitarian law to curb the war's excesses.

During the early 1920s the political battlelines over chemical weapons gradually became more entrenched as institutional interests in the continuation of chemical armament grew stronger, on the one hand, and sharp differences between idealists and pragmatists over how to counter future chemical threats coloured the opposition debates, on the other hand.

Apologists within the military-scientific community deflected any argument that no battle had been decisively influenced by gas. They argued that early means of dissemination had been crude and highly dependent on wind factors. In later stages of the war, so they claimed, artillery was still highly inaccurate. Moreover, more potent toxicants, such as lewisite, an organoarsenic vesicant, did not reach the front lines in time to prove their worth. Time and time again they saw their view on the effectiveness in war proven right in the colonial campaigns. (They, however, usually failed to mention that the attacked could not retaliate and hardly possessed any protective equipment and shelters.) They built the core of their arguments on a line followed by Captain Alfred Thayer Mahan, US naval delegate at the 1899 Hague Peace Conference, when he argued that future weaponry may still prove decisive and not cause superfluous suffering in wars to come.[67]

Advocates also maintained that toxicants are humane compared to classical weapons. Essentially, they countered emotional repugnance with the mathematical rationale of statistics. For example, the British officially listed 180,983 of their soldiers as gassed, of whom no more than 6,062 or 3.3 per cent were killed.[68] The popular press maintained similar arguments for many years after the war. One American piece published in 1935 posited that 24 per cent of US soldiers who had been injured by shrapnel or bullets subsequently died, while only two per cent of gas casualties proved fatal.[69] Such figures enabled them to present gas as a humane weapon that wounds rather than kills. That many casualties appeared to recover completely after a more or less prolonged span of time, reinforced their argument. At that time there were of course no statistics on long-term effects. The humane characteristic weighed heavily in the discussions between the two wars. Only later declassified documents revealed that whole categories of victims never made it into official statistics.[70]

In contrast to these macro-level arguments, opponents drew attention to the individual suffering of victims, which went beyond the acceptable to put a soldier *hors combat*, and the indiscriminate nature of gas clouds, which had caused innumerable civilian casualties. Already during the early 1920s strategic thinkers on air power, such as Italian General Giulio Douhet and US General William 'Billy' Mitchell, were advocating the integration of chemical weapons in aerial warfare.[71] Their writings led

A dump of chemical shells shortly after the First World War. (Jean Pascal Zanders, Private Collection)

some to envisage apocalyptic chemical bombing raids against cities, leading to human losses beyond anything experienced thus far. Having listened to a presentation by a chemical expert a few days earlier, Ellen Wilkinson, MP, predicted in a speech to the House of Commons on 11 July 1927 that 'the next war will be so destructive as to threaten the very existence of European civilisation', adding that 'our cities will be not merely decimated but rendered utterly uninhabitable by chemical bombs'.[72] A split in the opposition to chemical warfare emerged when some people and organisations advocated peacetime preparations to protect populations from chemical warfare and assist gas victims. In the eyes of those seeking a total ban, such humanitarian pragmatism allowed for the possibility of chemical warfare. They viewed this as totally unacceptable.[73]

Caught between these macro and micro levels of the humanitarian argument were many politicians and diplomats. While they still desired to strengthen the humanitarian laws of war, they had lost faith in their value once the war demons were unleashed. Those rules might give the victor a ground of action, but they could not mitigate the horrors of war.[74] They came to realise that armaments rather than bolstering national security were actually a source of instability in international relations. If war was to be abolished as means to resolve disputes among nations, states would have to accept limits on national armament. The *General Treaty for Renunciation of War as an Instrument of National Policy* (1928), more commonly known as the Kellogg–Briand Pact, concretised the first ambition.[75] The principle was to become a cornerstone of the Charter of the United Nations in 1945. Reining in technology-driven armament dynamics had been the original, but futile goal of the 1899 Hague Peace Conference.

US President Warren G. Harding called for ambitious reductions in naval and land armaments when he invited nine powers to the Washington Conference (12 November 1921 to 6 February 1922). His opening address captured the dual ambition of war prevention and arms control:

> I can speak officially only for our United States. Our hundred millions frankly want less of armament and none of war. Wholly free from guile, sure in our own minds that we harbor no unworthy designs, we accredit the world with the same good intent.[76]

Besides arms limitation, the conference also covered two other areas: territorial and political settlements in the Asia–Pacific region and the development of rules for control of new agencies of warfare. The conference took place outside the auspices of the League of Nations because the United States had not yet decided on whether to join the international organisation. France, Great Britain, Italy, Japan and the United States comprised the powers discussing limits on armament. Belgium, China, the Netherlands and Portugal joined the five for the other issue areas.

While one might have expected that a mere three years after the Armistice humanitarian considerations and opposition to war would dominate the Washington Conference, balance-of-power politics drove the discussions. Great Britain ostensibly played to preserve its favourable quantitative ratio in surface ships relative to other naval powers, but in the end accepted parity with any other single country. The outcome was actually less of a concession. In March 1920, following the scuttling of the German fleet in Scapa Flow in June 1919 and in view of the restriction placed on German naval rearmament by the Versailles Treaty, the British Admiralty had already announced the sufficiency of parity. France refused second-tier status and insisted on an authorised tonnage for submarines equal to that tabled for Great Britain and the United States, a proposition wholly unacceptable to its cross-Channel rival. In addition, France refused to consider reductions in land armaments as long as, in the words of Prime Minister Aristide Briand on 21 November, Germany was not morally as well as materially disarmed.[77] French fear of revanchism effectively removed the matter from further deliberation. The United States seemed the only Allied victorious power willing to consider serious armaments limitations, even though attendants could observe that Washington and Tokyo were already viewing each other as geopolitical competitors in the Asia–Pacific region.[78] In this context, it fared poorly according to some observers because it accepted limitations on the size of its fleet and agreed to the non-fortification of the Pacific Islands.[79]

Relative to the original ambitions the net outcome of these negotiations may have appeared meagre to contemporaries, but the Washington Conference nevertheless set a precedent for multilaterally agreed limitation and reduction of national armaments. The meeting also made some headway in the forum on Rules for Control of New Agencies of Warfare. It appointed three subcommittees to consider chemical weapons, aircraft and the rules of international law. The three topics in themselves reflected the confusion and doubts among political leaders and diplomats about the value of international laws of war in armed conflict, but pressed by public opinion (as invoked by President Harding in his opening address) they had no choice but to improve and expand the rules.

The subcommittee on aircraft came to the conclusion that it was impossible to prohibit the use of aeroplanes in war or effectively limit the number of planes or pilots. As noted in the introduction to this chapter, governments had already built great stakes in the militarisation of the skies before the war. Curbs on the further development and expansion of air power they would therefore tend to resist. A resolution declared that 'the use of aircraft in war should be covered by the rules of warfare as adapted to aircraft by a further conference which should be held at a later date'.[80] With the exception of a limitation on the tonnage of aircraft carriers in the Naval Treaty, the conference failed to impose any constraint on the competitive development of air forces.

Shifting from arms limitation to humanitarian law was the way the Washington Conference proceeded with regard to submarines. In view of the French objections to the proposed aggregate tonnage for its submarine fleet, the only restriction in the Naval Treaty pertained to the size of the vessels. Besides balance-of-power considerations in seeking restrictions, there was the obvious experience from the First World War that submarines had principally attacked merchant vessels and thereby caused harm to neutrals and non-combatants. Great Britain, depending on sea lanes for its supplies, thus managed to safeguard in principle its merchant fleet through war regulations instead of arms limitation. However, even this outcome remained unsatisfactory in view of the lack of confidence in effective enforcement.[81]

Contemporary confusedness about the value of international regulation was on greatest display on the issue of poison weapons. As noted earlier, Article 171 of the Versailles Treaty banned the use of modern chemical weapons without any qualifications. While this treaty did not apply universally, the five states participating in the arms limitation talks – France, Great Britain, Italy, Japan and the United States – were either party to the Versailles Treaty or to other bilateral peace agreements containing the same provision with the former Central Powers. It seems implausible that the US president intended to have the ban reconsidered. More likely, he wanted to reinforce the norm against gas in view of the experiences in France and Belgium. The Subcommittee on chemical warfare, however, developed logic similar to that in the Subcommittee on aircraft, concluding in its report of 6 January 1922:

(c) Research which may discover additional warfare gases cannot be prohibited, restricted or supervised.

(d) Due to the increasingly large peacetime use of several warfare gases. It is impossible to restrict the manufacture of any particular gas or gases. Some of the delegates thought that proper laws might limit the quantities of certain gases to be manufactured. The majority of opinion was against the practicability of even such prohibition. [...]

(f) The kinds of gases and their effects on human beings cannot be taken as a basis for limitation. In other words, the committee felt that the only limitation practicable is to wholly prohibit the use of gases against cities and other large bodies of noncombatants in the same manner as high explosives may be limited, but that there could be no limitation on their use against the armed forces of the enemy, ashore or afloat.[82]

The US experts in the subcommittee, in the words of US-educated Japanese writer Sotokichi Katsuizumi, 'were firmly for the unrestricted use of poison gases'.[83] The US delegation drew on national public opinion as a deft manoeuvre to check its own experts without open confrontation and overcome the potential legitimisation of chemical warfare. The General Board of the United States Navy recommended unreservedly that gas warfare be prohibited, because it 'threatens to become so efficient as to endanger the very existence of civilization'. The Advisory Committee of the American Delegation also argued that 'chemical warfare, including the use of gases, whether toxic or non-toxic, should be prohibited by international agreement, and should be classed with such unfair methods of warfare as poisoning wells, introducing germs of disease, and other methods that are abhorrent in modern warfare'.[84] On the same day of the subcommittee's report, Elihu Root, former Secretary of State and member of the US delegation, tabled a resolution drawing on the language in the Versailles Treaty to counter the report's conclusion.[85] With a few minor editorial modifications it became Article V of the Treaty Between the United States of America, the British Empire, France, Italy, and Japan, to Protect Neutrals and Non-combatants At Sea in Time of War and to Prevent the Use in War of Noxious Gases and Chemicals:

> The use in war of asphyxiating, poisonous or other gases, and all analogous liquids, materials or devices, having been justly condemned by the general opinion of the civilized world and a prohibition of such use having been declared in Treaties to which a majority of the civilized Powers are parties,
>   The Signatory Powers, to the end that this prohibition shall be universally accepted as a part of international law binding alike the conscience and practice of nations, declare their assent to such a prohibition, agree to be bound thereby as between themselves and invite all other civilized nations to adhere thereto.[86]

The outcome merely reaffirmed an already established rule, but it denied chemical warfare future legitimacy on the battlefield. Article V also defeated the idea that international law could not restrain the use of gas. At the Sixth Plenary Session on 4 February 1922 the Washington Conference agreed to constitute a Commission to consider the rules of international law respecting new agencies of warfare, but in a separate resolution determined 'to exclude the said Commission from reviewing the rules already adopted by the Conference relating to submarines or the use of noxious gases and chemicals'.[87] The latter decision foreclosed a possible replay of the logic driving discussions in the Subcommittee on chemical warfare.

Besides the diplomatic jockeying in the pursuit of national interests, two other elements seem to have contributed to the negotiation dynamic: pessimism about the ability of international law to restrict novel war fighting technologies and abandonment of regulating specific weapons or modes of combat in favour of more general principles of warfare. The diplomats concluded with respect submarines, aeroplanes and chemical weapons that the laws of war could not govern specific weapon types used to devastating effect in the First World War. They felt that the technologies had not yet fully matured. They could not control national programmes to further investigate their full potential and, as a consequence, halt the arms competition between nations. If anything, the 1899 Hague Declaration (IV, 2) on asphyxiating gases had proved to them how easily battlefield imperatives could circumvent a specific rule. France's forceful rejection of any limitation of land armaments – Prime Minister Briand had especially sailed to the United States to make that point – and refusal to accept quantitative limits on submarines attested to the primacy of peacetime national interests over international laws of war. It reinforced perceptions of the impossibility of restricting national armaments (which after all had been a key goal of the Washington Conference).

Meeting records and post-conference considerations actually reflected the disarray about how to address the challenges posed by modern chemical weapons and peacetime preparations for chemical warfare, all the while realising contemporary humanitarian law's futility in constraining the use of gas on the European battlefields. In a review of the achievements, Canadian delegate Sir Robert Borden captured the resigned scepticism about Article V's utility or added value:

> The question is not free from difficulty. Every investigation into the subject has shown the practical impossibility of preventing in time of peace preparations that would enable noxious gases to be produced on a great scale in time of war; so that it is impossible for nations that have no intention of employing this weapon, to abandon inquiry into the means by which its attacks may be resisted and if necessary countered. Doubtless the rule will not have the effect of preventing such preparation. On the other hand, those who are anxious to make war more humane should not be deterred by these considerations from condemning the misuse of scientific discovery for such purposes. In any case the rule does no more than to reaffirm existing international law.[88]

With multilateral arms control an idea whose time had not yet arrived, diplomats were left with sole recourse to the general principles and rules of armed combat. Protection of neutrals and non-combatants are age-old cornerstones of international humanitarian law. Safeguarding these categories of people from the worst consequences of new technologies was the best they felt they could achieve. For aeroplanes, they determined that a future conference had to adapt the principles of land warfare to the skies. The flow of logic also explains the oddity why restrictions on submarine warfare and noxious gases ended up in a single, self-contained document. Both rules were the Washington Conference's only contributions to the development of the laws of war. In the case of chemical weapons, the new elements – small as they may have appeared to contemporaries – were the framing of the prohibition outside of the context of the peace conditions on Germany and Article V's call for universal adherence.

Another effort during the early 1920s was the Convention for the Limitation of Armament agreed at the Conference on Central American Affairs. Five countries signed it on 7 February 1923 and the accord entered into force on 24 November 1924. Its Article V adopted the essence of the prohibition on chemical warfare in the Washington Treaty:

> The contracting parties consider that the use in warfare of asphyxiating gases, poisons, or similar substances as well as analogous liquids, materials or devices, is contrary to humanitarian principles and to international law, and obligate themselves by the present convention not to use said substances in time of war.[89]

In addition the Pan-American Conference, which held its fifth summit meeting in Santiago, Chile from 25 March until 3 May 1923, recommended in a resolution that its members become a party to the Washington Treaty.

Confronting technology

France baulked at the restrictions on submarine warfare against merchant shipping and refused to ratify the Washington Treaty. While in 1925 some hope still existed that the agreement might yet come into effect, reality was that seven years after the end of the First World War a mere single treaty banned chemical warfare, and it only had regional effect. Otherwise nothing constrained chemical warfare. In 1919 British forces intervening in the Russian civil war used their so-called M-device for the first time against Bolshevik forces. Between 1921 and 1927 Spain deployed various chemical warfare agents against the Berber rebels during the Rif War in Spanish Morocco. France's intervention in this colonial war saw mustard agent bombing runs near Fez. There were also claims of aerial CW use in British-controlled territories, including Iraq and India's North-West Frontier.

The ways in which a well-developed chemical industry symbolised national puissance in the first quarter of the 20th century also shaped attitudes to chemical warfare preparedness. Statesmen could not leave their country unprepared for future chemical warfare, but they also shared a widespread sense that smaller or lesser-developed societies should not be left vulnerable. In a wider reflection of France's attitude to proposed reductions in land armaments, they considered the disproportionate accumulation of chemical weapons by a single state as a major threat to peace and security. Amid calls for chemical armament and projections of unconstrained gas use in future conflicts, several European governments thus saw international assistance in offensive and defensive aspects of chemical warfare as beneficial to their own national security. They pursued chemical weapon proliferation as a preferred security policy option. As a matter of interest, never was the percentage of independent states with an active chemical warfare programme higher than on the eve of the Second World War.

Amid threat perceptions and insecurity of continental European states, as well as balance-of-power manoeuvres at the Washington Conference, the League of Nations was considering questions of chemical warfare in some of its committees. Questionnaires tried to delineate the problems and identify possible solutions to address them. In September 1922 Colombia recommended that the League's Assembly adopt a convention based on Article V of the Washington Treaty. It later endorsed Australia's alternative for a Council recommendation that League members adhere to the Washington Treaty. In 1924 a Temporary Mixed Commission prepared a scientific and technical report for the Third Committee of the Assembly. It was to contribute significantly to the debates in the next year.[90]

Although no new international agreement relating to chemical warfare came out of the League of Nations in the first half of the 1920s, its approach injected scientific and technical considerations into the deliberations. Committee members and national experts explored different routes to defining chemical weapons and laid links to science and industry in efforts to understand how the arms category could be restricted beyond a mere ban on its use in war. Whereas the Versailles Treaty tied chemical weapon capacity to a chemical industrial base, the Subcommittee on chemical warfare at the Washington Conference linked peacetime restrictions on the production of warfare agents to the control of civilian production of toxic chemicals. As noted earlier, it was a key finding in support of the Subcommittee's conclusion that international law could not restrain chemical warfare.

Despite their efforts, the diplomats and experts were making little headway. Their limited understanding of what exactly they ultimately wanted to control – battlefield use, weapon stockpiles, production capacity or volumes, etc. – affected their deliberations. Absent clear purpose, deciding which proposed definition serves the armament limitation goal best was impossible. Unbeknown to them, they were closing in on the security dilemmas posed by 'dual-use technologies'. These comprise knowledge, skills, equipment, processes and artefacts that may have both civilian and military application. Dual-use questions arise when the attempts to control a particular type of weapon-relevant technology confront the non-military commercial and scientific interests in such technology. Rather than treating arms, science and industry as separate spheres, arms control and disarmament require their integrated consideration.

Diplomats and technical experts came rather unexpectedly face to face with the dual-use dilemma in 1925, because the question of CW control got reframed as one of arms trade regulation. The Conference for the Supervision of the International Trade in Arms and Ammunition and in Implements of War opened in Geneva on 4 May 1925 and lasted until 17 June. The initial proposals concerned solely conventional weaponry. Expressing US concerns about the permissibility of chemical warfare, Senator Theodore

H. Burton submitted an amendment at the start of the deliberations on 5 May:

> The use in war of asphyxiating, poisonous or other gases and all analogous liquids, materials or devices has been justly condemned by the general opinion of the civilised world, and a prohibition of such use has been declared in treaties to which a majority of the civilised Powers are parties. The High Contracting Parties therefore agree absolutely to prohibit the export from their territories of any such asphyxiating, poisonous or other gases, and all analogous liquids, intended or designed for use in connection with operations of war.[91]

He also advanced an alternative text that called for 'adequate penalties, applicable in all places where such High Contracting Parties exercise jurisdiction or control'.[92]

The other delegates responded favourably. However, Burton's framing of chemical weapon control as an arms trade matter raised immediate questions about non-military applications of toxic compounds. In his statement welcoming the US proposal, French delegate Colonel Réquin noted the need 'to define, if possible, the characteristics of gases and chemicals which cannot be utilised in war, or of those which can be utilised both for warlike and non-warlike purposes'.[93] The comment captured the dual-use challenge. Conventional weapons, the intended subject of the conference, are single use and did not require diplomatic assessment of the nature of the technology.

The conference's Military, Naval and Air Technical Committee investigated the issue in detail, but was unable to overcome the dual-use challenges. As reported by General A. De Marinis Stendardo Di Ricigliano (Italy), the committee had sought expert opinion from notably bacteriological experts, physiologists and chemists:

> The data and opinions of these scientists show conclusively that all the materials required for chemical warfare are in everyday use in peace industries.
>
> Professor Mayer of the Collège de France says that 'such substances are not by any means rare; the majority are common materials ordinarily manufactured and employed in large quantities for peace-time requirements, so that there is very little difference between the manufacture of pharmaceutical products and that of injurious substances used in war.'
>
> All the chemical products which can be used in war, either as gas or in other forms, are more or less necessary in commerce, and it was pointed out during our discussions that a number of chemical products which were originally manufactured during the war solely for military purposes are now used in agriculture.
>
> As the deleterious substances are in common use in peace-time, the chemical weapon is within the reach of any great industrial Power possessing chemical factories. Professor Zanetti, of the University of Columbia, New York, states that "the extreme facility with which these factories can be transformed, almost overnight, into factories for chemical warfare material introduces an

element of fear and distrust towards a chemically powerful neighbour. This facility, indeed, gives a country with flourishing chemical industries as [sic] superiority if that country harbours hostile designs.

Having proceeded thus far the Military Technical Committee, though desirous of making an immediate advance which might satisfy the conscience of the civilised world, had to recognise that the prohibition of the trade in chemical products is not practicable in the majority of cases, and that, even if it could be effected, it would prove of no avail against Powers possessing a highly developed chemical industry. In addition, although this argument is not of a technical character and is not mentioned in the Committee's report, I should like to point out that such a prohibition would place non-producing countries in a dangerous position of inferiority as against producing countries. Your Committee was unanimous in thinking that this illusory method should be rejected and that the radical solution of the terrible problem would be found in a solemn and universal undertaking on the part of all the peoples of the world to regard chemical warfare as prohibited by the law of nations. [...][94]

During the committee discussion of the report, Colonel Réquin pointed out that the delegations had paid particular attention to political considerations and expressed his opinion that from a technical viewpoint, the prohibition of the export of chemical and biological arms was impossible, because 'all products used in chemical warfare were merely part of the economic necessities of a country'.[95] At best, a provision might be included to ban the export of certain types of shell filled with CW agents, but the foreign sale of the chemical substances itself could never be forbidden. Following the argument and in line with De Marinis' personal recommendation to outlaw chemical warfare, the Military, Naval and Air Technical Committee adopted a compromise resolution, thus preparing the ground for a ban on the employment of chemical warfare materials rather than on their international trade.[96]

A variation of the dual-use issue manifested itself when delegates raised the question whether methods or implements for the defence against chemical weapons should also be subjected to export prohibitions. Hungary proposed to make the means to defend oneself accessible to everyone in order to make chemical weapons ineffective.[97] This suggestion too ran into difficulties because of the lack of a global ban on chemical warfare. In line with those elements in public opinion who wanted to banish chemical warfare rather than prepare for the consequences of chemical weapon use, critics contended that regulating methods of defence might be construed as admitting to the possibility of chemical warfare, which in turn – as Colonel Réquin phrased it – would undermine the 'moral and effective scope of the desired prohibition'.[98] Hungary consequently withdrew the proposition, while reserving the right to present it at another occasion.

As noted earlier, in the 1920s a single country possessing a disproportionate advantage in chemical warfare capacities posed a far greater security threat than the number of countries with an offensive chemical warfare programme. Equal access to chemical weapon technologies and defence and protection informed national security policies. This core principle of equality conformed to the spirit of the League of Nations. When submitting his amendment, Senator Burton was fully aware of the problem:

> [...] The prohibition of exportation would make it possible for producing nations to supply themselves with these very barbarous implements of warfare while the non-producing nations would be denied the opportunity of doing so. I am sure it will be one of the main objects of this Conference to place the producing and non-producing countries, if possible, on the same footing, in accordance with the principle of equality.[99]

Greece submitted to the conference's General Committee that the principle of equal treatment between producing and non-producing countries alike ought to be the touchstone for the convention under consideration.[100] The Turkish representative Colonel Mehmed Tevfik Bey, echoing some earlier remarks by his Brazilian colleague Admiral de Souza e Silva,[101] summarised the security dilemma with specific reference to the American proposal to prohibit the transfer of chemical weaponry:

> [...] A country with a developed chemical industry will, in time of war, always have a great advantage over an enemy which is not in an equally favourable position in this respect. It follows that if some States provide in time of peace for the possible use of gases in war, other States will be compelled to take measures to import them. And if, in the event of war, one party makes use of these substances and its use of them is definitely established, the opponent should also have the right to make free use of them, if only as a legitimate means of defence.
>
> It is important that a prohibition to export should not place a producing State in a position of advantage as compared with a non-producing State. [...][102]

Security concerns of possessors and non-possessors had to be addressed simultaneously. In view of the just-discovered dual-use dilemma, the US proposal to restrict the transfers of chemical weapons and related materials could not meet this fundamental criterion of equality among all states.

Participants realised that they could not regulate a specific aspect of the preparations for chemical warfare in the absence of an overarching prohibition on the use of chemical weapons in war. They were not in a position to resolve the various core issues they had uncovered in their deliberations withing the time frame at their disposal. Therefore, they proceeded to formulate the multilateral ban on chemical warfare, termed a 'protocol' in anticipation of a more substantive resolution of the issues in the disarmament conference envisaged for the 1930s.

The lasting legacy of the Geneva Protocol

The Geneva Protocol was but a stepping stone on the route towards an all-encompassing disarmament treaty. At first sight, the one-page document appears little more than yet another iteration of the ban on the chemical warfare. However, the debates that led to its adoption had a completely different quality. The US proposal to outlaw the trade in chemical weapons shifted the focus from humanitarian considerations to the weapon technology and everything this technology implied from security, scientific, industrial and commercial perspectives. Consciousness of those various fields' interconnectedness not only gave diplomats and experts focus – total elimination of the weapon category – and thus helped them to frame the challenges with a precision that had eluded them in earlier deliberations.

In 1926 preparations for the disarmament conference began in earnest. The preparatory Commission comprised two sub-commissions dealing respectively with purely technical questions of disarmament and the financial and economic dimensions of disarmament. Drawing on the findings of the Arms Trade Conference, it presented each sub-commission with a list of questions on issues such as the time required to convert a chemical plant from civilian to military productions, time frames for the development of chemical agents or to convert civilian planes to bombers, how to protect the civilian population from gas attacks, and so on. The replies were highly discouraging. The sole option seemed acceptance of deterrence and retaliation with chemical weapons, but as the technical replies to the questionnaire revealed, the clear inability to protect civilians from gas made it unpalatable. Increasingly the diplomats began to realise that to prevent future chemical warfare, they had to constrain peacetime preparations.[103] With the Geneva Protocol in place, they now had the legal foundation to do so.

The choice for disarmament presented the delegates with different types of questions. How does one define chemical weapons, particularly in view of the civilian application of many toxic agents? While consensus was quickly established on barring riot control agents (such as tear gas) as a military instrument, how does one legitimise them for police purposes? How does one address the inevitable discovery of new toxic chemicals? How does one authorise the development of defence and protection against chemical weapons, while prohibiting all preparations for offensive chemical warfare?

By the end of May 1932 the Special Commission for Chemical and Biological Weapons, established to address specific questions concerning both arms categories, submitted its first report, which contained several novel insights.[104] First, it came with a definition of chemical weapon based on the agent's physiological impact on living organisms. Conscious of the fact that the definition had to capture all possible future compounds, they rejected approaches based on the chemical composition of compounds or their toxicity. The former approach would have implied a necessity to update the list with newly synthesised chemicals, a process deemed far too laborious to be effective for disarmament. The latter entailed a serious risk that if soldiers on the battlefield were

A chemical shell of the First World War waiting to be cleaned, identified and disposed off at the Belgian Army's disposal facilities in Poelkapelle, 2014. (Jean Pascal Zanders)

exposed to some poisonous substance, an erroneous conclusion of enemy initiation of chemical warfare might lead to false accusation and retaliatory action.

Second, the report offered a solution to the dual-use conundrum. Initially, the delegates tried to trace a sharp dividing line between legitimate and illicit applications of toxic chemicals. However, all efforts ran into problems of legal enforcement as ambiguities could not entirely be eliminated. The impossibility to achieve juridical precision eventually led them to the insight that *all* activities involving *any* type of harmful chemicals must be banned as the default position. Only a limited number of activities would then be explicitly exempted from this blanket prohibition. Throughout the debates in the late 1920s and early 1930s, delegates proposed lists with activities they considered licit. They included chemical and pharmaceutical manufacture, and scientific research (with the exception of theoretical studies on the development and application of warfare agents). This principle would eventually become known as the 'general purpose criterion': rather than banning objects as such, the prohibition focused on the goals to which they may be applied. The British draft disarmament convention submitted to the League of Nations on 16 March 1933 contained the general purpose criterion's first incarnation. Article 51 established the default blanket prohibition on preparations for chemical warfare both in time of peace and in time of war, while Article 52 enumerated the types of legitimate activities. The principle of the general purpose criterion rested on the overall ban on the use of chemical weapons laid down by the Geneva Protocol and further elaborated in Article 47 of the draft convention. In particular, it expanded the prohibition to 'any war, whatever its character'.[105] Civilisational supremacy over other peoples was clearly losing its legitimacy as justification for chemical warfare.

Third, to have confidence in the proposed disarmament regime, a verification system had to be set up. As became clear after a Soviet proposal in 1929 to have labourers' committees verify the non-production of chemical weapons in civilian factories, an international disarmament treaty might impose legal obligations on natural or legal persons. This would have violated the strict separation between private and international public law. The British draft convention resolved this by assigning states parties reporting obligations, on the one hand, and establishing an international oversight body, the Permanent Disarmament Commission, among whose responsibilities would be the examination of complaints alleging treaty violations, on the other hand.

The fast worsening political situation in Europe in the middle of the 1930s doomed the League of Nations' disarmament project. Concerted efforts at biological and chemical disarmament would not resume until the late 1960s under the auspices of the United Nations. Negotiation of the Chemical Weapons Convention concluded in September 1992 and the treaty was opened for signature in January 1993. Just over four years later, in April 1997, it entered into force. As of October 2015, 192 out of 196 states (197 if the State of Palestine, which has special observer status at the United Nations and has joined several international treaties and organisations, is counted) are party to the treaty, making it the most universal disarmament or arms control treaty.

The Chemical Weapons Convention owes a lot to the debates in the League of Nations that shaped the Geneva Protocol and the formulation of solutions to the problems relating to the control of chemical weapons identified in the following years. Article I comprises the core prohibitions. Article II defines chemical weapons based on the general purpose criterion and includes a limited list of non-prohibited purposes. Many of those activities had already been recognised as legitimate in the late 1920s and early 1930s. The Chemical Weapons Convention also has an elaborate verification machinery, which includes tools, such as on-site inspections, that were inconceivable during the *interbellum*. However, the verification process rests on the division of labour between the international body, the Organisation for the Prohibition of Chemical Weapons (OPCW), and the state party, which has the obligation to operate an National Authority as interface for collaboration and transpose the international prohibitions and obligations into domestic law.

Notes

1 G. Hartcup, *The War of Invention. Scientific Developments, 1914–18* (Brassey's: London, 1988), Chapter 1.

2 J. P. Zanders, 'The Road to Geneva', in this volume.

3 M. W. Royse, *Aerial Bombardment and the International Regulation of Warfare* (Harold Vinal Ltd Publishers: New York, 1928), Chapter III, especially pp. 68–86.

4 J. Brown Scott (Under the supervision of), *The Proceedings of The Hague Conferences: The Conference of 1907, Volume I* (Oxford University Press: New York, 1920), p. 105.

5 As an indicator of the importance of aerial warfare during this early developmental phase, United States military officials estimated national expenditures for the five-year period up to 1913 as follows [in US$]:

Germany	28,000,000	Chile	700,000
France	22,000,000	Bulgaria	600,000
Russia	12,000,000	Greece	600,000
Italy	8,000,000	Spain	550,000
Austria	5,000,000	Brazil	500,000
Great Britain	3,000,000	United States	435,000
Belgium	2,000,000	Romania	200,000
Japan	1,500,000	Turkey	90,000

Equally important from the viewpoint of institutional interest in the development are the private subscriptions in the leading countries, which were listed as: Germany, $3,500,000; France, $2,500,000; Italy, $1,000,000; and Russia, $100,000. Source: *ibid.*, p. 98, fn. 141 on the basis of US Congressional documents.)

6 B. C. Hacker, 'Resistance to Innovation. The British Army and the Case Against Mechanisation 1919–1939', *Actes du XIIIe Congres International d'Histoire des Sciences,* vol. 2 (1974), p. 225.

7 *Ibid.*, p. 226.

8 Report of the (British) Committee on Chemical Warfare Organisation (the so-called Holland Committee), 1919, as cited in L. F. Haber, *The Poisonous Cloud. Chemical Warfare in the First World War* (Clarendon Press: Oxford, 1986), p. 293.

9 D. J. C. Wiseman (Lt. Col.), *Special Weapons and Types of Warfare. Volume I – Gas Warfare*, The Second World War 1939–1945, Army (The War Office: London, 1951) [Unclassified 16 February 1984], pp. 1–2; see also: P. Harris, 'British Preparations for Offensive Chemical Warfare 1935–39', *Journal of the Royal United Services Institute for Defence Studies,* vol. 75, no. 2 (June 1980), p. 57.

10 Haber, *The Poisonous Cloud*, p. 288.

11 Haber, *The Poisonous Cloud*, p. 283.

12 D. P. Jones, 'The Role of Chemists in Research on War Gases in the United States During World War I', Thesis submitted to the Graduate School of the University of Wisconsin in partial fulfilment of the requirements for the degree of Doctor of Philosophy, University of Wisconsin, 1969, p. 38.

13 J. P. Zanders, 'International Norms Against Chemical and Biological Warfare: An Ambiguous Legacy', *Journal of Conflict & Security Law*, vol. 8, no. 2 (2003), pp. 391–410.

14 R. Hanslian and F. Bergendorf, *Der chemische Krieg: Gasangriff, Gasabwehr und Raucherzeugung* (E. S. Mittler & Sohn: Berlin, 1925), p. 7.

15 J. L. Klüber, *Droit des gens moderne de l'Europe*. Revu, annoté et complété par M. A. Ott. Deuxième édition (Guillaumin et Cie, éditeurs: Paris, 1874), p. 348.

16 *Encyclopædia Britannica; or, a Dictionary of Arts and Sciences*, Vol. III (Edinburgh, 1771), pp. 152–53.

17 Expert opinion provided by Dr. Kriege to an investigative committee of the German *Reichstag*, as reproduced in: Untersuchungsausschusses der Verfassunggebenden Deutschen Nationalversammlung und des Deutschen Reichstages 1919–1928, *Völkerrecht im Weltkrieg 1914–1918*. Dritte Reihe im Werk des Parlamentarischen Untersuchungsausschusses, Vierter Band (Deutsche Verlagsgesellschaft für Politik und Geschichte m.b.H: Berlin, 1927), pp. 33–34.

18 Untersuchungsausschusses, pp. 13–14.

19 *Ibid.*, pp. 7–8.

20 J. Meyer, *Der Gaskampf und die chemischen Kampfstoffe* (Verlag S. Hirzel: Leipzig, 1925), pp. 37–38.

21 Louis Lewin was a notable exception. As a toxicologist, he strongly pleaded to extend historical moral constraints to any use of poison under any circumstance. Although he clearly had the First World War in mind, given the date of publication, he barely touched upon events in that war. L. Lewin, *Die Gifte in der Weltgeschichte* (Verlag von Julius Springer; Berlin, 1920).

22 F. von Liszt, *Das Völkerrecht* (Verlag von Julius Springer: Berlin, 1918), pp. 297–298.

23 F. von Liszt and M. Fleischmann, *Das Völkerrecht* (Verlag von Julius Springer: Berlin, 1925), p. 475.

24 Report dated 29 April, 1915 by Lt. Col. Geo. O. Squier, S. C., Military Attaché, London, entitled 'Asphyxiating Gases' transmitted to the War Department, Office Chief of Staff, War College Division, n° 2463–1, 11 May, 1915. (RG 165, WC 2463 series.)

25 The report was released by the Press Bureau by the Belgian Legation in London. Full English version in *ibid.*

26 The Commission stated that the Belgian authorities had received several intelligence reports regarding the German preparations, including field trials at Houthalen near Hasselt, several weeks before chlorine attack. See also L. Vandeweyer, 'The Belgian Army and the Gas Attack on 22 April 1915', in this volume. The accusation of premeditation was to justify any future act of reprisal, often itself an unjust act. H. Bonfils, and P. Fauchille, *Manuel de Droit international public (Droit des Gens)*, septième édition (Librairie Arthur Rousseau: Paris, 1914), §§ 1018–1019, pp. 727–28.

27 Having been included to avoid false accusations as a consequence of impurities or undesired side effects by some new types of munition, the phrase 'the sole object' seemed open to double interpretation. On the one hand, it could be construed to mean that if a projectile had, for example, an explosive action besides the dispersion of gases then the Hague Declaration (IV, 2) was not applicable. On the other hand, it was possible to interpret the clause in the expansive sense that 'projectiles, which kill and are *sometimes* accompanied by deleterious jets, are thus not prohibited', implying that the noxious gases cannot be an inherent or intended feature. P. Fauchille, *Traité de Droit international public. Tome II: Guerre et neutralité* (Librairie Arthur Rousseau: Paris, 1921), p. 121 (Emphasis added). Such an understanding was implicit in the Allied accusations. According to a further British charge, the Germans willfully exploited a translation error in the Hague Declaration (IV, 2). By clerical omission, the official British version did not include the word 'unique' from the French text and thus read: '... projectiles the object of which ...'. A. A. Roberts, *The Poison War* (William Heinemann: London, 1915), p. 19. Venting the passions of the moment, the author forgot or ignored that the French text was the only authentic one.

28 Commission on the Responsibility of the Authors of the War and on Enforcement of Penalties, *Report Presented to the Preliminary Peace Conference,* Versailles, March 1919, document reproduced in L. Friedman (ed.), *The Law of War. A Documentary History – Volume I* (Random House: New York, 1972), p. 852

29 Fauchille, *Traité de Droit international public*, p. 124.

30 See p. 242.

31 Meyer, *Der Gaskampf und die chemischen Kampfstoffe*, p. 273.

32 J. B. S. Haldane, *Callinicus. A Defence of Chemical Warfare* (E. P. Dutton & Company: New York, 1925), p. 20. The German military instructions of 1902 referred to the humane principles of the Hague Conventions as 'sentimentalism and flabby emotion'. See Zanders, 'The road to The Hague' in the present volume, p. 40.

33 Haldane, *Callinicus,* p. 23.

34 F. Stern, 'Fritz Haber: Flawed Greatness of Person and Country', *Angewandte Chemie*, International edition, vol. 51, no. 1 (2 January 2012), p. 52.

35 *Foulkes Papers* as quoted in R. Harris and J. Paxman, *A Higher Form of Killing* (Triad/Granada, UK, 1982), p. 43.

36 J. Putkowski, 'Toxic Shock: The British Army's reaction to German poison gas during the Second Battle of Ypres', in this volume, p. 98.

37 D. Omissi, 'The Indian Army at the Second Battle of Ypres', in this volume, p.125.

38 A. A. Fries and C. J. West, *Chemical Warfare* (McGraw-Hill Book Company, Inc.: New York, 1921), pp. 437–38.

39 F. Haber, 'Zur Geschichte des Gaskrieges', in F. Haber, *Fünf Vorträge aus den Jahren 1920–1923* (Springer-Verlag: Berlin, 1924), p. 39.

40 Haldane, *Callinicus,* pp. 45–46.

41 *Ibid.*, pp. 46–47.

42 *Ibid.*, pp. 50–51.

43 Zanders, 'International Norms Against Chemical and Biological Warfare', pp. 403–04.

44 F. Tanner, 'Versailles: German disarmament after World War I', in F. Tanner (ed.), *From Versailles to Baghdad: Post-War Armament Control of Defeated States* (United Nations: New York, 1992), p. 5.

45 H. Schmitt, 'The Treaty of Versailles: Mirror of Europe's Postwar Agony', paper published as part of the Internet Project 'The Paris Peace Conference', Northern Virginia Community College, 1989, available at URL <http://www.ctevans.net/Versailles/Papers/Schmitt/Schmitt_paper.html>. Accessed 1 October 2015.

46 The Treaty of Peace between the Allied and Associated Powers and Germany, signed at Versailles, 28 June 1919, Part V. Military, naval and air clauses, pp. 155 ff., document available from UK Treaties Online, Treaty Record at <http://treaties.fco.gov.uk/treaties/treatyrecord.htm?tid=4034>.

47 The Treaty of Peace between the Allied and Associated Powers and Germany, pp. 161 and 163.

48 Treaty concerning the re-establishment of Peace between Germany and the United States, signed in Berlin on 25 August 1921 and entered into force on 11 November 1921.

49 S. J. Lee, *The Weimar Republic* (Routledge: London, 1998), pp. 36 and 37.

50 Haber, *The Poisonous Cloud*, p. 157.

51 The Treaty of Peace between the Allied and Associated Powers and Germany, p. 163.

52 F. J. Brown, *Chemical Warfare. A Study in Restraints* (Greenwood Press: Westport, CT, 1968), p. 53.

53 *Ibid.*, p. 57.

54 J. P. Perry Robinson, *The Problem of Chemical and Biological Warfare. Volume I: The Rise of CB Weapons* (SIPRI and Almqvist & Wiksell: Stockholm, 1971), p. 235.

55 Cf. the telegram from Mr Francis Garvan, Alien Property Custodian and later President of the Chemical Foundation, as cited in Brown, *Chemical Warfare*, pp. 54–55:

> Explain to President [the objectives of the Chemical Foundation and] [...] the fact that there must be no possibility of injuring the industry upon which rests, first our defence against explosive, gas, and germ future offensive of Germany; second, five hundred millions invested in the dye industry itself; third, the independence of all textile, paint, varnish, and other industries dependent upon the American dye industry; fourth, destruction of the present espionage system, only partially destroyed by war, through the German dyers' 'agents and representatives' in America; fifth, the general chemical development upon which modern industry so greatly relies; and sixth, the future of chemical medicine in America; in other words, the wresting from Germany of her destructive use of chemical science and turning it to our defence and the betterment of humanity.

The telegram was representative of the Chemical Foundation's position. For other examples: *ibid.*, 1968, p. 55, fn. 5.

56 During the First World War all governments of countries with a CW production programme eventually had to establish 'national factories' because of the weaknesses or incompetence in the private sector. Haber, *The Poisonous Cloud*, p. 156. The contracts proposed to the private industry were nevertheless huge. By the end of the war, the United States were manufacturing as much warfare agent as France and Great Britain combined and four times as much as Germany. Perry Robinson, *The Problem of Chemical and Biological Warfare. Volume I*, p. 276, n. 9. Government agencies thus assumed full responsibility for testing and manufacturing. Furthermore, they continued to run or maintain special plants after the war in case of a future chemical warfare threat.

57 Haber, *ibid.*, p. 167; Perry Robinson, *ibid.*

58 Brown, *Chemical Warfare*, p. 55.

59 *Ibid.*, p. 55 and fn. 6.

60 *Ibid.*, p. 56.

61 International Military Tribunal, Judgement of 1 October 1946, 'Criminal activities in Czechoslovakia', as reproduced in Friedman (ed.), *The Law of War*, p. 961.

62 Rome Statute of the International Criminal Court, adopted at Rome on 17 July 1998 and entered into force on 1 July 2002, Article 8, 2b(xvii) and Review Conference document RC/Res.5, Amendments to Article 8 of the Rome Statute, 10 June 2010.

63 Cf. T. Cook, *No Place to Run. The Canadian Corps and Gas Warfare in the First World War* (UBC Press:

Vancouver, 1999), p. 177.

64 L. van Bergen and M. Abbenhuis, 'Man-monkey, monkey-man: neutrality and the discussions about the "inhumanity" of poison gas in the Netherlands and International Committee of the Red Cross', in this volume at p. 220; P. Van den Dungen, 'Civil Resistance to Chemical Warfare in the First World War', in this volume at pp.192–96.

65 International Committee of the Red Cross, Appeal against the use of poisonous gases, 8 February 1918, available from <https://www.icrc.org/eng/resources/documents/statement/57jnqh.htm>.

66 Van Bergen and Abbenhuis, 'Man-monkey, monkey-man', p. [at note reference 53 and 54].

67 Captain A. T. Mahan, Report to the United States Commission to the International Conference at the Hague, on Disarmament, etc., with Reference to Navies, in J. Brown Scott, *The Hague Peace Conferences of 1899 and 1907. A Series of Lectures Delivered before the Johns Hopkins University in the Year 1908, Volume II* (The Johns Hopkins Press: Baltimore, MD, 1909), p. 37.

68 Harris and Paxman, *A Higher Form of Killing*, p. 34.

69 W. Gilman, 'Devastating poison gas – the Army planes' ally', *Popular Aviation*, vol. 17, no. 3 (September 1935), p. 145.

70 Harris and Paxman, *A Higher Form of Killing*, p. 34.

71 G. Douhet, *The Command of the Air* (1921), Translated from Italian by Dino Ferrari (Coward-McCann: New York, 1942), reprinted in Project Warrior Studies, Office of Air Force History, Washington, DC, 1983, p. 58. William Mitchell, Statement before the House Appropriations and Naval Affairs Committees, 28 January 1921, as cited in T. Wildenberg, *Billy Mitchell's War with the Navy: The Army Air Corps and the Challenge to Seapower* (Naval Institute Press: Annapolis, MD, 2014). Further examples of claims about the destructiveness of chemical bombs in T. H. Greer, *The Development of Air Doctrine in the Army Air Arm 1917–1941* (USAF Historical Division, Research Studies Institute, Air University: Maxwell Air Force Base, AL, 1955), reprinted by Office of Air Force History, Washington, DC, 1985.

72 Ms Ellen Wilkinson (MP), *Hansard*, Series 5, Vol. 208, Commons, Sittings of 11 July 1927, pp. 1859–61, available at <http://hansard.millbanksystems.com/commons/1927/jul/11/foreign-office#column_1859>.

73 Van Bergen and Abbenhuis, 'Man-monkey, monkey-man', p. 230.

74 Q. Wright, 'The Washington Conference', *American Political Science Review*, vol. 16, no. 2 (1922), p. 292.

75 League of Nations, *Treaty Series*, vol. 94 (1929), pp. 57–64.

76 W. G. Harding, Opening Speech of the Conference on Limitation of Armament, 12 November 1921, Miller Center, University of Virginia, URL <http://millercenter.org/president/harding/speeches/opening-speech-of-the-conference-on-limitation-of-armament>.

77 Address by Mr Briand, Third Plenary Session, 21 November 1921, as reproduced in Conference on the Limitation of Armament, Held At Washington, November 12, 1921, to February 6, 1922. Report of the Canadian Delegate, Including Treaties and Resolutions (F. A. Acland Printer to the King's Most Excellent Majesty: Ottawa, 1922), pp. 92–99, especially at pp. 95 and 98.

78 Wright, 'The Washington Conference', pp. 287–89.

79 R. L. Buell, 'Review: M. Sullivan, The Great Adventure at Washington: The Story of the Conference', *Political Science Quarterly*, vol. 37, no. 4 (December 1922), pp. 695–96.

80 R. L. Buell, *The Washington Conference* (D. Appleton and Company: New York, 1922), p. 210.

81 *Ibid.*, p. 228.

82 'Text of the Conference discussions', *New York Times*, 7 January 1922, p. 3.

83 S. Katsuizumi, *Critical Observation on the Washington Conference* (Ann Arbor, MI, 1922), p. 25.

84 Reports as reproduced in 'Text of the Conference discussions'.

85 Buell, *The Washington Conference*, pp. 208–09; also Katsuizumi, *Critical Observation on the Washington Conference*, pp. 25 and 28. Katsuizumi attributed the diplomatic manoeuvre to the US having been outvoted by other subcommittee members and unwilling to recognise the more principled stance of other nations, Japan foremost.

86 D. Schindler and J. Toman, *The Laws of Armed Conflicts* (Martinus Nijhoff Publishers: Dordrecht, 1988), pp. 877–79.

87 Resolutions reproduced in Conference on the Limitation of Armament, Report of the Canadian Delegate, p. 214.

88 Conference on the Limitation of Armament, Report of the Canadian Delegate, p. 25.

89 A. Boserup, *The Problem of Chemical and Biological Warfare, Volume III: CBW and the Law of War* (SIPRI and Almqvist & Wiksell: Stockholm, 1973), p. 154.

90 J. Goldblat, *The Problem of Chemical and Biological Warfare. Volume IV: CB Disarmament Negotiations, 1920–1970* (SIPRI and Almqvist & Wiksell: Stockholm, 1971), pp. 43–57.

91 League of Nations, *Proceedings of the Conference for the Supervision of the International Trade in Arms and Ammunition and in Implements of War, Held at Geneva, May 4th to June 17th, 1925*, Document A.13.1925.IX, Geneva (September 1925), p. 155.

92 League of Nations, *Proceedings*, p. 161. In addition, the Polish representative General Casmir Sosnkowski proposed that 'any decisions taken by the Conference concerning the materials used for chemical warfare should apply equally to the materials employed for bacteriological warfare', *ibid.* Diplomats thus accepted for the first time biological weapons as a separate arms category in an international agreement.

93 *Ibid.*, p. 156.

94 *Ibid.*, pp. 308–09. See also the account of deliberations (pp. 531–32) and the Report of the Military, Naval and Air Technical Committee on Chemical and Biological Warfare (pp. 739–40).

95 *Ibid.*, p. 540.

96 *Ibid.*, p. 780.

97 *Ibid.*, p. 530.

98 *Ibid.*, p. 533.

99 *Ibid.*, p. 155.

100 *Ibid.*, p. 161.

101 *Ibid.*, p. 156.

102 *Ibid.*, p. 162.

103 Goldblat, *The Problem of Chemical and Biological Warfare. Volume IV*, pp. 74–88.

104 *Ibid.*, pp. 113–15.

105 British draft disarmament convention, text reproduced in *ibid.*, pp. 167–69.